The Politics of Gun Control

The Politics
of Gun Control
Sixth Edition

Robert J. Spitzer

Routledge
Taylor & Francis Group

LONDON AND NEW YORK

First published 2015 by Paradigm Publishers

Published 2016 by Routledge
2 Park Square, Milton Park, Abingdon, Oxon OX14 4RN
711 Third Avenue, New York, NY 10017, USA

Routledge is an imprint of the Taylor & Francis Group, an informa business

Library of Congress Cataloging-in-Publication Data

Spitzer, Robert J., 1953–
  The politics of gun control / Robert J. Spitzer.
    pages cm.
  Includes bibliographical references and index.
  ISBN 978-1-61205-721-7 (pbk. : alk. paper) — ISBN 978-1-61205-722-4 (ebook)
  1. Gun control—United States. I. Title.
  HV7436.S68 2015
  363.330973—dc23

                                                                                    2014033325

Designed and Typeset by Straight Creek Bookmakers.

ISBN 13: 978-1-61205-721-7 (pbk)

To Ted Lowi, mentor, friend, bon vivant
and to the memories of Bill Spitzer (1921–1996)
and Ed Artinian (1936–1997)
and to my wonderful Tess

Contents

Preface

Every now and then, the name of a location or a hitherto anonymous person's name becomes famous, whether for good reasons or bad. In the case of gun policy, sudden fame or infamy is readily identifiable to most. This new, sixth edition of *The Politics of Gun Control* was motivated in part by the sudden notoriety of several such names: a formerly anonymous elementary school in Connecticut called Sandy Hook, a typical shopping mall movie theater in Aurora, Colorado, an African American teenager named Trayvon Martin, and a neighborhood watch volunteer named George Zimmerman. Because of a brief altercation between Martin and Zimmerman, the phrase "stand your ground" entered the American gun debate. In a similarly controversial situation, an action movie franchise series with the zippy title *Fast and Furious* (there have been seven such movies to date, starring Vin Diesel) suddenly took on a second, very different meaning when the title was chosen by the federal Bureau of Alcohol, Tobacco, Firearms, and Explosives (ATF) to name what became a botched gun-running operation into Mexico that may have resulted in the death of an American agent and that gave the ATF a new political black eye.

But this study of gun policy in America is more than a collection of stories about horrifying tragedies or tragic mistakes. Policy analysis means, in part, careful analysis of cases, trends, and policy change to discern meaning and insight. This new edition examines the aforementioned cases in detail in order to understand their consequences for gun policy. In addition to examining these cases, this book includes significantly expanded analysis of recent "stand your ground" laws; new developments with the ATF, the agency charged with administering federal gun laws; the spread of the concealed-gun-carry movement on college campuses, where seven states now, more or less, allow such carrying, despite vehement opposition from college leaders; the rise of a new, and for the first time well-financed pro-gun control movement; and recent trends in school shootings, shifts in public opinion, and in the ongoing debate over gun homicides, suicides, accidents, and self-defense. This new edition also examines the most important, if unsuccessful, effort in over a decade to buttress America's gun laws, launched by President Barack Obama within days of the Sandy Hook shooting, only weeks after his successful bid for re-election. Gun politics is indisputably tumultuous, yet no less instructive as a barometer of our politics, culture, and life.

This project began in classic academic style. Three decades ago a colleague contacted me to inquire about my interest in writing a chapter for a policy issues book. I was offered a choice of topics and settled on gun control, in large part because I knew little about the topic aside from what I read in the occasional newspaper article. One of the joys of academic life is the opportunity to examine and research subjects for the sheer pleasure of exploration. So it was with gun control. Since that time, I have continued to accumulate materials, write articles, and reflect on the singular nature of the gun debate as well as the continuing need for analytical writing on this subject.

One interesting phenomenon I observed through the research process was a few writers' almost frantic yet very conscious penchant to embrace, or run away from, ideological labels on the gun issue. The polemical undergrowth of the gun issue is certainly one reason for such proclamations, as is the penchant for ad hominem rather than substantive arguments; yet such proclamations are unusual in scholarly literature, and I was trained to let arguments and facts speak for themselves. Some lawyers and writers' statements declaring that they were good liberals or not members of various gun associations seemed anxious and diversionary efforts to protest too much. Nevertheless, in the spirit of such personal declarations, let me state for the record that I am, as of this writing, a member both of the National Rifle Association (NRA) and the Brady Campaign to Prevent Gun Violence (formerly Handgun Control, Inc., also known as the Brady Campaign). These memberships have been edifying for me in that they have helped provide a keener view of the gun issue from the trenches on each side.

I wish to acknowledge the advice, assistance, and thoughtful comments of several SUNY Cortland colleagues and friends, including Seth Asumah, Bruce Atkins, Erik Bitterbaum, Frank Burdick, James Clark, Deb Dintino, Herb Haines, Hubert Keen, Bruce Mattingly, Carol McPhee, Peg Murphy, Loretta Padavona, Tom Pasquarello, Len Ralston, Tim Shannon, Judson Taylor, and Don Wright. Two Cortland colleagues read significant portions of the original manuscript. My particular thanks go to Craig Little and Jerry O'Callaghan. John Mearsheimer of the University of Chicago also offered crucial suggestions and advice. I also wish to thank Kathleen Burke and Mark Prus, both highly skilled economists at SUNY Cortland, for their expertise. Additionally, Patrick

Pierce, Saint Mary's College; Donald Davison, Rollins College; and Melissa Buis Michaux, Willamette University, offered many useful suggestions in their past reviews. I was very grateful for the opportunity to work with Chatham House's then-publisher, the no-nonsense Ed Artinian, and one of its former editors, Chris Kelaher, on the original edition. At Paradigm Publishers, I wish to thank Jennifer Knerr, Terra Dunham, and Mary Kay Kozyra.

I also wish to acknowledge Gail Spitzer, Jason Popa, Mellissa and Aaron Mitchell, Olivia Mitchell, Shannon and Scott Fuller, Alexis Long, Luke Fuller, Cassandra Fuller, and Skye Wilson—who enjoys seeing her name in print, and who is also the Queen of Everything. And as always, I thank Jinny Spitzer and my wonderful wife, Teresa.

Introduction

GUNS—OR AT LEAST THE RIGHT to carry them—have made small but notable inroads onto some of America's college campuses from 2012 to 2014 (see chapter 3). The reasons have little to do with any burgeoning crime epidemic and much more with the intrusion of national and state gun disputes into some university communities. Still, serious gun violence is not unknown to campuses.

The worst gun massacre in modern American history began on an otherwise ordinary Monday morning in the middle of the spring semester on the campus of Virginia Polytechnic Institute and State University, also known as Virginia Tech, in Blacksburg, Virginia. At 7:15 a.m., two students were shot and killed in a campus dormitory. As local police tracked a possible suspect off campus, a disgruntled and mentally disturbed student, twenty-three-year-old English major Seung Hui Cho, left campus to mail a multimedia package containing a rambling diatribe to NBC News in New York City; he then returned to campus and entered a classroom building. At about 9:15 a.m., armed with two hand-guns and numerous large-capacity bullet magazines, Cho moved methodically from classroom to classroom, shooting rapidly and randomly. When he was done, thirty-two students and faculty members lay dead; twenty-five others were wounded. Cho reserved a final bullet for himself as police closed in on him, becoming the thirty-third and final fatality.

The April 16, 2007, massacre shocked the country and especially college campuses. Largely immune to gun violence, virtually all campuses maintain strict no-gun policies. Apparently, that tactic worked until the Virginia Tech shooting spree, as the last mass shooting on a college campus occurred in 1966, when Charles Whitman climbed to the top of the high tower of the University of Texas campus and killed sixteen people before police shot him. As has occurred throughout recent history in the aftermath of gun violence, the Virginia Tech shootings prompted a spate of questions related to gun control.

The Virginia Tech shooter's choice of weapons—a 9mm Glock 19 pistol and a .22-caliber Walther P22—were both semiautomatic handguns purchased legally at local stores. Cho ordered the Walther over the Internet and had it sent to a Blacksburg pawnshop, where he then completed the purchase. He bought the Glock at Roanoke Firearms. He also obtained large-capacity bullet magazines for the guns that held about thirty bullets. (The assault-weapons ban of 1994 barred such magazines, but when Congress failed to extend the measure in 2004, they again were legal.) The only acquisition obstacle he faced in a state with few gun restrictions was a one-handgun-purchase-per-month rule (he bought the Glock just over a month before the shooting, and the Walther a month before that). Yet Cho had a long history of behavioral and emotional problems as a college student, and in 2005 a judge declared him mentally ill and a danger to himself. This information should have been sufficient to disqualify him from making a handgun purchase, but Virginia's state criteria for disqualification were narrower than the federal standard. Even though he was ordered to obtain counseling, he was not institutionalized, which under Virginia law at the time kept his name from being placed on a state list barring him from buying a gun. Therefore, he was not flagged under the federal Brady law that does bar gun sales to those identified as mentally incompetent. In fact, data problems relating to mental competence existed in many states. According to the FBI, only twenty-two states at the time submitted any mental health records to the National Instant Criminal Background Check System (NICS) to which gun sales records are sent.[1]

One important feature of gun laws in America is that relatively few exist at the national level; at the state level, they vary widely. Thus, the gun purchases Cho made easily in Virginia probably could not have occurred in a state with stricter gun laws, such as New York. In the Empire State only those with a valid, state-issued permit can purchase handguns. Applicants can only obtain that permit after being fingerprinted, paying several fees, undergoing an extensive background check that includes police interviews with acquaintances, and successfully persuading a local judge that they have a good reason for wanting to own a handgun. It is highly unlikely that Cho would have met these standards in New York; indeed, most who came in contact with him reported that he seemed deeply troubled. Although this might have caused him to purchase a long gun—a rifle or shotgun—instead, that too might have changed the outcome. Cho was able to easily conceal the two handguns he carried as he traveled around the large Virginia Tech campus on foot. Had he been carrying one or more long guns, he would have been far easier to spot—and perhaps stop—before the shootings occurred. Cho's preference for handguns also mimics national gun crime trends: although there are twice as many long guns in

America as handguns and long guns are easier to obtain in most places, 80 percent of all gun crimes are committed with handguns.

In addition, Cho used large-capacity bullet magazines during his shooting rampage. A Glock handgun can accommodate one that holds up to thirty-three bullets. Yet a federal law enacted in 1994, known as the assault-weapons ban, barred new bullet magazines holding more than ten bullets. Congress allowed the ban to lapse in 2004, making the possession of such items again legal. The larger capacity meant that Cho needed to reload less often, thus diminishing the possibility that someone could have jumped him during reloading. In all, he fired nearly two hundred bullets in roughly ten minutes.[2]

In the aftermath of the mass homicide, many called for new, stricter gun laws. Gun rights activists argued against new restrictions. Some argued that there were already enough gun laws on the books or that existing gun laws should be weakened to allow citizens to legally carry guns on campuses for self-protection. This proposal met with little favor from most of the law enforcement and higher education communities, who feared more gun violence with legal campus gun carrying, including shootings arising from accident, rage, suicide, and gun thefts. Others argued for a measure to close the "gun show loophole," a reference to a gap in federal law that excludes private gun sales (those not involving federally licensed dealers) from any background checks. Such sales account for about 40 percent of all gun purchases.

Finally, despite an apparently sympathetic national political climate—a majority of the public has consistently supported tougher gun laws—the prospects for new gun laws were dim (although federal law was changed to improve state data gathering and reporting; see discussion in chapter 5). President George W. Bush denounced any effort to enact new restrictions, as had been his position throughout a presidency more in tune with the preferences of the powerful National Rifle Association than any in history. Some in Congress favored tougher gun laws, but the majority Democrats were divided on the issue, as some of the new Democrats elected in the 2006 midterm elections came from conservative areas of the country where gun regulations were viewed with suspicion. And to many Democrats the gun issue was more trouble than it was worth; many believed their party's presidential nominee in 2000, Al Gore, had lost the election at least in part because of his support for tougher gun laws.[3]

On the morning of January 8, 2011, Arizona Democratic Representative Gabrielle Giffords convened a "Congress on Your Corner" constituent meet-and-greet in front of a local supermarket in Tucson. As she was speaking with constituents, a twenty-two-year-old man with a recent history of mental disorders walked up to Giffords after weaving his way through the crowd of people around her, pointed a 9mm Glock 19 handgun a couple of feet from her head, and pulled the trigger. The bullet passed through her head, but, miraculously, she not only survived but also showed immediate and dramatic improvement in the days and weeks that followed. After shooting Rep. Giffords, Jared Lee Loughner proceeded to empty the thirty-one-bullet magazine, killing six people and wounding thirteen others. When he stopped to insert a second bullet magazine, a diminutive sixty-one-year-old woman snatched a second, bullet-filled magazine he had dropped on the floor from his grasp, and several bystanders proceeded to restrain the man. Among those killed were a federal judge who had stopped by after church to speak with Giffords, a nine-year-old girl interested in visiting with her congressional representative, and a Giffords staff member. As the shooting unfolded, an armed bystander, Joe Zamudio, heard the commotion and ran to the scene. "I had my gun in my hand," he said later. The first person Zamudio encountered was holding a gun, but it turned out that that person wasn't the shooter, but the man who had disarmed the shooter. Thankfully, Zamudio didn't shoot the heroic bystander. In fact, although Zamudio's hand was around his gun, he wound up keeping his own gun in its holster because, in the confusion of those few seconds, he "didn't want to be confused as a second gunman." In testimony before Congress in 2013, Giffords's husband, Mark Kelly, a career military man and former astronaut, testified that if the shooter had been limited to 10-round bullet magazines, fewer people would have been shot, including a nine-year-old girl killed at the scene with the thirteenth bullet he fired, because he was stopped when he changed magazines after emptying the 33-round magazine he had obtained legally.[4]

Many of the circumstances of this shooting resembled those of Virginia Tech. Loughner had exhibited increasingly erratic and threatening behavior in the years before the attack. For example, in 2010 the local community college where he had been enrolled suspended him for bizarre and threatening behavior, including multiple classroom disruptions that unnerved those in class who witnessed his behavior. His readmission was made dependent on psychological counseling. He was also rejected for military service, in part because he had flunked a drug screening test. He had had encounters with the police in the past, including an arrest for possession of drug paraphernalia in 2007, and he had posted extended diatribes on YouTube that raised further concerns that he suffered from serious mental problems, including perhaps schizophrenia. Yet because no one ever took formal action to see that he be institutionalized or receive mandatory counseling, no red flags were raised when he legally purchased his handgun the previous November.[5] Once again, in the aftermath of the shooting, public outrage prompted many to call for new regulations, including the reimposition of the ban on the sale of large-capacity magazines and better data gathering and reporting for would-be gun buyers having mental problems. As with the 2007 Virginia Tech shooter, any attempt by Loughner to purchase a gun in a state with more extensive background check criteria would have immediately revealed his severe problems, which were well known to all who knew him, including his family.

Aside from the horrifying nature of this attack, some pointed fingers at the hypercharged political atmospherics during and after the 2010 midterm elections when, for example, political opponents used gun-shooting language and symbols against Giffords and other Democrats running for election. Giffords's opponent publicized one campaign event this way: "Get on Target for Victory in November. Help remove Gabrielle Giffords from office. Shoot a fully automatic M16 with Jesse Kelly." Former Alaska governor and Republican activist Sarah Palin was accused of inciting violence against some Democrats during the 2010 elections through ads that depicted gun bull's-eye crosshair targets superimposed on maps of selected districts around the country where Democrats were "targeted" for defeat, urging followers to "reload" and "aim" to defeat them.[6] Though a defender of gun rights, Giffords herself had criticized such gun-based rhetoric during the campaign. As for Loughner, no clear evidence supported the charges of some that his actions were the specific result of such gun-oriented political rhetoric.

On July 20, 2012, twenty-four-year-old James Holmes entered a shopping mall movie theater in Aurora, Colorado, shortly after the start of its midnight showing of the latest Batman movie, *The Dark Knight Rises*. In the darkened movie theater, Holmes rapidly killed twelve and injured fifty-eight. Later, some in the audience said that they initially thought his actions were part of the movie before realizing that he was firing live rounds. He possessed four legally purchased guns: an AR-15-type semiautomatic assault rifle with an attachable 100-round drum magazine; two .40-caliber Glock handguns, each of which can receive magazines holding more than thirty bullets; and a Remington 12-gauge pump-action shotgun. In all, Holmes purchased six thousand rounds of ammunition anonymously through the Internet. Federal law formerly barred ownership of the AR-15, along with the high-capacity magazines—that law lapsed in 2004. The previous year, Holmes suffered what some called a "psychotic break" around the time that he dropped out of graduate school. Reports at the time of his arrest were that Holmes's mother said, "You have the right person" when first told of the assault, although she later denied making that comment. Holmes's significant emotional problems in the months before the attack either preceded or roughly coincided with his gun-buying binge.[7]

The facts and consequences of these horrifying shootings touch on many of the most important questions pertaining to American gun policy: the criminological appeal of handguns; the Brady law's background check provision; the problem of tracking and categorizing those with mental deficiencies; the lapse of the assault-weapons ban; variations in state gun laws; gaps in the compilation of mental health data that might otherwise prevent those with significant mental problems from purchasing guns; the role of guns in homicide, suicide, and self-defense; and the political fallout from this contentious issue. All of these topics, and more, are the subject of this book.

THE FUROR OVER GUN CONTROL has raged across the American landscape for decades, with a sustained intensity and intractability found among few other issues. Despite all that has been written on the subject, no comprehensive political and policy analysis on gun control existed at the time of this book's initial publication, even though the gun debate is precisely a political dispute over the proper scope and consequences of government policy.

At its heart, the gun debate is about the citizen, the state's power to regulate, and the maintenance of public order. All these relationships come together under the public policy umbrella and are thus amenable to a policy analysis that has as its central question, Should gun possession and use be significantly regulated? In raising this question, I am less concerned with the efficacy of each and every regulatory alternative—although most receive treatment here—than with the regulation principle as it applies to the gun issue. This is no esoteric exercise; every political dispute over some new effort to regulate guns invokes broader questions of government regulation.

The regulatory question is given coherence and context within a larger framework of policy analysis. Far from being an idiosyncratic issue that defies generalized analysis, the gun issue fits into a broader policy pattern, labeled social regulatory policy, that provides considerable predictive and explanatory power for the observed political trends.

This framework provides the organizational pattern for the analysis in this book. Chapter 1 lays out primary traits of the gun controversy, its social and cultural roots, and the social regulatory policy framework. Chapter 2 is devoted exclusively to the meaning, interpretation, and consequences of the Second Amendment to the Constitution, the much-cited yet little understood right to bear arms. The talismanic quality of the Second Amendment extends its importance beyond the narrow, arcane confines of constitutional and legal interpretation. The Constitution frames political rights, but constitutional imagery and symbolism frame political discourse.

Chapter 3 digests the wide-ranging arguments concerning the criminological consequences of guns and gun control in society. Most gun analysis and debate concentrate on the links between guns and crime, yet any such analysis is incomplete unless it incorporates suicide, accident, and self-defense questions as well.

Chapter 4 turns to the political patterns that spring from and are indeed typical of social regulatory policy. Needless to say, one giant player, the National Rifle Association, has dominated gun politics. Yet other, emergent political forces have deprived the NRA of its monopoly control in recent years, including a well-organized opposition led by the Brady Campaign. Serving as background for this struggle has been a surprisingly constant public disposition favoring control and an enduring party split.

Chapter 5 focuses on the key national institutions—Congress, the presidency, and the federal bureaucracy—that have been, at best, unwilling participants in the furious gun debate. All three institutions have behaved contrary to conventional belief regarding this issue—something that loses its power to surprise when considered within the social regulatory framework of these institutions.

Chapter 6 brings together the separate policy strands of the other chapters to synthesize the policy dilemma and propose a new way to approach the gun issue. This chapter draws on international relations theory to assess the arguments of gun control supporters and opponents and propose a new way to achieve political accommodation despite enduring hostility and mutual suspicion. The idea that political accommodation can be reached between hostile, intransigent opponents unwilling to give ground, much less negotiate, is a difficult and unwieldy phenomenon in American politics but a commonplace one in international relations.

Only two elements of the gun debate receive less detailed attention here: gun policy at the state level and comparative analysis of gun policies in other nations. Recent developments in both areas have required the addition of material on these subjects in subsequent editions, yet neither subject receives separate chapter treatment here, as the focus of this book continues to be American national gun policy.

Chapter 1

Policy Definition and Gun Control

> When a young person throws a rock across the [Mexican] border toward the [US] border or border agents, some agents respond with a gun and other agents don't respond at all. There seems to be some need for some consistency in the response to these incidents and how we treat it.
>
> —*Robert Menendez, Senator (D-NJ), commenting on US Border Patrol agents who deliberately stepped in the way of moving vehicles or who fired on Mexicans throwing rocks at agents across the US-Mexico border, based on an independent examination of sixty-seven cases of border firings that resulted in the deaths of nineteen Mexicans through 2014.*

THE CONTROVERSY OVER GUN CONTROL revolves around two related questions of government authority: does the government have the right to impose regulations, and, assuming the existence of such a right, should the government regulate guns? It is perfectly obvious that numerous gun control regulations already exist, from the national to the local level. Indeed, gun control opponents are quick to point out that thousands of gun laws exist throughout the country, a fact usually quoted to underscore their belief that such regulation is futile. A pamphlet produced by the National Rifle Association (NRA) mentions "an estimated twenty thousand local, state, and federal firearms laws," but that oft-repeated number is incorrect. A careful count of gun laws in the United States in the early 2000s produced an actual number of about four hundred.[1] Gun control opponents also argue that further gun restrictions could impinge on constitutional rights and the innate rights of the citizenry in a free nation. These arguments

1

reappear in every presidential election. In 2008, for example, Democratic presidential nominee Barack Obama was pilloried for his past support of gun regulations, and gun rights advocates translated that support as alarmist claims that Obama would be a "gun-grabber" as president. Obama's response was emphatic that he supported Second Amendment rights and had no intention of interfering with legitimate gun activities, including hunting and sporting. Yet Obama's reassurances did not assuage the critics. In fact, the Brady Campaign, a pro-gun control organization, gave Obama a failing grade of "F" for his performance on the gun issue during his first term. Before proceeding with these key questions, we must begin with the role and purpose of government regulation.

Regulation, Public Order, and Public Policy

The fundamental purpose of government—indeed, its first purpose—is to establish and maintain order. As many political thinkers have noted, human existence before the establishment of governments was chaotic and anarchic. Writing in the seventeenth century, the British political theorist Thomas Hobbes noted in his *Leviathan* that life in such a "state of nature" was "solitary, poor, nasty, brutish, and short." The only "law" in this situation was that of self-preservation, when one could expect only the "war" of "every man, against every man." To stave off such an anarchic condition, people formed governments, to which citizens traded some of their freedom, including the "freedom" to kill or be killed, in exchange for the order of civil society. In such a "civil state," according to Hobbes, "there is a power set up to constrain those that would otherwise violate their faith."

Writing several decades after Hobbes, the British political thinker John Locke in his *Of Civil Government* concurred, noting that "God hath certainly appointed government to restrain the partiality and violence of men. I easily grant that civil government is the proper remedy for the inconveniences of the state of nature." That we in America largely take the value of order for granted is a testament to the remarkable stability of American life.[2] Order is not the only priority for government, of course, because democratic nations also value freedom and the protection of basic rights and must continually strive to strike an appropriate balance between these values.[3] Nevertheless, order is the first purpose of government because without order there can be no freedom in society (aside from the "freedom" of anarchy to which Hobbes and Locke referred). As the political scientist Samuel Huntington once noted, "men may, of course, have order without liberty, but they cannot have liberty without order."[4] And, as James Madison wrote to Thomas Jefferson in 1788,

"It is a melancholy reflection that liberty should be equally exposed to danger whether the Government have too much or too little power."

Governments' maintenance of public order occurs through public policy, defined most simply as "whatever governments choose to do or not to do."[5] The interesting semantic fact that "policy" has the same linguistic root as "police" underscores the close link between order and public policy.[6] Note the link between the two in this definition of public policy offered by the British constitutionalist William Blackstone in 1769: "the due regulation and domestic order of the kingdom, whereby the inhabitants of the State, like members of a well-governed family, are bound to conform their general behavior to the rules of propriety, good neighborhood, and good manners, and to be decent, industrious, and inoffensive in their respective stations."

The techniques or tools of public policy take many forms, from the dispensing of benefits to strict regulation of individual conduct. Yet basic questions of public order usually involve direct regulation—power exercised by the government "for the protection of the health, safety, and morals of their citizens."[7] Beyond the simple maintenance of order, "government is the guarantor of the public good. Ideally, this is achieved as government regulates private functions to maximize public welfare."[8] The regulation of individual conduct may include that considered harmful to others, such as driving under the influence of alcohol, or conduct considered immoral, such as gambling or prostitution.[9] This returns us to the question of the regulation of firearms. (In this analysis "guns" and "firearms" are treated as synonymous.) The fierce and protracted debate over gun control raises a variety of issues about individual behavior and the role of the government. Nevertheless, at its core the gun debate turns on a single, central question of public policy as it relates to both order and personal conduct: should gun possession and use be significantly regulated? This central question of public policy guides the organization of this book.

Guns and Regulation

Why has gun control been such a difficult, controversial, and intractable issue in American politics? The first answer is because of the nature of regulation. Whenever the government seeks to apply its coercive powers directly to shape individual conduct, the prospect of controversy is great, especially in a nation with a long tradition of individualism. According to the policy analyst Theodore J. Lowi, when the likelihood of government coercion is immediate—that is, when the behavior of individual citizens is directly affected, as in the case of regulation—the prospect of controversy is high.[10] When the likelihood of government coercion is remote—that is, when the primary purpose of the policy in question is, say, to provide benefits rather than regulate individual conduct—the prospect of controversy is low. Examples of policies in which government coercion is low include public works projects (construction of roads, harbors, buildings, and the like) and subsidies to farmers (labeled "distributive"; see Figure 1.1). Government can influence behavior by providing these benefits, but the primary emphasis is on the awarding of benefits, not the shaping of conduct.

In addition to immediate coercion, regulatory policy shares a characteristic that fans the flames of political controversy: it seeks to control individual conduct. When the government imposes highway safety regulations, pure food and drug requirements, cable television rates, criminal laws, or laws regulating abortions, it is regulating the conduct of individuals (not only individual citizens but also individual companies or other entities). Because of these direct consequences to individuals, regulatory policies are more controversial than policies that seek to shape the "environment of conduct," such as fiscal and monetary policy, the progressive income tax, and welfare programs. Even though these latter policies (labeled "redistributive"; see Figure 1.1) affect individual citizens, the policies themselves are designed to shape broad classes or groups of people—the poor, certain categories of wage earners, homeowners—or even the entire society.[11] Thus, the individual citizen feels the hand of government less directly than policy designed to regulate the conduct of individuals.

Figure 1.1 Government Coercion and Political Controversy among Types of Policy

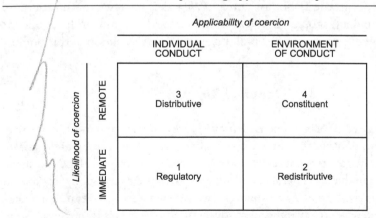

Note: 1 = most controversial; 4 = least controversial.

The fourth and least controversial form of policy is that for which government coercion is remote and seeks to shape the environment of conduct. Labeled "constituent" policy (see Figure 1.1), such policies include, for example, those pertaining to the administration of the government, the budgeting process, and the civil service.

Figure 1.1 summarizes the relationship between these four kinds of policies. Among the four, regulatory policy is the most likely to spawn controversy. Immediate coercion applied to individual conduct usually involves specific rules or sanctions with accompanying punishments, such as fines or imprisonment. The other kinds of policies are progressively less likely to include such specific and individually felt sanctions, as reflected in the numerical rank ordering in Figure 1.1.[12]

We can make an even finer distinction within the category of regulatory policy by distinguishing between two primary types of regulation: economic regulation and social regulation.[13] Economic regulation dates back to the late nineteenth century, when the national government began to become involved with regulating elements of the nation's economy. The first modern regulatory agency, the Interstate Commerce Commission (ICC), was created in 1887 to regulate railroad rates, control prices affecting consumers, require the publication of rail rates, and bar collusive practices.[14] Economic regulation then accelerated in the twentieth century, incorporating a wide variety of business, market, and economic sectors.

Social regulation dates back many decades. Government, usually at the state level, has long been concerned with regulating prostitution, marriage and polygamy, alcohol consumption, and the like. Nevertheless, social regulation greatly expanded at the national level in the 1960s. It differs from economic regulation in that it is less concerned with narrow economic questions and more concerned with broader issues of public safety, health, or morals. The focus is social relationships, not economic transactions. According to the political scientists Raymond Tatalovich and Byron Daynes, social regulatory policy is "the exercise of legal authority to affirm, modify, or replace community values, moral practices, and norms of interpersonal conduct."[15] Tatalovich and Daynes cited examples of such issues, including abortion, crime control, women's rights, pornography, school prayer, gay rights, civil rights, affirmative action, and gun control. As this laundry list of "morality policies" suggests, these issues are among the most controversial facing American society. Social regulation is especially controversial and may provoke even greater controversy than economic regulation for the fundamental reason that it is concerned with values. Moral issues often inspire even stronger feelings than economic issues.[16]

Although government involvement in some social regulatory policies predates the 1960s (notably crime control), considerable governmental and societal interest has focused on these issues in recent decades as the federal government has moved into this area, spawning intense and even explosive political antagonisms. The political characteristics of gun control conform closely to this characterization. But why is gun control an issue of social regulation? Or, to rephrase the question, what is it about gun control that provokes such sharp, deeply held feelings? What values underlie guns?

The Gun Controversy

In order to understand the dynamics of the gun issue, we need to begin with the admittedly narrow common ground of opponents and proponents. Despite the enormous differences that separate gun control advocates and opponents, they do share a few common assumptions:

- The primary and unique purpose of firearms is to provide an efficient means of destruction of people, animals, and objects. Although some may admire firearms for aesthetic, artistic, sporting, or other qualities, no one can dispute this central purpose of firearms. Indeed, they evolved from the pressures of war during the Middle Ages.[17] Other objects in society cause great destruction, of course, ranging from knives to automobiles, but these objects exist or were created to serve other purposes.[18] Knives, for example, serve a nearly infinite variety of other purposes; automobiles exist for the primary purpose of transporting people and commodities across vast expanses. That injury, destruction, or death arise from these or other objects is incidental or at least secondary to the primary and necessary purpose for which they exist. The same cannot be said for firearms, so they are distinctive for this reason alone.
- Existing gun laws have, at best, limited effects in curtailing gun-related deaths and injuries nationwide. Gun control advocates argue that the relative ineffectiveness of gun laws lies with their weakness and the problem of jurisdiction. The vast majority of gun laws exist at state and local levels, and states and cities with tougher gun laws find them at least partly neutralized by the ease with which guns can be transported from areas with weak gun laws. Stronger and more inclusive federal laws could address this problem—whether they could succeed is a separate question—but existing federal regulation is considered both limited

and weak, although some gun control opponents find even existing law too restrictive. Gun control opponents argue that government simply cannot succeed in such regulation either for practical reasons—that is, too many Americans already own weapons—or because stronger laws would violate fundamental American values, beliefs, and practices.

- Although gun ownership has been gradually declining, guns still permeate American society. In the early 1960s about half of all homes reported having at least one gun. By the first decade of the twenty-first century that number had dropped to about a third of all homes, amounting to around ninety million gun owners. With the decline in gun ownership has come a rise in the average number of guns owned: in the 1960s it was about two and a half guns per household; by this century, it had increased to more than four guns per gun owner.[19] Thus, whatever one's view on gun regulation, any government effort to significantly alter gun ownership and use patterns must be prepared to cope with the ubiquity of guns.[20]
- Part of America's social and cultural tradition includes an identifiable "gun culture," a phrase popularized by the historian Richard Hofstadter in his "America as a Gun Culture."[21] Many gun control proponents decry America's long association with and affection for the gun; gun control opponents for the most part embrace and celebrate the connections between guns and America's heritage. Regardless of one's personal or political feelings about guns, however, the gun culture is an undeniable component of American history and the gun debate.[22]

Despite this common ground, those who square off over gun control disagree on nearly everything else. Indeed, they cannot agree on the interpretation of laws and court cases about guns, on the validity of comparisons between the United States and other democratic nations (nearly all of which have stricter gun laws than those of the United States), or even on the effects of gun control on such basic issues as crime and public safety. Of course, many issues in American politics provoke sharp disagreement. Abortion, for example, provokes at times even greater passion than gun control. However, unlike gun control, those on opposing sides of the abortion question can at least agree on how abortions are performed, the desirability of avoiding unwanted pregnancies as a way to avoid the problem of abortion entirely, and the consequences of varying degrees of government regulation. Their disagreement turns primarily on the normative question of whether various restrictions should be imposed. Those on opposing sides of the gun debate cannot even agree on the basics.

The Gun Culture

To return to an earlier question: why do relatively simple metal-and-wood objects that do nothing more than propel small bits of metal at high speeds evoke such strong feelings? The first answer is obvious: in recent years more than thirty thousand Americans have been killed annually as the result of the homicidal, accidental, and suicidal use of guns; in all, Americans wielding guns intimidate, wound, and kill hundreds of thousands of people every year.[23] These actions disrupt American lives, inflame public sentiment, and interrupt the societal concept of ordered liberty. Although the absence of guns would not end violence and mayhem in America, the presence and easy availability of guns magnify the violent strain in the American character, multiplying its deadly consequences. These concerns are the ones gun control advocates typically express.[24]

The second answer is both less obvious and more important: the just-mentioned American gun culture. This phrase usefully summarizes the long-term sentimental attachment of many Americans to the gun, founded on the presence and proliferation of guns since the earliest days of the country; the connection between personal weapons ownership and the country's early struggle for survival and independence followed by the country's frontier experience; and the cultural mythology that has grown up about the gun in both frontier and modern life, as reflected in books, movies, folklore, and other forms of popular expression.

Not all Americans, by any means, embrace this gun culture, and most who do acknowledge in some respect the destructive consequences of weapons. Yet strong personal feelings about guns counterbalance these concerns. Beyond this, the gun culture is generally recognized, rightly or wrongly, as a key component of the American mythic tradition.[25] Recent research has demonstrated that although gun ownership dates to America's beginnings, it was far less ubiquitous in colonial and early federal life than popular impressions and mythology suggest. As a practical matter, most of the firearms in civilian hands were guns suited to farming use, often called fowling pieces—small-caliber weapons suitable for killing small game and nuisance animals, rather than military-grade weapons. Moreover, early guns were expensive, cumbersome, difficult and even dangerous to operate, and made from materials (mostly iron) that deteriorated rapidly even with regular maintenance. And subsistence agriculture, including the raising of crops and domestic animals, was the main source of sustenance for most Americans, not the hunting of wild game. Gun ownership and use became more widespread after the Civil War, in part because gun manufacturers such as Samuel Colt developed advertising campaigns that deliberately romanticized the attachment to guns and also because technological improvements made guns cheaper, more reliable, easier to use, and more durable. Further, relatively few Americans possessed the marksmanship skills so often attributed to them in folklore, a fact underscored by the common observation of America's military leaders during this period, who consistently bemoaned American males' lack of acquaintance and skill with firearms.[26] Regardless of its origins, the American gun culture as it exists today contains at least two elements that have survived since the country's early history: the hunting/sporting ethos and the militia/frontier ethos.

The Hunting/Sporting Ethos

The first of these elements sprang from a time when the United States was an agrarian, subsistence nation existing in a hostile environment. Hunting game was one source of food for American settlers (although domesticated animals were a far more important food source than game), just as it was a method of protection from animal predators, including bears, panthers, and wolves, although mounting evidence indicates that wolves posed no direct threat to humans. In addition, the growing market for furs encouraged hunting and trapping as a source of income. Noting the connection between shooting skills, survival, and the acquisition of these skills as a "rite of passage" for boys entering manhood, one colonial observer commented that "a well grown boy at the age of twelve or thirteen years, was furnished with a small rifle and shot-pouch. He then became a fort soldier, and had his port-hole assigned him. Hunting squirrels, turkeys and raccoons, soon made him expert in the use of his gun."[27] For at least some Americans, guns were a necessity of everyday life for reasons of subsistence alone. That they were used for self-protection from Native Americans and other hostiles is equally evident. The role of guns as a mark of maturity is one that lingers to this day.[28]

As American society evolved, becoming more urban and more developed, the necessity for and practice of hunting declined. In fact, as settlements grew, the practice of carrying arms declined along the nation's eastern coast. Even "during the colonial period, the urban areas were relatively free of the consistent use of firearms."[29] Yet the hunting tradition survived, especially in rural areas. So too did the element of competitive/sport shooting, a form of recreation also dating back to the country's earliest days. Such competitions occurred in part to improve shooting skill and aim, for despite the much-vaunted reputation of the American sharpshooter, even during the Revolution the sharpshooting reputation exceeded actual American shooting skills. According to one observer, shooting matches in the country's early history were "the major sport of America."[30] Although the accuracy of this claim is questionable, some shooting matches certainly occurred.

A 2006 federal survey of hunting in America reported 12.5 million hunters in the country, with perhaps as many as 18 million people who hunt occasionally. About 90 percent of hunters are male. These numbers reflect a long-term decline in hunting, both in absolute numbers and as a percentage of the total population: in 1975 the hunting population was 17 million.[31] Based on a study of hunters by Stephen Kellert of the Yale School of Forestry and Environmental Studies, the reasons for hunting vary, but the primary motivations include procurement of food, pursuit of sport, and the desire to commune with and participate in nature.[32] Beyond a mere activity, hunting survives as a central component of the gun culture. According to a variety of studies, the decline in hunting first predicted in the 1960s has resulted from and is continuing primarily because of the decline in farming and rural populations, the greater array of leisure activities available to rural residents, the reduction of land where hunting is allowed, and changing social attitudes. Indeed, some predict that the "hunting heritage" may disappear entirely by the middle of the twenty-first century. In 1983 the number of hunting licenses issued was 16.4 million; in 2013 the number was 14.6 million, even as America's population increased over the same time. In 2005 over 90 percent of all hunters were thirty-five years of age or older.[33]

The Militia/Frontier Ethos

The second tradition, the militia/frontier ethos, has more direct political antecedents and consequences. Early Americans had to rely on their wits and skills to protect themselves and their families from hostile Native Americans and foreign armies. Necessity dictated that anyone capable of carrying and using a weapon (excluding blacks and, for the most part, women) participate in local defense. Neither the budget nor the manpower existed to maintain a full-time army, so the armed citizen-soldier bore this responsibility. Nor did the government have the resources to arm its citizens; in fact, from the earliest days of the colonies, able-bodied men were pressed, even required, not only to serve but also to provide their own arms and ammunition because the colonies' very survival depended on these citizen militias. And the mother country was of little help. Even though the colonies were under British rule, England did not begin to send troops to America until the 1740s.[34]

As is well known, citizen-soldiers serving in state-based militias fought and won American independence against what was considered the finest standing army in the world (more is said about this in chapter 2). Yet by the 1790s the many drawbacks of citizen militias accelerated the reliance on volunteer units and a professional, full-time army. The death knell of the citizen militia was its abysmal performance in the War of 1812, after which it ceased to play any active role in national defense.[35] Despite this fact, the militia tradition has survived.

Closely related to the militia tradition is the frontier tradition, which linked westward movement with weaponry. Just as the Pennsylvania-Kentucky-style rifle was closely associated with the American colonial and revolutionary experience,[36] nineteenth-century firearms became readily identifiable symbols of westward expansion. The principal enemies of westward-moving settlers, said to be outlaws and Indians, necessitated an armed citizenry ready and willing to use their Winchesters, Smith & Wessons, Remingtons, and Colts to defend hearth and home at a time when allegedly the only reliable justice came from the barrel of a gun: "Men who wanted to hold their own against all comers carried their law with them—a Colt peacemaker, slung from their belt or in an arm-pit holster."[37] Axiomatic expressions such as "the guns that won the West" and "arm[s] that opened the West and tamed the wild land" typify what in actuality is a romanticized and wildly exaggerated assessment of the importance of guns in the settling of the West. Indeed, some have gone so far as to claim that "the American experiment was made possible by the gun."[38] These characterizations can be faulted for ignoring the central role of homesteaders, ranchers, miners, tradesmen, businessmen, and the generalized movement of "civilization," to label it thus, across the Western plains. The so-called taming of the West was in fact an agricultural and commercial movement, attributable primarily to ranchers and farmers, not gun-slinging cowboys.[39] In fact, the six-shooter and rifle played relatively minor roles in the activities of all these groups, even the cowboys. According to Richard Shenkman,

> The truth is many more people have died in Hollywood Westerns than ever died on the real frontier.... In the real Dodge City, for instance, there were just five killings in 1878, the most homicidal year.... In the most violent year in Deadwood, South Dakota, only four people were killed. In the worst year in Tombstone, home of the shoot-out at the OK Corral, only five people were killed. The only reason the OK Corral shoot-out even became famous was that town boosters deliberately overplayed the drama to attract new settlers.[40]

Even in the most violence-prone towns, the Western cattle towns, vigilantism and lawlessness were only briefly tolerated.[41] In his sweeping history of the West, the historian Ray Allen Billington noted that local businesspeople and other leaders quickly pushed for town incorporation in order to establish local police forces, which were supported by taxes levied against local bars, gambling establishments, and houses of prostitution. Prohibitions against carrying guns were strictly enforced, and there were few homicides. The gun "disarmament" that was routinely practiced in newly formed Western towns was well understood as a sign of civilization and an improvement in public safety. Ironically, such measures provoke more political heat and outrage in the twenty-first century than they did in the nineteenth century. The Western-style shoot-outs glorified in countless books and movies were literally "unheard of."[42] In the most violent cow towns of the old West—Abilene, Caldwell, Dodge City, Ellsworth, and Wichita—a total of forty-five killings were recorded between 1870 and 1885, and only six of these killings were from six-shooters; sixteen were by police. Outside populated areas, cowboys and other range riders who carried six-guns almost never used them in Hollywood-style gunfights or to enforce some brand of Western justice. As the cowboy experts Joe B. Frantz and Julian E. Choate observed, "the six-shooter has been credited with use entirely disproportionate with the facts."[43] Even Western outlaws illustrate the extent to which myth has replaced fact with respect to guns and lawlessness. Many studies of the famed Western outlaws demonstrate that "they were few, inconspicuous, and largely the invention of newspaper correspondents and fiction writers." Moreover, "the Western marshal [was] an unglamorous character who spent his time arresting drunks or rounding up stray dogs and almost never engaging in gun battles."[44] Most of the killing that took place on the frontier involved the wars between the US Cavalry and those Native Americans who rebelled against harsh and duplicitous treatment at the hands of whites.[45] The hunting/sporting and militia/frontier views converge to produce a certain mythical elevation of the gun. This mythologizing parallels—indeed draws strength from—the broader mythologizing of the American frontier tradition. As the American cultural analyst Richard Slotkin observed,

> The Myth of the Frontier was developed by and for an America that was a colonial offshoot of Europe, agrarian in economy, localistic in politics, tentative as to nationality, and relatively homogeneous in ethnicity, language, and religion; yet the Myth has been most thoroughly and impressively set forth in the ninety years that followed the closing of the Wild West, in and for an America that is a preeminent world power, urban-centered and fully industrialized, centralized in government, and heterodox in culture.[46]

This veneration of guns, with all its attendant symbolism and mythology, drives a powerful and deeply felt belief that guns are not only an integral part of but also a force responsible for America as it exists today. Although the percentage of Americans who aggressively embrace this tradition and consider it applicable to modern life is relatively small, the myths composing the gun culture survive and thrive in major elements of mass culture.

For example, one can hardly count as coincidence the fact that the very first feature film, *The Great Train Robbery,* sent moviegoers ducking for cover when an outlaw in the 1903 film aimed his six-gun at the camera and fired. From that day to this, the admittedly ambivalent relationship between movies and guns has, nevertheless, helped cultivate America's gun tradition, as have other forms of mass culture.[47]

The Modern Gun Culture

In contemporary society, the gun culture revolves around those who continue to own and use guns for legitimate hunting, sporting, and related purposes, although there are those who would include urban street gangs, gun-toting criminals, and other antisocial individuals and groups in this category. Modern social science has carefully identified the core of those who continue to promote a legitimate gun culture, based on both practice and attitude (these qualities are discussed in greater detail in chapter 4).

Those who compose and support the active gun culture are overwhelmingly white males (fewer than 15 percent of gun owners are female), live in rural areas (especially in the South), are likely to be Protestant, and are from "old stock" (that is, have ancestors who came to this country longer ago than the more recent immigrant waves). Naturally, they are highly likely to own and use guns. Conversely, those for whom the gun culture carries the least appeal are likely to be females, from larger metropolitan areas, from the Northeast, and from more recent immigrant descent. Despite impressions to the contrary, levels of education and income bear little relation to the gun attachment.[48] Those most likely to embrace and carry on the gun tradition are socialized early in their lives by other family members into patterns of gun ownership and use.[49] Despite the gradual decline in recreational gun activities, the gun culture persists even in areas typically thought of as less than "gun-friendly," or dominated by urban-suburban life. Even in states with strict gun regulations, the typical minimum legal hunting age is twelve (although an adult must accompany the children). In New York State, for example, some rural counties still cancel public school on the first day of deer-hunting season, held in mid-November—an acknowledgment of the many students who would otherwise be absent if school were held. In Vermont a hunting instructor established a "dream hunt" competition for children, offering all-expenses paid hunting trips to kids in order to interest more children in hunting activities. One winner in 2005 was nine-year-old Samantha Marley, a Massachusetts fourth grader who won a bear hunt using her own 20-gauge shotgun. A hunter from Preble, New York, eloquently expressed the social and familial link to hunting activities when he explained to a reporter why he was going to bypass his annual deer hunt: "I didn't feel like going hunting today. My son is away at college and I just didn't feel like going out without him." But to make up for that, the hunter said that he planned on taking off work the following week so the two could go hunting. "We will have a lot of fun; it's early in the season," he explained.[50] Having explored the basis of deep-seated feelings about guns—and therefore about gun control—we return to the contemporary political debate. That debate incorporates two features: stridency and immobility.

Policy Gridlock

The political pattern typifying the gun debate is one in which repetitive political scenarios play themselves out with great fury but astonishingly little effect. The cycle of outrage, action, and reaction usually begins with the sensational and the horrific.

Outrage

The first modern gun regulation, New York State's Sullivan law, was enacted in 1911 in reaction to an attempt to murder New York City mayor William Gaynor.[51] The shooting deaths of Senator Robert F. Kennedy and the Reverend Martin Luther King Jr., both in 1968, were more recent instances when public outrage over deaths from guns prompted a significant political reaction—passage of the federal Gun Control Act of 1968.

In the 1980s and 1990s highly publicized incidents of senseless mass slaughter and urban gang violence (with the latter often related directly or indirectly to drugs) again fanned the flames of public outrage. In 1989, for example, a man named Patrick Purdy opened fire with an AK-47 assault rifle on an elementary school playground in Stockton, California, killing five children and wounding thirty-three others. In 1991 a man using a semiautomatic pistol fired into a crowded cafeteria in Killeen, Texas, killing twenty-two people in the worst peacetime massacre of its kind in American history up until that time.[52] In 1999 two boys shot and killed twelve students and one teacher at Columbine High School in Littleton, Colorado, a crime that shocked the nation. The 2007 mass shooting at Virginia Tech State University and the 2011 shooting of Representative Gabrielle Giffords in Tucson (both discussed in the introduction) fueled similar rounds of national outrage and calls for change.

Action

Building on popular outrage, gun control proponents pressed for stronger gun laws in Congress and many state legislatures, meeting with some success. In the early 1990s, for example, states enacted laws that banned the sale and possession of assault rifles, barred those under the age of eighteen from possessing handguns, and held parents criminally liable for the gun-related actions of their children. In 1993 and 1994 Congress enacted new federal gun control laws (see chapter 5). After the Columbine massacre, national outrage pushed the US Senate to approve the first new federal gun control measure since 1994 (the bill eventually died in the House of Representatives).

Reaction

Anti–gun control forces, spearheaded by the National Rifle Association, have fought all these efforts. These forces were mostly successful in blocking gun control measures in the states and at the federal level in the 1970s and 1980s, but toward the end of the 1980s public sentiment shifted more strongly toward gun control, and the NRA's political inflexibility and stridency began to make more enemies than friends. As a consequence, the political fulcrum began to shift in favor of gun control proponents, spearheaded by the Brady Campaign to Prevent Gun Violence.

Still, the net policy change has been, for the most part, marginal, even in the states. A major federal battle revolved around the so-called Brady bill, named after the former White House press secretary and gun control supporter James Brady, who was critically wounded when shooter John Hinckley attempted to assassinate President Reagan in 1981. As enacted in 1993, the bill imposed a five-day waiting period and background checks for handgun purchases. Most agree that the Brady law is an extremely modest, even marginal effort at regulation,[53] yet the political struggle over this law was nothing less than furious.

The key policy question for the moment is not whether these policies are wise or prudent, but rather whether wise or rational policy is likely to result from this outrage-action-reaction cycle. Do sensational killings exemplify a larger problem, or are they simply extreme cases? If the latter, do they provide adequate justification for stricter gun laws? Although good policy may result, it surely cannot be attributed to a sound process in a policy sense.

The outrage-action-reaction cycle is symptomatic of the fundamental value conflict at the heart of the gun issue. As the policy analyst Thomas R. Dye noted, "policy analysis is not capable of resolving value conflicts."[54] Yet the machinery of politics cannot abandon its pursuit of better policy simply because of its degree of political difficulty. What policy analysis can do, however, is formulate its best analysis of the issue and use that analysis both to instruct and to provide a basis for reasonable policy prescription. Theodore J. Lowi framed this effort as

> develop[ing] a political science of policy analysis.... Political science may best make its pro rata contribution to good government on the basis of its ability to help define what government is ... and to evaluate the significance and impact of each form of government action *on the political system itself.*[55]

Lowi's first step, to "define what government is," translates for our purposes to a definition of "what gun control is." The social regulatory policy formulation provides the necessary theoretical tool for addressing this question. Lowi's second step, to "evaluate the significance and impact" of policies on the political system, constitutes the other analytical component of this book. It serves to bring together policy options and political realities, as reflected in the central question posed at the start of this chapter: should gun possession and use be significantly regulated?

Social Regulatory Policy Analysis

As discussed earlier, social regulatory policies seek to apply governmental authority in a direct and immediate way to shape individual actions in the realm of values, morals, and norms. As with other forms of government regulation, the enactment of specific rules accompanied by specific sanctions or penalties usually accomplishes this shaping.

According to social regulatory policy theory, certain distinctive political patterns and characteristics are associated with social regulatory issues. These patterns are observable among the major elements of the political process, including the political behavior of the courts, interest groups, the presidency, political parties, Congress, public opinion, federal agencies, and intergovernmental relations. The specific predicted patterns include the following:

- The *courts* provide a key avenue for defining and changing the issue.
- *Single-issue groups* are prevalent in the politics of the issue, and they behave in an absolutist, polarizing fashion; that is, they are singularly strident, they seek and defend extreme positions, and they are reluctant to compromise.

- *Presidential leadership* plays a relatively marginal role and operates primarily on a symbolic level.
- The *political parties* generally seek to exploit differences over social regulatory policy, with Republicans using such issues to mobilize conservatives and Democrats seeking to mobilize liberals.
- *Congress* is more heavily involved in this kind of issue than the president, but it tends to support the status quo, often following the lead of state legislatures instead of setting the course for the states.
- Rallying and mobilizing *public opinion* behind change is difficult; at the same time, for change to occur, it must be linked to and draw support from social/community norms and values.
- Federal *government agencies* exercise limited control and jurisdiction over the issue, and political winds from Congress, the president, and interest groups buffet these agencies.
- *Federalism* defines the structure and politics of the issue. That is, unlike many issues on which the federal government has become the primary actor, state and local governments continue to operate with a high degree of autonomy and control, even in the presence of federal regulations.[56]

The rest of the book relies on these predicted patterns to organize and explain the politics surrounding the gun control issue. The next chapter examines constitutional and legal issues, converging on court rulings and the much-discussed but poorly understood Second Amendment to the Constitution.

Chapter 2

The Second Amendment

Meaning, Intent, Interpretation, and Consequences

> A well regulated Militia, being necessary to the security of a free State, the right of the people to keep and bear Arms, shall not be infringed.
> *Second Amendment, US Constitution*

ANY CONSIDERATION OF THE GUN control debate inevitably turns to questions of the Constitution and the law. This quotation from the constitutional scholar Lucilius Emery illustrates that the two are inextricably linked:

> The greater deadliness of small firearms easily carried upon the person, the alarming frequency of homicides and felonious assaults with such arms, the evolution of a distinct class of criminals known as "gunmen" ... are now pressing home the question of the reason, scope, and limitation on the constitutional guaranty of a right to keep and bear arms.[1]

That Emery raised this issue in 1915 underscores the long and important connection between the gun debate and the Second Amendment. As with many aspects of constitutional interpretation, the debate over the meaning of the Second Amendment accelerated in the final decades of the twentieth century, especially within the legal community, as advocates of the so-called individualist view of the Second Amendment (discussed later in this chapter) achieved a monumental victory in 2008 when, for the first time in American history, the Supreme Court ruled in the case of *D.C. v. Heller* that the

.nendment protected a personal or individual right to own a handgun for personal self-protection in the home. Up until this time the verdict of the Supreme Court, as well as of lower federal courts, was that the amendment only protected citizen gun ownership in connection with citizen service in a government-organized and -regulated militia (known as the "collective" or "militia" view).

The Second Amendment warrants detailed treatment for two reasons. First, it is essential as a matter of public policy to know what the law does and does not allow because public policy springs from and is defined by law. Specifically, does the Second Amendment pose any obstacles to gun control? If so, what are they? If not, why is the Second Amendment so often cited as a barrier to gun control?

Second, an understanding of the Second Amendment and its consequences is essential precisely because it is a touchstone of the gun debate. In American political discourse, claims to rights abound. Some rights, such as free speech and religious freedom, are indeed cornerstones of American life, springing directly from the Bill of Rights. Yet Americans claim a bevy of other rights as well. Some, such as the right to privacy, are deemed to arise from the Bill of Rights even though privacy is not actually mentioned there. Other rights claims are far less supported, among them the right to smoke, the right to drive, the right to drink (but not to drink and drive), and the right to burn leaves in one's yard. The constitutional scholar Mary Ann Glendon has labeled this phenomenon "rights talk," a reference to "our increasing tendency to speak of what is most important to us in terms of rights, and to frame nearly every social controversy as a clash of rights."[2] This singularly American habit is founded in our historical tendency to view law as the preeminent vehicle for articulating American values, enshrining political legitimacy, and emphasizing individual rights. Rights language is "universal, inalienable, inviolable." Rights claims tend to be absolutist; thus, this kind of debate "heightens social conflict, and inhibits dialogue"; it erodes mutual respect and elevates the individual at the expense of social responsibility.[3] As Glendon notes, these attributes describe the gun control debate as well.

This chapter will assess the history, meaning, and consequences of the Second Amendment. (Because this book is principally concerned with federal gun issues, the chapter does not deal with state court rulings or Second Amendment–like provisions found in many state constitutions.[4]) Only after this assessment can we judge the abundant "rights talk" surrounding the gun control debate. Following up on the social regulatory policy analysis introduced in chapter 1, we would expect the courts to provide a key avenue for definition and change of the issue.

In order to clarify the meaning and consequences of the Second Amendment, I examine the circumstances and thinking that led to its insertion in the Bill of Rights, its interpretation by the courts, and its connection to the modern gun control debate. In order to accomplish this, I examine political and constitutional history leading up to and including the federal period, incorporating the thinking of the authors of the Bill of Rights; pertinent court cases; and the writings of Bill of Rights and Second Amendment specialists, including standard legal reference works. I then discuss the theories of those who take issue with the verdict of history and law. Above all, the reader should remember that claims to constitutional legitimacy hold special importance in American politics. Sometimes, the claim is even more important than the fact.

Historic Roots

As discussed in chapter 1, firearms possession (whether common or rare) was a part of colonial and frontier life. Settlers found it necessary to band together to provide for mutual defense from foreign armies and hostile Native Americans. This reliance on part-time militias, instead of on a regular, professional standing army, was based on two facts of life. First, the emerging American nation did not possess the manpower or resources to raise, finance, supply, or maintain a large professional army. Second, Americans shared a profound mistrust of standing armies. This suspicion stemmed from their knowledge of and experiences with standing armies in European history, in which, with depressing regularity, professional armies had subverted or overthrown civilian governments and deprived people of basic rights.

The British Heritage

Great Britain had recently experienced such turmoil. For thirteen years in the middle of the seventeenth century, professional military forces under the control of Oliver Cromwell ruled England. The country was, in the words of the great British historian Thomas Babington Macaulay, "governed by the sword," in that "the civil power" was "subjected to military dictation." Under Cromwell's standing army "the King had been murdered, the nobility degraded, the landed gentry plundered, the Church persecuted."[5] Only a few years after Cromwell, King James II, a devout Catholic, promoted the cause of "papism" by filling the leading ranks of the army with Catholics, to the exclusion of Protestants. James's oppressive practices in the cause of advancing Catholicism, including the threat of a swelling Catholic-led army that might overwhelm local Protestant militias (controlled by local landed gentry), eventually led to his overthrow and replacement by William of Orange, an event dubbed the Glorious Revolution of 1688.

Thereafter, in 1689 Parliament enacted the British Bill of Rights, in which various grievances against James II were enumerated, including that he "did endeavor to subvert and extirpate the Protestant Religion and the Laws and Liberties of this Kingdom.... By causing several good Subjects, being Protestants, to be disarmed at the same Time when Papists were both armed and employed contrary to Law." The right defined in Article VII of this document was "that the Subjects which are Protestants may have Arms for their Defence suitable to their Conditions, and as allowed by Law."[6] The law to which this sentence referred stipulated that only the nobility, wealthy landowners, and members of the militia executing their duty to defend the country could own firearms. As the historian Lois Schworer noted of Article VII, "Englishmen did not secure to 'ordinary citizens' the right to possess weapons."[7] This provision from the British Bill of Rights is cited as the forerunner of America's Second Amendment, although there is no direct evidence that it served as the model for the Second Amendment.[8] Foreshadowing the American experience, the British recognized the superior fighting capabilities of standing armies, but for political and historical reasons they found it necessary to pay the militia its due. In Macaulay's words, the British "were forced to acknowledge that, dangerous as it might be to keep up a permanent military establishment, it might be more dangerous still to stake the honour and independence of the country on the result of a contest between plowmen officered by Justices of the Peace, and veteran warriors led by Marshalls of France. In Parliament, however, it was necessary to express such opinions with some reserve; for the militia was an institution eminently popular."[9] These important episodes in British history revealed the actual and feared mischief of standing armies of which British subjects in America were keenly aware. They also underscored the government's connection of firearms ownership and regulation with militia or military service.[10]

The Colonial Heritage

The mistrust of standing armies was a pervasive sentiment during the revolutionary period and was directly related to the bearing of arms by citizens.[11] James Lovell wrote in 1771 that "the true strength and safety of every commonwealth or limited monarchy, is the bravery of its freeholders, its militia. By brave militias they rise to grandeur; and they come to ruin by a mercenary army." In 1776 Samuel Adams wrote that a "standing army, however necessary it may be at some times, is always dangerous to the liberties of the people." Samuel Seabury characterized the standing army as "the monster." George Washington observed that "mercenary armies ... have at one time or another subverted the liberties of almost all the Countries they have been raised to defend." At the same point, however, John Adams spoke bluntly to one American general when he said, "We don't choose to trust you generals, with too much power, for too long [a] time."[12]

In this way, the reliance on the citizen-soldier became synonymous with the revolutionary spirit. The Virginia Declaration of Rights, written in 1776, said that "standing armies, in time of peace, should be avoided, as dangerous to liberty." The other states copied Virginia's wording.[13] The public myth prevailing at the time concerning the military effectiveness of militias buttressed sentiments favoring the militia as more compatible with democratic values. What the political scientist Clinton Rossiter labeled "the Cincinnatus complex" was the belief that no professional army could fight as effectively as a citizen militia.[14] This and related sentiments were reflected in the political thought of such philosophers as Voltaire, François Quesnay, Anne-Robert-Jacques Turgot, and Jean-Jacques Rousseau. As was true in Britain, military reality would prove this politically popular myth to be hollow indeed.[15] Not only had the Americans inherited the mistrust of standing armies from the British, but ironically, the behavior of British troops on American soil magnified that mistrust. American outrage over the behavior of British troops found specific expression in the Declaration of Independence, wherein Thomas Jefferson complained that "He [the King] has kept among us, in Times of Peace, Standing Armies, without the consent of our Legislatures. He has affected to render the Military independent of and superior to the Civil Power." The 1776 Declaration also complained that the British were "quartering large Bodies of Armed Troops among us" and "protecting them, by a mock Trial, from Punishment for any Murders which they should commit on the Inhabitants of these States." The British only compounded these grievances and suspicions by "transporting large armies of foreign mercenaries [Hessians] to compleat the works of death, desolation, and tyranny." Not surprisingly, the British also took any and every opportunity to seize American weapons and ammunition.

As a consequence, American prosecution of the Revolutionary War relied for the most part on citizen militias that, according to the historian Merrill Jensen, were really "fourteen armies: the thirteen state militias and the Continental Army."[16] Although the reliance on militias was politically satisfying, it proved to be an administrative and military nightmare. State detachments could not be easily combined into larger fighting units, soldiers could not be relied on to serve for extended periods and desertions were common, officers were elected according to their popularity rather than experience or training, and discipline and uniformity were almost nonexistent. All too often militia units would enter the American army camp, consume scarce supplies, get drunk, quarrel, fight with each other, and then melt away the night before battle.[17] The commander in chief, George Washington, defended the militia in public, but he made his real sentiments brutally clear in correspondence with Congress:

> To place any dependence upon Militia, is, assuredly, resting upon a broken staff. Men just dragged from the tender Scenes of domestick life; unaccustomed to the din of Arms; totally unacquainted with every kind of military skill, which being followed by a want of confidence in themselves, when opposed to Troops regularly train'd, disciplined, and appointed, superior in knowledge and superior in Arms, makes them timid, and ready to fly from their own shadows.... [I]f I was called upon to declare upon Oath, whether the Militia have been most serviceable or hurtful upon the whole; I should subscribe to the latter.[18]

At a later point, Washington said of the militias that they "come in, you cannot tell how; go, you cannot tell when; and act, you cannot tell where." Despite the militia handicap, America did, of course, eventually win its independence, owing to the durability of the core group of soldiers composing the Continental Army that maintained the force's continuity as militias came and went; the large size of its force (more than four hundred thousand men participated during the course of the war); the adoption of tactics appropriate to American terrain; the assistance of the French; British difficulties related to distance and supply; and the American "home court advantage."

The Constitution

America's first constitution, the Articles of Confederation (1777–1789), reflected suspicion not only of standing armies but also of a strong national government. The Articles specifically granted sovereignty to the states and severely limited the power of Congress. Formulated and adopted during the Revolution, the Articles placed the primary burden of national defense on the states, stipulating that "every state shall always keep up a well regulated and disciplined militia, sufficiently armed and accoutred" (Article VI) and that Congress's military powers could be exercised only by a vote of nine of the thirteen states (Article IX). No specific provision was made for a national standing army.

These and other shortcomings of the Articles led to the Federal Convention of 1787 and the adoption of the modern Constitution. The military issue was resolved by establishing federal government power over both militias and a standing army. In Article I, Section 8, Congress was given the power to "raise and support armies," "provide and maintain a Navy," and finance and regulate both. In an important departure from the Articles, Congress would now have key authority over the state militias, as it could "provide for calling forth the Militia" in order "to execute the Laws of the Union, suppress Insurrections and repel Invasions," and it could "provide for organizing, arming, and disciplining the Militia, and for governing such Part of them as may be employed in the Service of the United States." The states retained only limited control, as the Constitution reserved "to the States respectively, the Appointment of the Officers, and the Authority of training the Militia according to the discipline prescribed by Congress." In addition, the president would serve as commander in chief of the military forces, including the militia (Article II, Section 2).

The founders recognized the long-standing mistrust of standing armies but accepted the reality that the militia was no substitute for a trained professional force controlled by the national government.[19] Those at the Constitutional Convention of 1787 who feared too much federal control over the military won two small concessions: limited control over the militias, which were primarily put under control of the federal government, and militia mobilization by Congress could occur only under the three circumstances listed above.

The overriding necessity for an effective fighting force was keenly felt in the country's early history, as it faced not only hostile European and indigenous forces on all sides but threats from internal rebellion. As the colonial historian Max Farrand noted, "Shays's rebellion [January 1787] had taught a much needed lesson. It was not sufficient to place the state militia under some central control. The central government must be empowered to maintain an efficient army and navy to protect the states against internal disorders, as well as against external dangers."[20] Reflecting the prevailing political view of the time, Virginia delegate George Mason also spoke for many at the Constitutional Convention when he said during debate that "he hoped there would be no standing army in time of peace, unless it might be for a few garrisons. The Militia ought therefore to be the more effectually prepared for the public defence."[21] James Madison said that "as the greatest danger to liberty is from large standing armies, it is best to prevent them by an effectual provision for a good Militia."[22] At the same time, the Virginians Madison and Edmund Randolph recognized that the states had often neglected their militias, making them unreliable unless the federal government could impose uniformity and discipline. Mason attempted to codify the warning against the liberty-eroding tendencies of standing armies when he proposed (unsuccessfully) an amendment to Article I, Section 8, to add the phrase "That the Liberties of the People may be the better secured against the Danger of regular Troops or standing Armys in time of Peace" preceding "To provide for organizing arming & disciplining the Militia."[23] Many of the issues raised during the Constitutional Convention arose in state-ratifying conventions. During the Virginia-ratifying convention in 1788, Edmund Randolph (also a delegate to the federal convention) said, "With respect to a standing army, I believe there was not a member in the federal convention who did not feel indignation at such an institution."[24] From a distance of two decades, founder Gouverneur Morris reflected the contrary sentiment in a singularly blunt fashion when he wrote in 1815:

> An overweening vanity leads the fond many ... to believe or affect to believe, that militia can beat veteran troops in the open field and even play of battle. This idle notion, fed by vaunting demagogues, alarmed us [the founders] for our country, when in the course of that time and chance ... she should be at war with a great power.... To rely on militia was to lean on a broken reed.[25]

Defenders of the new Constitution sought to assuage fears and counter criticisms in *The Federalist*. In *Federalist* number 24 Alexander Hamilton argued that it would be a mistake to restrict or ban standing armies in times of peace, citing the constant threats the young nation faced along its vast frontiers and the necessity of allowing Congress appropriate latitude to meet variable but persistent military threats. In number 25 Hamilton argued forcefully that standing armies were naturally superior on the battlefield, the Revolutionary War notwithstanding, and in number 28 that they were similarly superior in dealing with civil unrest. Further, Hamilton noted in number 29 that the federal government must have the power to impose uniformity on the militias in order for them to be effective and efficient. Both he and Madison dismissed the fear that a standing army would deprive the states of their sovereignty or citizens of their liberties. To "those who prophesy the downfall of the State governments," Madison, in number 46, computed that the United States could at the time raise at best an army of thirty thousand men—a force that could be opposed by state militias totaling a half million men. And in Hamilton's number 29 this wording presaged what would later become part of the text of the Second Amendment: "If a well-regulated militia be the most natural defense of a free country, it ought certainly to be under the regulation and at the disposal of that body which is constituted the guardian of the national security."

The Bill of Rights

The adoption of the Constitution codified the dual militia and standing army military system, but it did not resolve the nagging question of federalism; that is, the new Constitution not only countenanced a national standing army but also gave the federal government vast new power over the militia. Anti-Federalists were extremely concerned that this power might be used not only to undercut the effectiveness and independence of state militias (e.g., by the federal government's refusal to organize, arm, or train them—although Federalists asserted that the states would retain such powers if the federal government failed to act) but also to gut state power entirely. Convention delegate and anti-Federalist Luther Martin predicted nothing less than the demise of the states if the Constitution were adopted with federal control of militias included:

> They [supporters of the Constitution] said, that ... if the militia was under the control and the authority of the respective States, it would enable them to thwart and oppose the general [federal] government.... If after having retained to the general government the great powers already granted, and among those, that of raising and keeping up regular troops without limitations, the power over the militia should be taken away from the States, and also given to the general government, it ought to be considered as the last coup de grace to the State governments; that it must be the most convincing proof, the advocates of this system design the destruction of the State governments.[26]

These fears found voice in several state ratifying conventions, most particularly that of Virginia, where the anti-Federalist cause found no more eloquent champion than the revolutionary firebrand Patrick Henry. Profoundly suspicious of the concentrated federal governmental power provided in the new Constitution, Henry spoke for many who preferred a weak national government and strong states when he asked, "Have we [in Virginia] the means of resisting disciplined armies, when our only defence, the militia, is put into the hands of Congress?" Henry sought assurance that "with respect to your militia, we only request that, if Congress should refuse to find arms for them, this country may lay out their own money to purchase them."[27] Setting an example for other states,[28] the Virginia convention passed this wording, modeled on Virginia's Declaration of Rights of 1776, when it ratified the Constitution:

> That the people have a right to keep and bear arms; that a well-regulated militia, composed of the body of the people trained to arms, is the proper, natural, and safe defence of a free state; that standing armies, in time of

peace, are dangerous to liberty, and therefore ought to be avoided, as far as the circumstances and protection of the community will admit; and that, in all cases, the military should be under strict subordination to, and governed by, the civil power.[29]

In short, "the advocates of state sovereignty wished the main reliance to be upon militia, while their opponents [Federalists] saw the need for an effective standing army."[30] The central question giving rise to the Second Amendment was whether congressional authority over state militias could eclipse that of the state governments and whether this new federal military power (over both the militia and the federal-controlled professional army) might be used to abrogate state sovereignty and power. Although this might seem like an arcane or irrelevant issue to modern Americans, it went to the very core of the dispute over the new Constitution of 1787.

The pressure for a Bill of Rights to limit federal authority became all but irresistible. On June 8, 1789, Madison introduced in the House of Representatives of the First Congress a proposed list of rights to be added to the Constitution. Drawn heavily from Virginia's 1776 Declaration of Rights, the list included this, to be inserted in Article I, Section 9 (a section of the Constitution that lists several limits on the federal government and that followed the section dealing with military matters): "The right of the people to keep and bear arms shall not be infringed; a well armed, and well regulated militia being the best security of a free country: but no person religiously scrupulous of bearing arms, shall be compelled to render military service in person." As reported out of House committee on July 28, the amendment said, "A well regulated militia, composed of the body of the people, being the best security of a free State, the right of the people to keep and bear arms shall not be infringed, but no person religiously scrupulous shall be compelled to bear arms." On August 24, the House passed this wording: "A well regulated militia, composed of the body of the People, being the best security of a free State, the right of the People to keep and bear arms, shall not be infringed, but no one religiously scrupulous of bearing arms, shall be compelled to render military service in person." This and the other amendments then went to the Senate, where the final wording of what became the Second Amendment emerged: "A well regulated militia, being necessary to the security of a free State, the right of the people to keep and bear arms, shall not be infringed."[31] The sparse debate over the Second Amendment in the First Congress dealt with a few familiar questions, all concerning military matters: whether the amendment wording should codify the right of conscientious objectors to opt out of military service for religious reasons; the relationship between militias, standing armies, and liberty; the need to subordinate the military to civilian authority; and the military unreliability of the militia as compared with a professional army.[32]

To judge by the brief debate about and modest wording changes in the amendment's four versions, the basic sentiment was held throughout: that citizens have a constitutionally protected right or duty to serve in state militias when called into service by and in defense of state and country, and that the militias cannot be disarmed so as to render them ineffectual. The aim was to ensure the continued existence of state militias as a military and political counterbalance to the national army and, more broadly, to national power (the federalism question). Southerners in particular were very concerned about maintaining state militias to suppress slave rebellions because they were doubtful that a national government dominated by Northern interests would be willing to commit federal troops and supplies to keep African Americans in the bondage of slavery. All of the debate over the Second Amendment dealt with military questions. As Massachusetts delegate Elbridge Gerry said during congressional debate,

> What, sir, is the use of a militia? It is to prevent the establishment of a standing army, the bane of liberty.... Whenever government mean to invade the rights and liberties of the people, they always attempt to destroy the militia, in order to raise an army upon their ruins. This was actually done by Great Britain at the commencement of the late revolution.[33]

Thus, the Second Amendment is founded on federalism, balancing powers between the federal government and the states, and on military necessity, developing a political compromise between politically popular militias and a politically unpopular but militarily necessary national professional army. Most believed that the nation's very survival had to involve the entire adult male population. Absent from this extended history is any connection between the Second Amendment and any personal use of weapons for purposes including hunting, sporting, recreation, or even personal protection (a matter common law had already addressed in the eighteenth century).[34] Its purpose, like that of the Bill of Rights as a whole, was to place limits on the federal government and strike a balance between national and state power.

The Militia Transformed

Soon after the ratification of the Bill of Rights in 1791, Congress moved ahead to establish rules and procedures governing the militias. Titled "An Act more effectively to provide for the National Defence by establishing an Uniform Militia throughout the United States," the Uniform Militia Act of 1792 (I US Stat. 271) defined the nation's militia (in keeping with American militia tradition) as "every free able-bodied white male citizen of the respective states" between the ages of eighteen and forty-five.

Also in keeping with the militia tradition, the militiamen were legally obligated to provide their own weapons, ammunition, and accoutrements: "That every citizen so enrolled ... shall ... provide himself with a good musket or firelock, a sufficient bayonet and belt, two spare flints, and a knapsack, a pouch with a box therein to contain not less than twenty-four cartridges ... each cartridge to contain a proper quantity of powder and ball."[35] It is not hard to understand why the Second Amendment was so careful to protect the right to keep and bear arms when militiamen, by law and tradition, bore the burden of arming themselves. Indeed, even though the Constitution said that Congress bore responsibility for arming the militia (Article I, Section 8), Madison "observed that 'arming' as explained did not extend to furnishing arms." Massachusetts delegate Rufus King elaborated that arming meant providing "for uniformity of arms," including "authority to regulate the modes of furnishing" them.[36] In the two years following the passage of the Uniform Militia Act, all fifteen states passed their own laws to bring their militia systems into line with federal guidelines. Both the wisdom of and fears prompting the militia system seemed borne out in the country's first few years. Some key battles with Native Americans were successfully won with militia forces in 1794, and the Whiskey Rebellion of the same year was suppressed with a militia force of fifteen thousand.[37] In 1794 Georgia militiamen literally faced federal troops with weapons loaded and aimed in a dispute over the treatment of the Creek and Cherokee peoples. A dispute over the Alien and Sedition Acts of 1798 nearly precipitated a similar encounter between federal troops and the Virginia militia in 1798.

Despite these events, by the close of the eighteenth century it was already clear that the militias were impractical, if not obsolete. Almost without exception, the states failed to implement the terms of the Uniform Militia Act. The system of fines imposed to impel men to arm and uniform themselves, as well as to ensure that they showed up for drills, failed to achieve these objectives. Neither the states nor the federal government took much interest in continuing universal militia training and service, although the social structure of the militia system continued for decades.[38] Indeed, the "history of the state militias between 1800 and the 1870s is one of total abandonment, disorganization, and degeneration." Instead, the government relied on its professional army and elite corps of volunteers, called the select (later, "organized") militias.[39] The reputation of the citizen militias suffered a final, crippling blow as the result of their terrible performance in the War of 1812. According to the military historians Donald M. Snow and Dennis M. Drew, this conflict shattered the illusion that general militias were militarily effective and reliable. The War of 1812 revealed militias to be "generally ineffective" and any successes were the result of "overwhelming odds or the incompetence of the adversary," factors that help explain why this conflict was "the closest thing to a decisive military defeat the United States has ever suffered." The American forces' "unpreparedness" and "amateur military leadership" was "a national disgrace."[40] As the political historian Stephen Skowronek noted in his important study of the evolving military system of the nineteenth century: "By the 1840s the militia system envisioned in the early days of the republic was a dead letter. Universal military training fell victim to a general lack of interest and administrative incompetence at both the federal and state levels."[41] Thus, subsequent references to the militia pertained to the select or volunteer militia, not to the more well-known system of universal male service (the unorganized or general militia). The idea of universal militia service would persist, however, because Congress retained the theoretical power to mobilize such a force; more important, it persisted as part of the political symbolism and mythology surrounding the Second Amendment.

No significant legal changes occurred until the start of the twentieth century. In a 1901 message to Congress, President Theodore Roosevelt called for long-overdue legal change, saying that "our militia law is obsolete and worthless."[42] In 1903 Congress passed the Militia Act, which legally separated the "organized [also known as volunteer or select] militia, to be known as the National Guard," from the "reserve militia," also called the unorganized militia, even though the unorganized militia had by now been discarded as a viable military entity for the simple reason that fighting could no longer be given over to untrained amateurs. The balance of the act provided for federal arming, training, and drilling of the National Guard. It made no provision whatsoever for the unorganized militia.[43] In 1916 Congress passed the National Defense Act, which mandated that the National Guard would be organized in the same method as the "Regular Army." It also placed state Guards under federal guidelines.[44] Thus, from 1903 onward America's active militia in law was the National Guard, which, though now under federal regulation, is still trained by the respective states.[45] Congress retained for itself the theoretical option of calling up the reserve militia—all able-bodied men from seventeen to forty-five[46]—but America's now substantial regular army, plus the National Guard, constituted formidable and ample military forces to meet national needs. Any gaps in those needs have been met in modern times by the military draft rather than by activation of the old-style militia. As the historian Saul Cornell demonstrated, the Second Amendment embodied a "civic right," meaning that citizens were obligated by and to the government to participate in a well-regulated militia, as militias existed and functioned in the country's first century. Attendant to that obligation was the citizen's "right" to keep and bear arms to the extent that citizen arms bearing was necessary to ensure the military viability of the government's militias.[47]

In sum, the possession of firearms referred to in the Second Amendment comes into play only at such time as the unorganized militia is activated by a state or the federal government, a practice effectively abandoned before the Civil War, and when the government fails to provide weapons for that force.[48] Thus, the historical Second Amendment was rendered essentially irrelevant to modern American life, as is the prospect of, say, National Guard troops from New York and Pennsylvania squaring off against each other, weapons at the ready, along state borders.[49] Its irrelevancy in law was reversed, however, when the Supreme Court infused the amendment with a new, gun rights–based interpretation in 2008.

Supreme Court Rulings

The Second Amendment has generated relatively little constitutional law. In six instances, however, the Supreme Court has ruled directly on this amendment.

In the first case, *US v. Cruikshank,* 92 US 542 (1876), William Cruikshank and two other defendants were charged with thirty-two counts of depriving blacks of their constitutional rights, including two claiming that the defendants had deprived blacks of firearms possession, in violation of the Force Act of 1870. Speaking for the Court, Chief Justice Morrison Remick Waite wrote,

The second and tenth counts are equally defective. The right there specified is that of "bearing arms for a lawful purpose." This is not a right granted by the Constitution. Neither is it in any manner dependent upon that instrument for its existence. The Second Amendment declares that it shall not be infringed; but this ... means no more than that it shall not be infringed by Congress. This is one of the amendments that has no other effect than to restrict the powers of the National Government.[50]

The Court in this case established two principles that it (and most other courts) consistently upheld: that laws may be properly enacted to restrict or regulate the carrying of weapons, including firearms, and that the Second

Amendment was not "incorporated," meaning that it pertained only to federal power, not state power (this is what the Court meant when it referred to the Second Amendment not being "infringed by Congress"). Admittedly, the Supreme Court did not begin to incorporate parts of the first ten amendments (i.e., use the wording of the due process and equal protection clauses of the Fourteenth Amendment to extend parts of the Bill of Rights to the states) until 1897.[51] But the Court has never accepted the idea of incorporating the entire Bill of Rights,[52] and until 2010 it declined numerous opportunities to incorporate the Second Amendment long after it had incorporated most of the rest of the Bill of Rights.

Ten years later the Court ruled in *Presser v. Illinois*, 116 US 252 (1886), that an Illinois law that barred paramilitary organizations from drilling or parading in cities or towns without a license from the governor was constitutional. Herman Presser challenged the law after he was found guilty of illegally marching and drilling his (armed) fringe group, Lehr und Wehr Verein, through Chicago streets. In upholding the Illinois law, the Court reaffirmed that the Second Amendment did not apply to the states (citing *Cruikshank*).[53] Speaking for a unanimous Court, Justice William Burnham Woods went on to discuss the relationship between the citizen, the militia, and the government:

> It is undoubtedly true that all citizens capable of bearing arms constitute the reserved military force or reserved militia of the United States as well as of the States; and, in view of this prerogative ... the States cannot, even laying the constitutional provision in question out of view, prohibit the people from keeping and bearing arms, so as to deprive the United States of their rightful resource for maintaining the public security, and disable the people from performing their duty to the General Government. But, as already stated, we think it clear that the sections under consideration do not have this effect.

The Court then went on to ask whether Presser and his associates had a right to organize with others as a self-proclaimed and armed military organization against state law. No, the Court answered, because such activity "is not an attribute of national citizenship. Military organization and military drill and parade under arms are subjects especially under the control of the government of every country. They cannot be claimed as a right independent of law." In other words, militias exist only as defined and regulated by the state or federal government, which in Illinois at the time was the eight thousand–member Illinois National Guard (as the Court noted in its decision). To deny the government the power to define and regulate militias would, according to the Court, "be to deny the right of the State to disperse assemblages organized for sedition and treason, and the right to suppress armed mobs bent on riot and rapine [looting]." Thus, the *Presser* case confirmed the understanding that the right to bear arms came into play only in connection with the formation and conduct of the militia, as formed and regulated by the government. The Court emphatically rejected the idea that citizens could create their own militias, much less that the Second Amendment protected citizens' rights to own weapons for their own purposes.

In 1894 the Supreme Court unanimously ruled in *Miller v. Texas,* 153 US 535 (1894), that a Texas law "prohibiting the carrying of dangerous weapons" did not violate the Second Amendment. Again, the Court said that the right to bear arms did not apply to the states. The Court ruled similarly in *Robertson v. Baldwin,* 165 US 275 (1897).[54]

In 1939 the Supreme Court addressed the meaning of the Second Amendment in *US v. Miller,* 307 US 174 (the first significant case on the Second Amendment handed down after the Court began the process of incorporation). The *Miller* case was founded on a challenge to the National Firearms Act of 1934, which regulated the interstate transport of various weapons. Jack Miller and Frank Layton were indicted under the 1934 act for transporting an unregistered 12-gauge sawed-off shotgun (having a barrel less than eighteen inches long) across state lines. They challenged the act's constitutionality by claiming that it was a violation of the Second Amendment and that it represented an improper use of the commerce power. The Court turned aside these claims and ruled that the federal taxing power could be used to regulate firearms and that firearm registration (as required under Section 5(a) of the 1934 law) was constitutional. Beyond this, the Court was unequivocal in saying that the Second Amendment must be interpreted by its "obvious purpose" of ensuring an effective militia as described in Article I, Section 8, of the Constitution (to which the Court referred in its decision). Speaking for a unanimous court, Justice James Clark McReynolds wrote,

> In the absence of any evidence tending to show that possession or use of a "shotgun having a barrel of less than eighteen inches in length" at this time has some reasonable relationship to the preservation or efficiency of a well regulated militia, we cannot say that the Second Amendment guarantees the right to keep and bear such an instrument. Certainly it is not within judicial notice that this weapon is any part of the ordinary military equipment or that its use could contribute to the common defense.

In the next paragraph the Court noted that the Constitution gave to Congress the power to call forth and regulate the militia, quoting from Congress's Article I, Section 8, powers. It then said this:

With the obvious purpose to assure the continuation and render possible the effectiveness of such forces the declaration and guarantee of the Second Amendment were made. It must be interpreted and applied with that end in view.

Thus, the Court stated that citizens could possess a constitutional right to bear arms only in connection with service in a government-organized and -regulated militia. In addition, it affirmed the constitutional right of Congress as well as the states to regulate firearms. Most of the rest of the decision is an extended discussion of the antecedents of the Second Amendment. Justice McReynolds cited various classic works, colonial practices, and early state laws and constitutions to demonstrate the importance of militias and citizen-armies to early America as the explanation for the presence and meaning of the Second Amendment.

Critics of this case have on occasion taken the wording quoted above to mean that the Court would protect under the Second Amendment the ownership of guns that do bear some connection with national defense. Such an interpretation is foolish on its face because, first, such reasoning would justify the private ownership of such militarily useful weapons as machine guns, bazookas, howitzers, and even tactical nuclear weapons. Second, the Court decision states that possession of such weapons as sawed-off shotguns could be allowed under existing law only if that possession were connected with militia service. Because the two men charged under the 1934 law obviously did not have the gun for the purpose of or while they were serving under an organized militia, their prosecution was justified; the Second Amendment would apply only in the context of militia service. And as *Presser* clearly stated, citizens may not create their own militias independent of the government. Ironically, sawed-off shotguns can and do have some military value.[55] The Court's point in this case arose from the challenge to the National Firearms Act (the source of the Court's definition of a sawed-off shotgun),[56] and its remedy lay in the failure of *Miller* and *Layton* to claim any credible connection to Second Amendment–based militia activities. The Second Amendment also received brief mention in two other Supreme Court cases, *Adams v. Williams*, 407 US 143 (1972; the comment on the Second Amendment was in a dissenting opinion), and *Lewis v. US*, 445 US 95 (1980), when the court specifically cited the 1939 *Miller* case to uphold gun regulations as long as there was some "rational basis" for them.[57] Both of these cases supported the logic of the earlier four.

Responding in part to a rising tide of writing in support of an "individualist" view of the Second Amendment (discussed later in this chapter) buttressed substantially by gun rights groups[58] and because of a more conservative court sympathetic to this viewpoint, the Supreme Court reversed course on the Second Amendment in 2008 in the landmark case of *D.C. v. Heller* (554 US 570). In this case the court majority set two firsts: for the first time in history a federal court overturned a gun regulation as a violation of the Second Amendment; in addition, it adopted the individualist interpretation of the amendment,[59] reversing course on its prior rulings, all of which supported some version of the militia-based interpretation of the amendment.

The *Heller* case arose as a challenge to the District of Columbia's strict gun law, first enacted in 1976 (and drafted, ironically, with the assistance of the National Rifle Association), which banned the new registration of handguns, banned handgun carrying, and required that firearms in the home be kept unloaded and locked. Police officers and security guards were exempted. The law was challenged as a violation of the Second Amendment. The fact that the federal government directly governs the nation's capital meant that the Court's past refusal to incorporate the Second Amendment did not keep the case from proceeding, as the entire Bill of Rights has always applied to actions of the federal government.

On appeal from the District of Columbia Circuit,[60] the Supreme Court ruled 5–4 against the DC law, striking it down as inconsistent with the court majority's individualist reading of the Second Amendment. Writing for the majority, Justice Antonin Scalia concluded that the amendment now protected a personal right of civilians to own handguns to protect themselves in their homes. This right is by no means unlimited, however. Scalia noted that "nothing in our opinion should be taken to cast doubt on longstanding prohibitions on the possession of firearms by felons or the mentally ill, or laws forbidding the carrying of firearms in sensitive places such as schools and government buildings, or laws imposing conditions and qualifications on the commercial sale of arms."[61] In addition to lending support for long-standing gun regulations, the court also suggested that certain types of especially powerful weapons might also be subject to regulation and that laws regarding the safe storage of firearms would also be allowable. As for the court's past reading of the Second Amendment as militia based, the majority decision rejected the idea that the first half of the Second Amendment, referencing a "well regulated militia," explained the second half of the sentence (referencing the right to bear arms), arguing instead that the first half of the sentence in effect merely offered an example of the right mentioned in the second half of the sentence. Indeed, most of the text of this lengthy opinion dealt with the history of the right to bear arms. The decision did not overturn the 1939 *Miller* case (previously discussed), but dealt with it instead by saying that it was only about "the type of weapon" at issue in the case. "Beyond that,"

Scalia concluded, "the opinion [i.e., *Miller*] provided no explanation of the content"[62] of the Second Amendment.

The four dissenting justices filed two dissents, authored by Justices John Paul Stevens and Stephen Breyer. Stevens's opinion disputed Scalia's historical analysis, arguing in a similarly lengthy historical analysis that the amendment was indeed a militia-based right and that the Supreme Court had said so in *Miller* and *Presser* (Scalia argued that the prior court rulings either supported or were not inconsistent with the individualist view). Stevens wrote that "The text of the [Second] amendment, its history, and our decision in United States v. Miller … provide a clear answer"[63] to the meaning of the amendment. In Stevens's view, that answer was that the amendment "was adopted to protect the right of the people of each of the several States to maintain a well-regulated militia."[64] Stevens's interpretation of *Miller* was that "it protects the right to keep and bear arms for certain military purposes."[65] Stevens also noted that this was how literally hundreds of federal judges in dozens of cases had interpreted *Miller*. Breyer's dissent argued that even if the individualist interpretation were correct, DC's strict gun law was still allowable as a legitimate effort to control crime. In all, the *Heller* decision is notable for three reasons: first, for carving out a new, individual right to own guns, even if the right is subject to limitations and regulation; second, for its heavy reliance on history; and third, for the fierce controversy it engendered. In the aftermath of *Heller*, scores of legal challenges were mounted against gun laws around the country.

Finally, the Supreme Court completed its establishment of this new right two years later in the case of *McDonald v. Chicago* (561 US 742; 2010), in which the high court, by the same 5–4 vote, applied or "incorporated" the Second Amendment to the states. The *McDonald* case arose from a Second Amendment–based challenge to Chicago's strict law that essentially banned handguns and any other gun not already registered with the city (Chicago's law was very similar to the DC law struck down by *Heller*). The majority opinion, written by Justice Samuel Alito, did two primary things. First, it affirmed the qualified *Heller* individual right, saying that "the right to keep and bear arms is not 'a right to keep and carry any weapon whatsoever in any manner whatsoever and for whatever purpose.'"[66] Further, this ruling was not to cast doubt on "longstanding [gun] regulatory measures"[67] such as those cited in *Heller*. Second, the majority opinion incorporated or applied the Second Amendment to the states while cautioning that "incorporation does not imperil every law regulating firearms."[68] The means by which the Court chose to effect incorporation was through the Fourteenth Amendment's "due process" clause, which had been the basis for past incorporation decisions regarding parts of the Bill of Rights. It rejected the argument that it should use the Fourteenth Amendment's "privileges or immunities" clause (a much-discussed but controversial method that the Court discarded in the nineteenth century[69]), and it rejected the idea of "total incorporation," a theory arguing that the entire Bill of Rights should be applied to the states as a whole. *McDonald* produced five opinions: three in the majority and two in the minority. Although the majority argued that this individual right to guns was a "fundamental" right "necessary to our system of ordered liberty"[70] (the standard for incorporation), Justice John Paul Stevens, in his dissent, argued that guns "destabilize ordered liberty."[71] He and the dissenters continued to argue that *Heller* was wrongly decided and that incorporation itself was not warranted in this case. As for the Chicago law, the Court did not strike it down but instead sent it back to the lower court for review in the light of its new ruling. In the first six years following *Heller* more than 700 challenges to gun laws around the country have been brought; to date, virtually all have failed. Further, the Supreme Court has generally refused to hear Second Amendment-based appeals. From 2008 to mid-2013, it turned aside more than sixty such appeals.[72] Yet at least two major questions remain unresolved: whether citizens have a Second Amendment right to carry firearms in public and the degree of restrictiveness the courts should apply when gun laws are challenged.

Other Court Rulings

The Supreme Court cases up to *D.C. v. Heller* represented an unbroken line of Court thinking—one that lower courts have consistently followed. Challenges to gun regulations and related efforts to win a broader interpretation of the Second Amendment (including efforts to incorporate the Second Amendment) were uniformly turned aside—with a single exception. In more than forty cases from *US v. Miller* to *Heller,* federal courts of appeal "analyzed the Second Amendment purely in terms of protecting state militias, rather than individual rights."[73] Of those, the Supreme Court declined to hear appeals in nearly half of these cases, thus letting the lower court rulings stand. The inescapable conclusion is that the Supreme Court considered the matter settled and had no interest in crowding its docket with cases that merely repeated what has already been decided. An article written by retired chief justice Warren Burger that appeared in *Parade* magazine confirmed this.[74] Lower federal courts and state courts generally followed this pattern.[75] In the most famous of these cases the Supreme Court declined to hear an appeal of two lower federal court rulings upholding the constitutionality of a strict gun control law passed in Morton Grove, Illinois, in 1981 that banned the ownership of working handguns by anyone except peace officers, prison officials, members of the armed forces and National Guard, and security guards as long as such possession was in accordance with their official duties.[76] The one pre-*Heller* federal court case that produced a finding different from the others discussed above was *US v. Emerson* (270 F.3d 203, 5th Cir. 2001), in which two members of a three-judge panel embraced the individualist view but failed to use it to uphold an individual's right to own guns.[77] So many lower federal court rulings' unanimous acceptance of the militia view buttresses the conclusion that the 1939 *Miller* case did indeed embrace the militia view and that it was the accepted legal interpretation. In the post-*Heller* world the Supreme Court's new standard for Second Amendment cases will guide lower courts, but as suggested earlier, the likely outcome seems to be that most existing gun laws will continue to pass constitutional muster.

Bad History Makes Bad Law

The *Heller* and *McDonald* rulings have established as a matter of law an individual-rights interpretation of the Second Amendment. But although judges can change the law, they cannot change history, and the historical record largely contradicts the bases for these two recent rulings.

The militia-based understanding of the Second Amendment is that found in most standard historical texts on the Bill of Rights. From classic nineteenth-century analyses such as those of St. George Tucker, Joseph Story, and Thomas M. Cooley, to modern treatments, the verdict is the same.[78] In his classic book on the Bill of Rights, Irving Brant wrote, "The Second Amendment, popularly misread, comes to life chiefly on the parade floats of rifle associations and in the propaganda of mail-order houses selling pistols to teenage gangsters."[79] Similar, if less sarcastic, sentiments are found in other standard works. In the words of Robert A. Rutland, the Second Amendment (along with the Third, having to do with the quartering of troops in private homes) had become "obsolete."[80] Moreover, standard legal reference works that lawyers and judges use paralleled this perspective.[81] The fact that standard historical treatments of the amendment have long accepted the militia-based view lends credence to the criticism that the *Heller* ruling played fast and loose with history. As one legal historian noted about *Heller*, Scalia's opinion "is at best confused" and presents "an historical argument that is limited and wrongheaded."[82] To cite but one example, Scalia supported his nonmilitary reading of the Second Amendment by saying in his majority opinion that "there is no evidence whatsoever to support a military reading of 'keep arms.'" He added that "we find no evidence that it [i.e., the phrase 'keep and bear arms'] bore a military meaning."[83] The historical consensus, however, is the reverse. Contrary to Scalia's categorical assertion, not only is there evidence that the Second Amendment phrase had a military meaning, but most colonial and military historians say as much. For example, as the Pulitzer Prize–winning historian Garry Wills has written, "'Bear arms' refers to military service . . . 'arms' means military service in general." The historical evidence of the military usage of bearing arms, Wills said, is "overwhelming." Wills's overall conclusion about the Second Amendment is clear: "History, philology, and logic furnish no solid basis for thinking the Second Amendment has anything to do with the private ownership of guns."[84]

As the conservative federal judge Richard A. Posner noted, "professional historians were on Stevens's side" (Stevens defended the militia-based view) in *Heller*. Scalia's distortion of history, according to Posner, is an example of "law office history," meaning that it is the product of lawyers "tendentiously dabbling in history, rather than by disinterested historians." Posner archly concludes that Scalia's decision "is evidence of the ability of well-staffed courts to produce snow jobs."[85] Other commentators, notably prominent conservatives, accused Scalia of unwarranted judicial activism (a criticism usually reserved for liberals) and distortion of history, arguing that an accurate "originalist" reading of the Second Amendment leads to the militia-based understanding of the amendment, not the individualist view.[86]

The "Individualist" View

As mentioned, the *Heller* court decision embraced the individualist view—that is, that the Second Amendment was meant to bestow on every American citizen a right to have guns for personal self-defense, aside from the militia principle. This view suffers from several problems.

The first problem with the individualist view in *Heller* is that it often relies on quotations pulled out of context.[87] The historical issue of the bearing of arms *as it pertained to the Constitution and the Bill of Rights* always came back to military service and the balance of power between the states and the federal government, as seen in the two most important historical sources: the records of the Constitutional Convention and those of the First Congress, when the Bill of Rights was formulated (see earlier discussion). Scalia dismisses the First Congress's deliberations and debate over the Second Amendment by saying that it is of "dubious interpretive worth."[88] Second, the definition of the citizen militias at the center of this debate has always been men roughly between the ages of seventeen and forty-five.[89] That is, it has always excluded a majority of the country's adult citizens—men over forty-five, the infirm, and women.

Therefore, it was not a right enjoyed by all citizens, unlike such Bill of Rights protections as free speech, religious freedom, or right to counsel.

Scalia argued in *Heller* that the reference to "the people" in the Second Amendment has the same meaning as it does in other parts of the Bill of Rights, as in "the right of the people [to] peaceably assemble" in the First Amendment or the "right of the people to be secure in their persons, houses, papers and effects" in the Fourth Amendment. Because all citizens are considered to have such First and Fourth Amendment protections, why shouldn't the Second Amendment be read as meaning that all citizens have a right to bear arms? In support of this claim Scalia referenced a 1990 Supreme Court case, *US v. Verdugo-Urquidez* (494 US 259), for support.[90] This claim is false on four grounds. First, militia service, from colonial times onward, always pertained only to those capable and eligible to serve in a militia—that is, healthy young to middle-age men (excluding the infirm, old men, and nearly all women). Second, the courts (especially in the *Presser* case) and federal law up until *Heller* clearly defined and interpreted the Second Amendment as having this specific meaning. Third, no evidence suggests that the authors of the Bill of Rights attempted or succeeded in imposing a single, uniform definition of "the people" in the document; the Bill of Rights was the product of many hands and many ideas, a fact reflected in the variety of ideas, interests, and concerns addressed in the first ten amendments. Fourth and most important, the *Verdugo-Urquidez* case has nothing to do with interpreting the Second Amendment. In fact, the case deals with the Fourth Amendment issue of whether an illegal alien from Mexico was entitled to constitutional protection regarding searches (the court ruled that non–US citizens were not "people" as the term is used in the Fourth Amendment). In the majority decision, Chief Justice William H. Rehnquist, in order to determine its applicability to a noncitizen, discussed what was meant by the phrase "the people," given that the phrase appears not only in several parts of the Bill of Rights but also in the Constitution's preamble. Rehnquist speculated that the phrase "seems to have been a term of art" that probably pertains to people who have developed a connection with the national community. Rehnquist's speculations about whether the meaning of "the people" could be extended to a noncitizen and his two passing mentions of the Second Amendment in that discussion shed no light, much less legal meaning, on this amendment.

Third, the fact that the individualist view is of modern origin contradicts Scalia's central claim that it reflects an originalist reading of the Second Amendment. The individualist view first appeared in print in a law review article published by a law student in 1960.[91] Prior to 1960 the militia or collective view of the Second Amendment discussed in this chapter was the basis for understanding and analyzing the Second Amendment in thirteen law journal articles published from 1874 to 1959.[92]

Self-Defense

The overriding goal and purpose of *Heller* is to establish a Second Amendment–based personal right of civilians to own guns for self-protection. As Scalia wrote, "individual self-defense ... was the *central component*" of the Second Amendment.[93] As others have noted, Scalia reached this conclusion by "dismembering"[94] the Second Amendment—that is, by essentially ignoring or removing the first half of the amendment referring to a well-regulated militia. Scalia does this in part by intermixing the defense needs of early Americans (e.g., against Native Americans or predators) with modern personal self-defense against robberies, assaults, rapes, intrusions into people's homes, or other life-threatening circumstances. Yet as the discussion in this chapter shows, the Second Amendment by design and interpretation has nothing to do with these very real modern-day threats but rather with the threats posed by armies and militias.

This does not mean that the law affords no legal protection to individuals who engage in personal self-defense—far from it. American and British common law has recognized and legally sanctioned personal self-defense for hundreds of years prior to and independent of the Second Amendment. But this arises from the area of criminal law, not constitutional law,[95] a fact that Scalia largely ignored. A standard, long-accepted definition of self-defense from common law reads:

> A man may repel force by force in the defense of his person, habitation, or property, against one or many who manifestly intend and endeavor, by violence or surprise, to commit a known felony on either. In such a case he is not obliged to retreat, but may pursue his adversary until he find himself out of danger; and if, in a conflict between them, he happen to kill, such killing is justifiable. The right of self-defense in cases of this kind is founded on the law of nature; and is not, nor can be, superseded by any law of society.[96]

Even in the light of *Heller* and *McDonald*, the Second Amendment is as superfluous to legal protection for personal defense or defense of the home today as it was more than two centuries ago. Indeed, as defined in the common law tradition, the self-defense principle supersedes even constitutional guidelines.

The "Right of Revolution" and Oppression

At least twice Scalia's opinion in *Heller* links the right to bear arms with citizen resistance to tyranny.[97] Given the decision's individualist view of the Second Amendment, it infers that citizens, armed and acting independently of the government (not as part of a government-organized and -regulated militia), somehow may use force against tyranny—government tyranny. This assertion harkens to a so-called right of revolution, which, though not expressly endorsed by *Heller,* has been an important component of how many supporters of the individualist view have interpreted the Second Amendment. That is, proponents of a right of revolution (also called "insurrectionism") have argued that the amendment is meant to provide a right of citizens to threaten or use force against their own government to somehow keep the country's rulers responsive to the citizens.[98] Although these theories pose interesting intellectual questions about the relationship between citizens and the state, they do not translate into meaningful policies for modern America. Most citizens recognize the importance of using democratic institutions and values to express their opinions by participating in elections, juries, expressions of public opinion, and participation in interest groups rather than by pointing guns (whether by threat or deed) at congressional leaders or the White House. Few Americans approve of those few groups in America that actively pursue something resembling a right of revolution—the Ku Klux Klan, the skinheads, the Branch Davidians, Los Angeles rioters, those responsible for bombing the federal office building in Oklahoma City in April 1995, or elements of the modern so-called Patriot movement. As the legal scholar Roscoe Pound noted, a "legal right of the citizen to wage war on the government is something that cannot be admitted.... In the urban industrial society of today a general right to bear efficient arms so as to be enabled to resist oppression by the government would mean that gangs could exercise an extra-legal rule which would defeat the whole Bill of Rights."[99]

In any event, any so-called right of revolution is carried out against the government, which means against that government's constitution as well—including the Bill of Rights and the Second Amendment. In short, one cannot carry out a right of revolution against the government and at the same time claim protections within it. This fact was well understood by the country's founders, for in 1794 the government, through its militias, moved to suppress the Whiskey Rebellion, an uprising that was denounced by Federalists and anti-Federalists alike. As historian Saul Cornell noted, in the 1790s there was "widespread agreement that the example of the American Revolution did not support the rebels' actions" because Americans at the start of the Revolution "did not enjoy the benefits of representative government," whereas those who fomented the Whiskey Rebellion "were represented under the Constitution."[100] The Constitution itself makes this point forcefully, as Congress is given the powers "to provide for calling forth the Militia to execute the Laws of the Union, *suppress Insurrections* and repel Invasions (emphasis added)" in Article I, Section 8; to suspend habeas corpus "in Cases of Rebellion or Invasion" in Section 9; and to protect individual states "against domestic Violence" if requested to do so by a state legislature or governor in Article IV, Section 4. Further, the Constitution defines treason in Article III, Section 3, this way: "Treason against the United States, shall consist only in levying War against them." (The United States was originally referred to in the plural.) In other words, the Constitution specifically and explicitly gives the national government the power to suppress by force anything even vaguely resembling revolution. Such revolt or revolution is by constitutional definition an act of treason against the United States. The militias are thus to be used to suppress, not cause, revolution or insurrection.

These powers were further detailed and expanded in the Calling Forth Act of 1792 (1 *US Stat*. 264), which gives the president broad powers to use state militias to enforce both state and federal laws in instances when the law is ignored or in cases of open insurrection. This act was passed by the Second Congress shortly after the passage of the Bill of Rights.[101] In current law these powers are further elaborated in the *US Code* sections on insurrection (10 *US Code* 331–34). Still, the link between guns and freedom has become an ever-more entrenched component of the individualist view of the Second Amendment. For example, the 2010 Republican nominee for the US Senate from Nevada, Sharron Angle, said during her campaign, "our Founding Fathers, they put that Second Amendment in there for a good reason and that was for the people to protect themselves against a tyrannical government . . . if this Congress keeps going the way it is, people are really looking toward those Second Amendment remedies."[102] Angle lost her Senate race, but her assertion that the Second Amendment gives people the right to use violence against Congress if they disagree with its decisions embodies a fanciful and dangerous idea that bears no sane relationship to the intention or purposes of the Second Amendment. Gun rights groups like the NRA have been leading exponents of this "insurrectionist" view of the Second Amendment.[103]

Along these lines, others have argued that traditionally oppressed groups, such as women and African Americans, should aggressively claim for themselves a right to bear arms.[104] Blacks in particular have been subject to race-based violence for hundreds of years and were unquestionably denied arms "as a means of racial oppression."[105] Yet the key handicap for blacks and other oppressed groups has not been the denial of Second Amendment rights but the denial of *all* basic Bill of Rights freedoms, not to mention denial of the basic common law principle of self-defense. Further, an article by the legal scholar Carl Bogus presents substantial evidence that Southern state leaders supported inclusion of the Second Amendment to ensure that they could use their state militias to suppress slave revolts.[106]

Conclusion

The Second Amendment emerged from the great political struggle in the latter part of the eighteenth century between those who wanted a strong national government (the Federalists) and those who believed that the states should retain more power over their own affairs (the anti-Federalists) in order to protect a system they believed would keep government both more responsive to the people and less likely to usurp individual liberties.[107] The sweeping new powers given to the national government in the modern Constitution included not only the authority to create and maintain a standing army but also the ability to organize and regulate militias. The inclusion of the Bill of Rights as a means of limiting national governmental power was the political compromise the Federalists accepted in order to win support for the new Constitution. The inclusion of the Second Amendment embodied the Federalist assurance that state militias would be allowed to continue as a military and political counterbalance to the national army at a time when military takeovers were the norm in world affairs. Yet it soon became apparent that the politically popular but militarily inefficient state militias were of little military value. The country's civilian and military leaders realized that American security needs could not and should not be left to the ineffective and unreliable unorganized militias. And in one of the great triumphs of American democracy, civilian control of the military became a fixture of our system. Thus, the fears that gave rise to the Second Amendment never materialized.

Up until the 2008 *Heller* decision, this key fact was reflected in court decisions and congressional enactments in which the Second Amendment applied not to civilian citizens with weapons but only to individuals enrolled in militia service to the government. As the historian Garry Wills noted about the pre-Constitution period, "at no time preceding the passage of the Second Amendment could any man be considered a militia member just by picking up his gun and proclaiming himself one."[108] The *Heller* case, of course, changed that interpretation, vesting the Second Amendment with a new, individual right of citizens to own guns for personal protection. The 2010 *McDonald* case extended that right to the states, making it the first instance when any part of the Bill of Rights was applied to the states since 1969. As mentioned earlier, the courts have the ability to change the law, as indeed the Supreme Court has with regard to the Second Amendment. But it cannot change history, and the *Heller* decision can be faulted for at least four problems: first, it rewrites the Second Amendment by, in effect, ignoring or striking out the first half of the sentence ("A well regulated Militia, being necessary to the security of a free State"); second, it is based on an interpretation of history that contradicts the views of most historians and a plain reading of the historical record; third, the core right of personal self-protection *Heller* carves out in the Second Amendment essentially ignores the fact that citizens have always had such a right aside and apart from the Second Amendment; and fourth, personal self-defense and guns are not identical—yes, guns can be used for personal self-defense (see discussion in chapter 3), but there are many, many ways for citizens to effect self-defense aside from guns.

To return to the primary policy questions guiding this book, the Second Amendment, even as viewed through the *Heller* and *McDonald* cases, now establishes a personal right that the Supreme Court has described as limited. Although one must assume that at least some gun laws around the country will eventually be struck down as incompatible with these rulings, the Court has gone to great pains to say that most existing gun laws are presumptively constitutional. Consistent with social regulatory policy theory, the courts have indeed provided a key avenue for defining—and redefining—the issue. Yet these actions by the courts have occurred against the backdrop of abundant and frenetic activity in the "political" branches of government—Congress and the presidency. Before turning to those arenas, however, we first examine the criminological debate over gun control, which picks up on many of the issues of gun use in society that the courts have addressed.

Chapter 3

The Criminological Consequences of Guns

> Guns don't kill people—people do.
>
> *NRA slogan*

> Guns don't die—people do.
> *—Pete Shields, founder, Handgun Control, Inc.*

Case 1: ON OCTOBER 14, 1989, three teenage boys were examining a .38-caliber automatic pistol that belonged to the father of one of the boys. Thinking that the gun was unloaded because the ammunition magazine had been removed, one of the boys pulled the trigger, accidentally shooting and killing fourteen-year-old Michael J. Steber of Clay, New York. The boys had not realized that a round was still in the gun's chamber. Two years later the parents of the dead boy filed a civil suit against the gun's owner (and father of the shooter), Gordon Lane, a former Syracuse police officer and head of the state's chapter of Vietnam Veterans of America, and against the gun manufacturer for failing to include a 75-cent safety feature that would have prevented the gun from firing without the bullet magazine. Lane had several guns in the home and had guided his son's use of them. The father of the dead boy questioned the justification for keeping such weapons in the home. "I'm a Vietnam veteran too," said Mr. Steber, "and I don't have a gun around the house. I don't need it."[1]

Case 2: One evening, Marion Hammer was on her way to her car, located in a parking garage in Tallahassee, Florida, when she noticed a car carrying six drunken men following her. Less than five feet tall and weighing 111 pounds, she feared trouble when some of the men made comments that amounted to a threat of rape. Reaching into her purse, Ms. Hammer produced a Colt .38 Detective's Special. When the car's driver spied the gun, he stopped the car, turned around, and peeled out of the garage. "Had I not had my gun," said the fifty-one-year-old woman, "I might not have lived to talk about it."[2]

Case 3: The school day began like any other at Cleveland Elementary School in Stockton, California. But shortly before noontime, on January 17, 1989, a twenty-four-year-old drifter named Patrick Edward Purdy opened fire on the crowded schoolyard with a Chinese-made AK–47 assault rifle (purchased in Oregon) fitted with a "drum" magazine holding seventy-five bullets (purchased in Rhode Island). Purdy laid down a line of fire that killed five students and wounded thirty-three others. After firing 105 rounds, Purdy fired one final shot from a Taurus 9mm semiautomatic pistol, killing himself on the spot. Purdy's motives were never entirely discovered, but investigators did find a history of drug and alcohol abuse, mental instability, brushes with the law, and a fascination with weapons of all kinds.[3]

Case 4: A mother and son returned home one Saturday night in October of 2009 to find the contents of their home turned upside down. As twenty-five-year-old Adam Candee headed toward the basement, his mother, forty-eight-year-old Deanna, entered the house, where a man later identified as thirty-nine-year-old Timothy Hartigan confronted her. The two struggled; Hartigan grabbed the woman's hair. Hearing the noise, Adam came to his mother's defense, which allowed her to retrieve her legally licensed pistol, whereupon she shot and killed the man. The police investigation in the tiny upstate New York town of Schroeppel in Oswego County concluded that robbery was not Hartigan's motive for entering the home, although the home had been thoroughly vandalized, and the intruder had cooked bacon and eggs. Although Hartigan had no prior criminal past, he had been diagnosed with schizophrenia ten years earlier. Hartigan's former wife said of her husband that "he wouldn't have done any harm to anyone if he was on his medicine. He wouldn't hurt a fly." A grand jury determined the shooting to be justified.

As is true with public debate over the Second Amendment, most public debate and much policy discourse on the criminological consequences of guns are fragmentary in the treatment of fact, polemical in tone, and narrow in consideration of options. The four cases that begin this chapter typify some of the key criminological consequences of guns. They also exemplify the nature of public discourse on the gun issue, in that tragic incidents such as the Stockton shooting massacre receive considerable attention and therefore rivet public attention; moreover, the increase in such incidents in the past two decades has fanned reformist flames, supporting the call for stronger gun control as well as for stiffer penalties for gun-related crimes.

Although such incidents may serve the purposes of particular policymakers and interest groups, confidence that good policy will result from a knee-jerk reaction to an unanticipated disaster is difficult to maintain. Yet this is a common pattern for the gun control issue, as summarized in the outrage-action-reaction cycle described in chapter 1. To be sure, disasters have prompted desirable policy change in such areas as coal mine safety, automobile safety, and earthquake preparedness. In these and many other instances, necessary policy changes occurred only after significant human disasters.

The criminological debate assessed in this chapter is also politically significant for how the gun problem is defined. The "rights talk" surrounding the Second Amendment, discussed in chapter 2, is a political means that foes of gun control use to blunt criminological analysis that supports stronger control. "Even if guns are harmful," the argument goes, "I have a right to own and lawfully use them as I see fit." Such an argument parallels others in which questionable behavior that might otherwise be controlled or prohibited is allowed because it falls under the Bill of Rights umbrella. For example, a wide array of hateful, hurtful, and otherwise objectionable speech is nevertheless protected by the courts because of the preeminent importance attached to the First Amendment's free speech protection. As noted in chapter 2, the Second Amendment's location in the Bill of Rights encourages gun control opponents to use "rights talk" to political advantage.

Arrayed against this view is a growing effort that emphasizes the gun problem as a public health issue. Spearheaded by public health and medical professionals, this effort dates to 1983, when the Centers for Disease Control and Prevention (CDC) declared firearms violence to be a significant public health threat. That year the CDC created a unit to gather and encourage research on gun-related violence, which in turn has spawned considerable public health and medical research (much of it discussed in this chapter) underscoring the public health threat posed by guns.[4] President Ronald Reagan's surgeon general, C. Everett Koop, and President Bill Clinton's first surgeon general, Joycelyn Elders, both weighed in strongly to push the public health definition of the problem. By tagging guns with the "public health threat" label and comparing them to such public health risks as smoking and automobile accidents, members of the medical community have sought to redefine the gun issue in order to alter public policy outcomes. It is a classic example of what the political scientist Murray Edelman has labeled symbolic politics—that is, shaping language and perception to political advantage: "The words a group employs and on which it relies ... can often be taken as an index of group norms and conceptual frameworks."[5] The concern expressed by the public health community became sufficiently threatening to gun control opponents that the National Rifle Association launched an effort in 1995 to get Congress to stop funding for CDC research on gun issues, which that year amounted to $2.6 million. The following year and in each succeeding year, Congress barred the CDC from engaging in any research that "may be used to advocate or promote gun control." This eliminated most gun-related research. By 2009, however, the National Institutes of Health had regularized some funding for public health studies of gun violence, amounting to under $5 million for the previous seven years. Still, the gun research funding bar has, according to one researcher, "largely succeeded in choking off the development of evidence upon which that [gun] policy could be based."[6]

Just as I examined the Constitution in chapter 2 to see if it imposed any obstacles to gun control, so too will I examine the criminological consequences of guns to see whether they pose obstacles or encouragement to gun control. It may be, for example, that the best available analysis points toward stricter regulation as a feasible means for stemming gun-related violence. Conversely, data and evidence may suggest that regulatory efforts are fruitless or even counterproductive. It also may be that existing analysis cannot offer any clear direction. No matter what the conclusion, it is impossible to understand the gun issue and, therefore, its place in the larger policy framework without considering this central issue. Although the connections between guns and crime discussed here suggest a panoply of possible policy responses, this chapter focuses primarily on the general criminological picture. Specific policy options are discussed in chapters 5 and 6.

As noted in chapter 1, maintaining public order and safety are primary, even primordial purposes of government. Regardless of one's view of guns, it is clear that firearms are intimately associated with a variety of disruptions of public order in American homes and on American streets. Thus, we begin with the nature of those disruptions.

America and Violence

America has long reigned supreme in levels of violence among the developed nations of the world. As Table 3.1 shows, America leads the world in total firearm deaths by a wide margin over similar Western nations, but also over many developing nations where lawlessness and gun violence are significant problems—many of the nations of Central and South America have far higher gun homicide rates than the United States.[7]

Table 3.1 Total Firearm-Related Deaths and Gun Ownership Rates in Twenty-Seven Nations*

	Total firearm-related deaths per 100,000 people**	Guns per 100 people***
United States	10.2	88.8
South Africa	9.41	12.7
Switzerland	3.84	45.7
Finland	3.64	45.3
France	3.00	31.2
Austria	2.94	30.4
New Zealand	2.66	22.6
Canada	2.44	30.8
Belgium	2.43	17.2
Malta	2.16	11.9
Israel	1.86	7.3
Luxembourg	1.81	15.3
Norway	1.78	31.3
Portugal	1.77	8.5
Greece	1.50	22.5
Sweden	1.47	31.6
Denmark	1.45	12.0
Italy	1.28	11.9
Iceland	1.25	30.3
Germany	1.10	30.3
Australia	1.04	15.0
Ireland	1.03	8.6
Turkey	0.72	12.5
Spain	0.63	10.4
Netherlands	0.46	3.9
United Kingdom	0.25	6.2
Japan	0.06	0.6

*Source: Sripal Bangalore and Franz Messerli, "Gun Ownership and Firearm-Related Deaths," *American Journal of Medicine* 126 (October 2013): 875.
**Total gun deaths includes from all causes, including homicide, suicide, and accident.
***The "guns per 100 people" is an average of total guns owned by civilians, divided by total population.

An incident that occurred on Halloween night in 1992 dramatized the gulf between the United States and other nations, when a Japanese exchange student was shot and killed at a home near Baton Rouge, Louisiana. The student, sixteen-year-old Yoshihiro Hattori, was looking for a Halloween party in the neighborhood of Rodney Peairs when he mistakenly approached the Peairs door. As the student (costumed as John Travolta from the movie *Saturday Night*

Fever) and a friend approached the door, Mrs. Peairs yelled to her husband to get his gun, apparently believing the two to be assailants. When the students entered the family's carport, Mr. Peairs ordered them to "freeze." When Hattori continued to advance toward the man, Peairs shot the student once with a .44 Magnum revolver. Peairs was tried for manslaughter in 1993 but was acquitted on the grounds that he believed the threat to be legitimate (the student carried a camera in his hand, which Peairs took to be some kind of weapon). It turned out that Hattori spoke little English and probably considered Peairs's actions to be consistent with Halloween traditions.[8]

The man's acquittal sent shock waves throughout Japan, which had followed the trial closely. One Japanese professor, an expert on American studies, said, "We are more civilized. We rely on words." The incident "seemed to confirm the Japanese view of America as a place rife with guns." A major Japanese newspaper said that the town where the student was killed "is like an old-frontier town of the old wild west." To the Japanese, the killing and its justification were almost beyond understanding and seemed to confirm the belief that America was a nation of lawless, gun-toting vigilantes. The parents of the dead student did prevail in a civil action, winning $650,000 in damages in September 1994. The judge observed that "there was absolutely no need for the resort to a dangerous weapon."[9]

In image as well as in fact, guns are closely linked to American patterns of violence. The homicide rate began to rise dramatically in the 1960s, as did the production and sale of handguns. Two-thirds of homicides and three-fifths of suicides are committed with guns, as are one-third of robberies and one-fifth of aggravated assaults. At its high point in the 1990s, guns were used in more than one million violent crimes each year. By the end of the first decade of the twenty-first century, that number had dropped to about a half million.[10]

Americans are by no means unmindful of gun and violence problems. Concerns about crime, violence, and law and order have been important political issues for decades. In 1968 Richard Nixon won the presidency on a tough law-and-order platform that resonated with voters who were concerned about crime and lawlessness. With some fluctuations, the issue has continued to be potent from the national to the local level, with a notable upswing in 1993 and 1994, when crime and violence were considered the second-most important problem facing the country, exceeded only by the economy and jobs.[11]

In every year since 1972 guns have accounted for roughly 30,000 deaths annually. For nearly all those years, more gun deaths were attributable to suicide than to homicide. In 2010, for example, of 31,672 reported gun deaths, 19,302 were suicides, 11,078 were homicides, 606 were accidents, and 686 undetermined. Also, in 2010, 73,505 people were treated for nonfatal gunshot wounds in hospital emergency rooms. In 2011, a total of 478,400 fatal and nonfatal firearm crimes were reported. In 2011, 393 gun deaths were the result of justifiable homicides by law enforcement personnel. Of 13,636 reported murders in the United States in 2009 (from all causes, including but not limited to guns), law enforcement concluded that only 215 were killed by firearms in circumstances judged to be justifiable (i.e., justifiable self-defense). In 2010, firearms were the third leading cause of injury-related deaths, behind poisoning and automobile accidents. Motor vehicle fatalities in 2010 were 32,788.[12] To provide a different comparison of loss of life, about 400,000 Americans were killed in World War II, and about 58,000 in the Vietnam War.

The fact that gun suicides consistently exceed gun homicides is especially significant from a policy standpoint because the primary, almost exclusive, focus of public and governmental attention has been the crime/homicide problem. A primary purpose of this chapter is to provide a unified examination of all three gun-related problems: homicide, suicide, and accident. The failure to consider all three, along with the role of guns in self-defense, represents a failure to examine the full scope of the policy problem at hand.

In demographic terms, gun homicides do not affect the population uniformly but instead occur disproportionately among youths, males, African Americans, and residents of the South.[13] These groups in particular have experienced a rapid rise in gun deaths. From 1981 to 1999 adolescents and young adults were the most likely to die from firearms compared with other age groups. In the decade of the 1990s, on average about seven adolescents between the ages of fifteen and nineteen were murdered with guns daily. Males accounted for 83 percent of all gun-caused homicide victims in 1999; that same year African Americans accounted for 51 percent of all firearm homicide victims, despite the fact that blacks made up only 13 percent of the population. According to the CDC, firearms are the second-highest cause of unnatural death among children and adolescents. In 2006, 84 percent of all gun deaths (including homicide, suicide, and accident) were males, and 27 percent involved African Americans. A 2008 study of nonnatural deaths in Fulton County, Georgia (including the city of Atlanta), reported that half of all violent deaths for those aged ten to nineteen were homicides; firearms were involved in 88 percent of these deaths.[14]

According to a US Department of Justice report, "firearms play a large role in juvenile violence," reflected in the facts that firearms played a role in more than 80 percent of juvenile violence incidents discussed in the report and accounted for 83 percent of juvenile homicides in Milwaukee, 85 percent of juvenile homicides in the District of Columbia, and 91 percent of such homicides in Los Angeles.[15] Further, these changes have occurred at a time when the proportion of young people as a percentage of the total population has actually been declining. According to the criminal justice expert Scott Decker, the "decreasing age of both offenders and victims is the most profound change in homicide rates since World War II." According to one police figure, the explanation is "population [shifts], gangs and easy accessibility of weapons." A government report in 2000 noted that the sharp increase in juvenile homicides from the mid-1980s through the early 1990s and the subsequent drop in such homicides in the late 1990s were both "firearm-related" and "linked to gun use."[16]

In addition to gun deaths, guns injure a far larger number of people each year, whether by intention or by accident. For every gun death there are an estimated five to seven gun injuries. Despite the vagueness of this figure, it is generally accepted. (The imprecision of this ratio is attributable to the lack of systematic national record keeping on gun-related injuries.[17]) The public policy and public health consequences of gun injuries are substantial: the annual national cost of intentional and unintentional gun injuries was estimated in 1993 to be more than $14 billion, with most of those costs covered directly or indirectly by public monies. Direct costs to hospitals were about $1 billion. According to the policy analysts Philip J. Cook and Jens Ludwig, the total yearly costs of all gun violence nationwide, taking into account the full range of costs borne by society, including health care, security, prevention efforts, familial consequences, and other factors, are a staggering $100 billion.[18] When gun-death rates are compared by states, the five with the highest per capita firearm death rates are Louisiana, Alaska, Nevada, Mississippi, and Alabama (these states also have few gun regulations). The five states with the lowest per capita gun-death rate are Hawaii, Massachusetts, Rhode Island, Connecticut, and New York (all have among the strictest gun laws).[19]

Some consider these death and injury figures sufficient in and of themselves to justify much more stringent gun control laws. Others argue that they simply represent the inevitable by-product of a modern, complex society that is also armed and for which the justification for having guns outweighs these negative consequences.

Choice of Weapons

Most guns owned in America are long guns—rifles and shotguns. Yet handguns have become more prevalent. In the 1950s only about one-fifth of all gun purchases were handguns. But starting in the 1960s handgun sales began to rise in proportion to other guns. By 1992 almost 50 percent of new gun sales were handguns. In 2010–2011, about half of all guns sold were handguns. Still, the overall ratio of long gun to handgun ownership has stayed at about two-to-one.

In the first decade of the twenty-first century Americans owned about 260 million guns; at the same time, however, about a third of all households reported having at least one gun (down from about half of all households in the 1960s). About a quarter of all adults report owning at least one gun. Three-quarters of these people owned more than one gun. By the start of the twenty-first century households with guns reported an average ownership of 4.4 guns, an increase from the 1960s. Gun owners were most likely to be white, male, older, from the South, and living in rural areas or small towns; they were least likely to be women, from large cities, from the far West or Northeast.[20] The decline in gun habits is seen in gun ownership rates examined by age. Those least likely to own guns are the young (historically, most gun owners acquire the habit while young through family ties; few acquire gun habits as adults). In 1998 23 percent of those aged eighteen to twenty-nine reported owning a gun. In 2013 that number had dropped to 16 percent. Ownership rates generally increase by age category, but over time ownership rates dropped between 1998 and 2008 in every age category except the two oldest: in 1998 41 percent of those sixty to sixty-nine years of age reported owning a gun, a percent that increased to 44 percent in 2008. For those seventy and older, gun ownership increased from 32 percent in 1998 to 48 percent in 2008.[21]

As shown in Table 3.2, gun ownership is far more prevalent in the United States than in any other nation. This is clear both as to rate of ownership (guns per hundred people) and to absolute numbers of guns, whether developed or developing.

Given America's population of about 317 million, its predominantly urban-suburban nature, and its enormous diversity, that guns pose a uniquely important issue for this country is not surprising. The particular public policy concern with handguns arises from the fact that they are far more likely than long guns to be used to intimidate, injure, and kill. Even though handguns account for only about one-third of all guns owned in the country and are generally more difficult to obtain than long guns, they consistently account for about 80 percent of gun homicides, about 60 percent of all homicides (including homicides from other weapons and instruments), and about 80 percent of robberies involving firearms. Of the 1.4 million incidents in which Americans were victimized by criminals carrying guns and committing crimes such as rape, robbery, and assault in 1993, 1.1 million (86 percent) involved handguns.[22] By one estimate, a handgun has a one-third chance of being used in a crime over the life of the weapon.[23] The appeal of handguns for criminal use arises from their smaller size (allowing for easy concealment), portability, and ease of use. In fact, long guns are actually more deadly because they usually use a larger-caliber bullet and always propel their bullets at a higher rate of speed.

Table 3.2 Nations with Highest Gun Ownership Rates, by Country*

Country	Guns per 100 people	Total Civilian guns
United States	88.8	270,000,000
Yemen	54.8	11,500,000
Switzerland	45.7	3,400,000
Finland	45.3	2,400,000
Serbia	37.8	3,050,000
Cyprus	36.4	275,000
Saudi Arabia	35	6,000,000
Iraq	34.2	9,750,000
Uruguay	31.8	1,100,000
Sweden	31.6	2,800,000
Norway	31.3	1,400,000
France	31.2	19,000,000
Canada	30.8	9,950,000
Austria	30.4	2,500,000
Germany	30.3	25,000,000

*Source: "Gun Homicides and Gun Ownership By Country," *Washington Post*, December 17, 2012, http://www.washingtonpost.com/wp-srv/special/nation/gun-homicides-ownership /table/. Accessed August 28, 2014. Data is from 2009 or 2010, depending on the country.

Both factors increase the likelihood of injury.[24] Even so, handguns continue to be the firearm criminals prefer.

Similarly, handguns are far less useful for hunting and other recreational purposes. Handguns are, however, more convenient for self-protection. Even so, only 20 percent of gun owners and 40 percent of handgun owners cite self-protection as their reason for gun ownership, although self-protection is the most commonly cited reason among those who purchase handguns.[25]

Guns, especially handguns, clearly have far-reaching consequences for American life. Yet these summary statistics merely outline the scope of the gun issue. What follows is a more detailed consideration of guns' criminological consequences.

Homicide and Malicious Injury

Many weapons can be used to kill, injure, and intimidate. Yet guns are different from weapons such as knives (the second-most commonly used weapon) in that guns can be used from a distance, they act quickly and require little effort, and they pose a universally understood threat.[26]

A study of prisoners conducted in the 1980s confirmed the attractiveness of guns for criminals.[27] When asked why they carried guns, the prisoners surveyed cited wanting to avoid hurting the victim as the most important reason (as did those who carried other kinds of weapons). Several other responses emphasized the convenience and ease of gun use as well as the gun's deterrent value (a consideration underlying the desire to avoid harm to the victim). The prisoners surveyed also reported a preference for handguns that were more rather than less expensive, and most of the handguns were purchased rather than stolen.[28]

The unique significance attached to guns is summarized by the "weapon instrumentality effect." This phrase refers to the independent effect of weapon type on crime and likelihood of injury, a factor dramatically illustrated in cases 3 and 4 at the beginning of this chapter. That is, the death rate and degree of injury associated with crimes involving guns is far higher than it would be if guns were not involved.[29] One study concluded that assaults with guns were five times more likely to result in death than knife assaults. Comparable findings have emerged from other studies.[30] In addition, in the case of robberies, the successful completion of the crime is more probable when guns are used as compared with other weapons.[31] Some evidence also supports the idea that the mere presence of guns sometimes precipitates violence that would not otherwise occur.[32]

A 1998 study of the impact of guns on homicide concluded that the sharp increase in the homicide rate in the 1980s and early 1990s occurred because "the weapons involved in settling young people's disputes have shifted dramatically from fists or knives to handguns, which are much more lethal. The growth in homicides by young people, which accounted for the entire growth in homicides in the post-1985 period, was all due to handguns." The study also noted that the decline in homicides in the 1990s was similarly attributable to reduced handgun availability and use by the young.[33]

Thus, guns in and of themselves wreak more havoc in regard to violence and death. Were guns less available, fewer deaths and serious injuries would result. As the policy expert Philip Cook said, "guns don't kill people, they just make it much easier." Nevertheless, there is little reason to believe that the overall amount of crime would appreciably diminish. Less availability of guns might bring about less serious harm, but it might prompt more nonfatal injuries.[34] This fact takes on greater significance with the realization that about three-fifths of handgun murders are committed against relatives, friends, neighbors, or other acquaintances. About half of handgun killings escalate from arguments that get out of control. Only a small proportion of murders are the result of careful and methodical planning. When anger or impulse is the norm, guns prove too easy a means to translate rage into death.[35]

Suicide

As mentioned earlier in this chapter, gun-related deaths from suicide account for more annual fatalities than do those from homicide, a fact that receives little attention in news accounts or from policymakers. Roughly 60 percent of all suicides are committed with guns. Those who use guns for this purpose are most likely to be white males; women are much more likely to rely on poison, although the rate of gun use among women has increased.[36] Guns are by no means the only means for committing suicide, but they are the most lethal. The success rate for gun suicide attempts is about 90 percent, compared with about 80 percent for hanging, 77 percent for carbon monoxide asphyxiation (usually from car exhaust), 70 percent for drowning, and 23 percent for poisoning.[37] Analysts generally agree on the accuracy of these numbers but disagree as to whether the difference between gun suicides and those from other forms is significant. One considers the differences "slight"; another considers them "impressive."[38] Still, considerable evidence supports the proposition that the mere presence of guns increases the number of successful suicides. For example, men attempt suicide only one-third as often as women, yet men are four times more likely to die in the attempt as women, a disparity explainable in large part by men's preference for guns over other methods. Contrary to popular impression, suicide for most individuals arises from impulse, not long-term planning. A study of people who survived a suicide attempt found that, when asked how much time had passed between the decision to kill themselves and the actual attempt, 24 percent said that the time gap was five minutes; 48 percent said it was less than twenty minutes; 70 percent said less than one hour; and 86 percent said it was less than eight hours. Moreover, 9 out of 10 who attempt suicide but survive do not die from suicide later.[39]

Gun suicide has proven to be a significant problem with troops returning from combat in Iraq and Afghanistan in the 2000s. The US Army reported that soldier suicides occurred at a lower level in the military than in society until 2004 (America invaded and occupied Iraq in 2003), when the soldier suicide rate began to rise. By 2008 soldier suicides exceeded the civilian average, a pattern generally attributed to interrelated factors including posttraumatic stress disorder, head trauma, and increased stress. According to suicide researcher Mark Kaplan of Oregon State University, the death rate by natural causes and interpersonal violence of veterans was the same as the civilian population, but veterans are more than twice as likely to commit suicide, with firearms the most frequent method employed. Kaplan concluded that easy gun access plays a key role because veterans are familiar with their use and are likely to own guns.[40]

Does the Presence of Guns Matter?

Regardless of the interpretation, guns clearly result in a higher death rate than other methods. It may be true, however, that those who choose guns are more serious about ending their lives than those who select other methods.[41]

The key policy question is whether the availability of guns in and of itself enhances the likelihood of suicide. That is, if guns were not available, would individuals simply turn to other means (a phenomenon labeled "displacement")?[42] This question takes on added importance when we note that from 1968 to 1985, firearms suicides increased 36 percent, whereas the suicide rate from all other methods remained constant.[43]

A growing number of studies have addressed this question. First, virtually all researchers agree that restricting gun availability does result in fewer gun suicides. This finding is significant from a public health and public policy standpoint because other means of suicide are less lethal, and only about 10 to 15 percent of suicides are the result of an unyielding determination to end life; therefore, some lives are or would be spared because of the switch to nongun methods. This finding aside, some have concluded that gun availability bears no significant relationship to the overall suicide rate among the adult population. That is, when guns are less available, the suicide-prone simply turn to other means.[44] Other studies have concluded the contrary—that gun availability has an independent effect on the suicide rate.[45] A large and ambitious study of suicide, a book-length analysis based on fourteen separate studies and the extant literature, concluded that states with stricter gun control laws have a lower suicide rate (although some "displacement" was observed) and, specifically, that firearms availability as measured by strict gun laws was the most powerful explanatory variable, accounting for about 30 percent of the variation in suicide rates among the states.[46] A subsequent study relying on different methodology concluded that the presence of one or more guns in the home increased the likelihood of suicide by a factor of five.[47] In contrast, a study relying on comparable methodology concluded that restricting access to handguns decreased the suicide rate of the young but not of adults.[48]

None of these studies can claim to offer final proof for their arguments, and much research in this area is yet to be done. Philip Cook offered probably the most reasonable synthesis when he concluded that "the argument here is *not* that the availability of lethal means is the *sole* determinant of suicide rates but, rather, that the availability of lethal means influences the extent to which suicidal impulses are translated into completed suicides. Depriving a suicidal person of a lethal and attractive means of self-destruction may well save his [or her] life."[49] As the public health specialist David Hemenway concluded, "one of the best strategies for reducing suicide appears to be the removal of firearms from the home, particularly where there are adolescents or young adults."[50] Recent studies confirm that higher suicide rates are associated with greater gun availability in homes.[51]

Suicide and the Young

Although the question of the impact of guns on adult suicide is still open to debate, the impact of guns on youthful suicide is not. Ample research indicates that the presence of guns has had a profound effect on youthful suicide. This fact takes on particular and alarming significance with the realization that the adolescent suicide rate tripled from the 1950s to the 1980s, whereas that for all ages increased only slightly. In the 1990s and 2000s, suicide was the second-leading cause of death among older teenagers and the third-leading cause among those between the ages of ten and nineteen.[52] Jane E. Brody has noted that "Nationwide, the presence of a loaded handgun in the house is the most potent risk factor for successful suicide among children."[53] A study of adolescent suicide in Chicago found, for example, that children of law-enforcement officers accounted for an unusually large number of adolescent suicides, an alarming statistic buttressed by the results of a study showing that 44 percent of police officers kept their weapons unlocked and loaded when at home; one-third of all gun owners who had children under the age of six reported keeping guns in the home unlocked. This finding regarding law enforcement personnel is striking because nearly all the law-enforcement officers kept guns in the house and are carefully trained about the use, care, and dangers of weapons in the home.[54]

The young are especially susceptible to the suicide impulse, precisely because they are more likely to act impulsively in a wide range of behaviors. However, although they may exhibit symptoms of suicidal depression, they do not approach suicide with the same determination as the elderly, who, by comparison, are more likely to "have a clear and sustained intent" to find an alternate suicide method if guns are not available.[55]

In the comparative study of suicide rates in King County, Washington, and in the Vancouver metropolitan area in Canada, the comparative suicide rate reflected the displacement principle; that is, with guns less available in Canada, those committing suicide turned to other means. The sole exception to this trend was the fifteen-to-twenty-four age group, where the 1.38 times greater suicide rate among the American group was attributable almost entirely to the presence of handguns. The *Journal of the American Medical Association* reported that the odds of suicide-prone adolescents actually succeeding increase seventy-five times when guns are present in the home. A study published in 2002 examined suicide rates of young African Americans (ages fifteen to twenty-four) from 1979 to 1997 and observed a quadrupling of that rate up to 1994, when rates then began to drop off. The study concluded that a contributing factor to this pattern was gun availability among a population where impulse-based action was high.[56] A 2004 study comparing eighteen states that had "child access prevention" (CAP) laws, making it a crime to store firearms in such a way that they are accessible to young people, found that the suicide rate among the young was 8.3 percent lower than in states not having such laws. Homes where guns are properly stored and locked away have lower firearm deaths, including suicides, than those where guns are present but not properly stored.[57]

The impulsive nature of adolescent suicide is reflected in a study of adolescent suicide and alcohol consumption. Although it comes as little surprise that the combination of alcohol and guns is associated with a dramatic increase in suicide, researchers found evidence that those intending suicide did not consume alcohol to "brace" themselves for death but that being intoxicated when guns were present or readily available increased the likelihood of suicide attempts. This behavior is generally consistent with the depressant effects of alcohol.[58] In sum, the most plausible conclusion regarding guns and suicide is that the presence of guns probably results in a moderate increase in the overall suicide rate and a significant increase in the rate for adolescents.

Accidents

As reported earlier in this chapter, the accidental discharge of weapons accounts for a relatively small percentage of gun deaths—roughly 5 percent. In addition, the accident-related fatality rate has been declining on a per capita basis since the early 1970s, although accidents account for about 40 percent of all gun injuries.[59] This comes as little surprise because, by definition, injuries caused by accident are not prompted by any intent to kill (unlike suicide and, to a lesser extent, homicide, where the victim generally seeks to avoid death). More than half of all gun accidents occur in and around the home; most of the rest are hunting related. Male adolescents are most likely to die in such accidents, and indeed, accidental deaths from guns are most common among children and young adults; 60 percent of those killed by accidental shooting are under the age of thirty, and about 33 percent are younger than twenty. These statistics have put greater focus on stemming gun accidents among the young, given their preventability.[60] As is true of some other gun-related data, gun-accident data are often ambiguous or imprecise.

One study of accidental shootings by children in California found that three-quarters of the accidents occurred when children played with guns alone or with friends. In about half the incidents the children were playing with guns stored loaded and unlocked in the house.[61] Unsafe storage of guns in the home increases the likelihood of accidents, yet children have demonstrated that they can unlock and load weapons unless they are completely inaccessible. For older adolescents, no number of locks may suffice. In one embarrassing instance in 1994, the twin sixteen-year-old sons of the former Syracuse, New York, police chief Leigh Hunt stole seven handguns from their father and illegally sold them. In order to get to the guns, the boys had to break through a locked door and into a locked cabinet holding the guns. The theft of the guns was discovered only when one was used to commit a crime. This problem of gun storage and access raises still another paradox because the possibility of using a weapon for self-protection (discussed later in the chapter) is greatly diminished if too much time or effort is required for the owner to obtain access to the gun.

Accidents are directly attributable to three factors: gun availability or density (the number of guns in a locality), the accessibility of guns (the ease or difficulty in operating a gun), and conduct (how guns are actually handled, including frequency and skill). Accidents are most likely to occur when availability is high, guns are handled often, and skill is low; they are least likely to occur under the reverse circumstances. In particular, one study of handgun purchases in Detroit over a twenty-six-year period found a "remarkable" and "strong" relationship between handgun purchases and fatal firearm accidents.[62]

Some critics argue that too much is made of gun accidents because the numbers are small, are declining, and involve high-risk populations.[63] Yet the involvement of innocents in unintentional or, at worst, reckless actions underscores the special issue accidents raise, especially given the disproportionately high accident rate involving minors; the ease of preventability (e.g., the use of gun locks or devices to prevent gunfire when magazines are removed and the growing availability of "smart guns" that can only be fired by the owners); and the high nonfatal injury rate. These three features explain the emphasis on policy intervention, especially as advocated by health professionals. In addition, gun injuries often focus on the young. From 1993 to 2000, 2,261 children required hospital emergency room treatment for nonfatal gun wounds. Of those, 43 percent were known to be accidental, and 41 percent were known to be deliberate. A 2013 study concluded that the number of accidental deaths of children caused by guns is significantly underreported—by as much as half—indicating that the accidental shootings of children pose a far greater hazard than previously reported. In its analysis of hundreds of child shooting deaths, the study found that medical examiners and coroners tend to categorize any shooting death of one person by another as a homicide. The common denominator in these accidental shootings was "the almost magnetic attraction of firearms among boys." In virtually every instance studied, the shooter was male, and boys accounted for over 80 percent of the victims.[64]

Few would dispute the assertion that anyone who owns or has legitimate access to a gun should be properly skilled in its use and safe storage. The just-mentioned issue of availability is both more complex and more controversial, for it goes to the question of why citizens own guns.

By far the most common reasons for gun ownership are hunting and related recreational uses, a fact consistent with the prevalence of long guns over handguns. Self-protection is the second-most frequently cited reason, and it is the main reason cited for handgun purchases. In 2013, for the first time, self-defense was given as the most common reason for gun ownership. Regarding public policy, legitimate hunting purposes are not questioned, aside from issues related to safety. The self-protection issue, however, poses a different problem. Specifically, how does the injury and death rate compare with that found in the defensive use of guns?

Self-Defense

Those who acquire or own guns for self-protection are reacting to the perceived and real threats of modern American life. One study of those who own guns for self-protection found key explanations in feelings of vulnerability to crime and police ineffectiveness. In addition, men are more likely to purchase guns for security, as are those who have been victimized by crime or who believe the risk of crime is increasing.[65]

The fear of crime is certainly real, although it is also often unrelated to actual crime rates. From 1979 to the mid-1990s roughly one million residential burglaries occurred per year while at least one member of the household was at home (this figure represents a minority of all burglaries). About one-third of these intrusions included assault, robbery, or rape. Nevertheless, fear of crime remained high and even increased in the late 1990s and early 2000s, even though crime in virtually every category declined during the same period. In the aftermath of the September 11, 2001, terrorist attacks in New York City and Washington, DC, handgun purchases rose dramatically, despite there being no direct connection between actual threats against individuals and the overall terrorist threat against the United States.

Clearly, the value of a gun to a potential victim parallels that to the criminal; that is, a potential victim can use a gun to "equalize" differences in size or strength or simply to deter or thwart the commission of a crime against his or her home or person, assuming that the victim can get the drop on an assailant. Anecdotal information, such as case 2 at the beginning of this chapter, illustrates the intuitive plausibility of the self-defense logic. The National Rifle Association reprints many such anecdotes in its magazines *American Rifleman* and *American Hunter* under the heading "The Armed Citizen." Yet anecdotes do not answer the safety-versus-self-defense paradox.

National statistics reveal that people who use guns to defend themselves are usually able to thwart crimes. Yet such instances are rare—only about 1.2 percent of incidents—for the simple reason that victims are usually not present during home robberies and are rarely armed during attacks away from home. Moreover, even if the victim is armed, the criminal initiates the encounter, making it difficult or impossible for the victim to deploy a gun first.[66] This raises an immediate question: is it rational to escalate the process of arming the population in order to deter or otherwise thwart crime? Although the Wright and Rossi study of prisoners reports concern by some over the prospect of confronting an armed victim, two studies based on crime statistics concluded that there was no statistical relationship between the prevalence of guns in an area and the robbery rate nor any evidence that burglaries were deterred by higher gun ownership rates.[67] Moreover, there is reason to believe that more guns in the home are an enticement rather than a deterrent to theft. In the 1990s, about 500,000 guns were reported stolen annually (at least 60 percent were handguns). In recent years, that number has dropped to about 250,000 annual gun thefts. Alternatively, the prospect of confronting an armed victim simply pushes crime into other areas or invites the escalation of violence.[68] Still, a number of related questions require attention.

Defense Data

In 1991 the criminologist Gary Kleck produced an estimate that yielded what he characterized as "implying 606,000–960,000 defensive uses of all guns" per year. This "implied" figure was subsequently rounded up to one million and publicized by gun control opponents such as the NRA. Indeed, in the introduction to his own book, Kleck rounds his own data up to "as many as a million times a year" instead of proposing a midpoint of 783,000 for data that are, by his own assessment, speculative.[69] Yet his estimates are at odds with national crime data and suffer from severe methodological problems.[70] According to the National Crime Victimization Survey, about fifty thousand defensive gun uses in violent crimes were reported annually between 1979 and 1985. Although these data probably represent an underestimation, Philip Cook examined this issue by obtaining special calculations from the federal Bureau of Justice Statistics. Cook concluded that guns were used for self-defense in roughly eighty thousand instances (including robbery, rape, assault, and burglary) per year. Cook's estimate is generally consistent with the simple fact that "most crimes do occur in what might be referred to as nondeterrable situations."[71] More recent studies verify a defensive gun use rate of about one hundred thousand to two hundred thousand times per year.[72]

In a follow-up study conducted in 1993, Kleck and a coauthor produced an estimate of as many as 2.5 million self-defense uses of guns each year. Kleck argued that his estimates are more accurate because his survey was anonymous and included follow-up questions to determine the accuracy of reported instances of self-defensive uses of guns. He criticizes the lower National Crime Victimization Survey (NCVS) estimates by saying that they are from "a single source of information," the results of which are inconsistent with the several polls he cites. He also argued that people interviewed may be reluctant to tell the truth to the in-person government interviewers in part because their use of a gun under such circumstances might be illegal.[73]

Yet Kleck cited no evidence to support his allegation that interviewees systematically lied to NCVS interviewers or that NCVS methods produce results that are less accurate than his own poll. Indeed, it is just as likely that those interviewed in Kleck's survey were more prone to exaggerate because the interviews were conducted anonymously over the telephone and deliberately focused on obtaining anecdotes from people concerning potentially justifiable uses of guns. If the alleged defensive uses cited in Kleck's poll are actual events that were illegal, however, then the justifiability of the acts themselves is suspect. Moreover, the NCVS survey is not "a single source," as though its results came from a single poll, but rather an annual survey of one hundred thousand people in fifty thousand households. The validity of the survey methods used has been examined repeatedly. Highly trained interviewers conduct seven separate, on-site, confidential interviews with respondents over a three-year period. These surveys have been conducted since 1973, producing numerous, voluminous data sets that are widely used and accepted in the realm of criminology. According to Cook, the NCVS approach "reflects the best thinking on how to get reliable answers to sensitive questions about crime."[74] Further, Kleck's figure of 2.5 million defensive gun uses seems dubious because it is almost twice as high as the total number of all gun crimes in 1993, 1.3 million. An additional criticism several researchers have raised pertains to so-called false positives in the Kleck survey, a common problem in surveys that attempt to identify a phenomenon based on a small percentage of a larger survey. To illustrate, if a survey reported a phenomenon occurring at a rate of 60 percent but the actual rate of occurrence was 62 percent, the statistical difference or significance would be small. Yet if only 2 percent reported a phenomenon, but only 0.2 percent actually engaged in the phenomenon, the 2 percent poll estimate would be inflated by a factor of ten, yielding a gross distortion of reality. As the researcher Tom W. Smith noted, "the rarer the event the greater the over-reports because there are many more true negatives than can be 'accidentally' misclassified as false positives than there are true positives that could by chance be misreported as false negatives."[75] Smith concluded that defensive gun uses most likely number one hundred thousand to four hundred thousand per year.

Defense versus Accident

Guns are useful for self-defense only if individuals have them at the ready or are at home when a crime (e.g., burglary) is committed. Under such circumstances, guns used for self-defense are "associated with a reduced risk of physical attack and injury."[76] But the small number of instances when guns are actually used for defense (a little more than 1 percent of all incidents) may be attributable to the victim's ability to get the jump on the assailant rather than the simple presence of a gun. Even among trained professionals, the presence of a gun for defense is no guarantee of safety or success. Police officers carry guns as part of their job, and they receive regular training. Yet among all police officers killed in the line of duty from 1980 to 1995, about 16 percent were killed with their own weapons or those of their partners. Since that time, this percentage has declined significantly, to 8.3 percent from 2000 to 2009.[77] The drop is attributable to improved holster technologies that make gun stripping much more difficult, improved officer training, and a general drop in violent crime. Nevertheless, gun carrying, even by highly trained professionals, carries a certain degree of risk to the carrier and innocent bystanders. In an armed confrontation on the street outside of the Empire State Building in New York City in 2012, police drew and fired on an armed man who had just killed a former associate. The perpetrator was fatally shot by police, but, in the process, nine bystanders were also shot and wounded (none fatally). A study of police shootings in major cities found that more than half of the bullets fired by police miss their targets because "even the best marksmanship training programs do not prepare officers for the stress that affects accuracy in real-life situations."[78] An eleven-year study of New York City police officers' firearms-discharge reports found that officers who discharged their weapons in the line of duty hit their targets about 34 percent of the time. Studies of other police forces report hit rates of around 20 percent.[79] Obviously, the prospect of unintended and undesired harm from gun use by civilians in potential crime situations, when those civilians do not possess the kind of regular training given to police, is far greater. And contrary to the usual assumption that police are victimized by guns obtained illegally, a study of 511 police officers killed with guns in the line of duty nationwide from 2000 to 2010 found that 46 percent of the traceable guns were legally purchased or otherwise legally owned by the assailants; 35 percent involved guns that were stolen or otherwise illegally obtained (72 percent of the 511 gun killings were with handguns).[80]

A few studies have attempted to compare directly the benefits of guns in deterring or thwarting crimes with the costs of accidents and other gun-related harm. One estimate from the 1970s, based on FBI data, concluded that a gun "kept in the home for self-defense is six times more likely to be used in a deliberate or accidental homicide involving a relative or a friend than against a burglar or unlawful intruder."[81] A study of all gun deaths in King County, Washington, from 1978 to 1983 concluded that for every instance of justifiable homicide, there were 1.3 accidental deaths, 4.6 criminal homicides, and 37 suicides with guns.[82] A subsequent study of homicides in homes in the most populous counties in Ohio, Tennessee, and Washington states concluded that the presence of guns in the home increased the risk of homicide by nearly three times. In three-quarters of the homicides, the victims were killed by family members or acquaintances. Even in instances of forced entry or victim resistance, guns were of little value, the researchers concluded.[83] Similarly, a comparative study of homicide rates and gun use in Seattle, Washington, and Vancouver, British Columbia, found that only about 4 percent of gun homicides from 1980 to 1986 were justifiable or committed in self-defense.[84] A more recent study of home invasion crimes in the Atlanta area concluded that in homes where criminal entry took place but where guns were also present, homeowners rarely deployed the guns. A subsequent study of 239,000 handgun owners in California found that the presence of the guns increased the likelihood of violent death, including homicide, suicide, and accident. A study published in 2002 found that gun availability was associated with a higher rate of gun deaths among children ages five to fourteen. A 2001 study also found that general gun availability was directly related to fluctuations in gun accidents and gun homicides, meaning that when availability increased, gun-related deaths increased; when availability dropped, gun deaths dropped. The researcher concluded that the continuing drop in the percentage of American homes with guns could explain one-third of the decrease in gun homicides since 1993.[85] Studies continue to report that guns in the home are significantly more likely to result in a suicide, homicide, or accidental shooting than in use for justifiable self-defense, as is true for guns in the workplace. In addition, about a half million guns are stolen each year.[86]

For the circumstance of gun-related incidents outside the home, most in law enforcement reject the prospect of encouraging citizens to carry guns as a general policy as being an invitation to even greater street violence. Even so, arguments for an armed citizenry often accompany instances of public violence.

For example, two years after the assassination of President John F. Kennedy, a lawyer writing in the *American Bar Association Journal* opined that it was "conceivable that an armed witness in Dallas might have been alert enough after the first shot to have prevented the fatal shot."[87] Leaving aside the fact that the highly trained Secret Service agents guarding the president were themselves unable to protect him from the final, fatal shot, no serious expert on safety would argue that the president would be safer if random citizens in a large crowd were allowed to carry handguns or rifles, for the simple reason that the risk of being shot by intention or accident would *increase,* not *decrease,* with an armed crowd. In any case, it is impossible to imagine an individual on the Dallas street on that day being able to identify the source of the shots, aim at, and disable or kill Lee Harvey Oswald in a six-to-eight-second time frame.

Similar comments appeared in the aftermath of a massacre on a New York commuter train that occurred on December 7, 1993, when Colin Ferguson killed six passengers and wounded nineteen others with a semiautomatic pistol he had purchased in California.[88] Undeniably, the massacre could have been avoided or minimized had one of the passengers on the ill-fated train been carrying a gun. Yet because such random attacks are unpredictable and infrequent, some kind of policy first would have to be established regarding designated passengers carrying guns (leaving aside a different and arguably more sensible policy solution of placing armed professional guards on passenger trains). But if, *as a matter of policy,* train authorities allowed or encouraged passengers to carry guns, the likelihood of gun injuries and deaths would certainly escalate. And suppose Ferguson himself (a man without a criminal record) or someone with similar intentions was the designated passenger gun carrier?

Concealed–Carry Laws

As of 2014, forty-one states had enacted liberal laws allowing qualified citizens to carry concealed weapons. Such "shall carry" laws, most enacted since 1988, require local police to grant carry permits to anyone who applies unless the individual is a convicted felon (nine states, plus the District of Columbia, have stricter "may carry" laws that require justifiable reasons and expertise for permission to carry guns, and where the state has discretion as to whether to grant a permit). Four of the forty-one states—Alaska, Arizona, Vermont, and Wyoming—actually require no permits for gun carrying. Enacted in large part because of political pressure exerted in state capitals by the National Rifle Association, supporters view such laws as a proper extension of rights to law-abiding citizens as a means of self-protection and as a method of deterring or thwarting crime. Relatively few citizens have availed themselves of this carry option, yet even a modest rise in lawful carrying may pose an increased safety problem. A study of homicide rates in urban areas in Florida, Mississippi, and Oregon found that homicide rates rose after the enactment of liberalized carry laws. In Florida about 18 percent of five hundred concealed-carry licensees used a firearm to commit a crime. In Texas licensees were arrested for a total of 2,080 crimes between 1996 and 1998, including 15 charges of murder or attempted murder, 6 charges of kidnapping or false imprisonment, 28 charges of rape or sexual assault, and 103 charges of assault or aggravated assault with a deadly weapon. These crimes occurred at a time when Texas residents had about 184,000 concealed-carry handgun permits, representing about 1.4 percent of the state's population of thirteen million. In 2006 about 247,000 Texans had concealed-carry permits. Most of the increase in concealed carrying tends to occur in low-crime rural and suburban areas among white, middle-class, middle-aged males. While supporters of liberalized concealed carry argue that permit holders are law-abiding citizens, a nationwide study of permit holders from 2007 to 2014 reports that permit holders have killed 14 law-enforcement officers and 622 private citizens, including 27 mass shootings and 39 murder-suicides. Nationwide, about 11 million people reportedly held concealed-carry permits in 2014, although it is likely that most are not carrying firearms at any given time.[89]

Critics cite such evidence to argue for repealing concealed-carry laws. Conversely, proponents of such laws argue that lawful carrying has not resulted in an increase in crime but instead has had beneficial effects. In this instance both claims are at least partially correct. Without a doubt, people who have concealed-carry permits have committed some crimes. Yet, as the numbers for Texas and throughout the nation suggest, these criminals probably represent a statistically small percentage of licensees and a small number of crimes in comparison with total crime rates, meaning that any increase in crime among those with permits would be statistically invisible.

Beyond this, local law enforcement efforts have been moving in a contrary direction; that is, police forces have been escalating efforts to force guns off the streets to reduce crime. Police in such cities as Boston, Indianapolis, Kansas City, and New York have directed patrol officers to watch for any infraction that might allow for a stop-and-search of individuals and cars. Their aim is to seize illegal guns, discourage gun use in crime, and keep guns in general off the streets. Kansas City reported a 50 percent drop in gun crimes when the program was carried out; New York City reported a 41 percent drop in handgun murders. In Philadelphia local law-enforcement officials blame a loosening of the gun-carry law in 1995 for an upsurge in homicides in the subsequent two years. In 1994, before passage of the new law, 1,500 gun-carry permits were issued; by 1996 that number had risen to 11,500. The number of crime-linked guns purchased locally also rose significantly during this period of time. In general, police disapprove of liberal gun-carry laws even though such laws are supposed to be limited to law-abiding citizens.[90]

More Guns, Less Crime?

Economist John R. Lott militates against these arguments. In a highly publicized and controversial study first published in 1998, Lott summarized his argument in his book's title: *More Guns, Less Crime*.[91] Using highly complex models drawn from economics (referred to as "econometric" models), Lott argued that states that have adopted "shall issue" concealed-carry laws (meaning that individuals seeking to carry guns need only apply for permission to do so) have seen reductions in violent crimes without any increase in gun accidents. In fact, he estimated that a 1 percent increase in gun ownership causes a 3 percent decrease in murder as well as declines in rapes, robberies, and aggravated assaults. Lott graphed some of his data, which seemed to show sharply rising crime rates, followed by steep drops in crime rates after the passage of concealed-carry laws in selected states. These conclusions derive from Lott's statistical analysis of county data from all 3,054 counties in the United States from 1977 to 1992 (he later extended the data to 2000). Such a massive database, accompanied by such precise numerical predictions, would seem to imply a high degree of accuracy and objectivity. Yet critics have assailed both.

Students of statistics understand well that precise numbers are no guarantee of accuracy because the numbers that any statistical model produces are only as good as the assumptions of the model itself. The looming problem with Lott's analysis is that many factors account for fluctuations in crime rates, including poverty, drug use, gang activities, numbers and practices of police, and unemployment. Further, the reasons for crime rate fluctuations in states with concealed-carry laws are likely to be different from those in states without such laws. Lott argued that his models are able to quantify all these factors and control for the numerous differences among the states, thereby allowing him to isolate the impact of concealed-carry laws. Yet the first problem with Lott's claim is that his models never establish a causal relationship between concealed-carry laws and declining crime rates.

This problem was illustrated when two researchers, Dan A. Black and Daniel S. Nagin, analyzed Lott's data and concluded that there was "no statistically significant evidence that RTC [right to carry] laws have an impact on any of the crime rates." Among their criticisms, they noted that Lott's model over- or underestimates crime rates in states that adopted concealed-carry laws; that his model erroneously assumes "uniform impact" of concealed-carry laws across states that enacted them; and that when the single case of Florida (a state where crime rates are highly volatile) is removed from the total analysis, all the beneficial consequences Lott attributes to the enactment of concealed-carry laws disappear. In sum, Black and Nagin concluded that Lott's model is "inappropriate" for his stated purposes and that his findings "cannot be used responsibly to formulate public policy." Even Gary Kleck, whose arguments are discussed above, doubts the veracity of Lott's claims. After discussing the speculative nature of Lott's findings, Kleck concluded, "More likely, the declines in crime coinciding with relaxation of carry laws were largely attributable to other factors not controlled."[92]

An additional reexamination of Lott's data raised similar questions. The economists Hashem Dezhbakhsh and Paul H. Rubin objected to two bedrock assumptions in Lott's analysis: (1) that "behavioral parameters" are fixed, meaning that social, demographic, and other traits, including arrest rates in the counties, do not change over time; and (2) that the effects of concealed-carry laws on crime patterns are assumed to be exactly the same in every county. Dezhbakhsh and Rubin said that these assumptions are "unwarranted" and therefore undercut Lott's conclusions because the purpose of the model is to observe how or whether enacting concealed-carry laws alters the behavior of citizens and criminals, and because the effects of such laws will surely vary from county to county because of population, age, education level, income level, poverty rate, racial composition, male-female ratio, and the like. Recalibrating Lott's model to allow for these changes, including the separation of places that enacted concealed-carry laws from those that did not, Dezhbakhsh and Rubin found that concealed-carry laws produce, at best, mixed results—modest drops in certain crimes in a few places, increases in more crimes in more places, and no significant effect in most places and most crimes. An important lesson learned from these studies is that minor changes from one model to another produce results that are statistically small but may produce major changes in public policy recommendations, a trend that raises doubts about using such models to formulate policy.[93]

Problems arising from Lott's statistical weighting techniques are revealed in his chapter, "Gun Ownership, Gun Laws, and Gun Crime." Therein, Lott used an unusual source of data to examine the nature and extent of gun ownership in America. Rather than relying on conventional public opinion polls that regularly ask questions about gun ownership, he instead uses 1988 and 1996 election-day exit polls, which in those years included a question about gun ownership. Lott's use of exit polling is puzzling because the main purpose of such polling is to give the news media data on the likely outcome of federal and state elections. Exit polling occurs when questioners stop voters as they leave polling places around the country to ask them how they voted and a few other questions. Needless to say, such polls are not only brief but also relatively haphazard, as many people refuse to talk to pollsters as they hurry from the voting booth. A larger problem with using these data for purposes other than predicting election outcomes is that only about half of eligible adults have actually voted in recent national elections, making such polls a poor choice to examine the entire American public, for the obvious reason that half of the adult public is excluded from the sample. In 1988 nationwide voter turnout was about 53 percent; in 1996 it was about 48 percent.

Lott claimed to control statistically for the fact that his data excluded half of the country's adult population by "weighting" the responses given to the interviewers so that the sample would statistically resemble the total adult population. But weighting procedures fail to give him an accurate picture of the general public, so his subsequent analysis is unreliable. This fact is evident in his results: according to Lott's reconfiguration of these exit poll data, gun possession *rose* significantly in America, from 26 percent in 1988 to 39 percent in 1996. Yet several other polls designed to measure the opinions of the entire national adult population allow for independent verification. These other results show that Lott's statistical manipulations have, in this case, generated a false conclusion. To cite two of the nation's most reliable and respected polls, Gallup reported gun ownership rates of 47 percent in 1989 (the data were not available for 1988) and 38 percent in 1996. The National Opinion Research Center reported national gun ownership rates of 40 percent in 1988 and 40 percent in 1996 (in the intervening years, the rate fluctuated 6 percent). Kleck's compilation of survey data from a variety of polling organizations (including CBS/*New York Times, Los Angeles Times,* Harris, and the Center for Social and Urban Research) posing the same question reveals a general downward trend with percentages in roughly the same range. None of these polls reveals the upward trend Lott alleges nor does any report a possession number as low as 26 percent (Lott's figure for 1988) at any point between 1959 and the end of the 1990s. Further, it is well understood (as these and other data show) that gun ownership in the United States gradually declined from the 1960s, when about half of all households had at least one gun, to the end of the 1990s, when a little more than one-third of households reported having a firearm. This downward trend is generally accepted[94]; there is no reason to believe that gun ownership rose 13 percent from 1988 to 1996, either as a temporary spike or as part of an upward trend, as Lott asserted. Lott did not explain why he declined to use other, more reliable data to examine gun ownership in America. We can conclude, however, that the kind of statistical analysis that undergirds his book yields a conclusion that is demonstrably false.

Another critic noted that Lott's data set of all counties in the country was inappropriate to his task, in part because counties vary so widely in population and in social, demographic, and other characteristics. Further, only a very small percentage of counties account for most major crime, including murder, which receives special emphasis in criminal justice analysis, and most of these high-crime urban areas are found in states that do not have concealed-carry laws. According to the sociologist Ted Goertzel, Lott "had no variation in his key causal variable—'shall issue' laws—in the places where most murders occurred"; therefore, "Lott's massive data set was simply unsuitable for his task" even though Lott claimed he had controlled for population size. Yet statistical controls cannot conceal the fact that Lott "simply had no data for the major cities where the homicide problem was most acute." Goertzel concluded,

> What actually happened was that there was an explosion of crack-related homicides in major eastern cities in the 1980s and early 1990s. Lott's whole argument came down to a claim that the largely rural and Western "shall issue" states were spared the crack-related homicide epidemic because of their "shall issue" laws. This would never have been taken seriously if it had not been obscured by a maze of equations.

Using a different data set to examine the impact of concealed-carry laws, researcher Mark Duggan found no evidence to support Lott's claims, arguing instead that "More Guns" mean "More Crime."[95]

Finally, researchers Ian Ayres and John J. Donohue reexamined Lott's data (including updated data that extended the analysis through the 1990s) and found that it contained numerous coding errors. When these errors were corrected, the positive results of concealed-carry laws that Lott alleged disappeared. In fact, the most prominent statistical association they discovered was an increase in some types of crime in the aftermath of enacting liberalized concealed-carry laws.[96]

These criticisms emphasize the considerable difficulty in isolating the effect of a single law among states of the union that are otherwise very different from each other. Yet Lott's own analysis reveals still other problems. In his book he gave little credence and even less attention to the many studies (some of which are cited in this chapter) that examine the social and criminological costs of guns and offer conclusions at odds with his own. Lott mentioned only two such studies, which he dismissed because of what he considered to be their limited scope. He also failed to consider the social costs of gun availability relating to suicide, a subject that receives only the briefest mention in his book. Even though more Americans die annually from gun suicide than gun homicide, he swept aside the suicide question as statistically insignificant "if a person becomes depressed while away from home." That is, his analysis assumes that concealed-carry guns pose a suicide risk only when they are being carried on the street, ignoring their presence in the home, possible use or misuse by the owner or others when the gun is not being carried on the street, theft risks, and the like. Such assumptions are symptomatic of analysis that is disconnected from actual human behavior.[97]

When one considers the very small percentage of people who actually obtain carry licenses—in North Carolina, for example, only 0.3 percent of the state's population acquired a concealed-carry permit within a year after enactment of such a law there[98]—the smaller-still percentage of people who actually carry guns with any regularity (even police officers often do not carry their service weapons with them when off duty) and the little attention most citizens pay to state politics, simple common sense suggests that the likelihood that such laws could produce any measurable decrease in crime is extremely small. Further, on a per capita basis most concealed gun carrying occurs in low-crime rural areas, whereas most crime occurs in urban areas, enforcing the disconnect between the enactment of concealed-carry laws and any possible drop in crime. Guns have been used, at least on some occasions, for successful defensive or other crime-thwarting purposes. But Lott's study fails to alter the continuing debate over the relative costs and benefits of gun possession and carrying.

Finally, Lott's reputation suffered fatal blows when he repeatedly said that "98 percent of the time that people use guns defensively, they merely have to brandish a weapon to break off an attack."[99] After first claiming that the number came from national surveys, none of which actually reported such a number, he then claimed that it came from a survey he conducted. Yet he later claimed that he lost the data from the survey, and its existence was never verified. And in 2003 Lott critics discovered that a person named "Mary Rosh," who wrote frequent, highly praiseworthy Internet comments about Lott, his written work, and his teaching during the previous three years, was in fact Lott himself (although he claimed it was actually his teenage son's doing). The last name "Rosh" was derived from the first two letters of the names of two of his four sons (Roger and Sherwin).[100]

Gun Thefts

One other consideration in this already complex equation is the theft of legally owned guns. Gun control opponents are quick to point out that stricter gun laws would result in less gun availability for law-abiding citizens but that criminals would continue to get guns anyway because most obtain them by illegal means. The problem with this logic (leaving aside for the moment the self-defense side of the equation) is that it begs the question of where the guns used by criminals come from. Stolen guns and guns used to commit crimes begin as weapons produced and sold legally. In addition, one core purpose of law is to retard, inhibit, or stop behavior that society deems wrong—in this case, gun possession by criminals. And studies of criminal behavior support the idea that when legal barriers are erected to prevent guns from falling into the wrong hands, it indeed becomes more difficult, expensive, and risky for criminals to try to obtain guns.

According to studies of prison inmates who reported having used guns to commit crimes, most of the guns were obtained from friends and family members, or from the "secondary" market (such as informal exchanges from acquaintances). In a 2004 report, 41 percent said they got guns from a friend or family member; 32 percent said they got guns off the street from a drug dealer or black market source; 12 percent from a pawn shop or gun shop; 2 percent from a gun show or flea market; 2 percent from the victim; 1 percent from a burglary; and 9 percent reported getting guns by other means. In recent years, the best estimates suggest that about 250,000 guns are stolen annually. This represents a decline from around a half million gun thefts per year, a decline explainable because of the decline in crime since the early 1990s as well as the decline in gun ownership. Over 60 percent of all guns stolen are handguns. And guns are reported to be one of the top four items burglars seek to steal.[101]

Gun Availability

More to the point, the general prevalence of guns (especially handguns)—that is, the density of gun ownership in an area—is directly related to criminal gun access. One study noted that the percentage of burglaries that include gun thefts rises with the proportion of households in which guns are owned. Another study found that, holding other factors constant, burglary rates rise with the rate of gun ownership.[102] A third study found gun density to be directly related to the homicide rate. Moreover, overall gun density in a locality is a matter of major concern to local law enforcement agencies.[103]

It is well understood that guns, especially handguns, are valued prizes for criminals because of their street and crime value. Thus, a general reduction in gun (especially handgun) availability is directly related to gun availability for criminals and criminal use, although firearms may pass through many hands between the point of legal purchase and illegal use. Stated another way, any effort to impose meaningful handgun or other gun control has to address the flow of firearms from all sources, not just thefts. Several studies have found a close connection between the availability of guns and the homicide rate, as discussed earlier in this chapter.[104] One analyst observed a 5 percent drop in gun robbery and a 4 percent drop in robbery murder with a 10 percent drop in local gun ownership—although there was no discernible drop in the overall rate of robbery.[105]

In addition, the enormity of the existing pool of handguns in the United States does not necessarily mean that efforts at regulation are futile. Several studies of the flow and use of handguns concluded that new handguns are proportionately more likely to be involved in crimes than older guns, suggesting that the regulation of new handgun manufacture and sale would have a proportionately greater impact on gun-related crime. As the law professor Franklin Zimring noted, "Older handguns include a large number that are packed away in attics or kept in homes for self-protection. Such weapons show up in crimes or confiscations only if used by their owners or transferred by sale or theft to other individuals."[106] Guns used in crimes are likely to be disposed of or to be confiscated by police. Law enforcement authorities have speculated that even though there are more than 200 million guns in America, "far fewer—perhaps 100,000 or so—firearms are used to commit crimes." In addition, according to studies published in 1998 and 1999, about half of the handguns used in crimes had been obtained within the previous three years.[107] According to a report of the Police Executive Research Forum, the general availability of guns—accelerated by the relaxation of gun laws in the 2000s—"is a growing factor in the commission of many types of crimes."[108]

The Feeling of Safety

Various surveys have reported that many citizens believe they are safer or feel safer by possessing guns. A 1990 survey of gun owners found that 42 percent reported feeling safer, 2 percent less safe, and 56 percent said it made no difference. From this type of data the criminologist James D. Wright and colleagues asserted that this feeling, whether objectively true or not (i.e., whether gun-owning individuals actually are safer, statistically) is in itself a benefit of weapons ownership because such people will "lead happier lives because they feel safer and more secure."[109]

In contrast, a 1994 survey came to a different conclusion. From the population as a whole, 71 percent reported that they would feel less safe if more people in their communities acquired guns, compared with 19 percent feeling more safe. Among non–gun owners, 85 percent reported feeling less safe, compared with 8 percent feeling more safe. Among gun owners the split was even, with 41 percent feeling less safe and 40 percent feeling more safe. A study published in 2001 found similar results: 59 percent of respondents in a 1996 national survey would feel "less safe" if more people in their local communities carried guns; and 88 to 94 percent interviewed in 1999 said that citizens should not be allowed to carry guns into various public places.[110]

Although such feelings are not without significance, the evident problem is that such feelings by themselves count for little when fundamental issues of public safety, welfare, or morals are at stake. Some motorists continue to feel safer driving without seat belts; some smokers do not feel that the smoking habit diminishes their quality of life or that of those around them; consumers of pornographic materials believe such materials to be benign in their effects; racial segregationists believed that both they and African Americans were better off when the races were kept apart. Yet in these and many other instances, government has concluded that the feelings of some citizens should be set aside and various regulations imposed as a matter of public policy. So too with guns, assuming that the weight of data and argument is sufficiently persuasive.

Alternative Means of Defense

Most discussion of the role of guns in self-defense neglects the consideration of alternatives. Guns aside, home defense may be effectively implemented through the use of locks, alarm systems, safes, improved lighting and landscaping, window bars, dogs, the activation of neighborhood watch groups, increasing neighborhood policing, and the like. Attacks and assaults away from the home can be minimized or fended off by modifications in behavior and the use of alternative means of defense, such as mace or pepper spray, and general improvement of street safety (e.g., more police on the beat, better street lighting). The point is not that guns should never be used for defense but that any consideration of personal defense and deterrence should not be limited to guns.

Guns and School Violence

In the late 1990s the country's attention was riveted by a series of schoolyard shootings committed by school-age boys in small cities, towns, and rural areas, including Jonesboro, Arkansas; Springfield, Oregon; Pearl, Mississippi; Bethel, Alaska; Edinboro, Pennsylvania; Johnston, Rhode Island; Pomona, California; Fayetteville, Tennessee; and West Paducah, Kentucky. This seeming crescendo of schoolyard mayhem reached its peak on April 20, 1999, when two teenage boys shattered the relative security and placidity of their public school, Columbine High, located in Littleton, Colorado, by bringing four guns to school and shooting. When they were done, twelve students and one teacher had been killed in the space of less than fifteen minutes. Twenty-three others were wounded. As police closed in on eighteen-year-old Eric Harris and seventeen-year-old Dylan Klebold, the two turned the guns on themselves.

The guns had been purchased on the teens' behalf in 1998 by Klebold's eighteen-year-old senior prom date and friend, Robyn Anderson, who purchased two shotguns and a 9mm Hi-Point carbine for them at the Tanner Gun Show in nearby Denver. They supplied the money; she supplied the identification. At the time of Anderson's purchases, neither boy was old enough to buy the guns (Harris was still seventeen at the time). Another friend, twenty-two-year-old Mark Edward Manes, later provided to them the fourth gun, a TEC-DC9 semiautomatic pistol, which he bought at a different gun show and then resold to the boys for $500. All four of the gun show purchases were conducted by private sellers exempted from background check requirements—the so-called gun show loophole that allows sales at gun shows by unlicensed dealers to be conducted without checks or waiting periods. When Anderson purchased the guns on behalf of the boys, she was acting as a "straw buyer," a practice outlawed in some states but not in Colorado. Repeated efforts to close the gun show loophole had been defeated in the Colorado State legislature, although the political momentum the Columbine shooting generated led to a statewide referendum on the measure, which won approval by a wide margin in November 2000 (Oregon also adopted by referendum a measure to close the gun show loophole in the 2000 election).[111]

The extensive national attention given to these shootings undoubtedly fed public concerns about crime. Indeed, polls revealed that the fear of crime rose throughout the 1990s, including fear of school-related crime. Yet this rise has occurred at the same time that crime in virtually every category has been declining, both in schools and in society. Student attitudes about school safety follow a similar, contradictory pattern. In 1989, according to the *1998 Annual Report on School Safety* produced by the US Departments of Education and

Justice, 6 percent of students ages twelve to nineteen reported fear of attack or harm at school. By 1995 this figure had risen to 9 percent. And in the aftermath of the 9/11 terrorist attack in 2001, fears also increased. Yet actual school crime rates reflect the opposite trend. In fact, American public schools are relatively safe places, as compared with local communities and even homes. By itself this is remarkable, given that American public schools enrolled over fifty million students during the late 1990s and early 2000s and that teens and young adults compose the most crime-prone segment of the population.

More specifically, school shooting deaths (which account for three-quarters of all violent deaths in schools) are both rare and have, on average, declined in number, as the data in Table 3.3 show. The heightened attention given to schoolyard shootings has no doubt fanned fears about school safety, coupled with their occurrence in low-crime rural areas and the rise in attention-grabbing multiple-victim shootings, from two in 1992–1993 to six in 1997–1998. Yet in the fall of 2006 a series of four school shootings occurred in the space of a month, turning the country's attention again to such violence, with the worst of these involving a man who entered an Amish school in Pennsylvania and killed five schoolgirls and himself.

Generalized downward crime trends apply to other school crime patterns as well. According to the government's *1997 Annual Report on School Safety*, in 1996 children ages twelve to eighteen were subjected to serious violent crime at a rate of 26 crimes for every 1,000 students away from school, totaling about 671,000 incidents nationwide. That same year the same age group was victimized by violent crime within schools at a rate of 10 per 1,000 students (about 255,000 incidents, or 38 percent of the out-of-school crime rate). In addition, overall crime rates have been declining since the mid-1990s, both within and outside of schools. From 1993 to 1996 the overall crime rate in schools for this age group dropped from 164 incidents per 1,000 students to 128 per 1,000. From 1995 to 1999 the number of students reporting that they had been victimized by crime in school dropped from 10 percent to 8 percent. According to the National Center for Education Statistics, from 1992 to 2003 violent crime victimization in schools dropped from 48 per 1,000 students to 28 per 1,000. Outside of schools, the rate dropped comparably, even though students were twice as likely to be victims of serious violence away from school as in school. These trends are more significant given that nationwide crime rates such as homicide are proportionately highest among eighteen-to-twenty-four-year-olds, followed by fourteen-to-seventeen-year-olds.[112]

School violence continues to be a serious national concern; nevertheless, it is also important to note that violence occurs in schools at lower rates than in society at large and has followed a downward trend from the 1990s to the 2000s.

Table 3.3 Public School Shooting Deaths, 1992–2014

Year	Shooting deaths
1992–1993	45
1993–1994	41
1994–1995	16
1995–1996	29
1996–1997	15
1997–1998	36
1998–1999	25
1999–2000	16
2000–2001	19
2001–2002	4
2002–2003	14
2003–2004	29
2004–2005	20
2005–2006	5
2006–2007	16
2007–2008	3
2008–2009	10
2009–2010	5
2010–2011	8
2011–2012	15
2012–2013	32
2013–2014	13
TOTAL	**416***

*Deaths by guns at schools amounted to 74 percent of all violent public school deaths. Total public school violent deaths from all other causes from 1992–2010 was 120. The second leading cause across this time period was stabbing/slashing (67 deaths).

Sources: "Report on School Associated Violent Deaths," National School Safety Center, www.schoolsafety.us; John Light, et al., "Guns in America After Newtown," Moyers and Company, June 10, 2014, http://billmoyers.com/2013/05/03/gun-violence-since-newtown/. Some data also examined at "List of School Shootings in the United States" on Wikipedia .org. URLs accessed August 28, 2014.

Part of the reason for greater fear concerning school safety arises from the "moral panic" that accompanies reports of school shootings—that is, an exaggerated sense of alarm over perceived threats. Such was the case after the December 2012 shooting of twenty elementary school students and six faculty and staff at Sandy Hook Elementary School in Connecticut, a shooting that genuinely shocked the nation (see chapter 5). Yet it is important to note that public schools across the nation have taken aggressive steps to make schools safer through such measures as improved mental health screening, violence prevention curricula, enhanced security, and communication procedures, including regular safety drills and the presence of "resource officers"—police or other trained individuals who are present at schools. Since the Sandy Hook shooting, 90 percent of school districts report having tightened security. From 1992 to 2006, over 50 times as many murders occurred among school-age children away from school as occurred at school. During the 2010–2011 school year, the combined suicide-homicide rate in schools was 1 per 3.5 million enrolled students—far lower than the rate outside of school.[113]

Aside from children's safety, an added concern is violence against schoolteachers. From 1992 to 1996 an average of 30 teachers per 1,000 were victims of violent crimes at school, amounting to about 123,000 per year. Concerns persist over weapons carrying by students. According to the US Department of Education's Institute of Education Sciences, in 2011 about 5 percent of students reported carrying a weapon (including guns, knives, and clubs) to school within the previous thirty days. That represented a long-term decrease in school weapons carrying (in 1993 the number was 12 percent). Guns represented less than a third of all weapons reportedly carried to schools. A scattered few would like to see armed teachers and administrators, and support for such measures has increased since the 2012 Sandy Hook school shooting. To date, 18 states have laws that allow adults to carry guns in public schools under certain circumstances. In practice, however, there are a few reasons such carrying rarely occurs: because of other safety measures already in place, because schools are objectively relatively safe places, and because of generalized opposition from the vast majority of teachers and administrators. The obvious problems with the introduction of guns into schools include the risk of gun theft, accident, suicide, intentional violence, and the tacit encouragement of even more guns in schools.[114]

Several observations emerge from these events. Schoolyard shootings have occurred in urban areas in the past, but those incidents received less attention than the spate of shootings discussed here because the latter have occurred in suburban or rural areas, where crime rates are generally lower and arguably because urban shootings are more likely to affect ethnic populations, a pattern that supports preexisting racial stereotypes. Schoolyard shootings are overwhelmingly committed by young white males. These boys all exhibited warning signs of depression, suicidal tendencies, or alienation, and others often picked on the boys. In most cases, their plans for violence were known to others. And, most pertinent to the subject of this book, they all had ready access to guns. To suggest that no harm would have been done had these boys not been able to arm themselves easily would be unrealistic, but the degree of death and injury would undoubtedly have been reduced if they had had less firepower. Typical is the case of fifteen-year-old Kip Kinkel, who fired fifty-one shots in his school cafeteria in Springfield, Oregon—a state with higher gun ownership rates than the national average—with a .22-caliber Ruger semiautomatic rifle, killing two and injuring twenty-two others. Kinkel was subdued only when he stopped to reload. Kinkel's weapon increased the "lethality" of the attack when compared with, say, an attack with a knife or even compared with guns that hold fewer rounds of ammunition or with single-loading, bolt-action models. Along with their guns the two boys involved in the Columbine shootings also brought about fifty explosive devices to school with them, but all the deaths and injuries came from gunshots, emphasizing both the ease and lethality of gun use.

Although adults commit similar crimes, such school incidents heighten public concern because they involve the young, both as innocent victims and as impulsive perpetrators. Society controls or restricts children's access to many products, from alcohol to automobiles, precisely because of the inherent dangers attendant on their use and the resulting need for adult judgment. Even though most of the child assailants, including Kinkel, were trained in the proper handling of firearms, by their nature children are more likely to respond on impulse and less likely to understand the consequences of their actions. These facts are of great importance in understanding the link between young people and suicide, as discussed earlier. As argued in this chapter, tighter control of guns would not eliminate violence, but it would render many criminal acts less lethal and also increase the degree of difficulty in committing crimes—observations borne out in the schoolyard attacks.[115]

Gun Carrying on College Campuses?

The mass shooting on the Virginia Tech State University campus in 2007 (discussed in the introduction) and a similar shooting on the Northern Illinois University campus in 2008, when a deranged former student shot and killed five people and wounded eighteen in a large lecture class before killing himself, fanned calls by some for student or faculty gun carrying on college campuses. The arguments on behalf of doing so are familiar: that an armed civilian on campus could confront a shooter or other serious threat more quickly than campus or local police; that concealed carrying reduces crime (an assertion generally based on John Lott's discredited analysis, discussed earlier); that criminals can easily enter campuses to wreak mayhem; that the Supreme Court's 2008 and 2010 rulings establishing a personal right to have a gun for personal self-protection (see chapter 2) provides a constitutional basis for campus carrying; and that gun-free zones like college campuses are "magnets for killers bent on maximizing their body count."[116] A student group supported by gun rights groups, Students for Concealed Carry on Campus (www.concealedcampus.org), is lobbying for concealed carry on campuses and in state legislatures around the country.

Despite these pressures, including legislation offered in more than half the states, to allow college campus gun carrying, only seven states have adopted some kind of concealed-carry law as of 2014. Utah was the first state to allow gun carrying on college campuses (students must be twenty-one), and it has the only state law that specifically names its state campuses as places that cannot ban concealed carrying of firearms. The laws in six other states—Colorado, Idaho, Kansas, Mississippi, Oregon, and Wisconsin—impose various conditions or qualifications. For example, the Kansas law says gun carrying must be allowed unless campus buildings have adequate safety measures. Wisconsin allows its campuses to exempt buildings if they post signs barring gun carrying; such signs are indeed now posted on every campus. Mississippi limits carrying to those with special training. Aside from the seven states that allow gun carrying in some manner, twenty-one states ban concealed weapons on campuses, and campuses in the remaining twenty-two states can decide for themselves whether to bar or allow concealed carry. Overwhelmingly, campuses have opted to bar firearms.[117]

Campus administrators, faculty, campus law enforcement agencies, and most students have uniformly opposed such measures. Opponents note, first, that despite a handful of horrifying mass shootings, college campuses are very safe places. According to the Bureau of Justice Statistics, violent campus crimes dropped 9 percent and property crimes dropped 30 percent from 1994 to 2004. In 2004 campuses reported 62 instances of serious violent crime (the national average is 462 per 100,000) and 1,625 instances of serious property crime per 100,000 students—rates significantly lower than those of the campuses' surrounding communities. A study comparing campus crime rates with those in society from 1997 to 2010 found that rates of violent crime on campuses were about 10 percent of those in society during this period. It also noted that crime rates continued to drop throughout this period. The odds of a campus homicide in 2010 were 1 in 875,000, far lower than in society. Even Students for Concealed Carry acknowledges that crime rates on college campuses are lower than in society at large.[118]

Second, campuses have increased security measures in recent years, including the hiring of more campus police, better lighting and patrolling practices, safety awareness training for students and staff, installation of notification systems and cameras, and implementation of campus lock-down plans. Over two-thirds of campus police carry guns, and those who do not are usually found in urban areas or other places where local police provide armed backup. Third, students who live on campuses live in densely populated dormitories and are mostly young adults subject to periods of intense stress, impulsive behavior, and alcohol and drug use. All of these factors invite problems when firearms are also present in the form of gun suicides, thefts, out-of-control altercations, and accidents. Property theft in dormitories is by no means uncommon. Fourth, the Supreme Court's two rulings establishing gun rights carved out specific exceptions for long-standing laws against gun carrying and possession, especially in places such as schools and government buildings. Fifth, college campuses are places of learning, and although they are not immune from crime, the vast majority of criminal or other activity subject to penalty is nonviolent. For most connected to university campuses, civilian gun carrying on campuses is a solution in search of a problem.[119]

"Stand Your Ground" Laws: Extending the "Castle Doctrine" to America's Streets

In 2005 Florida enacted a law that expanded the right of citizens to use deadly force in the streets of that state. Enacted with little attention, the law represented a significant expansion of the "Castle Doctrine." Since the 1600s criminal law has generally protected the right of citizens to defend themselves in their own homes (reflected in the old expression that "one's home is one's castle") against intrusion and attack, even if such defense results in the death of the attacker. On the streets and in other public places, however, the law generally requires citizens to retreat if threatened, unless retreat is unsafe or not feasible. The new Florida law, however, dubbed the "kill bill" by critics, allows citizens to meet force with deadly force without fear of either criminal or civil prosecution because of special immunities and protections written into the bill for the person making a self-defense claim. These include a legal presumption that the individual has acted in self-defense and cannot be prosecuted, and that this presumption need to be based on nothing more than the person's belief that he or she faced a dire threat. These presumptions thwart or inhibit typical prosecutorial investigations.

Enacted in large measure because of pressure by the National Rifle Association, defenders argued that the law would improve the ability of citizens to protect themselves in public places rather than wait for the police to show up. Critics contended that the law would encourage vigilante justice; increase the likelihood that everyday confrontations, from drivers with road rage to drunken sports fans, would turn deadly; and take police responsibilities out of the hands of local law enforcement. After its victory in Florida, where about a million of the state's seventeen million citizens have permits to carry guns on the streets (Florida also has the second-highest crime rate in the nation), the NRA pursued the enactment of such laws in other states. By 2012, twenty-five states had enacted similar laws, with ten of those state laws pretty much identical to that of Florida. NRA vice president Wayne LaPierre called the effort part of "a multi-state strategy" that, when implemented in states with concealed-carry gun laws, would increase the likelihood of street gunplay.[120]

Early tests of the new law fanned critics' concerns. In Tampa, Florida, a tow truck operator shot and killed a man he claimed was trying to run him over, even as the local district attorney evaluated evidence that the victim was shot from behind. In another Florida case, a prostitute shot and killed a client with his own gun after the man threatened the woman. According to the prosecution, before the law, the woman would have been obliged to retreat instead of using deadly force. In another instance, a cab driver killed a drunken man to whom he had given a ride, claiming that the man had threatened him with a knife after being driven to his destination but refused to exit the cab. No knife was found, and relatives of the dead man criticized the cabbie for failing to use his car radio.[121]

These changes garnered little national attention until the shooting death of seventeen-year-old African American Trayvon Martin by neighborhood watch volunteer George Zimmerman in Florida. Zimmerman was patrolling a local neighborhood in Sanford, Florida, on a rainy night in February 2012 when he saw a tall, African American male wearing a hooded sweatshirt wandering the neighborhood. When Zimmerman called in the sighting to police, the dispatcher advised him to remain in his vehicle. Instead, Zimmerman left to follow the person he had seen. Zimmerman was armed with a handgun, which he carried legally (although police authorities urge neighborhood watch volunteers not to carry firearms). Within minutes, the two had some kind of encounter, during which Zimmerman shot and killed Martin with a single bullet to the chest at close range. Martin was unarmed; Zimmerman suffered cuts to his head and face. Martin had been visiting his father, who lived in the neighborhood where he had been seen wandering, and had gone to a local store to purchase a drink and a bag of candy, but had become disoriented in the darkened, unfamiliar neighborhood. Zimmerman was charged with murder, but was found not guilty in a jury trial in July 2013.

Zimmerman's lawyer did not expressly invoke Florida's "stand your ground" law in his defense, but rather relied on a standard self-defense claim; however, the new Florida state law had a significant effect on the case from start to finish. First, while Zimmerman was read his Miranda rights and questioned on the night of the shooting, he was not arrested and held, because police are not allowed to do so if there is probable cause that Zimmerman acted in self-defense, which was established by Zimmerman's self-defense claim. Second, the initial police investigation was not as thorough as it could have been (for example, neighborhood canvassing, witness interviewing, and crime scene preservation were all considered inadequate). While initially attributed to police incompetence or lack of zealousness, it was later attributed, at least in part, to the potency of the Florida self-defense claim law, and the attendant reluctance of police to proceed with a full-bore investigation under such circumstances. It is also the likely reason why the local prosecutor declined to bring any criminal charges against Zimmerman. Charges were eventually brought six weeks after the shooting when the governor named a new prosecutor.

Third, the judge's instructions to the jury included the statement that if Zimmerman "was not engaged in an unlawful activity and was attacked in any place where he had a right to be, he had no duty to retreat and had the right to stand his ground and meet force with force, including deadly force if he reasonably believed [it justified]." Before 2005, Florida law called for safe retreat in public places. This is clear from the jury instructions read to Florida juries in such cases before the 2005 law change, which included asking whether the defendant "used every reasonable means within his power and consistent with his own safety to avoid the danger before resorting to that force. The fact that the defendant was wrongfully attacked cannot justify his use of force likely to cause death or great bodily harm if by retreating he could have avoided the need to use that force." When that wording was dropped in 2005, it resulted in an important added benefit to Zimmerman's case and one of the Zimmerman jurors said after the trial that the "stand your ground" law was a factor in their decision.

Fourth, Florida's law protecting individuals making self-defense claims from civil suits makes such an action by Trayvon Martin's family highly unlikely. Fifth, when a Florida-style "stand your ground" law is combined with citizens carrying concealed handguns, the circumstances become even more complicated when an altercation takes place. It becomes more likely in a state like Florida (which has issued more than one million concealed-carry permits and has a higher handgun ownership rate than other places in the country) that the opponent may also be carrying a gun, and if the survivor believes that the opponent is reaching for a gun—or reaching for that of the survivor—that provides the basis for the perceived fear that the survivor's life was in danger. As one analyst noted, "Since your fear needs only be reasonable, not correct, a mistaken but reasonable fear that the other person is reaching for a gun legally justifies killing an unarmed person." This was just the set of events described by George Zimmerman. Several studies have sought to systematically examine the impact of these laws.

A Florida newspaper, the *Tampa Bay Times*, conducted an extensive analysis of self-defense claims in the state since the "stand your ground" law's enactment in 2005 through 2013, identifying almost 200 such cases. The *Times* found that the law was administered in widely varying ways across the state, such that circumstances in which persons were found not guilty in some jurisdictions were convicted in other cases involving virtually identical circumstances. According to the paper, which called these outcome disparities "shocking," defendants who have benefited the most from the "stand your ground" law were those with criminal and violent records: almost 60 percent of those claiming self-defense when a death resulted had been arrested at least once before; a third had been accused of violent crimes or drug offenses in the past; and over a third had threatened others with a gun in the past or had been found to carry guns illegally. In dozens of cases, both the defendant and the victim had criminal records. In the prosecution of these cases, the results varied widely from county to county as to whether they resulted in charges, trials, convictions, or acquittals.

A Harvard University researcher studied the impact of the Florida law on its state homicide rates and concluded that the enactment of Florida's law not only did not deter homicides, but instead resulted in between 1 and 1.5 extra homicides per year from 2006 to 2010. A nationwide analysis of killings dubbed "justifiable homicides" by the *Wall Street Journal* in 2012 found that, from 2000 to 2010, they nearly doubled, even though the homicide rate declined during this period. Among the states that enacted Florida-style "stand your ground" laws, justifiable homicides doubled in Texas and Georgia, and tripled in Florida (increasing from an average of twelve per year in the five years before the new law to thirty-three per year in the five succeeding years). Florida and Texas alone account for a quarter of all justifiable homicides during this ten-year period. On the other hand, in five other states that enacted the new "stand your ground" laws during this period, justifiable homicide rates did not appreciably change.

Researchers from Texas A&M University drew on FBI Uniform Crime Report data to examine the effects of newly enacted "stand your ground" laws. Their analysis of the period from 2000 to 2010 found no evidence that such laws deterred crimes, including burglary, robbery, or aggravated assault. They did, however, find an increase of about 8 percent in the homicide rate (about 600 additional homicides per year) in states with the new "stand your ground" laws, and an increase in justifiable homicides of between 17–50 percent, leading them to conclude that "stand your ground" laws led to significant increases in homicides. At the same time, they found little evidence that criminals were more likely to carry guns than before the enactment of these laws. In all, they concluded that "stand your ground" laws reduce the costs associated with the use of lethal force, thereby encouraging greater use of it.

A 2012 study from the National Bureau of Economic Research found that the enactment of "stand your ground" laws was associated with a significant increase in homicides, averaging from 336 to 396 additional deaths per year, or a 6.8 percent increase in the homicide rate, and that the laws did nothing to thwart or deter crime. Finally, an Urban Institute study found wide racial disparities in the handling of "stand your ground" cases during the 2005 to 2010 period. In non–"stand your ground" states, African Americans who killed whites were ruled to have justifiable self-defense claims in 1 percent of cases, whereas when the killer was white, and the person killed was African American, 9.5 percent of the claims were judged justifiable. In "stand your ground" states, African Americans who claimed self-defense in killing a white were judged justifiable in 1.4 percent of cases. When the killer was white and the person killed was African American, however, the justifiable rate was 16.8 percent. These numbers do not establish causality, but strongly suggest systematic race bias in the criminal justice system when it comes to killings where "stand your ground" claims are made, and far greater race bias in "stand your ground" states than in states without such laws.

Conclusion

What does this survey of the criminological consequences of guns lead us to conclude about the regulation of guns in the United States? Without question, guns are inextricably linked to violence in America. The available evidence does not, however, answer the causal question of whether guns cause violence or whether those prone to violence simply turn to guns. The answer to this riddle is probably a combination of both conclusions. If guns disappeared tomorrow, violence would surely continue. But it would probably be less devastating, especially for such at-risk groups as the young and African Americans.

Beyond this, we can reasonably come to the following conclusions:

- Handguns are a disproportionate component of gun harm. Even though long guns are more abundant and usually easier to obtain, the handgun is the weapon of choice for criminals.[123] Handguns are useful for self-defense, but the opportunity for a victim actually to deploy a handgun is so small a percentage of the more than one million an٬ (much less of all crimes) that it cannot be considered an ad٬ balance to the handgun crime problem. In addition, a lonᵍ substitute for the handgun for purposes of home defense. ٬ have suggested that an across-the-board restriction of handguns would at best only push criminals to greater long gun use, the existing ratio of handgun to long gun use in crime, the greater difficulty in obtaining handguns, and handguns' greater concealability undercut this argument.

- Homicide attempts would continue regardless of gun regulations. But the "weapon instrumentality effect" alone makes clear that significantly fewer would die and that injuries would be less severe—although the total nonfatal injury rate might rise without guns because of the greater difficulty of controlling a situation with weapons other than guns. In addition, there is reason to conclude that guns facilitate some homicides that would not occur were guns absent.

- The suicide rate among the adult population would probably undergo a measurable reduction without guns because some would not seek other methods, and guns are more lethal than other suicide methods. The suicide rate of young people would certainly undergo a significant drop. Indeed, specialists interested in reducing suicide from all means have focused increasing attention on restricting access to lethal agents, including guns, carbon monoxide (notably, eliminating this toxic gas from automobile exhaust, as was done in Britain in the 1960s and 1970s), and drugs. Gun control in this area is thus consistent with what is known about suicide prevention.

- A reduction in gun availability would probably have some effect on the accident rate, but the numbers are small enough (and have been declining for some years) that any degree of change would likely be modest. More effective here would be regulations to require added safety features and improved training.

- The most reliable estimate suggests that guns are used in self-defense more than one hundred thousand times each year. Even if that number is doubled or tripled, it does not come close to matching or counterbalancing criminal gun uses, much less the thirty thousand gun deaths logged each year and the tens of thousands of gun injuries reported each year. Remembering that about one-third of all American homes already have at least one gun, there is little reason to expect any dramatic rise in successful defensive uses if the rest of the population suddenly decided to obtain guns. One could, however, expect an appreciable rise in homicides, suicides, accidents, and injuries from guns.

- Greater gun availability in an area is associated with greater gun availability for criminals. Far from serving as a deterrent to crime, guns in the home are especially tempting targets for theft, particularly because most burglaries occur when no one is home. On an individual level, a gun in the hand of a victim can thwart or stop a crime. On an aggregate level, however, more guns mean more gun problems, even though many citizens believe that guns make them safer.

- It makes no sense to consider self-defense, deterrence, or related issues of gun ownership without considering the numerous other means by which citizens may protect themselves and their homes, both individually and collectively. Even though citizens often feel alone in the fight against crime, allies are to be found in neighbors, local governments, and law enforcement. To isolate defense and safety issues from this larger context is to fail to understand the dimensions of the problem to which guns are related.

- School violence continues to be a national concern even though schools and especially including colleges are statistically safer for children than are their local communities or even their homes. School crimes, including school shootings, have been declining since the early 1990s, although this is not to suggest complacency on the part of families, teachers, and others involved with schools. And the "stand your ground" laws' record provides no confidence that they help the innocent, deter crime, or improve safety. In fact, all the available evidence to date supports the conclusion that such laws increase harm and the likelihood of harm.

Considering the role of guns in homicide, suicide, accident, and self-defense as reviewed in this chapter, the regulation of guns is a rational policy step not because it represents a panacea or because the results of research all point in the same direction but because the weight of evidence significantly favors societal benefits over the likely costs. Admittedly, this conclusion begs the question of the kind, degree, and practicality of regulation. These are, of course, vital questions, but they cannot be addressed before we examine the contemporary politics of the gun control issue.

Chapter 4

Political Fury

Gun Politics

> The truth is that this legislation would effectively create a NATIONAL GUN REGISTRATION system. And if this bill becomes law, it could set the stage for gun-banners to achieve their ultimate goal—confiscation of our firearms and end of the Second Amendment!!!
>   *From a letter from NRA Director Chris Cox to NRA members, 2010*

> The gun lobby has gone off the deep end! I mean, we've always known the gun pushers were a little unhinged, with their obsession with getting as many firearms in as many hands as possible, but I've never seen anything so reckless as the stunts they're trying to pull right now.
>   *From a letter from Brady Campaign spokesman Jim Brady, sent to members of the Brady Campaign to Prevent Gun Violence, 2010*

WHITE-HOT RHETORIC IS NO STRANGER to American political discourse. Yet one would be hard-pressed to find an issue that has provoked more anger and vitriol through the years and even decades than the gun debate. The legislation mentioned in the National Rifle Association letter excerpt above that prompted such outrage and alarm was a bill introduced by Democratic Senator Frank Lautenberg (NJ) that would have preserved for ten years the gun background check data of applicants identified as suspected or actual terrorists and preserved other criminal background check records for 180 days. The Brady Campaign letter was sparked by an NRA-backed bill to allow loaded guns to be carried onto Amtrak trains in stowed luggage (President Obama later approved the measure once it had passed Congress). Such heated, even hysterical language is, in fact, typical of the tone and style of the messages these groups transmit to their members as well as of much of the political discourse on gun control.[1]

Admittedly, these strident appeals are not unusual in the world of targeted mailings; in fact, the standard wisdom on effective direct mail is that it be both emotional and personal.[2] Needless to say, the NRA and the Brady Campaign are likely to pull out all the stops when it comes to mobilizing their members. Yet this kind of rhetoric spills beyond the groups themselves and into the wider public debate, as is often true of the rhetoric used in other social regulatory policy debates. To state the matter in its simplest terms: rational policymaking recedes from view when the political combatants spend most of their time screaming political obscenities at each other.

As I argue in chapter 1, these traits are symptomatic of social regulatory policies in which the primary focus is on social relationships rather than economic transactions. The political traits of social regulatory policy, which are the focus of this chapter, include the following:

- The prevalence of single-issue groups. The significance of these groups, which have proliferated in recent decades, is that they maintain a narrow and intense focus on a specific issue of morality or set of related concerns. This narrow focus, combined with intense feelings associated with a value issue such as gun control, cultivates absolutism within the group, which in turn polarizes the larger public debate. Because the policy battleground revolves around activities viewed in moral terms, those engaged in the political struggle are highly motivated to defend what they believe are fundamental and very personal values. One consequence of this pattern is that it enhances the internal cohesiveness of the organization because the existence of external "enemies" sustains and cultivates the "we-feeling" (sense of unity and solidarity) of the group. This in turn can make the group a zealous participant in the political process.[3] Conversely, Raymond Tatalovich and Byron Daynes have noted that single-issue groups bring "a disruptive influence to normal political discourse and consensus building because ... moral discourse is polarizing."[4] The evidence of this intense struggle is readily visible for such issues as abortion, school prayer, and gay rights. It is no less true for gun control.
- Grassroots activism. Social regulatory politics is not confined to an "inside the beltway" struggle in Washington, DC. It emerges in states, cities, towns, and villages across the country. Unlike issues on which national political figures may provide leadership for the rest of the

country, pressure from the political grassroots can have a profound effect on how national political leaders respond to these issues.

- Public opinion. Public opinion can be mobilized behind change, but such mobilization is likely to be sporadic. Most citizens hold opinions on social regulatory issues but do not share the same intense feelings of interested groups. Thus, pivotal events, such as an assassination or a mass murder, or longer-term issue shifts, such as the rising fear of crime, play a vital role in public-issue consciousness. More important, the outcome of a political controversy may vary according to the ability of key groups to mobilize and sway popular sentiment in the aftermath of a pivotal event.
- Political parties. The political parties often seek to exploit differences over social regulatory issues. Republicans are likely to use such issues to appeal to core conservative constituencies, whereas Democrats seek to appeal to traditional liberal constituents. The significance of this trait lies in the fact that American political parties are noted primarily for their tendency to seek the political center and to minimize rather than maximize their differences on most issues.

As I argue in chapters 2 and 3, constitutional prohibitions or any straightforward conclusion from the criminological evidence cannot explain the present state of American gun policy. Unquestionably, gun policy continues to be defined by its politics.

Single-Issue Gun Groups: The NRA

A handful of groups have played the primary role in defining and shaping gun politics. Although several groups focus on the gun issue, this chapter concerns itself with those that have had important political effects: the National Rifle Association and the Brady Campaign.[5]

Looming like the fierce three-headed watchdog from Greek mythology, Cerberus, the NRA dominated and defined gun politics for most of the last century. By one assessment, the NRA is "the prototypic single-issue interest group in America."[6]

NRA Background

Col. William C. Church, editor of the *Army and Navy Journal,* and Capt. George W. Wingate, an officer in the New York National Guard, formed the NRA in 1871. Its original stated purpose, reflecting concern over the Union

Army's poor marksmanship skills during the Civil War, was "improvement of its members in marksmanship."[7] The group languished in its early years, prompting New York State to withdraw its subsidy of NRA shooting matches in 1880 (from which the NRA had benefited since its founding). In 1900 the moribund group served as the vehicle for a revival in marksmanship (prompted partly by the Spanish-American War in 1898) when Albert Jones, an officer in the New Jersey National Guard, promoted its involvement. With the assistance of the gun enthusiast Theodore Roosevelt, Congress was prompted to create the National Board for the Promotion of Rifle Practice as part of the Militia Act of 1903. At its first meeting in 1905, this board authorized the sale of government surplus weapons and ammunition to rifle clubs, and this proved to be a critical boost for the organization. Two years later the NRA moved its headquarters to Washington, DC. In 1921 the still small NRA (it had about thirty-five hundred members) took on new life thanks to the efforts of C. B. Lister, the organization's promotions manager, who affiliated the NRA with two thousand local sporting clubs. By 1934 membership had grown tenfold, making the organization the largest and best-organized association of firearms users in the nation. By the start of World War II membership was fifty thousand.[8]

Although the NRA played a role in limited political efforts to alter national gun policy in the 1920s and 1930s, its primary focus continued to be marksmanship and related sporting activities. NRA leaders did, however, play an active role in shaping what became the National Firearms Act of 1934, the first major national law to regulate guns (see chapter 5). At the end of World War II the influx of returning soldiers provided a significant membership boost. Within three years of the end of the war, membership had tripled, although most of these new members had a greater interest in hunting than in marksmanship. The NRA quickly adapted to this new priority. In the mid-1950s, with a membership of 300,000 and 140 paid employees, the organization moved from its old Washington location to an eight-story building in downtown Washington, which it occupied until the end of 1993, when it moved to a new location in Fairfax, Virginia.[9] When Congress turned its attention to gun control in the 1960s, so too did the NRA. From that point on, the NRA devoted increasing time and resources to its political agenda.

These shifting organizational priorities are confirmed in a content analysis of the NRA publication the *American Rifleman*, in which the proportion of space given over to target shooting declined from about 40 percent before World War II to about 20 percent after the war. Similarly, the percentage of space devoted to legislation rose from less than 4 percent before 1965 to about 10 percent after that time.[10] By the mid-1970s membership reached 1 million. It hit 2 million by the early 1980s, peaked at more than 3 million in the mid-1980s, declined to about 2.5 million about 1990, and then climbed to about 3.5 million by 1995 but dipped again to 2.7 million by 1997. By 2001 membership again rose, this time to a peak of about 4 million, where the membership level stayed through the mid-2000s. By 2010 membership was reportedly about 4.3 million. Yet, there is reason to believe that the NRA artificially inflates its membership numbers. An examination of NRA magazine circulation rates in 2007 (all members receive a free magazine) found that their total circulation was 2.7 million, not the 4 million members they claimed at the time. At roughly the same time, an NRA letter to members referred to "about 3 million NRA Members," which, of course, could have been a simple mistake, but it does conform to the magazine circulation number. Further, the NRA gives out free, unsolicited memberships with gun purchases. It also turns out that "life members"—those who pay a large fee to be members for life—may not be removed from the rolls when they pass away. In 1992 the organization's annual budget was about $90 million, most of which came from membership dues. By 1995 its total budget had risen to about $150 million, but it had also run up a debt of about $60 million. By 2000 its budget was $168 million, and much of its debt had been retired. Its office maintains a staff of more than 300 employees, including 65 devoted specifically to lobbying efforts. The organization's 2011 budget was $230 million. The NRA Foundation had revenues of $27 million.[11] The NRA's political significance is best understood through an analysis of its links to the government and industry as well as its targeted political operations.

Government Subsidies

Ironically, the NRA probably owes its existence to its long-term, intimate association with government subsidies and other forms of support, illustrating how government actions can prompt the formation and cultivation of interest groups. According to interest-group specialist Jack Walker, the NRA "was launched in close consultation with the Department of the Army."[12] The irony stems from the NRA's contemporary fierce government-is-the-enemy rhetoric. Only a year after its founding, the New York State assemblyman David W. Judd, an NRA ally, pushed through the state legislature a $25,000 appropriation to purchase a hundred-acre site on Long Island for NRA use as a rifle range.

The National Board for the Promotion of Rifle Practice made possible the NRA's rebirth in the early 1900s. As mentioned, the board's first action was to authorize the sale of surplus weapons and ammunition, at cost, to gun clubs sponsored by the NRA. In 1909 the NRA amended its bylaws to include five additional governing board members selected by the secretaries of war and navy along with the heads of the state National Guards. In 1910 the army decided to give away the surplus rifles and ammunition, but again only to NRA members and their recognized groups. Needless to say, these giveaways provided a powerful incentive for gun enthusiasts to join the organization.[13] Two years later Congress began to fund NRA marksmanship contests and allowed the army to provide soldiers to assist in running the annual events, all at government expense.[14] In the 1912 army appropriations bill, $25,000 was allocated to fund the NRA matches. The National Defense Act of 1916 appropriated $300,000 for civilian marksmanship training, opened army rifle ranges to civilians, and allowed military instructors to teach shooting skills to civilians. It also created the Office of the Director of the Division of Civilian Marksmanship under the Rifle Practice Board to supervise civilian marksmanship activities.

By the 1960s the office was spending $5 million a year; yet some complained when, during the Vietnam War, the office was using three thousand troops at Camp Perry, Ohio, for the NRA-sponsored events. The primary rationale for the program—to provide a pool of trained shooters for possible military induction—was never borne out; a survey in 1965 revealed that only about 3 percent of military inductees had participated in the program before joining the military, and less than half of those who participated in the contests were of military draft age. A 1990 study by the General Accounting Office reported that only two hundred civilian graduates of the marksmanship program entered the military each year, meaning that the program was spending $23,000 per recruit—hardly an efficient use of government dollars.[15] Weapons sales continued to escalate. From 1959 to 1964 the army sold five hundred thousand guns to civilians. By the end of the 1960s the Rifle Practice Board was providing sixty million rounds of ammunition free and was selling M-1 rifles for $17.50. The sale of guns was then sharply curtailed, however, at least in part due to concern that weapons were falling into the hands of such fringe groups as the Ku Klux Klan and the Minutemen. In another ironic twist, four hundred members of the Detroit Police Department had to join the NRA in 1967 in order to obtain surplus army carbines for riot control.[16] A 1979 lawsuit filed by the National Coalition to Ban Handguns (NCBH) challenged the NRA's exclusive agreement with the Department of Defense. A federal court agreed, striking down the NRA membership requirement. Those eligible to obtain surplus guns would still have to belong to a government marksmanship club, however, and many continued their NRA affiliation.[17]

Despite periodic exposés and public criticism, the Division of Civilian Marksmanship continues to operate more than two thousand clubs with about two hundred thousand members. The clubs are also affiliated with the NRA. About forty million rounds of ammunition are made available free each year, at a cost of about $1 million. The civilian participants continue to have free access to military shooting ranges, and Camp Perry continues as the site of the annual NRA competition, at government cost of about $2.5 million. In all, the program costs about $5 million annually. An effort to kill the program was brought to the floor of the House of Representatives in October 1993, but it failed. Although this program today represents a small component of the NRA agenda, it was instrumental in the organization's early development and continues to represent a unique benefit for the NRA that critics consider to be unjustifiable pork barrel, providing for nothing more than "a subsidy of a hobby."[18]

The NRA also continues to benefit from special concessions from other government agencies. Both the Bureau of Land Management and the National Forest Service granted the NRA permission to build target ranges on federal land in 1990. The opportunity to use the hundreds of millions of acres of federal land (found in most states) controlled by these agencies allows the NRA to avoid zoning and other problems in securing shooting sites; it also provides an additional recruitment tool for the organization. The NRA has also pressed to repeal the century-long ban on hunting in national parks. Opposition to this effort swelled in 1994 as environmentalists and others worried about the effects of such hunting on other park users as well as on park wildlife. In 2009 Congress enacted legislation allowing park visitors to carry loaded firearms in national parks, despite the objections of parks officials and law enforcement.[19]

Finally, the NRA benefits in another way from the government. Although it is a political organization, the NRA has set up several related organizational entities to which citizens may make tax-exempt contributions. These include the Firearms Civil Rights Legal Defense Fund, the International Shooter Development Fund, the National Firearms Museum Fund, the NRA Special Contribution Fund, and the NRA Foundation, a nonprofit corporation that includes within it the Junior Programs Fund and the Range Development Fund. The NRA's Firearms Civil Rights Legal Defense Fund has been particularly active in funneling money to support legal challenges to gun control laws. In 1994 it contributed more than $500,000 to this purpose. In 1996 it contributed $20,000 to the legal defense of Bernhard Goetz, who shot four men in a New York City subway in 1984 after they allegedly threatened to rob him. Goetz lost the civil suit. The NRA also offers various estate planning and will services, hoping to encourage gifts and donations to it from "life insurance, securities or real estate gifts and charitable remainder trusts."[20]

The Gun Industry

The NRA has also had a long and intimate relationship with gun makers and sellers. Policy analyst Josh Sugarmann has gone so far as to conclude that the

NRA "has evolved into the unofficial trade association for the firearms industry."[21] The link between the two is pragmatic, in that general gun advocacy on the part of the NRA helps generate and sustain a market for the firearms industry's products. Similarly, gun sales benefit gun users, who compose the core NRA constituency. The link is also ideological because both manufacturers and the NRA embrace and extol the gun culture (described in chapter 1) for emotive, symbolic, and patriotic reasons. Two specific interests have animated the NRA-industry link: first, the desire to maintain or boost firearms and ammunition sales at a time when the percentage of gun users in America has been declining, and second, the desire to avoid any gun regulations that might impinge on sales. The first goal is facilitated through the extensive weapons advertising found in NRA publications; the second constitutes the core of the NRA's political agenda.

As early as the start of the twentieth century, a "revolving door" commonly existed between personnel in the NRA and the weapons industry. Indeed, from 1927 to 1935 the NRA actually sold firearms supplies to its membership through the NRA Service Company. The practice was halted, however, when the discounted pricing and overhead expenses pushed the organization into the red.

In the 1950s and 1960s the then–$1.5 billion arms industry accelerated its political and advertising efforts to boost sagging gun sales and fight proposed government regulations.[22] Yet the industry was able to curtail its direct foray into politics by the early 1970s because, at the same time, the NRA assumed a more aggressive political role. The acceleration of campaign finance reform in the 1970s also made this desirable for the gun industry. Symptomatic of the embarrassment the industry sought to avoid was the revelation in 1973 that the Olin Mathieson Corporation, owner of the Winchester-Western Division (the nation's second-largest gun producer), had made the fourth-largest single contribution to Richard Nixon's 1972 reelection campaign.[23] The *New York Times* noted, "Many firearms manufacturers have chosen to remain in the background of the raging debate over tighter restrictions on the sale and possession of guns, preferring to leave their public talking to the National Rifle Association."[24]

Aside from the NRA's conventional political activities, it also helps boost the firearms industry through invariably favorable reviews of various weapons in its publications. In addition to NRA publications, more than a dozen other magazines are devoted to promoting guns and gun products. The NRA provides extensive advertising space in its publications, and this also accounts for a significant percentage of NRA revenues. In 1990, for example, about $7.5 million in revenues (about 8 percent of the organization's total budget) was generated from industry ads.[25] Moreover, manufacturers insert NRA membership applications in their packaging, and the NRA provides discount gun purchase offers as well as advertising and publicity for a wide array of accessories—camping equipment, clothing, and the like. In recent years the NRA has provided a commission to gun dealers for every person they sign up as an NRA member. In addition, as a way to draw in more people as gun users and create markets for new gun designs, thereby combating what the gun industry considered sluggish sales in the 1980s and 1990s, the NRA and gun companies cooperate in tandem to generate "new kinds of target sports."[26] More important, the NRA has in recent decades assumed the political point on gun issues in the political arena, turning the spotlight away from industry. Not until 1989 did the gun industry hire a Washington lobbyist, and then only because of the concern that the NRA was losing some of its political clout.

The gun industry was pushed further into the public spotlight in the late 1990s when cities and counties around the country filed more than thirty lawsuits against gun manufacturers, charging them with manufacturing unsafe products and with marketing their products irresponsibly. Successful litigation against the tobacco industry during the 1990s spurred these legal efforts. Gun liability suits received a major boost in 1999 when, for the first time, a Brooklyn, New York, jury found nine gun manufacturers legally liable in a shooting incident because of the industry's marketing and distribution practices, which allegedly encouraged gun trafficking from states with weak gun laws to those with stricter laws, such as New York. The half-million-dollar verdict against the gun manufacturers was overturned on appeal in 2001, but numerous other suits around the country posed a considerable financial threat to the gun industry. Unlike the tobacco industry, whose deep pockets could afford financial payouts (in 1997 the tobacco companies generated almost $50 billion in sales), the ailing gun industry could ill afford to lose many such suits, as its total 1997 sales were only about $1.4 billion. For example, the city of Chicago filed a $433 million suit against gun manufacturers, which alone could have had a devastating effect on the industry if the effort had succeeded. In 2005, however, these efforts were essentially ended when Congress passed the Lawful Commerce in Arms Act (see chapter 5) that all but barred civil and criminal actions against the gun industry. Enactment of this measure was the NRA's top political goal. In response, the NRA also pushed legislation in many states to bar localities from filing suits or enacting other local gun regulations, having seen enactment of such "preemption" legislation in at least thirty-one states by 2003.[27]

Of particular interest to the firearms industry has been the Consumer Product Safety Commission's avoidance of gun regulation. This commission specifically exempted gun and ammunition regulation in the 1972 act creating the agency and helps maintain the continued ease in obtaining federal firearms licenses, which have allowed individuals to become weapons dealers for a modest fee. In the early 1990s only about 20 percent of licensed dealers operated a storefront; the rest were "kitchen table," noncommercial dealers who accounted for about one-quarter of all weapons sales. Monitoring and regulating such sales have been notoriously poor, prompting an increase in the licensing fee from $30 to $200 for a three-year license in 1994. The industry has also benefited from NRA resistance to the regulation of new, more destructive, compact, or undetectable weapons. The financial link between industry and the NRA has grown in the 2000s. According to a 2005 to 2010 report by the Violence Policy Center, corporations have contributed between $19.8 million and $52.6 million to the NRA through its "Ring of Freedom" corporate giving program. Most of the corporate participants are in the gun business. In 2011, large corporate and individual donors contributed $71.1 million to the NRA.[28]

The Institute for Legislative Action

In the late 1960s and early 1970s the NRA focused political efforts for the first time on specific legislative races, claiming credit for defeating two gun control proponents in the Senate, Joseph Clark (D-PA) in 1968 and Joseph Tydings (D-MD) in 1970.[29] Buoyed by these victories and persuaded to make politics a higher priority, the NRA reconstituted and concentrated its lobbying activities in 1975 with the creation of its Institute for Legislative Action (ILA). Focusing primarily on legislative efforts in the states and in the nation's capital, the ILA has become the primary power center in the NRA. Commenting on the ILA's effectiveness, the *Washington Post* admitted that "few lobbies have so mastered the marble halls and concrete canyons of Washington."[30] In 1988 the ILA spent $20.2 million on political activities. By 1992 its spending had risen to $28.9 million. In the 2000 election cycle the ILA raised and spent $30 million, and in 2008, $40 million. In recent years the ILA has consumed 25 percent or more of the NRA's total budget.[31]

Beyond its lobbying activities, the ILA has become the primary means through which the NRA mobilizes political support among NRA membership and sympathizers. In 1991, for example, the NRA spent about $10 million on "legislative alert," fund-raising, and other mass mailings. Journalist Osha Gray Davidson has labeled the tone of the politically charged mailings the "Armageddon Appeal." As a former NRA head said, "You keep any special interest group alive by nurturing the crisis atmosphere. 'Keep sending those cards and letters in. Keep sending money.'"[32] After the 1984 Bernhard Goetz subway shooting incident, the NRA ran afoul of the law when it printed on the outside of one of its mailings, "If you fail to respond to this letter you could face a jail term."

The New York State attorney general's office charged the NRA with fraud. After resisting New York's investigative efforts to examine its other mailings for two years, the NRA finally complied. The matter was resolved when the NRA promised to avoid such tactics in the future.[33]

A study of NRA advertising conducted by the Congressional Research Service found numerous inaccuracies in the way NRA literature described gun bills before Congress.[34] Even though the NRA is by no means the largest lobbying group in the country, its belief in membership mobilization for political purposes is most clearly reflected in its spending on internal communications designed not only to buttress support for the NRA agenda but also to rally support for political candidates sympathetic to the NRA perspective. In almost every year since the end of the 1970s, the NRA has spent more money on internal communications than any other comparable group. During the 1991–1992 election cycle, for example, the NRA spent $8.4 million on political mail and other related internal political spending aimed at members and others. This level of spending represented a 90 percent increase over its spending for the same purpose four years earlier. In 2008, NRA internal communications spending was $25 million. Unlike donations to candidate fund-raising committees, there are no federal spending limits on such internal communications, and the NRA is consistently one of the top-spending interest groups in this area.[35]

The NRA's Political Action Committee

The ILA also manages the NRA's political action committee (PAC), called the Political Victory Fund. Formed in 1976, its specific purpose is to channel campaign contributions to sympathetic officeholders and seekers. In 1988 it channeled $1.5 million into George H. W. Bush's presidential campaign (it refused to endorse Bush in 1992 because of his support for restrictions on assault weapons imports). In all, it spent $4.6 million during the 1987–1988 election cycle, making it the fifth-biggest PAC spender during that period. During the 1991–1992 election cycle the PAC contributed more than $1.7 million directly to US Senate and House candidates, ranking it the ninth-biggest PAC spender. In addition, it spent $958,000 on its own against or in favor of selected candidates. (Unlike contributions made directly to candidates, such independent spending is not limited by federal law.) In 1994 the PAC spent more than any other—$5.3 million in campaign contributions, independent expenditures, and other campaign activities. In the 1999–2000 cycle the NRA PAC raised and spent more than $20 million on federal and state elections. In the 2004 election it again raised and spent about $20 million at the national level alone. In the 2012 election cycle, the NRA PAC spent over $16 million.[36]

As is true of most PACs, the Political Victory Fund gives most of its money to incumbents. It also favors Republicans over Democrats. From 1978 to 2000 the NRA gave about 84 percent of its money to Republicans. This ratio shifted even more dramatically in the 2000 elections, when it gave 94 percent of its money to Republicans. This shift reflected the NRA's conscious decision to throw its lot in with the Republican Party, which it viewed as far more friendly to its agenda. In 2004 it endorsed George W. Bush's reelection bid and heavily backed Republican candidates around the country, with over 90 percent of its contributions going to GOP candidates. In the 2006 midterm elections, however, 16 percent of its contributions went to Democrats (and 84 percent to Republicans), anticipating, correctly, the Democrats' return to power in Congress. In 2008, 22 percent of its contributions went to Democrats. In 2010 (the year Republicans won back control of the House of Representatives) 29 percent went to Democrats. Although this rise in Democratic contributions may seem anomalous, it represented two realities: first, that the NRA continued to log political victories even with Democrats in charge of Congress and the White House, and second, that the Democrats all but abandoned their prior commitment to stronger gun laws, partly because a growing number of Democrats elected to Congress did so on an expressly gun-friendly agenda.[37]

The NRA's politicization came at a cost. Fewer NRA resources have been devoted to traditional hunting, shooting, and other programs. In 1980, 19 percent of the NRA budget went to hunter safety programs, police training courses, and the like. By 1988 only 11 percent of the budget was devoted to such programs. The dramatic upsurge in political spending ran the NRA deeply into the red in the early 1990s. In 1991 it posted a $9 million debt. In 1992 the debt was $34 million out of a total budget of about $84 million, and its liquid assets dropped from $91 million to $68 million. Its 1993 debt was $32.7 million; in 1996 it reported a debt of $43 million and laid off up to seventy of its four hundred employees. Clouding the financial picture further have been charges of mismanagement. In particular, Executive Vice President Wayne LaPierre was accused of awarding a no-bid contract to a direct-mail firm to which he had close contacts and upon which he had spent lavishly. Further, some in the NRA believe that membership recruitment has been mishandled, as the organization was spending more to recruit new members ($87 per new member) than it was receiving in dues from them ($35 per member).[38] These suspicions were fanned when internal NRA documents were leaked to the press in 1995. They revealed that the recent, intensive recruitment efforts were a money-losing proposition for the organization both because of cost and because only about one-quarter of these members renewed their memberships.

ILA spending, which in 1994 lavished $28.3 million on its various political activities, caused about 70 percent of the total deficit that the NRA accumulated between 1991 and 1994. (The NRA financed the budget gap by selling off more than half of the stocks, Treasury bonds, and corporate bonds that constituted the organization's nest egg. The NRA also borrowed $32 million to cover the costs of its new headquarters in Virginia.) In the 1994 elections, when the NRA's PAC was the biggest-spending PAC in the country, insiders characterized its bookkeeping practices as "sloppy." At the time, the chair of the NRA's finance committee wrote that the "disintegration of the assets of the N.R.A. under current spending policies have eroded our future viability."[39] The private credit-rating agency Dun & Bradstreet gave the NRA its lowest possible rating on its credit risk scale in a report delivered June 30, 1995.[40] A few months before the release of the credit report, the Internal Revenue Service informed the NRA that it would be audited. In the late 1990s, however, the NRA's financial picture improved as it trimmed costs, increased membership (more than half of the NRA's revenues come from membership dues), and accelerated fund-raising activities.

The NRA Goes International

In the midst of these changes, the NRA expanded its political efforts to the international stage. Joining with gun manufacturers and gun groups from eleven countries in 1997, it sought to fight international efforts at gun control, including the enactment of tougher gun laws in such countries as Australia, Brazil, Britain, Canada, and New Zealand. Further, the NRA obtained advocacy (akin to lobbyist) status at the United Nations in 1997, and in 1998 it unsuccessfully opposed a UN resolution to curb illicit international firearms trade. In 2001, however, with NRA loyalist George W. Bush in the White House, the NRA and the Bush administration reversed the Clinton administration's position of restricting international arms trafficking. According to UN estimates, more than five hundred million small arms are responsible for at least five hundred thousand annual deaths worldwide. To the bewilderment of representatives from other countries, the Bush administration argued that such a UN effort would not only impinge on American gun habits but also on the US Constitution's Second Amendment. After several weeks of negotiations, the effort to impose restrictions was dropped, leaving only a no-sanction, voluntary agreement to reduce small arms trafficking. The NRA's stated goal is to pressure the UN to sidestep any involvement in gun control matters, and it regularly demonizes the UN in its publications for its efforts related to gun control. In 2009 the Barack Obama administration reversed Bush-era policy by endorsing an international treaty to regulate international arms sales. In 2008 the United States accounted for over two-thirds of the $55 billion in worldwide arms transfer deals. In 2013, the Obama administration signed off on a UN-sponsored international treaty to stifle illicit international arms trafficking. The NRA decried the agreement, saying that it would erode American gun rights, even though domestic laws trump international agreements and the treaty reaffirms "the sovereign right of any State to regulate and control conventional arms" within its borders. The only nations to oppose the treaty were Iran, North Korea, and Syria. Objective evaluations of the treaty made clear that it would have no effect on American gun rights.[41]

The NRA has also become increasingly aggressive in cultivating gun rights activities in nations where gun control efforts have met with greater success. In 2006 it helped achieve a major victory in Brazil when that nation voted down a referendum proposing a nationwide gun ban. As early as 2003 NRA political strategists traveled to Brazil to develop political strategies to counter those of gun control advocates. At the outset of the referendum movement, national polls showed over 70 percent support for the gun ban as a means to stem Brazil's high gun-death rate, the highest of any nation in the world. Yet referendum opponents adopted a page from the NRA playbook, arguing that the ban would be a denial of the rights of Brazilian citizens and that if the measure passed, the Brazilian government would encroach on other citizen rights. On election day the referendum was rejected by 64 percent of the vote. As one referendum supporter noted, "We gun control groups failed to anticipate this idea of focusing on rights."[42]

Explaining the NRA's Effectiveness

As mentioned previously, the NRA probably owes its existence to government support and largesse. Its long-term, intimate link to the gun industry—the NRA's political silent partner—was also important in its development and is a continuing source of political and financial support. Yet these two elements contribute little to an understanding of the NRA's contemporary political effectiveness.

Member Incentives

Standard wisdom on the influence of interest groups identifies a handful of key factors that explain a group's effectiveness. They include money, membership, reputation, and some combination of information, expertise, and skills. These factors are not all equal in importance, although the NRA excels in all these areas. Compared with similar groups, the NRA is considered to have a large, intense membership; a fat budget; and skilled, experienced leaders.[43]

Popular analysis in the press often points to the NRA's political spending through its PAC as a key explanation for its influence. Commenting on an NRA-supported bill successfully forced out of the House Judiciary Committee in 1986 by discharge petition (gun control proponents sought to keep the bill, the Firearms Owners Protection Act, in committee), the *Washington Post* noted that 84 percent of the members of the House who signed the petition had also received NRA PAC money within the previous two years. The paper editorialized that the NRA "has done a bang-up job of buying support in Congress."[44] The common assertion that PAC spending buys votes in Congress is one that is mostly unsupported by analysis.[45] In fact, contributions to members of Congress most often serve as a reward for supporting the position of the PAC rather than as a way of swaying or switching votes, although money is more likely to be important when the issue is narrower and of lower visibility. Some of the heaviest PAC spenders in Washington, such as the American Medical Association and the National Association of Realtors, are often big losers on Capitol Hill. The main consequences of PAC spending are reinforcement of existing loyalties and the acquisition of interest-group access to the legislator. These are important considerations in the interest-group process, to be sure, but PAC spending by the NRA's PAC, or that of any other, can rarely be tied directly to the purchase and subsequent casting of legislators' votes.[46]

The key to the NRA's effectiveness that distinguishes it from other interest groups lies in its highly motivated mass membership and the organization's ability to bring pressure from that membership to bear at key moments and places. Central to this effectiveness is the fact that gun control opponents are more likely to engage in political action—letter writing, contributing money, attending meetings, and the like—than gun control proponents. As Bill Keller observed in *CQ Weekly Report,* the NRA's strength rests with "a body of gun lovers linked by a common activity that continues even when the legislative front is quiet." And in the *New York Times* Steven Roberts said, "The real power of the rifle association stems from the fervor of its members, their apparent devotion to a single, overriding issue, and their determination to judge politicians on a 'for-us-or-against-us' basis."[47] The question of member motivation is central to understanding and gauging the effectiveness of interest groups.

The political scientist James Q. Wilson identified four kinds of member incentives: material, specific solidary, collective solidary, and purposive. Material incentives are tangible rewards, including money, services, or gifts. Specific solidary incentives include intangible rewards such as honors, the bestowal of rank or office, and the granting of special respect or deference. Collective solidary incentives are also intangible but can be acquired only through a group experience, such as the enjoyment, comradeship, and esteem one might feel by belonging to a group. Purposive incentives are those that might be most nearly considered ideological—those based on the support of a cause or ideal; the satisfaction of membership comes from belief in and advancement of a cause, not from receiving immediate concrete benefits.[48] In the case of NRA members, one can observe each of these incentives. People who join the NRA receive several concrete benefits for their $35 dues, including a magazine subscription (*American Rifleman, American Hunter,* or *America's First Freedom*), a cap bearing the NRA logo, travel and auto discounts, a Visa card (for which members must apply), $1,000 in firearms insurance and $10,000 in personal accident insurance (although the terms of these policies are very narrow), information on and access to hunter tours and sporting events, and other information and expertise on gun-related activities. Although certainly a draw to some, these modest incentives alone are hardly adequate to explain the zealotry of NRA membership.

Specific and collective solidary incentives can also be found in the organization. The NRA offers various awards, offices, and other forms of recognition to individual members who show particular devotion to the organization's political goals and to those who demonstrate marksmanship and hunting skills. Collective incentives include participation in the NRA's various marksmanship competitions and other meetings that bring together those who share a common interest in guns.

The final type of incentive, purposive, is certainly the most significant. Much of the analysis in this chapter illustrates the primacy of purposive motivations, in that the high and intense degree of NRA member involvement connects most directly to the NRA's ideological agenda. As Wilson noted, members animated by purposive incentives "care passionately about goals," which, for the NRA, focus preeminently on avoidance and repeal of gun controls.[49] The acceleration of the NRA's political agenda, dating to the 1960s, is both a cause and a reflection of member concerns—concerns that the NRA promotes in its numerous strident communications with its members. The NRA's use of mass mailings and electronic communications is especially important as a link between the national organization and the grassroots as well as a mobilizing tool to energize and direct member animus. That its mailing lists are organized by congressional district reveals the political importance of these mailings to the NRA.[50] As the political scientist Jeffrey Berry notes, the key to effective mass mail is to provoke anger or fear or both. For the NRA in 1993 and 1994, this included regular demonization and vilification of Bill and Hillary

Clinton; Attorney General Janet Reno; the Bureau of Alcohol, Tobacco, and Firearms (ATF); and Handgun Control head Sarah Brady. In the 2000s their chief demons included Hillary Clinton and Barack Obama. These efforts are enhanced when they are "tied to highly visible current events."[51] During the 1993–1994 period the salient current events included passage of the Brady bill and the assault-weapons ban. In the aftermath of the terrorist attacks on 9/11, the NRA rallied members, arguing that pro–gun control groups were trying to exploit people's fears of terrorism to increase gun regulations.

In short, the gun culture unites and motivates gun enthusiasts. No parallel force provides similar unity and motivation to gun control proponents, although groups such as the Brady Campaign have sought to replicate the NRA's organizing successes. The NRA membership has maintained its singular devotion for decades. Elected officials who support the NRA's position are motivated by a combination of grassroots pressure from constituents, the desire to avoid potentially nasty confrontations with NRA supporters (what has been labeled the "hassle factor"), and ideological sympathy.

Access

Closely related to explaining the NRA's influence is the question of access to the circles of decision making. Almost unique among interest groups, the NRA has counted among its members several presidents, including Theodore Roosevelt, Dwight D. Eisenhower, John F. Kennedy, Richard M. Nixon, Ronald Reagan, George H. W. Bush, and George W. Bush. Key congressional leaders, including former House Speaker Tom Foley (D-WA) and former House Commerce Committee chair John Dingell (D-MI), have been members. Dingell also served on the NRA board, as have other members of Congress.

The case of the Consumer Product Safety Commission (CPSC) makes evident the significance of the political access represented by these memberships. The CPSC was created in 1972 to test and regulate the production and marketing of thousands of products to determine if they posed a health or safety risk to consumers. Gun control opponents played no role in the legislation's initial consideration in committee; no one from the NRA, for example, testified about the bill in committee. Yet during the adoption struggle, Representative Dingell inserted a provision that specifically exempted guns and ammunition. Although the matter received some debate in the final stages of the bill's consideration, it prompted relatively little scrutiny or outcry outside Congress.[52] Twenty-two years later, the CBS news program *60 Minutes* ran a feature on the still-existing exemption, highlighting several popular guns that had caused injuries and death because of defective parts or workmanship. For example, the popular Remington Model 700 bolt-action rifle was shown to discharge even when the trigger was not pulled (the gun would sometimes fire, for example, by the act of unlocking the safety). More than a thousand such instances had been reported to Remington, suggesting a far larger number of incidents not documented. An internal company memo revealed that Remington had been aware of the problem as far back as 1979. The popular Chinese-made SKS semiautomatic rifle was also shown to fire in a fully automatic fashion, even when the trigger was not pulled, because of defective parts.

When asked why his bill to incorporate guns under the CPSC had failed to advance in Congress, Senator Howard Metzenbaum (D-OH), a gun control proponent, said, "The NRA's position is consistent. They're opposed to any legislation that has the word 'gun' anywhere in it." When asked what would happen if the NRA dropped its opposition to the bill, Metzenbaum replied, "We would pass the bill overnight." John Dingell had kept the bill bottled up in committee in the House in order to avoid a likely supportive vote on the floor. An NRA representative argued that the NRA continued to oppose the bill because it was simply a back-door method to regulate or ban guns entirely, even though legislative language could be written to avoid such a problem. By one estimate, regulation of defective or flawed guns and the use of inexpensive technology could prevent five hundred accidental gun deaths and numerous gun injuries every year.[53] Access has provided the NRA with the ability selectively to apply pressure effectively, particularly when relatively few others in the political process are paying attention or when the focal point of the pressure has been relatively narrow. Consider these illustrative examples:

- In 1965 Congress considered a bill to regulate mail-order gun sales, spurred in part by the fact that President John F. Kennedy's killer, Lee Harvey Oswald, had purchased his rifle through a mail-order ad in an NRA publication, the *American Rifleman*. The NRA alerted its membership, exhorting them to write to Washington against the bill. In the month preceding the NRA alert, the White House received fifty letters, split evenly for and against the bill. Within two weeks of the NRA alert the White House received twelve thousand letters, nearly all against the bill. The two key congressional committees considering the bill also received a sudden flood of angry mail—thirty-four hundred letters within two weeks. Senators expressed astonishment at the volume and angry tone of the letters. Gale McGee (D-WY) says, "I can recall no issue, either international or domestic, in my tenure in the Senate that has aroused the people of Wyoming as this one."[54] Gun mail-order regulation was averted until 1968, when public fury at the assassinations of the Reverend

Martin Luther King Jr. and Senator Robert Kennedy spurred the passage of the Gun Control Act of 1968. The pattern the NRA set in the 1960s has subsequently become its political signature.

- During the summer of 1982 the otherwise placid Long Island community of Brookhaven erupted in political controversy. The issue that rocked the New York township was an attempt by the Brookhaven Town Board to outlaw the possession of handgun bullets capable of piercing a bulletproof vest. The armor-piercing bullets, also known as KTW bullets, had been developed the previous decade to provide police with a means for piercing automobile engine blocks in order to provide literal stopping power.[55] Yet the police found the bullets to be unusable precisely because their ability to penetrate dense objects meant that the bullets' flight could not be controlled. Worse, such bullets could pierce the body armor worn by police. The president of the International Association of Chiefs of Police stated flatly that KTW bullets had "no legitimate use ... either in or out of law enforcement."[56] The Brookhaven Town Board's attempt to ban the bullets, an effort local police organizations supported, was defeated when hundreds of angry local residents turned out at a town meeting to denounce the proposal. NRA "alert" telegrams sent to local members prompted the outpouring. Speaking against the ordinance, NRA lobbyist James Baker commented, "You can't moderate behavior by controlling objects."[57] A toothless version of the ordinance was eventually passed.

  The armor-piercing bullet controversy spread to Washington, where the NRA's fear of any form of gun control prompted the organization to fight enactment of a federal law for nearly four years. Seeking to avoid antagonizing police organizations that supported the bill (and whose support the NRA sought for the Firearms Owners Protection Act, being considered at the same time), the NRA finally yielded in 1986, and a revised bill banning the import, manufacture, and sale of KTW bullets was signed into law in August that year.[58]

- Freshman representative Peter P. Smith (R-VT) felt NRA wrath in 1989 when he cosponsored a bill to ban semiautomatic weapons. This action prompted particular ire because Smith had signed a petition in 1988 saying he would oppose gun controls. NRA members in his district demanded his resignation, and the NRA spent $18,000 in the campaign to defeat him in 1990. "Impeach Peter Smith, Traitor" posters sprang up in his district. Flyers pairing his picture with that of Adolf Hitler were circulated. "I've never been through anything like this. It was astounding," he noted.[59] Speaking about his subsequent unsuccessful reelection bid, Smith said, "My mother was almost driven off the road. People were shooting my lawn signs at night. That is the level of emotion the NRA was able to stir up."[60] Smith was defeated by socialist Bernard Sanders, who had also expressed support for an assault-weapons ban. Yet the NRA was less concerned with Sanders's position than with punishing Smith. After election to the House, however, Sanders voted against a waiting period for handgun purchases in 1991 and again in 1993, when the measure passed.

- Michigan congressman Bart Stupak, considered one of the most conservative Democrats in the House of Representatives, had a long history of NRA support. The former Michigan state trooper, whose district included the state's rural and conservative Upper Peninsula, had received almost $50,000 in campaign contributions from the NRA in his four previous election bids. The NRA's support seemed well justified, as Stupak always voted with the NRA's position on gun issues; Stupak's voting trend was logical because hunting and sporting are important activities in that district, where more than 60 percent of households own guns. In the 2000 race, however, the NRA turned against Stupak. It was instrumental in recruiting his Republican opponent, Chuck Yob, to whom it funneled $5,000, and the NRA advertised for Stupak's defeat. His sin? Stupak voted in 1999 in favor of a House bill that would have imposed a three-day waiting period for background checks for firearms sales at gun shows. The measure failed to win enactment. In a closely watched campaign, Stupak won reelection with 58 percent of the vote, only slightly less than his 59 percent margin of victory in 1998. "I'm a hunter and I have been since I was a kid," said Stupak. "I've never voted to take away a single gun. Never."[61]

- "Access" was the name of the game for the NRA and the presidency of George W. Bush. During the 2000 election campaign the NRA's first vice president was caught on tape saying that Bush's election would mean that the NRA would have "a president where we work out of their office." In fact, the second Bush presidency proved to be the most NRA-friendly administration in history. In Congress, after several years of effort, the Bush administration won enactment of the NRA's chief policy objective, a bill to provide the gun industry and gun dealers with immunity from lawsuits (see chapter 5). It also allowed the assault-weapons ban to lapse in 2004. Bush's first attorney general, John Ashcroft, had been one of the NRA's chief allies in Congress when he served as senator from Missouri. As the nation's chief law-enforcement officer, Ashcroft broke with five decades of Justice Department policy, spanning both Democratic and Republican presidents, by adopting as policy the "individualist" view of the Second Amendment, claiming that it protected the right of individual citizens to own guns for their own purposes. Thanks in part to the administration's new view, the Supreme Court embraced it in 2008 (see chapter 2).

The administration also limited gun data record keeping and law enforcement access to gun-related data, even when other law enforcement agencies were seeking data on suspected terrorists after the 9/11 attacks. The problem of limiting access to gun-purchase records was not merely hypothetical: in 2005 a congressional investigation found forty-seven instances during eight months in 2004 when terror suspects were allowed to buy guns legally because of restrictions that prevented law enforcement from cross-checking such lists. This prompted one critic to say that the Bush "firearms policy [was] largely dictated by the National Rifle Association."[62] Further, the administration resisted all efforts to stem international arms trafficking by the United Nations. It even canceled the Department of Housing and Urban Development's gun buyback program, a program the NRA ridiculed as a "gun surrender program."[63] In 2009 a Government Accountability Office report revealed that although people on terrorist watch lists could be prevented from boarding airplanes, they could not be prevented from buying guns. In fact, from 2004 to 2009, 963 requests for gun purchases were made by people on watch lists; 865 (90 percent) of them were allowed to complete the purchases. In 2010, 272 people whose names appeared on the terrorist watch list (and who are not allowed to board an airplane) attempted to purchase guns; of those, only twenty-five were rejected. Legislative efforts to close this gap failed, according to one senator, because Congress was "knuckling under to the gun lobby."[64]

The Politics of Purity

Coupled with the fervor of its membership is a related key organizational trait: the increasingly polemical, ideological, and zealous nature of the organization's leadership, a tendency that further underscores the purposive motivations of the NRA's adherents. Long known for its zealotry, the NRA accelerated its insistence on absolute issue purity in the aftermath of a furious internal power struggle that came to a head in 1977.

Although it had opposed gun controls for decades, the NRA leadership had maintained the organization's primary focus on sporting, hunting, and other recreational gun uses. To the dismay of NRA hard-liners, Executive Vice President Franklin Orth had given at least partially favorable testimony before Congress on the 1968 gun control bill. The hard-liners tried but failed to remove Orth. Meanwhile, the old-guard moderates in control of the organization sought to turn the organization away from politics and back toward hunting and conservation.

Symptomatic of this effort were plans promoted by the old guard to create a national shooting center in New Mexico and move the NRA's headquarters to Colorado Springs. Meanwhile, the NRA's recently formed ILA, headed by hardliner Harlon Carter, complained bitterly at the devotion of organizational resources to these nonpolitical efforts. The response of the old guard was to fire seventy-four employees, most of whom were hard-liners. The simmering dispute surfaced at the NRA's 1977 convention in Cincinnati. Rallying a faction called the Federation of the NRA, Carter won organizational changes that gave the convention members greater control over decision making. He and his allies then used those rules to depose the old guard at the convention in what was dubbed the Cincinnati Revolt. From this point forward, the ILA became the primary power center of the NRA, and as Osha Gray Davidson noted, "the NRA became more than a rifle club. It became the Gun Lobby."[65] Since that time the hard-liners have pushed the organization toward total, unwavering opposition to all forms of gun regulation.[66] This emphasis on 100 percent purity has helped the organization mobilize and activate its faithful, but it has also alienated former and potential allies.

One of the most highly publicized consequences of this unyielding approach has been the alienation of most national police organizations. The split between these former allies can be traced to the NRA's opposition to any regulation of armor-piercing (so-called cop-killer) bullets in the 1980s. The stand infuriated many in law enforcement because the bullets had no sporting or hunting purposes—unless the quarry was a police officer wearing a bullet-proof vest. Police organizations began to side with HCI's lobbying efforts, spearheaded by Sarah Brady, to impose a waiting period for handgun purchases. In recent years police organizations have also opposed such NRA-backed efforts as liberalizing concealed-carry laws and the extension of the "Castle Doctrine" (expanding the right of civilians to use deadly force on the streets; see chapter 3) in many states around the country.

NRA purity-based attacks have targeted longtime allies as well. Most notably, President (and former NRA life member) George H. W. Bush was the focus of an unsuccessful effort of expulsion from the NRA as the result of his 1989 decision to ban the import of semiautomatic rifles. Bush's decision came in large part because of the recommendation of drug czar William Bennett, who was threatened with political retaliation from the NRA for his gun stand. According to a spokesperson for the Bush administration, Bennett said he was told through an intermediary that "if he has thoughts of a political future, he can forget them if he doesn't respect the power of the NRA."[67] Even though Bush's 1992 opponent Bill Clinton supported gun control more strongly, the NRA refused to endorse Bush (as it had in 1988) or contribute any money to his campaign. In 1996 the NRA turned its back on Republican presidential nominee and longtime NRA supporter Robert Dole because of his refusal to support repeal of the 1994 assault-weapons ban, even though the incumbent, Clinton, had become the NRA's arch foe.

Although the NRA is quick to project a tough crime-fighting image, it lobbied successfully in 1996 to kill key provisions in a counterterrorism bill that was introduced in response to the 1995 bombing of a federal office building in Oklahoma City. Among the provisions opposed by the NRA and successfully deleted from the bill were measures to make it easier to deport illegal aliens charged with terrorism, enhanced government powers to crack down on fund-raising by foreign terrorist groups, studies of armor-piercing ammunition and explosives, and measures that would have made it easier for the government to prosecute those who provide weapons that are used in crimes. A watered-down version of the bill was signed into law in April 1996.[68] Despite the shift in focus, the NRA's objective remained the same—to combat gun control advocates.

The NRA's most serious gaffe arose from a fund-raising letter sent out shortly before the bombing of a federal office building in Oklahoma City on April 19, 1995. In the six-page letter, signed by NRA executive vice president Wayne LaPierre, federal government agents were compared to Nazis in that they were said to wear "Nazi bucket helmets and black storm trooper uniforms" and to "harass, intimidate, even murder law-abiding citizens." In the wake of enhanced national sensitivity to the extremist antigovernment rhetoric of those believed to be responsible for the bombing and other acts of domestic terrorism, many expressed outrage at the letter. In particular, former president George H. W. Bush publicly resigned his life membership in the organization, noting that a Secret Service agent was killed in the bombing, ATF agents were killed in the line of duty, and the heads of these and other federal law enforcement agencies were not fascists. He called the NRA letter a "vicious slander on good people."[69] In response, NRA president Washington published a full-page written response in several prominent newspapers, defending LaPierre's incendiary letter. Shortly thereafter, however, LaPierre apologized for the letter and expressed regret for offending federal law-enforcement officials. Yet the apology did little to dampen criticism of the NRA's apparent sympathies for extremist groups. This criticism intensified when it was revealed that NRA official Tanya Metaksa had met with members of the Michigan Militia in a hotel lobby in Michigan a few months before the Oklahoma City blast (although no one suggested that the NRA knew of or discussed any plans to blow up the building or engage in other violent acts). Bemoaning the NRA's tarnished image, former NRA president Riley said, "now we're cast with the Nazis, the skinheads, and the Ku Klux Klan."[70]

Internal power struggles between NRA factions took a Hollywood twist in 1997 when the actor and gun activist Charlton Heston defeated the hardliner and then first vice president Neal Knox in his reelection bid (in 1999 Knox's protégée Metaksa was pushed out of power). Heston's nomination was propelled by Knox's nemesis LaPierre, whom Knox had targeted for defeat. Heston's election served several purposes. LaPierre was able to exploit Heston's celebrity status to beat back efforts by the more extremist elements within the organization, headed by Knox, to consolidate control. Heston's presence also provided a badly needed public relations boost to the organization, and indeed, Heston was a leading spokesperson for the NRA and its causes, lending his name to various paid advertisements, letters to national publications, and the like, extolling NRA positions. As a consequence, those positions likely received more attention than they would have otherwise. Most notably, Heston spearheaded a new campaign extolling gun rights as the most important of all civil liberties. Knox, however, continued to criticize Heston as insufficiently strong on the gun issue, and the extended intraorganizational struggles promoted criticisms that the NRA had become too politicized and too extremist, even for its traditional hunter-sportsperson base of support. At its June 1998 convention the NRA elected Heston to serve as its president, a further defeat for the Knox faction. Heston was reelected in 1999, 2000, 2001, and 2002, eclipsing the organization's two-term limit. Heston retired in 2003 when he was diagnosed with Alzheimer's disease.[71] First Vice President Kayne Robinson succeeded him. In 2005 Sandra Froman, a lawyer, became president. Former NRA president Warren Cassidy summarized the NRA's continuing single-issue zealotry: "You'd get a far better understanding if you['d] just approach us as if [we were] one of the world's great religions."[72]

Despite the NRA's legendary commitment to issue purity, it came under fire in 2009 and 2010 for wavering in its loyalty to gun rights and conservatism. For example, the gun rights movement's greatest success in decades, the 2008 *Heller* Supreme Court case establishing personal gun rights (see chapter 2), was not spearheaded by NRA lawyers but instead by other organizations, including the libertarian Cato Institute and the Gun Owners of America. As one account noted, "The NRA thought the *Heller* case was a bad idea and fought to kill it with various strategies."[73] The reason for the NRA's reluctance was its fear that a frontal Second Amendment–based legal challenge to gun laws might fail before the high court. The NRA's timidity earned it the ire of these more staunch groups, especially after the NRA jumped on the *Heller* bandwagon to share credit for the legal victory.

The NRA was also excoriated for abandoning its longtime opposition to campaign finance reform when it changed sides by supporting a bill in 2010 called the Disclose Act that would have imposed strict disclosure requirements on interest groups in exchange for a provision added to the bill that would have exempted the NRA and a handful of other interest groups from the law's requirements. Among other conservative critics, the *Wall Street Journal* called the NRA "arrogant and hypocritical," and House Republican leader John Boehner accused the NRA of "throw[ing] everybody else under the table so they can get a special deal."[74] The NRA caught additional fire from the right wing for endorsing some Democrats in the 2010 election, including Senate Democratic majority leader Harry Reid, even though he had been a longtime NRA supporter (Reid won his race); for failing to support open-carry gun movements around the country (where gun owners legally carried their guns in plain sight instead of concealed on their persons); for failing to vigorously oppose President Obama's two successful nominees to the Supreme Court, Sonia Sotomayor and Elena Kagan; and for being too willing to negotiate with the majority Democrats in Congress and the White House. Although criticism of the NRA from the ultraright was nothing new (the Gun Owners of America was formed in the 1970s because of the belief that the NRA was not being tough enough on gun issues), this larger flap over the NRA's conservative credentials reflected the NRA's political ascendance, demonstrable successes won in part because of negotiations with Democrats, the pro-gun turn of some in the Democratic party in the 2000s, and the right wing's general movement even further to the right, especially with the establishment of the Tea Party movement in 2009. From the perspective of the right wing, the NRA had sold out; from the NRA's perspective, it was and is hard to argue with success.[75]

The Brady Campaign to Prevent Gun Violence

The NRA's primary opponent is the Brady Campaign to Prevent Gun Violence, known as Handgun Control, Inc. (HCI) before 2001. Founded under the name the National Council to Control Handguns in 1974 by Chicago native Mark Borinsky, who had been robbed at gunpoint, the organization took off when Republican marketing manager Pete Shields (whose twenty-three-year-old son had recently been murdered) joined in 1975 and became chairman, whereupon the organization became HCI. The organization began in partnership with the National Coalition to Ban Handguns (NCBH), formed at about the same time. The groups soon parted ways. The NCBH, renamed the Coalition to Stop Gun Violence (CSGV) in 1990, has generally pursued a tougher stand on gun regulation than the Brady Campaign, but the Brady Campaign's greater size and visibility, especially since Sarah Brady became a prominent figure, has overshadowed it.[76]

In 1976, after establishing a friendly relationship with members of the House Judiciary Committee, HCI won early support for a ban on the manufacture of cheap handguns, called Saturday night specials. However, an NRA political counter-attack caused four members of the Judiciary Committee to withdraw their support for the ban, and the bill failed. HCI possessed relatively few resources until the murder of John Lennon in 1980 helped spark interest and fund-raising activities. By 1981 membership had surpassed 100,000.[77] In 1983 the organization created an education outreach organization, the Center to Prevent Handgun Violence, which became the Brady Center to Prevent Handgun Violence in 2001. In 1989 it established the Legal Action Project to push its agenda in the courts.

The organization contributed money to congressional campaigns for the first time in 1980, when it gave $75,000; in comparison, the NRA spent $1.5 million for campaigns that year. By the 1991–1992 election cycle HCI had spent $280,000. In the 1995–1996 election cycle HCI spent $315,000, but the NRA's spending of $6.6 million in those years dwarfed that figure. In the 1999–2000 election cycle the Brady Campaign spent at least ten times as much on campaigns as it had in 1996, amounting to more than $4 million; yet the NRA still dwarfed its spending. Even so, pro–gun control candidates generally fared well in the 2000 and 2004 elections (see below).[78] The Brady Campaign has sought to duplicate the tactical and organizational methodologies of the NRA, in particular by building a grassroots base of members willing to write letters, make phone calls, vote, and contribute money to support the gun control agenda. It too has sought to demonize the opposition, but it has not matched the NRA in volume or intensity. By 1990 membership reached 250,000; in 1998 it reported membership exceeding 400,000 and a mailing list of more than one million.[79] In 2010 it reported a membership of 600,000.

The Brady Campaign's main focus has been national and state lobbying efforts, spearheaded in recent years by Sarah Brady. The daughter of an FBI agent and a Republican activist, Brady achieved notoriety when her husband, Reagan's press secretary James Brady, was seriously injured in a 1981 assassination attempt against the president. Four years later Sarah Brady joined the board of HCI in reaction to a bill then before Congress that would have gutted much of the 1968 Gun Control Act. Two years later she helped initiate and subsequently led the successful charge to enact a waiting period for handgun purchases, enacted in 1993 as the Brady law (see chapter 5). HCI also claimed victory when Congress enacted the assault-weapons ban in 1994. Brady headed the Brady Campaign since 1989.[80] Former Maryland Democratic congressman Michael Barnes became organization head in 2000. In 2006 former Republican mayor of Fort Wayne, Indiana, Paul Helmke, succeeded Barnes.

The Brady Campaign can certainly claim some credit for the enactment of gun control measures in Congress and in many states in the late 1980s and 1990s, even though its size and resources are only about one-tenth of those of the NRA. For a brief time, however, the first genuine modern mass movement on behalf of stronger gun laws eclipsed this group's efforts.

The Million Mom March

In the aftermath of the 1999 Columbine school shooting (see chapter 3) and other highly publicized acts of gun violence, a grassroots movement of women in support of stronger gun laws sprang up and organized the first mass rally in modern times on the gun issue; it was one of the largest mass rallies ever held in Washington, DC. The idea originated with Donna Dees-Thomases, a New Jersey mother. Outraged by a 1999 shooting at a Jewish community center in California, Dees-Thomases, who also worked part-time as a publicist, recruited like-minded women who eventually established fifty state-based organizations to coordinate a march on Washington styled after the Million Man March held there several years earlier.

The organization, labeled the Million Mom March (MMM), converged on the nation's capital on Mother's Day in May 2000. It identified six policy goals: uniform "cooling off" periods and background checks for gun purchases; the licensing of handgun owners and registration of all handguns; mandatory safety locks for all handguns; one-handgun-per-month purchase limits; strict enforcement of existing gun laws; and help from corporate America. On march day, turnout exceeded all expectations, as the day-long event attracted about seven hundred thousand people. Rally speakers included public officials, celebrities, and women whose lives had been affected by gun violence. Smaller rallies were held simultaneously in at least twenty cities around the country. The rally received extensive attention, and it seemed to mark a turning point in the political dynamic of the gun issue. Much of the impetus for the event and its resonance among women arose from the fact that women support gun control in significantly greater numbers than men. During the 2000 elections, for example, polls showed that the "gender gap" between men and women on the gun issue was greater than on any other issue. After the march the organization reorganized itself as the Million Mom March Foundation, hoping to sustain its momentum and political impact in the way that Mothers Against Drunk Driving (MADD) eventually influenced drinking age laws in the 1980s. MMM activities won support from the US Conference of Mayors, the League of Women Voters, the National Parent-Teachers Association, and other groups in favor of gun control.

A counter-demonstration group that was formed during this period, the Second Amendment Sisters (SAS), sought to rally women in support of gun ownership at what it called the Armed Informed Mothers March. Closely paralleling the NRA's stand on gun issues, SAS argued that stronger gun laws would infringe on a woman's ability to defend herself. The NRA also launched a concurrent advertising campaign to counter the MMM's arguments. The SAS counter-demonstration, held on Mother's Day at the opposite end of the Washington Mall, attracted about a thousand protestors.

The MMM's dramatic initial event mushroomed for a time. Within a few months more than 240 MMM chapters opened in forty-six states. Yet its grass-roots base was unable to sustain its momentum and mass involvement. Identifiable membership shrank, offices were closed, thirty of thirty-five employees were laid off, and in 2001 the MMM organization was folded into the Brady Campaign. On the first anniversary of its landmark march, it was unable to rally more than a sprinkling of participants. Still, the MMM movement established a network of local and state organizations that has persisted. In 2005 about fifty active chapters operated in twenty states, and thousands of participants became directly involved in local politics through activities like lobbying, electioneering, and public education efforts. By 2009 the organization claimed chapters in all fifty states.[81] The MMM's political and organizational arc again underscored limitations on the ability of gun control groups to establish and maintain the kind of political loyalty that has sustained the NRA for decades, despite the fact that public opinion stands closer to the MMM than to the NRA.

New Gun Control Groups Enter the Fray

In 2006, New York City Mayor Michael Bloomberg and Boston Mayor Thomas Menino convened a summit of fifteen big-city mayors to coordinate an effort to combat the flow of illegal firearms into their cities from states with lax gun laws. The organization they formed, Mayors Against Illegal Guns (MAIG), also became a national lobbying force to press for stronger guns laws. By 2014, the group claimed more than one thousand mayors as members and—while its efforts initially focused on investigation and interdiction of arms trafficking that funneled guns into large cities (see chapter 6), as well as the production of reports on gun issues—it became a more political group, seeking to pressure lawmakers at federal and state levels to tighten gun regulations and investing money in electoral races. In 2012, Bloomberg's Super PAC, Independence USA, spent $10 million on ads supporting pro-gun control candidates. By the 2010s, Bloomberg had become the most recognizable nationwide proponent of stronger gun laws. The group had already begun to turn its attention and resources to political campaign activities when the Sandy Hook elementary school shooting in December 2012 (see chapter 5) proved to be a catalyzing moment. Decrying past inaction by the president and Congress on the gun issue, billionaire Bloomberg vowed to invest some of his personal fortune in counterbalancing the NRA's influence. Two other factors also facilitated his decision: the loosening of campaign finance laws by Supreme Court rulings that now allowed individuals to spend unlimited amounts of money on political campaigns and the conclusion of Bloomberg's third term as New York mayor at the end of 2013.

In the spring of 2014, Bloomberg officially launched a new umbrella group, Everytown for Gun Safety, which now combined MAIG with another new group, Moms Demand Action for Gun Sense in America. Formed by an Indiana mother of five with extensive public relations experience, Shannon Watts was moved to take action the day after Newtown with the goal of bringing together mothers' voices at the local level throughout the country. The grassroots group, claiming 125,000 members, had logged some successes by pressuring businesses through publicity and threat of boycott to not allow gun carrying in their places of business. These tactics had proven effective in persuading businesses like Starbucks, Chipotle, and Target to ban gun carrying. Bloomberg pledged to spend $50 million of his own money to advance his agenda, including the building of a grassroots organization and heavy spending in the 2014 midterm elections. For the first time, a pro-gun control group would not only match but exceed NRA spending (expected to be about $20 million). As noted earlier, there is no simple equation between dollars spent and favorable outcomes. Nevertheless, money is a prerequisite for influence, and Bloomberg pledged that he and his organization would continue their work in the years to come.[82]

The other significant gun control organization to emerge was formed by former congresswoman Gabrielle Giffords and her husband Mark Kelly, a retired Navy captain and former astronaut. After Giffords survived a near-fatal shooting in January 2011 (see Introduction), the two formed Americans for Responsible Solutions in early 2013; their organization was also spurred, at least in part, by Newtown. Both are gun owners and professed supporters of the Second Amendment who spend considerable time and resources reaching out to gun owners, though their organization focuses on solutions to gun violence.

In addition, they pledged and succeeded in raising $20 million for the 2014 elections—a significant accomplishment in and of itself. The duo's personal narratives and their longtime gun ownership provided a contrasting image to that of big city mayor Bloomberg. Despite these stylistic differences, their policy focus was on measures with wide and clear public support, including universal background checks for gun purchases, improved record-keeping, more effective crack-downs on gun trafficking, bullet magazine limits, and measures to keep guns from children. Their overall political goal, to break the NRA's hammerlock on decision makers at federal and state levels, opened a new and, for the first time, well-funded front in the ongoing political struggle over gun policy.[83]

The Gun Control Movement's Strategic Blunders

In an important study, political scientist Kristin Goss incisively analyzed the political defeats that the pro–gun control movement had suffered from its founding through the start of the 2000s.[84] In her view, the gun control movement (including but extending well beyond HCI/Brady Campaign) committed a significant strategic mistake when it sought a "comprehensive policy approach" to the gun issue in the 1970s and 1980s. That is, rather than pursue achievable but incremental policy change both at the national and state levels, it advanced a "rational national" strategy that sought nothing less than a major revamping of national gun policy.

Such an effort to enact sweeping national policy change is rarely effective in American politics because power in American governance is fragmented among the three branches of government at the national level (separation of powers and checks and balances), and between the national government and the states (the system of federalism). Instead, a more modest, incremental approach to policy change is both more typical and more successful. Yet the gun control movement mostly rejected small gun-policy steps. For example, the National Coalition to Ban Handguns pursued a nationwide handgun ban during this time period even though most Americans, although favoring most gun control initiatives, opposed such a ban. And when more limited gun measures were offered, they were often rejected as inadequate. In one instance President Gerald Ford proposed to Congress in 1975 a ban on "Saturday night specials" (cheap, small-caliber handguns), a one-gun-per-customer sales limit for licensed firearms dealers, background checks on prospective gun buyers, and improved gun dealer oversight. Yet congressional Democrats rejected this proposal from a conservative Republican president for not going far enough.

Instead, numerous other, tougher gun measures were introduced, including a nationwide handgun ban; the final result was that no gun control measures were enacted. The following year voters in Massachusetts rejected a statewide referendum to enact a handgun ban, despite early polls showing most voters in favor of the measure; a similar initiative in California in 1982 also met with unexpected defeat.

This string of defeats demoralized the gun control movement. Ironically, gun measures rejected as too limited by the pro-control movement in the 1970s, such as the Saturday night special ban and even uniform gun registration, might well have won enactment at the time. In the 1990s and 2000s the enactment of such measures seems beyond the reach of gun control groups. Since the 1980s, however, these groups learned from such reversals. That learning culminated in the enactment at the national level of a uniform background check for handgun purchases in 1993 and enactment of the assault-weapons ban in 1994 (see chapter 5). Both measures reflected small-scale, incremental policy changes, even though the political effort involved in their enactment was great. The public supported both measures by wide margins. Before considering public opinion, however, it is necessary to understand why the interest-group battle has been so asymmetrical; that is, why has the NRA enjoyed a near-monopoly over gun politics until recent years?

The Political Balance and the Invincibility Myth

It is evident, first, that the NRA faced no serious opposing single-issue group until the rise of HCI in the 1980s, a time when other groups (such as police organizations) also brought pressure to bear on the NRA. This has helped maintain a mythology of political invincibility concerning the NRA. Like any interest group, the NRA trumpets any successes, even if they are not attributable to NRA influence, and minimizes its reverses. For example, it worked with great vigor against 1988 Democratic presidential nominee and gun control proponent Michael Dukakis, considering his loss to George H. W. Bush a great victory that was attributable in substantial measure to NRA efforts. Yet the NRA's actual effect on the outcome was marginal.[85]

The spurious nature of the invincibility myth is even clearer in congressional elections. From 1983 to 1988, eleven Senate incumbents endorsed by the NRA lost their seats. During the same period no pro–gun control Senate incumbents were defeated, despite NRA opposition. The NRA's total Senate endorsement-opposition scorecard during these five years showed that candidates backed by the NRA lost in twenty-one instances and won in only five. In 1990 the only incumbent senator to lose a seat was NRA-backed Rudy Boschwitz (R-MN). And no House member that the NRA targeted for defeat lost his or her seat in 1986 or 1988.

NRA efforts helped forge the Republican takeovers of the Senate and House in 1994, but factors overshadowing the gun issue fueled that dramatic change. In 1996, despite a concerted effort to defeat those who supported the Brady bill and the assault-weapons ban, the NRA suffered significant losses, failing to unseat any of the top ten members of Congress it had targeted. Of the twenty-three incumbent members of Congress who lost in 1996, nineteen had voted in favor of repealing the 1994 assault-weapons ban. Staunch NRA supporters, including Representatives Harold Volkmer (D-MO), Steve Stockman (R-TX), Andrea Seastrand (R-CA), and Bill Baker (R-CA) were defeated. And a Republican, Carolyn McCarthy, switched parties to run against Long Island representative Dan Frisa (R-NY) because he had voted to repeal the assault-weapons ban. McCarthy, whose husband was killed and her son wounded in a 1993 shooting spree on a Long Island commuter train, defeated Frisa on a gun control platform.

During the 2000 elections the NRA worked furiously for Republican presidential candidate George W. Bush. It did not officially endorse him at first, though—not because of ideological objections, but because it felt that a loud endorsement might undercut the Bush campaign theme of "compassionate conservatism," Bush's effort to appear less archly conservative and more open to compromise. The NRA's only slip in strategy occurred when a comment appeared in the press quoting an NRA official as saying that a Bush win would mean that the NRA could set up shop in the Oval Office. The NRA's all-out support for Bush was amplified in part because the Democratic presidential nominee, Al Gore, campaigned expressly on a strong gun control agenda, including support for handgun licensing.

The NRA took credit for Bush's razor-thin victory over Al Gore (Gore actually received 540,000 more popular votes nationwide than Bush, but Bush received 271 electoral votes to Gore's 267), pointing in particular to his wins in Arkansas, Tennessee, and West Virginia. Yet Bush failed to win the large and key battleground states of Iowa, Michigan, New Mexico, Pennsylvania (the state with the second-largest NRA membership, next to Texas), and Wisconsin. Moreover, NRA-backed candidates lost in key US Senate races, five of whom were incumbents, in Florida (Bill McCollum lost to Bill Nelson), Michigan (incumbent Spencer Abraham lost to Debbie Stabenow), Minnesota (incumbent Rod Grams lost to Mark Dayton), Missouri (incumbent John Ashcroft lost to Jean Carnahan), and Washington State (incumbent Slade Gordon lost to Maria Cantwell). In addition, statewide referenda to close the gun show loophole in Colorado and Oregon passed by wide margins, despite expensive NRA-backed campaigns to defeat the measures. The NRA fared little better in races in the House of Representatives. For example, in California, in one of the most expensive House races in the country, the NRA-backed incumbent, Republican James Rogan, lost to Democrat Adam Schiff. Even so, the 2000 election persuaded at least some Democrats that the gun issue was a loser for them.

In 2004 many Democrats sought to avoid the gun issue entirely or to embrace gun practices. Democratic presidential nominee John Kerry, for example, emphasized his long interest in hunting, gun ownership, and use.[86] During Bush's successful reelection effort in 2004, the NRA threw its full weight behind his campaign, endorsing him and spending over $20 million on his and other races around the country. In 2006 NRA-backed candidates in Minnesota, Missouri, Montana, Pennsylvania, and Virginia all lost, despite NRA endorsements, internal communications, and spending of more than $1 million on their behalf. In the 2008 election the NRA's $40 million in spending, including $15 million earmarked to defeat Barack Obama, seemingly made little dent in that year's Democratic tide. And the major Republican gains in the 2010 midterm elections came at a time when the NRA backed more Democrats than it had in decades. Some prominent Senate candidates—including Sherrod Brown (Ohio), Kay Hagen (North Carolina), Tim Kaine (Virginia), Claire McCaskill (Missouri), and Bill Nelson (Florida)—won their races in swing states despite receiving failing ratings from the NRA. An analysis of the 2012 elections by the Sunlight Foundation reached a similar conclusion. Based on an analysis of Federal Election Commission data, the study found that the NRA got a less than 1 percent return on the over $11 million it spent directly on election races. The NRA backed twenty-seven winning candidates, but only .4 percent of its money went to them. The rest of its money went to defeat other candidates, yet the NRA only achieved its desired result in .39 percent of those races. And out of sixteen Senate races in which the NRA invested money and effort In 2012, thirteen of its endorsed candidates lost.[87]

This pattern does not mean that the NRA is without political influence—far from it. Rather, it reflects the simple American political reality that single issues rarely decide electoral outcomes. This observation does not, however, mitigate the fear, felt especially by potentially vulnerable members of Congress, that NRA influence can sway key votes in Congress or swing an election. The NRA's continuing fearsome reputation was reflected in *Fortune Magazine*'s pronouncement on May 28, 2001, that the NRA had become the most powerful lobby group in Washington, DC, taking the top spot from the powerful American Association of Retired Persons (AARP). The NRA continued to hold its number-one ranking. The perception of NRA strength and its "hassle factor" can in and of themselves be inhibiting forces. The NRA has been highly conscious of the potency of projecting an image of strength and an unlimited willingness to harass opponents. A confidential memo written in 1993 revealed how the NRA views its strategy: "We may not win a particular election, but our methods have an extremely efficient 'political cost exchange ratio' making it exceedingly expensive, difficult and unpleasant for the target [the NRA's political opponent] to remain in office. Victory springs from imparting excruciating political pain in unrelenting political attacks on a single politician as an example to others."[88] To cite an example of electoral success for the NRA, in 2013 the NRA and its allies engineered a successful effort to recall—that is, remove from office—two sitting members of the Colorado State Senate who voted in favor of the stronger gun control laws enacted earlier that year. While they failed to force recall votes against two other state senators (although one of them later resigned from office), the two successful efforts sent shockwaves through the state and beyond. Key to this effort was the fact that voter turnout in these two special elections was low (about 13 percent), so highly motivated gun rights voters were able to carry the day.

In contrast, gun control proponents have, indeed, operated in the political arena for decades—but not as single-issue groups. Both HCI and the NCBH sprang from a coalition of thirty national religious, educational, and social organizations, helped significantly by a grant from the United Methodist Church. Groups as diverse as Common Cause, the American Jewish Committee, the AFL-CIO, the National Women's Political Caucus, and the American Baptist Convention have devoted effort and resources on behalf of stronger gun control. Yet all these groups have multi-issue concerns that dilute their effectiveness and visibility on the gun issue. The NRA, in contrast, has benefited from and cultivated a single-issue mass constituency and political focus for decades. The NRA has therefore been able to consolidate and accelerate its mission.

The interplay of these groups does not occur in a vacuum. Gun groups as well as members of Congress and other government leaders are mindful of shifts and swings in public sentiment, and these help to explain the changing nature of the gun debate in recent years.

Public Opinion

The initial and most important fact about public opinion on gun control has been its remarkable consistency in support of greater government control of guns. As one opinion analyst has noted: "The vast majority of Americans have favored some kind of action for the control of civilian firearms at least as long as modern polling has been in existence."[89] This finding emerged with the advent of modern polling, when a 1938 Gallup poll showed that 79 percent of respondents favored "firearms control."[88] From then through the 1970s no less than two-thirds of Americans favored stronger controls.[91] As shown in Table 4.1, the size of the majority favoring stronger gun controls has varied, hitting a low point during the anti–gun control presidencies of Ronald Reagan and George W. Bush, with the number edging even lower, but then rising, during the Obama presidency. Although gun groups vilified Obama for his prior support of stronger gun laws, he took no interest in the gun issue until the start of his second term, reflecting the move of the Democratic party away from gun control advocacy in the 2000s. The decline is also notable as it coincides with the continuing two-decade decline in crime rates, and especially violent crime, which in 2010 hit its lowest level since 1973.[92] Nevertheless, the overall opinion trend has been consistent in its support for stricter laws. This broad trend does not reveal how Americans respond to particular varieties of controls and proposed controls, where results do, indeed, fluctuate, but it is remarkable not only for its consistency but also for its reversal of the pattern that public opinion usually supports existing government policy.[93] That is, one infrequently finds such strong and durable opinion supporting a policy option or options not already enacted.

Specific Policy Options

Beyond this general trend, pollsters have posed a variety of more specific questions gauging public reaction to particular regulations. The trend on these questions is predictable: public support generally fluctuates with the degree of government control being proposed.

Consistent and substantial majorities of Americans have favored universal handgun registration. According to a succession of Gallup polls, 66 percent supported registration in 1982, 70 percent in 1985, 81 percent in 1990, 81 percent in 1993, 76 percent in 2000, and 79 percent in 2006.[94] A series of Roper polls have found that, since the early 1970s, an average of 72 percent of Americans have favored a law requiring "a person to obtain a police permit" before buying a gun (in 2002 this number was 80 percent). In 2002 a National Opinion Research Center (NORC) poll found that 80 percent favored a law requiring police permits as a prerequisite for gun purchases. Americans have similarly voiced support for universal background checks for gun purchases. In a 2014 poll, 79 percent favored such checks, while 13 percent opposed.[95]

Even larger majorities have consistently supported the idea of a waiting period between the time a person applies to buy a handgun and the time it is actually sold. Gallup polls reported 91 percent support in 1988, 95 percent

Table 4.1 Public Opinion and Gun Control

Question: In general, do you feel that the laws covering the sale of firearms should be made more strict, less strict, or kept as they are now?*

	More strict	Less strict	Same	No opinion
2013	49	13	37	1
2012	58	6	34	2
2011	44	11	43	2
2010	44	12	42	2
2009	44	12	43	1
2007	51	8	39	2
2006	56	9	33	2
2005	57	7	35	1
2004	60	6	34	0
2001	53	8	38	1
2000	61	7	30	2
1999	65	5	28	2
1996	61	9	26	4
1995	63	13	23	1
1993	70	4	24	2
1991	68	5	25	2
1990	78	2	17	3
1986	60	8	30	2
1983	59	4	31	6
1981	65	3	30	2
1980	59	6	29	6
1975	69	3	24	4

*All figures in percentages.
Source: Leslie McAneny, "Americans Tell Congress: Pass Brady Bill, Other Tough Gun Laws," *Gallup Poll Monthly*, March 1993, 2. Updates from Gallup Organization.

in 1990, 93 percent in 1991, 88 percent in 1993 (the year Congress enacted a national five-day waiting period, known as the Brady law), and 93 percent in 2000. In 2006, 80 percent favored background checks for private gun sales. A Gallup poll taken immediately after passage of the Brady law revealed 87 percent support. A 2000 Gallup poll also found that 79 percent favored requiring all guns to be sold with trigger locks. A 2006 NORC survey found that 85 percent of Americans favored limiting the sale of .50-caliber high-powered rifles.[96]

The use of so-called assault weapons in some highly publicized killings focused special attention on attempts to regulate or ban such weapons. Although some critics have assailed polls mentioning these weapons, arguing that they are misrepresented to the public by pollsters in ways that elicit an artificially high degree of support for stronger controls, mainstream pollsters generally take care to define the question properly. For example, a 1992 *New York Times*/CBS News poll asked, "Would you favor or oppose a ban on assault weapons—that is, semiautomatic military-style rifles that can hold up to 30 bullets?" Seventy-nine percent responded they would favor such a ban, and only 19 percent said they would oppose it. A 1993 Gallup poll asked, "Would you favor or oppose a law banning the manufacture, sale, and possession of semi-automatic assault guns, such as the AK–47?" In response, 66 percent said they would favor such an action, and 30 percent said they would not. These percentages are notable not only for the clear preference they represent but also because the question poses the prospect of a ban on such weapons, not merely their regulation. Even gun owners support the ban. In a 1995 survey, 69 percent of gun owners favored keeping the assault-weapons ban in place, and only 24 percent supported removal of the ban. A 2009 CBS/*New York Times* poll reported 54 percent support for an assault-weapons ban, reflecting other poll results from the time showing less support for the measure than earlier reported. In early 2013, Gallup reported 60 percent favoring reinstituting the ban. In an unusual nationwide survey of gun owners taken in 2009 (five years after Congress failed to renew the ban; see chapter 5), 47 percent of gun owners reported favoring the ban, with 36 percent opposed, and 17 percent no opinion.[97] Even among the most pro-gun segment of the public, support for the ban persisted.

Surveys have also asked about support for an outright ban on the sale and possession of handguns (a handful of towns around the country enacted such a ban in the 1980s). A succession of Gallup surveys found rising support for a handgun ban (making exceptions for police and "other authorized persons"), starting at 31 percent in 1980 (with 65 percent opposed), rising to 42 percent support (54 percent opposed) in 1992.[98] In 1993 a Harris poll reported that 52 percent favored a handgun-possession ban (except for court-allowed permission), and 43 percent opposed one. Since then, support has declined, hitting a low of 29 percent supporting a handgun ban in 2010; in 2012 that number was 24 percent. Declining support for handgun bans also coincides with court rulings upholding the right of citizens to own handguns for personal self-defense (see chapter 2). As the survey results from questions on gun registration, waiting periods, assault weapons, and even a ban on handguns make clear, Americans' support for stronger gun control is not the product of misunderstanding or a failure to comprehend what the gun debate is all about. Most Americans may not possess the knowledge of a gun specialist, but the policy options under public discussion are straightforward and clear, as are public preferences, which in fact reveal a high degree of sophistication.[99]

Demographics

Not surprisingly, gun ownership and opposition to gun controls are closely related. Those most likely to oppose gun controls are male (about 75 percent of gun owners are men, as are 87 percent of hunters), reside in small towns and rural areas, are registered as Republicans, are white, and live in the South.[100] The important factors that tie these demographic traits together include the male "rite of passage" connection between guns and maturity (a value rarely found in the socialization of females), the rural setting where guns and hunting activities are more common, and "Southernness." The particular importance of Southernness was examined in a separate study that concluded that the Southern subculture was one where the sporting use of guns was emphasized, as was the "attribute of being more defensive"; that is, there was greater suspicion of outsiders and a stronger belief in the need to rely on personal self-sufficiency. Another study found that gun ownership was highly correlated with individuals who had little belief or confidence in the American national government.[101]

Gun Beliefs and Crime

Support for gun control is typically tied to the fear of crime, in that poll results often fluctuate in response to widely publicized acts of violence. Yet the underlying support for gun control does not rest solely on the crime issue. That is, unlike support for tougher sentencing and the death penalty, citizens seem to believe that greater gun control is no panacea for the crime problem, although citizens do see a connection between violence and guns. In a 2001 NORC survey, for example, only 8 percent agreed that passing stricter gun laws would reduce crime; 33 percent said that stricter enforcement of existing laws would help, and 54 percent said that both actions together would reduce crime.[102] Thus, support for stronger gun laws rests partly with concern over crime but more with the general sense that guns pose an inherent risk to society and ought to be more tightly regulated.

Perhaps even more impressive than the consistently high degree of support for gun control is that it extends even to gun owners. In the 2009 nationwide survey of NRA and non-NRA gun owners mentioned earlier, 85 percent of non-NRA gun owners favored background checks for all gun sales at gun shows (69 percent of NRA members favored this); 46 percent of non-NRA gun owners favored a national gun registry, with 42 percent opposed (this was favored by 30 percent of NRA members); only 33 percent of non-NRA gun owners favored allowing guns to be carried in bags on Amtrak trains (61 percent of NRA members favored the idea, which is now allowed). As this and previous polls have revealed, most gun owners tend to support gun control measures in numbers only modestly lower than the population as a whole. As this survey revealed, the four million members of the NRA hold more staunchly anti–gun control beliefs than the nation's roughly eighty million gun owners.[103] Thus, gun owners provide a surprising degree of support for the gun control agenda—surprising, given the stridency and inflexibility of the groups that claim to represent gun users in Washington, DC.

A final public opinion question brings us back to the NRA. In a national survey conducted in 2000 by the Survey Research Center at Ohio State University, respondents were asked to rate various interest groups from most to least liked. The NRA ranked as the third-most well-liked group, yet it also ranked as the third-most disliked. What these apparently contradictory findings reveal is that the NRA continues to arouse intense feelings of respect among its adherents and contempt among its opponents. Yet the NRA's public image has improved since the mid-1990s, when its unfavorability rating among the general public (48 percent) exceeded its favorability rating (44 percent). By 2007 its favorability rating had risen to 52 percent (unfavorability rating 32 percent). This change probably reflects the NRA's long-term effort to tone down its extremist rhetoric, its policy successes, and the decline in opposition from many Democrats.[104]

The Opinion–Policy Gap

The disjunction between broad popular support for firmer gun laws and the failure to enact most such laws might be interpreted as a failure of democracy. Yet the connection between public opinion and public policy is far more complex than such a conclusion suggests. In the absence of a national system of governance by nationwide referendum, it is all but inevitable that such disjunctions will exist. The explanation rests, first, with the difficulty of translating social regulatory policy preferences into policy enactments. Like trying to build a house in the middle of a hurricane, the effort to construct or alter social regulatory policy is notoriously difficult because of the passion and intensity surrounding such issues. This fact takes on added significance when we note that, other things being equal, the enactment of policy is always more difficult than blocking the enactment of policy. Thus the weight of political inertia rests with gun control opponents. Clearly, swings in public opinion in recent years have helped win passage of the Brady law, the ban on armor-piercing bullets, and the assault-weapons ban (see discussion in chapter 5). Yet the outrage-action-reaction cycle described in chapter 1 means that public outrage is limited in intensity and duration, especially because the gun issue is but one of many that compete for attention on the national issue agenda. Once the outrage has subsided, gun control opponents retain a political edge that generally works against a direct translation of public preferences into policy enactments.

The second and related reason for the opinion-policy gap is the consequence of pressure-group politics. It is well understood that Congress responds to pressures from organized interest groups, especially when broader public tides subside. As former senator J. William Fulbright (D-AR) once observed, the legislator does not serve "constituents as a community, but the best-organized, best-funded, and most politically active interest groups within the constituency." The political scientist Graham Wootton calls this "special-interest democracy." A central part of this special interest democracy is not only its effective use of pressure politics, but election mobilization, especially when the electoral contests are less visible and more local, such as primary elections and special elections (as was the case with the 2013 Colorado special election discussed earlier). Polls show consistently that, while consistent majorities of Americans support stronger gun laws, gun rights supporters are much more likely to vote based solely on the gun issue and are also more likely to engage in other political activities, such as attending a meeting or contributing money. According to one survey, 25 percent of those who support gun rights are likely to take political action based on the gun issue, compared with only 5 percent of those who support stronger gun laws. This "activism gap" is key to understanding the NRA's political successes.[105]

Political Parties and Guns

As in the case of other social regulatory policy issues such as abortion and women's rights, the national political parties have consistently disagreed with each other on gun control, although the degree and emphasis of the rhetoric used has varied according to the nature of the gun debate at the time and the political posturing of the party nominees. This disagreement takes on added significance with the recognition that America's two major parties have a long-standing reputation for seeking to minimize their differences and for addressing issues in broad, abstract terms rather than through unambiguous advocacy of specific policies. A study of party platforms by the political scientist Gerald M. Pomper found that less than 10 percent of the promises found in platforms involved conflicting positions between the Democrats and Republicans.[106] Not surprisingly, platforms have been ridiculed for their "mindless rhetoric." The 1972 Democratic platform went so far as to admit that "the people are skeptical of platforms filled with political platitudes."[107]

As measured by national party platforms, the Republicans have long expressed support for gun ownership free of government regulation (except for gun use by criminals), and the Democrats have exhibited a similar consistency in favor of gun regulations. The gun issue first surfaced in modern times in party platforms in 1968, reflecting the emergence of the issue at the national level in the late 1960s.[108] Both parties usually have addressed the issue in their platforms under the category of crime and criminal justice.

The Republicans

The 1968 Republican Party platform (of nominee Richard Nixon) urged "control [of] indiscriminate availability of firearms" but also "safeguarding the right of responsible citizens to collect, own and use firearms ... retaining primary responsibility at the state level." The 1972 platform, supporting Nixon's renomination, again endorsed citizens' rights to "collect, own and use firearms"; however, it also included "self-defense" as a purpose and emphasized efforts "to prevent criminal access to all weapons," especially cheap handguns, although relying mainly on state enforcement. The 1976 platform took a turn to the right; it simply stated, "We support the right of citizens to keep and bear arms." The platform also stated its opposition to federal registration of firearms and advocated harsher sentences for crimes committed with guns. If the previous GOP platforms contained at least a nod to gun regulation, the 1976 document, produced by the convention that nominated Gerald Ford, conformed closely to NRA policy.

In 1980 the Republican platform wording was duplicated from 1976, with an added phrase urging removal of "those provisions of the Gun Control Act of 1968 that do not significantly impact on crime but serve rather to restrain the law-abiding citizen in his legitimate use of firearms." This sentence foreshadowed the original purpose behind the Firearms Owners Protection Act of 1986. Reflecting the conservative views of party nominee Ronald Reagan, this platform language represented the zenith of NRA-style views in the party.

The 1984 convention, which renominated Reagan, adopted a platform that dropped any reference to the Gun Control Act or to the lifting of gun regulations and said instead that citizens ought not to be blamed for "exercising their constitutional rights," presumably a reference to the Second Amendment. The 1988 platform of the convention that nominated George H. W. Bush also indicated the party's support for "the constitutional right to keep and bear arms" and called for "stiff, mandatory penalties" for those who used guns in the commission of crimes. This wording was kept in the 1992 platform (despite the NRA's refusal to endorse Bush) along with additional wording tying gun ownership to national defense and criticizing efforts at "blaming firearm manufacturers for street crime." The 1996 platform again invoked the Second Amendment but added wording about the need for training programs for safe firearms use. It also supported presidential candidate Robert Dole's call for instant background checks, a proposal floated by the NRA the previous decade (even though the NRA refused to back Dole because of his opposition to repeal the assault-weapons ban). The platform also called for mandatory penalties for gun crimes.

The 2000 platform for nominee George W. Bush paralleled that of 1996, invoking the Second Amendment and citing the importance of self-defense; it also promised vigorous enforcement of existing gun laws. It further stated express opposition to gun licensing and registration. The 2004 platform for President Bush's reelection again contained an emphatic Second Amendment statement of gun rights, applauding the hunting tradition, the use of guns for self-protection, and administration efforts to open federal lands to hunting. It also supported quick destruction of gun-purchase documentation and the ongoing effort to protect the gun industry from lawsuits (enacted in 2005), and it opposed any gun licensing or registration. The 2008 platform accompanying the presidential nomination of Senator John McCain (R-AZ) extolled the pro–gun rights Supreme Court decision earlier that year in *D.C. v. Heller* (see chapter 2) and argued for the appointment of judges who would support this ruling. In a new twist, the platform called for "firearms training in federal programs serving senior citizens and women." There was no explanation for who would conduct such training, its purpose, or why it would be aimed at these groups. The 2012 platform applauded the *Heller* and *McDonald* cases, extolled the "God-given" right of self-defense, and provided a new laundry list of measures they supported or opposed, including any monitoring of ammunition sales, support for "stand your ground" laws (see chapter 3), support for a bill in Congress to allow the weakest state gun-carry law to be recognized by all the states (so-called "carry reciprocity"), opposed lawsuits against gun manufacturers and any limits on bullet magazine size, decried the Obama administration's botched Operation Fast and Furious (when the government tried to trace illicit arms trafficking into Mexico; two such weapons were used to kill an American agent), and opposed gathering of firearms sales information by the roughly ten thousand American gun dealers found along the US-Mexico border.

The Democrats

In its mention of gun control, the 1968 Democratic Party platform urged "the passage and enforcement of effective federal, state and local gun control legislation." Paralleling the nomination of liberal senator George McGovern (D-SD), a specific proposal appeared in the 1972 platform that, after calling for "laws to control the improper use of hand guns," recommended a ban on "Saturday night specials" (cheap handguns). The 1976 platform again called for strengthening existing handgun controls as well as banning Saturday night specials. But reflecting nominee Jimmy Carter's more conservative views, the platform also urged tougher sentencing for crimes committed with guns and, in a concession to gun owners, affirmed "the right of sportsmen to possess guns for purely hunting and target-shooting purposes." The 1980 platform advocated the same position and reaffirmed support for sporting uses of guns, reflecting the caution of incumbent president Carter.

The 1984 Democratic platform, reflecting the more liberal views of nominee Walter Mondale, dropped any reference to the sporting use of guns. The platform again called for tough restraints on small, cheap handguns. Despite Michael Dukakis's initial support for strong gun control, the 1988 platform retreated on previous tough language. Its only specific gun regulation proposal was a call for the enforcement of the ban on "cop-killer" bullets enacted two years earlier, a proposal notable for being both uncontroversial and inconsequential. It also made a vague reference to the procuring of weapons as an impediment to the jobs performed by police, teachers, and parents. This language probably reflected the belief in the Dukakis camp that it needed to backpedal on the candidate's gun control views in order to remain competitive with George H. W. Bush.

The 1992 platform assumed a much stronger and more specific stand on gun control. After asserting that it was "time to shut down the weapons bazaars," it endorsed a waiting period for handgun purchases and a ban on "the most deadly assault weapons." It also called for swift punishment of those who commit crimes with guns, shutting down the gun black market, and stiff penalties for those who sell guns to children. Reflecting nominee Bill Clinton's support for new gun laws but also respect for hunters (Clinton himself is a hunter), the platform stated that "we do not support efforts to restrict weapons used for legitimate hunting and sporting purposes." Clinton's 1996 platform again trumpeted the policy enactments sought in the 1992 platform, including the Brady law and the assault-weapons ban. It connected crime reduction to the restricted availability of certain weapons, but it also repeated the commitment to protect legitimate hunting and sporting gun uses.

The 2000 platform extolled candidate Al Gore's record of standing up to the "gun lobby," citing past successes of the Clinton-Gore administration, including the Brady law and the assault-weapons ban, reductions in juvenile gun crimes, and also promises of a continued tough approach to crime and especially gun crime. The platform also called for mandatory gun locks, a photo license ID system, full background checks, and more federal gun prosecutors and prosecutions. The 2004 convention that nominated John Kerry (D-MA) for the presidency called for protecting "Americans' Second Amendment right to own firearms," fighting gun crime, and efforts to extend the assault-weapons ban (it lapsed that year without renewal) and to close the gun show loophole that allows gun purchases at gun shows without background checks. The 2008 platform for Democratic nominee Senator Barack Obama (D-IL) also referenced protecting citizens' right to bear arms, but it also supported closing the gun show loophole, improving background checks, and reinstituting the assault-weapons ban. The 2012 platform acknowledged the individual right to bear arms, "subject to reasonable regulation," decried gun violence, and supported improved gun background checks, reenactment of the assault-weapons ban, and closing of the gun show loophole.

Presidential politics in an election year drives party platforms. The variations in emphasis and tone observed in the party platforms since 1968 reflect the ideological leanings of the party nominees as well as some assessment of the public mood. In 1992, for example, a waiting period for handgun purchases and regulations on assault rifles were prominent policy options that had gained much support in Washington and in many state capitals around the country since the late 1980s. Most important, in the past several decades the political parties have split on the gun issue rather than ignored the issue or mimicked the views of the opposition party. In recent platforms, however, the Democrats have adopted Second Amendment rhetoric and expressed support for hunting, whereas the Republicans have amplified the Second Amendment rhetoric and also emphasized crime fighting. The conservative Tea Party movement that coalesced in 2009 and 2010 also included a strong pro-gun commitment. Although the Tea Party movement did not formally ally itself with a single political party, it maintained close ties to the Republican Party, as its members played a key role in propelling pro–Tea Party candidates to Republican nomination in the 2010 midterm elections. The NRA moved to ally itself with and capitalize on the Tea Party's pro-gun proclivities, which sometimes included Tea Party members carrying guns to political events.

Conclusion

The NRA provides the prototypical example of single-issue interest politics at work. The lengthy and detailed attention it receives in this chapter reflects both the NRA's political importance and the extent to which it typifies the political maelstrom accompanying social regulatory policy. A zealous, highly motivated, and readily mobilizable grassroots base, animated mostly by purposive incentives, has been the NRA's key political force, whether applied in Washington, DC, or in the town of Brookhaven, New York; the organization's long-standing ties to key public officials have provided key entry points for the effective insertion of its political vector. Its influence is maximized when the public's attention is focused elsewhere. Yet in its continuing political battles, NRA leaders have consistently employed a Chicken Little ("the sky is falling") rhetorical style, especially aimed at its potential and actual constituency, with constant prophecies of imminent doom. As a consequence, the NRA has often sacrificed both a sense of perspective and the truth, leading to a general erosion of its credibility outside its own core constituency. Unquestionably, this is a tradeoff that most NRA leaders are willing to accept. Whether it is a "right" decision in purely political terms or not, it does place the NRA outside the mainstream interest-group tradition in American politics and even at the outer edge of group dynamics found in other examples of social regulatory policy.

Because the NRA's positions are largely at odds with public sentiment, its effectiveness has been reduced, even stymied at times, when national attention becomes aroused and focused on selected gun issues. Yet the window of opportunity for gun control proponents has typically been brief because of the limited duration of the public's attention to gun issues. This pattern began to change with the rise in the 1980s of an effective single-issue counterforce: HCI and its allies. Public support for stronger gun laws rests partly in concerns related to crime but more strongly in the public's sense that guns pose an inherent danger that ought properly to be subject to greater control by the state. The primary proposals of gun control supporters that constitute the gun policy agenda have found consistently wide support among the public, although with major NRA policy successes in the 2000s, continued declines in crime, and the retreat of many Democrats on the gun issue, public sympathy for stronger gun laws has waned.

The political parties have responded to the gun issue as well. Although their stands in particular years have been alternately modest and symbolic on one hand, and aggressively specific on the other hand, they have identifiably split—with consistency—since 1968, as we would expect for social regulatory policy: the Republicans have opposed new gun laws, and the Democrats have supported new laws. In this instance, at least, the parties have offered voters an identifiable choice on the gun control issue. These party differences have not had a greater effect on the national debate because single-issue appeals are rarely decisive in national politics and because the influence of the national parties has decreased in recent years.

In the next chapter the convergence of these political forces is observed at several key policy moments. As the social regulatory policy framework predicts, a primary convergence point is the legislative arena.

Chapter 5

Institutions, Policymaking, and Guns

REPRESENTATIVE McCORMACK: You have contacted such as you could and wired the members of the [National Rifle] Association?

GENERAL RECKORD: In each state, or practically every state, we have a state rifle association, and we advised a number of those people that the hearing would be held today ...

McCORMACK: Did you ask them to wire here?

RECKORD: I do not recall the exact language of the telegram; I would say yes, probably we did ...

McCORMACK: Did you wire the people telling them what the recommendations were going to be to the Committee?

RECKORD: No, except that the legislation was bad.

McCORMACK: And they blindly followed it?

RECKORD: I would not say blindly.

Exchange between Representative John W. McCormack (D-MA) and General M. A. Reckord, executive vice president of the NRA, Concerning the flood of mail members of Congress had received in response to an NRA message that erroneously claimed that pending legislation would lead to federal fingerprinting and photographing of all gun purchasers (1934)

THE INTEREST-GROUP PRESSURES DISCUSSED IN chapter 4 converge primarily on Congress. As the sparring from 1934 between Representative McCormack and General Reckord suggests, the political texture of gun issues in Congress has maintained an astonishing degree of similarity in the past eight decades. The NRA was actually far more amenable to gun regulations in the 1930s, however, than since the 1980s; for example, it helped draft a handgun waiting-period law for the District of Columbia in the 1930s, as well as DC's very strict handgun law written in the 1970s—which the Supreme Court struck down in 2008. Yet the policy line since that time reflects, one might argue, a regression (either desirable or undesirable, depending on one's point of view). In the 1930s national gun registration was openly advanced as an achievable national policy.[1] In the 1990s gun control supporters hailed as a great, even landmark, victory the passage of a modest, even marginal, policy change—enactment of a five-day waiting period for handgun purchases.

In this chapter I examine the political and policy roles of Congress, the president, and the key federal agency involved with gun regulation. As hypothesized in chapter 1, we would expect Congress to play an important and highly visible role in social regulatory policy, serving as a primary focal point for national policy conflict. In comparison, the president plays a relatively marginal role in social regulatory policy—marginal, that is, in comparison to the president's involvement with other kinds of policy. This does not mean that presidents are either indifferent to or impotent in the social regulatory area, but rather that other forces play a larger role and that key political conflict unfolds in the halls of Congress.

In addition, federal agencies involved with social regulatory policy find their work under close and critical scrutiny from the outside. As a consequence, political forces emanating from Congress, the president, and interest groups typically buffet such agencies. The significance of this assertion is that it differs from the general evaluation of the federal bureaucracy as a domineering force in American politics, relatively unimpeded by outside political forces, that suffers from too much, rather than too little, power.[2] The primary federal agency involved with gun matters, the Bureau of Alcohol, Tobacco, Firearms, and Explosives, is categorized as a regulatory agency, which supports the idea that its decisions and activities are subject to considerable political counterforce.

Early Legislative Efforts

The first congressional action pertaining to guns was the enactment of a 10 percent federal excise tax, passed as part of the War Revenue Act in 1919.[3] It was more significant as a revenue-raising measure than as a tool of regulation, and it survived the 1920s despite several efforts to reduce the tax.

In 1927, responding to popular fears of handgun use by criminals, Congress passed a bill to prohibit the sale of handguns to private individuals through the mail. This measure passed when other gun control efforts failed because its supporters justified it as a measure that supported, rather than eroded, state sovereignty. That is, proponents argued that such a federally imposed ban would prevent the US Post Office from unintentionally aiding in breaking the laws of states with tougher gun regulations. The significance of this argument lay in the prevailing reluctance to extend federal power over the states in the period preceding Franklin Roosevelt's New Deal. The Post Office was an enthusiastic supporter of the bill, but it found little support from President Coolidge or others in the executive branch. Thus, more ambitious efforts at handgun regulation, such as a bill to regulate the interstate commerce of handguns, never survived committee consideration. The mail ban on handguns enacted in 1927 was little more than symbolic, however, because no regulations were imposed on sending handguns via private express companies, and individuals were free to cross state lines to make gun purchases.

By the early 1930s gangsterism had become a national problem, fed by the Depression, Prohibition, and a new generation of powerful weapons. Responding to this new wave of crime and spurred by growing impatience with past federal inaction, the Roosevelt administration won passage of new crime legislation. As part of this effort, the Justice Department pushed strongly for more comprehensive gun control, including registration of machine guns, submachine guns, handguns, silencers, cane guns, sawed-off shotguns, and the like.[4] Yet the original bill was substantially weakened in committee. Most important, handguns were removed from the bill at the urging of the National Rifle Association and other gun groups. Ironically, the Roosevelt administration's emphasis on the gangster threat (the notorious gangsters Bonnie and Clyde were killed in May of 1934 and John Dillinger was hunted and gunned down in July of 1934) as a justification for the bill helped opponents to pare it down so that what emerged focused solely on gangster-type weapons. The National Firearms Act of 1934 (48 *Stat.* 1236) was signed in June of 1934 and was the last gun bill Roosevelt actively touted, although his Justice Department continued to press for national handgun registration. This year also marked the establishment of the NRA's Legislative Division.

A year later the Justice Department went to work on a new bill, which eventually became the Federal Firearms Act of 1938 (52 *Stat.* 1250). Once again, however, gun regulation opponents prevailed. The 1938 law gave the Treasury Department control over a national licensing system incorporating gun dealers, manufacturers, and importers. But the key power to prosecute those who bore responsibility for putting guns in the hands of criminals was effectively neutralized when language added in committee made successful federal prosecution dependent on being able to prove that the gun provider sold guns to criminals knowingly, a standard the Justice Department knew it could rarely if ever meet. (Indeed, those selling weapons were not required to verify the eligibility of those making gun purchases.) Recognizing this, the Justice Department withdrew from further involvement with the bill in Congress, discouraged at the outcome and fearing (correctly) that its association with the bill would undercut future efforts to enact tougher laws, including national firearms registration.[5] The Justice Department's withdrawal resulted in consolidation of the NRA's control over the bill, as the gun group moved "from coauthor to chief architect of the 1938 act." By the time of its enactment, the bill "had become the gun lobby's protégé."[6] Even so, the NRA continued to tout its fervent opposition to gun regulations.

Symptomatic of the impotency of this legislation is that fewer than one hundred arrests per year were made under any provision of the act from the 1930s to the 1960s. In addition, the low license fee for dealers ($1 in the 1938 act, increased to $10 in 1968) encouraged private citizens to acquire dealer licenses to circumvent the law by getting the cheap licenses to obtain dealer benefits even though they were not, in fact, dealers.

These early gun control efforts share several traits in common. First, the primary basis for support for such legislation came from the general public and elements of the executive branch. Second, these forces by themselves were relatively ineffective and unsuccessful in battling the well-organized and motivated forces opposing such controls as the measures moved through Congress. Even in this early stage, the NRA spearheaded the antiregulation movement. Third, the fates of these bills were all resolved in congressional committees. Unlike gun bills to come, no grand floor fights broke out over any of these bills in either the House or the Senate—again a reflection of the relative political weakness of gun control proponents. The bills that passed did so with little or no debate or public attention. Fourth, the opposition to these bills was fed less by material or business concerns than by the deep-seated, personal feelings of opponents who thought that these bills would impinge on the values identified here as the gun culture.[7] Thus, except for the absence of nasty floor fights, the political dynamics of these early bills clearly reflected those associated in this book with gun control as a social regulatory policy.

The Gun Control Act of 1968

The effort to revise and strengthen federal gun laws that concluded in 1968 began in 1963, when the Senate Judiciary Committee held hearings on a bill to ban mail-order handgun sales to minors. After the assassination of President Kennedy in November, the bill was expanded to include a ban on mail-order purchases of shotguns and rifles, but the bill never left committee, owing to pressure applied by the NRA and its allies.[8] President Lyndon Johnson proposed more sweeping gun control legislation in 1965 and in each subsequent year.

The difficulty Johnson faced in achieving enactment of a new gun control measure is underscored by comparing Johnson's failure to win passage of a gun bill until 1968 with his stunning legislative successes throughout his five years in office. No president in modern times has achieved passage of such a large volume of major legislation, and few presidents have had a higher percentage of bills enacted into law, despite the high volume. Johnson's legislative skills and mastery of the intricacies of Capitol Hill politics, acquired during his years as Senate majority leader, were legendary. Why, then, did Johnson fail to win enactment of this one bill until 1968, the last year of his presidency and a time when his political influence was at its lowest?[9] The answer lies in the nature of regulatory policy. Recalling the four types of policy discussed in chapter 1 (distributive, regulatory, redistributive, and constituent), previous analysis has shown that regulatory policy is both the most controversial and the one over which presidents have been able to exercise the least influence. This pattern was found to hold true not only for Johnson but for all presidents studied.[10] This does not mean that successful enactment of regulatory policies is impossible, but rather that the odds of enactment—much less enactment in the form presented—are longest for this type. And when one then factors in the unique characteristics of social regulatory policy in general and gun control in particular, the political "degree of difficulty" for Johnson or any president turns out to be very high.

Prelude

The first important gun control legislation Congress passed since 1938 was found in Title IV of the Omnibus Crime Control and Safe Streets Act of 1968 (82 *Stat.* 234). This provision banned the shipment of pistols and revolvers to individuals across state lines and forbade the purchase of handguns in stores in a state where the buyer did not reside. President Johnson found much of this omnibus bill to be highly objectionable, as it was very different from what his administration had proposed, and he nearly vetoed it. The gun control section was but a small element of what his administration had been pushing for, but it was not the primary source of his dismay over the bill.[11] The fact that this gun control provision was lodged in a crime bill accurately reflected the connection between popular anxiety over crime and the push for stronger gun control. Yet the final boost for this bill came from the assassination of Senator Robert F. Kennedy; the House voted for the bill on June 6, a day after the shooting of

Kennedy (the Senate had passed the bill the previous month) and two months after the assassination of Martin Luther King Jr.

More Gun Control?

Immediately after passage of the omnibus bill, Senator Thomas Dodd (D-CT), chair of the Judiciary Subcommittee on Juvenile Delinquency, introduced an administration-backed gun bill in the Senate that had as its centerpiece the registration of all firearms and licensing of gun owners. Representative Emanuel Celler (D-NY), chair of the Judiciary Committee, introduced the measure in the House. The bill that emerged at the end of the legislative gauntlet was still a gun control bill, but it failed to include these two central provisions.

President Johnson urged Congress "in the name of sanity . . . in the name of safety and in the name of an aroused nation to give America the gun-control law it needs."[12] After weakening Johnson's bill, the House Judiciary Committee initially voted 16–16 on the bill, thus failing to report it out of committee. An agreement was reached to reconsider the legislation, however, and it was finally reported out on June 21. The House Rules Committee approved a rule for the bill on July 9, after holding the legislation for nearly three weeks. Rules Committee chair William Colmer (D-MI), a gun control opponent, released the bill only after extracting a promise from Celler that he would oppose any efforts to add registration and licensing provisions to the bill on the floor of the House.

The House passed HR 17735 on July 24 after four days of vigorous floor consideration characterized by numerous attempts to amend the bill. Efforts were made to strengthen registration and licensing provisions, increase penalties, deregulate ammunition sales, provide exceptions for collectors, and curtail importation of foreign military weapons. Overall, forty-five attempts were made to amend this legislation on the House floor (eighteen accepted, twenty-seven rejected, with wins and losses for both sides), including four roll-call votes plus one more on final passage.

In the more sympathetic Senate the gun bill found greater support, and more debate centered on whether or not to strengthen the law. Subcommittee hearings began on June 26, and testimony was received from a wide variety of witnesses, including NRA president Harold W. Glassen, who said that the legislation was part of an effort to "foist upon an unsuspecting and aroused public a law that would, through its operation, sound the death knell for the shooting sport and eventually disarm the American public."

The Senate subcommittee approved the measure unanimously and forwarded it to the full committee, where the bill encountered stiff opposition. Gun control opponents, including Judiciary Committee chair James

Eastland (D-MI), delayed and weakened the bill. Further, the absence times of gun control supporters, including Senator Edward Kennedy who was still mourning the loss of his brother Robert, hampered e. push the bill through.

Finally, the bill was sent by committee to the Senate floor, where it was debated for five days. The opening salvo came from Senator Dodd, who accused the NRA of "blackmail, intimidation and unscrupulous propaganda." Debate centered on attempts to nationalize gun registration, strengthen criminal penalties, and create special exemptions for gun collectors and sportsmen. In all, seventeen formal motions were made to amend the bill on the floor (nine accepted, eight rejected, again with wins and losses for both sides). Eleven recorded votes were taken. After the bill's passage on September 18, a conference committee ironed out differences with the House, and Johnson signed the bill on October 22.

As enacted, the Gun Control Act of 1968 (Public Law 90-618; 82 *Stat.* 1226) banned the interstate shipment of firearms (handguns and long guns) and ammunition to private individuals; prohibited the sale of guns to minors, drug addicts, mental incompetents, and convicted felons; strengthened licensing and record-keeping requirements for gun dealers and collectors; extended federal regulation and taxation to "destructive devices" such as land mines, bombs, hand grenades, and the like; increased penalties for those who used guns in the commission of a crime covered by federal law; and banned the importation of foreign-made surplus firearms, except for those appropriate for sporting purposes. These measures represented a significant advance in law over previous federal gun regulation efforts, yet they were also modest and did not include the blanket registration and licensing proposals Johnson had sought—that is, the core of Johnson's gun agenda.

Political Assessment

The signs of a fierce and difficult political struggle for even this modest bill were everywhere. A useful way to think about political conflict in Congress for this or any bill is to envision each house of Congress as having two "arenas," or areas where important actions on bills are taken: in committee and on the floor. It is a truism of Congress that most important work on bills occurs in committees.[13] Sometimes, however, legislation that is either exceptionally important or very controversial continues to be the focus of deliberation, debate, and amendment on the floor of either or both houses. Thus, an important indicator of controversy and political struggle is the extent of debate and amendment on the floor.[14] A second important indicator is the bypassing of standard congressional procedures, such as normal committee consideration or use of such unusual procedures as the discharge petition in the House or the filibuster in the Senate.

The legislative history of the Gun Control Act reveals contentiousness both in committee and in floor consideration (to find no conflict in committee and great conflict during floor consideration is rare). Committees in both chambers made substantial changes to the bill, for the most part contrary to the president's wishes (this is particularly significant in the House Judiciary Committee, where the chair strongly supported Johnson's bill).

The many amendment efforts on the floors of both chambers further reflected controversy, as did the continued failure of the president and his allies in Congress to retain the core gun control provisions they sought. In more quantifiable terms, out of the 165 most important bills considered by both houses of Congress from 1954 to 1974, only 6 bills had more roll-call votes in the House than the Gun Control Act, and only 27 bills had more roll-call votes in the Senate.[15] One may therefore conclude that the Gun Control Act was one of the most controversial and contentious bills that Congress considered during this twenty-year period.

Given clear evidence of President Johnson's limited influence over the bill, why did it pass? First, as discussed in chapter 4, the public had long favored stronger gun controls. A second and necessary condition was that, like the omnibus act, latent public support was aroused and motivated by the rising fear of crime and was galvanized by the political shock waves caused by recent assassinations.[16] Third, support from the administration was still a factor and a contributing influence. And fourth, gun control supporters gave in on key elements of Johnson's original proposal to win the necessary support to enact some kind of gun regulation bill.

Consequences

The actual consequences of the 1968 act were several. The number of gun dealers increased, even though dealer regulations were tightened and gun dealer license fees were increased to $10. The importation of shotguns also increased, although that of rifles decreased. Even though handguns have little to no hunting purpose, handguns that did not fit the definition of the Saturday night special (defined by the ATF as those with a barrel length of three inches or less, that fired a .32-caliber or smaller bullet, and that sold for less than $50) continued to be imported. Nevertheless, total handgun imports dropped, but domestic handgun production increased. Finally, because the law regulated gun imports but not the import of gun parts, handgun parts imports increased dramatically.[17]

Thus, the Gun Control Act was the most sweeping federal gun regulation enacted up to that time. Yet its scope was modest, and as a consequence, its impact was minimal. Gun control opponents nevertheless immediately set to work to erode the act, if not overturn it entirely. One year later, for example, Congress repealed a provision of the act requiring sellers of shotgun and rifle ammunition to register purchasers.[18] The effort to neutralize the 1968 act climaxed with the Firearms Owners Protection Act.

The Firearms Owners Protection Act of 1986

The passage of this next important gun bill can be traced in large measure to the efforts of two gun control opponents: Senator James McClure (R-ID) and Representative Harold Volkmer (D-MO). In fact, the bill passed in 1986 came to be known as the McClure-Volkmer bill.

As early as 1978, Representative Volkmer proposed legislation to repeal much of the 1968 act. Senator McClure's efforts began in the early 1980s. These parallel efforts picked up important momentum from the election of gun control foe Ronald Reagan and the attendant more conservative mood of the country, as well as from the Republican control of the Senate after the 1980 elections (Republicans lost their majority in the 1986 elections). Intensive and serious pressure picked up in the two years preceding the bill's enactment, as did the protracted lobbying effort of the NRA, joined by the Gun Owners of America and the Citizens Committee for the Right to Keep and Bear Arms.

The Senate Judiciary Committee approved earlier versions of the McClure-Volkmer bill in 1982 and 1984, but full floor consideration was not obtained until 1985, when, at the urging of bill sponsors, Senate majority leader Robert Dole (R-KS) authorized the unusual move of bypassing the Judiciary Committee and placing the bill directly on the Senate calendar. Once on the floor, the bill was subjected to a barrage of amendments designed to strengthen gun controls; none of these amendments, however, was accepted. Senator Edward Kennedy proposed that the ban on the interstate sale of handguns be retained. Senator Charles McC. Mathias (R-MD) moved to eliminate a provision requiring that gun dealers be given prior notice before routine inspections by federal investigators. Senator Daniel K. Inouye (D-HI) proposed a fourteen-day waiting period between purchase and delivery of handguns, a provision many law enforcement groups supported.

But the bill's chief Senate sponsors, McClure and Orrin Hatch (R-UT), argued that the proposed restrictions would have no effect on crime fighting but instead represented unjustified limitations on sportsmen, hunters, and dealers. The one significant restriction the Senate adopted was a ban on the importation of Saturday night special gun parts.

Bill opponents, led by Kennedy and Howard Metzenbaum (D-OH), threatened a filibuster in June if some of the bill's provisions were not softened. Supporters yielded, and after intense negotiations, Senate bill 49 was passed on July 9, 1985. In all, four roll-call votes were taken.

The final vote for passage of the bill was 79–15, with the strongest support coming from senators from Western and Southern states. The relatively speedy passage of the bill was attributed to the pressure of the NRA and its allies and to a sympathetic Judiciary Committee chair Strom Thurmond (R-SC) and majority leader (Robert Dole).[19]

House Obstacles

Deliberations in the Democratic-controlled House posed a far greater problem for McClure-Volkmer supporters. Judiciary Committee chair Peter Rodino (D-NJ), a staunch gun control proponent, had announced early in 1985 that the bill arrived "D.O.A.—Dead on Arrival." Bill opponents were still confident that Rodino would succeed as he had in the past in keeping the bill bottled up in committee. Yet Rodino was unable to fulfill his prediction. By the fall of 1985 bill supporters had begun a discharge petition that, if signed by a majority of the House membership (218), would force the bill out of committee and onto the floor. The drastic and unusual nature of the House discharge petition is revealed by the success, from 1937 to 1986, of only twenty such petitions. Of those, only two of the affected bills were actually enacted into law.[20]

Despite their initial opposition, both Rodino and Representative William J. Hughes (D-NJ), chair of the Judiciary Subcommittee on Crime realized that unless they formulated a substitute compromise bill, the full committee would be forced to report McClure-Volkmer to the House floor. The committee thus held a markup session on a compromise bill and reported it to the floor by unanimous vote. This remarkable turn of events occurred in March 1986 as the result of a successful discharge petition. By reporting the Rodino-Hughes bill to the floor first (on March 11) before the actual filing of the discharge petition on behalf of McClure-Volkmer (on March 13), gun control supporters hoped to salvage some parliamentary flexibility that would allow priority consideration of the Rodino-Hughes bill. This maneuver failed because Volkmer

was able to offer his version of the bill as a substitute for that of the Ju
Committee in a vote on the floor.

On April 9, Representative Hughes offered a package of law enforcement
amendments to McClure-Volkmer, including a ban on interstate sale and
transport of handguns and stricter record-keeping regulations. The package
was rejected by a wide margin (176–248). During the vote police officers stood
in full uniform at "parade rest" at the entrance to the House floor as a sign of
their opposition to McClure-Volkmer. After several other votes on motions
to strengthen certain gun control provisions (all were defeated), the House
adjourned and then reconvened the next day. This time, on the third try the
House approved (233–184) a ban on interstate handgun sales after proponents
stressed the difference between sale and transport. A final amendment to bar
all future possession and sale of machine guns by private citizens also passed.
The bill was approved by a lopsided 292–130 vote on April 10. President Reagan
signed the measure into law on May 19, 1986 (PL 99–308). In all, seven roll-call
votes were taken in the House.

As passed into law, McClure-Volkmer amended the 1968 act by allowing
for the interstate sale of rifles and shotguns as long as the sale was legal in the
states of the buyer and seller. The act also eliminated record-keeping requirements for ammunition dealers, made it easier for individuals selling guns to
do so without a license unless they did so "regularly," allowed gun dealers to
do business at gun shows, and prohibited the ATF from issuing regulations
requiring centralized records of gun dealers. In addition, the act limited to
one per year the number of unannounced ATF inspections of gun dealers
and prohibited the establishment of any system of comprehensive firearms
registration. Finally, the act barred future possession or transfer of machine
guns and retained existing restrictions (except for transport) on handguns.

In a final move to tighten up elements of the bill, partly as a concession to
law enforcement groups that had opposed McClure-Volkmer, the Senate passed
a separate bill on May 6 that tightened licensing, record keeping, and interstate
transport requirements. That bill easily passed the House on June 24 and was
signed into law on July 8, 1986 (PL 99–360; 100 *Stat.* 449).

Political Assessment

The politics of McClure-Volkmer was distinctive in several important respects.
First, despite President Reagan's widely known sympathy for the NRA and
its causes—marked particularly by his continued opposition to gun controls
during his presidency even after the assassination attempt against him in

1981—his administration played a small role.[21] Officially, the administration supported the bill, but the Justice Department offered no testimony at committee hearings, and internal ATF memos released to the press revealed doubts about some of the decontrol provisions. Public comments by Attorney General Edwin Meese were similarly equivocal.

Second, the bill's passage represented the zenith of the NRA's influence on Capitol Hill until the 2000s. The *New York Times* noted, for example, that during House debate, "it was a measure of the power of the gun lobby that no member of Congress, in the day-long debate, spoke in favor of keeping all the existing controls. Rather, the question was the extent to which they should be eased."[22] Passage of the House bill prompted the comment that the NRA "won almost everything it had sought in a lobbying and advertising campaign that cost about $1.6 million."[23] By contrast, the police coalition spent about $15,000, and Handgun Control, Inc.'s spending was similarly modest. Even so, HCI and its allies acquired a first taste of success in the vote to retain the ban on interstate pistol sales and in the halt of the sale and manufacture of new machine guns (Sarah Brady reported being "thrilled" with this particular part of the bill).[24] Third, wrangling over the bill solidified the split between the NRA and police organizations. Beyond this, the McClure-Volkmer battle served as an important testing ground for the relatively inexperienced police groups. As one member of Congress observed, "The police misunderstood the force of lobbying. Lobbying is not standing in long lines at the door. Lobbying is good information early; it is a presence when minds are being made up."[25] Fourth, the bill represented the political coming of age of HCI as well as the establishment of Sarah Brady as primary spokesperson on behalf of gun control. Clearly, the battle over this bill was key to politicizing Brady on the gun issue.

Fifth, interest-group activity was intense and decisive. As a Senate aide who worked for a gun control supporter commented, "I have never gotten so many vituperative calls on any issue that we've ever dealt with as the gun issue. Violent, violent calls. People calling up threatening me, threatening the senator. Death threats."[26] On the political balance scales, the NRA dominated in a way it would not be able to replicate until the 2000s. Yet gun control supporters could also claim some victories.

Sixth, rhetoric aside, the highly controversial nature of the bill was reflected in the procedures followed in both houses. Even though the measure met less opposition in the Senate, the move to bypass the Judiciary Committee was highly unusual; the filibuster threat was a clear symptom of high controversy, as were the numerous efforts to amend on the floor. In comparison with the 1968 gun act and averages of roll-call votes for important regulatory bills, the four Senate roll calls represent a below-average number. Still, other signs of controversy support the social regulatory policy analysis. In the House the trends are even more marked. The use of a discharge petition, the extensive debate, and the many efforts to amend all follow the social regulatory policy pattern. And the seven roll-call votes exceed the average reported earlier for regulatory bills in the House. The passage of a special clarifying bill after passage of McClure-Volkmer was another unusual action.

Seventh, an analysis of congressional voting patterns reveals that key factors influencing their votes included region (strongest support for McClure-Volkmer came from Southern and Western representatives), constituency (those from rural districts were more likely to support the NRA's positions), and attendant ideological disposition toward the gun issue. The NRA's grassroots efforts were politically influential, as was its overall spending. Yet HCI's lobbying efforts conjoined with the police organizations also had some effect on the final outcome.[27]

The Tide Turns: The Assault-Weapons Ban

From 1972 (when the Senate passed a ban on cheap handguns) to 1988 no measure to increase gun controls reached the floor of either house of Congress. In the late 1980s and early 1990s, however, gun control proponents pressed their case for stronger national controls with progressively greater effectiveness and skill, often mimicking the lobbying and organizational tactics that had worked for the NRA. Simultaneously, the lurking national fear of crime, coupled with several sensational mass murders, pushed public opinion more firmly and strongly in favor of new gun regulations.

In the forefront of this effort was the move to regulate or ban various styles of semiautomatic assault weapons. The key event spurring control supporters was a senseless January 1989 schoolyard massacre in Stockton, California, when five children were killed and twenty-nine others were wounded in a shooting spree by drifter Patrick Purdy using a Chinese AK–47 assault rifle (see chapter 3). Within weeks thirty states and many localities were considering bans on these weapons.[28] Indeed, 1989 witnessed an explosion of interest in such weapons. Two years later the worst such massacre in American history occurred in a cafeteria in Killeen, Texas, when George J. Hennard killed twenty-two people and himself and wounded twenty-three others.[29] Regulation of such weapons posed a practical problem because the definition of a semiautomatic weapon is one that fires a round with each pull of the trigger, which would include wooden-stocked hunting rifles. Assault-style semiautomatic weapons are distinguished from others in that they are configured specifically for military use. They typically have magazines holding twenty to thirty bullets, are more compact in design, have barrels less than twenty inches in length, take intermediate-sized cartridges, include extensive use of lightweight stampings and plastics, and are therefore lighter in weight (six to ten pounds). In addition, they often have pistol grips or thumbhole stocks, flash suppressors, folding or telescoping stocks, grenade launchers, and bayonet fittings.[30] These are partly designed to facilitate "spray fire."

Responding to advice from within his administration and from the first lady, George H. W. Bush reversed his opposition to assault-weapons regulation within the space of a month, announcing a temporary ban on the import of certain assault rifles by executive order in March 1989.[31] The temporary ban was subsequently expanded to include a larger number of weapons and then made permanent, earning Bush the ire of the NRA. President Bill Clinton expanded the scope of the import ban in 1993, also by executive order, to include assault-style handguns, such as the Uzi. In 1998 Clinton announced a permanent import ban on fifty-eight additional assault weapons.[32] In Congress several bills aimed at curbing or banning assault weapons were introduced in 1989, but those bills languished in committee until 1990, when the Senate narrowly approved a provision to ban the production, sale, and possession of nine semiautomatic assault-type weapons. The provision was added to an omnibus crime bill. The House Judiciary Committee had approved a similar measure, but it never left committee. In conference committee the assault-weapons ban was removed from the bill that was enacted into law.

In 1991 the Senate again included an assault-weapons ban in a larger crime bill. A similar provision was included in the House version of the bill, but it was stripped out in a highly emotional floor vote that occurred one day after the massacre in Killeen, Texas.

In November 1993 the Senate passed a ban on the manufacture of nineteen assault weapons, but it also included a provision allowing gun dealers to sell guns that had already been produced. The measure, added to a crime bill, also exempted more than 650 types of hunting weapons. That same month the Senate also passed a measure making it a federal crime to sell handguns to minors.[33] In the spring of 1994 the House took up the assault-weapons ban. From the start, ban supporters shared little optimism that the House would approve the measure. In April President Clinton weighed in strongly for the ban, enlisting the help of several cabinet secretaries, most notably treasury secretary and gun owner Lloyd Bentsen. Ban supporters received unexpected help from Representative Henry Hyde (R-IL), a staunch conservative who had opposed gun measures in the past. Thanks in part to Hyde's support, the Judiciary Committee approved the measure on April 28, despite the opposition of committee chair Jack Brooks (D-TX).[34] As the House floor vote approached, bill supporters all but admitted defeat, noting that they were probably fifteen votes shy. Democratic leaders were split on the bill, as House Speaker Tom Foley (D-WA) opposed the measure, whereas Majority Leader Richard Gephardt (D-MO) favored it. Yet in a stunning finale, the assault-weapons ban managed to pass by a two-vote margin, 216–214, on May 5. The drama was heightened when Representative Andrew Jacobs Jr. (D-IN), at the urging of several colleagues, switched his vote from "against" to "for" in the final seconds of the roll-call vote.

As is true of other congressional votes on gun control, more Democrats supported the measure than Republicans, yet party was not the key dividing factor: 177 Democrats were joined by 38 Republicans plus 1 independent in favor of the bill, and 137 Republicans and 77 Democrats opposed. The bill's strongest opposition came from Southern and Western representatives. As with other gun bill votes, the politics was intense. A staffer for one freshman Republican representative who supported the bill commented, "You don't know the threats we received."[35] Because the assault-weapons ban was part of a larger crime bill that had passed in different versions in the two houses, a conference committee was called to iron out the differences. Typically, a bill that survives the legislative gauntlet up to the point of conference committee is all but assured final passage. Such was not the case for the assault-weapons ban.

Bill supporters initially predicted that the conference committee would complete its work by the end of May. Yet it did not report a bill back to the House and Senate until the end of July, during which time Representative Brooks, a member of the House-Senate conference, attempted repeatedly to kill the assault-weapons ban. Brooks's efforts failed, but he did succeed in inserting provisions that exempted pawnbrokers from the Brady law (see below) and barred all antihunting protests from taking place on federal lands. Meanwhile, Republican leaders launched a full-scale assault on the $33 billion crime bill, calling it a wasteful piece of legislation laden with pork-barrel spending. These criticisms took on added legitimacy when it was revealed that Representative Brooks had succeeded in slipping into the bill a $10 million appropriation to establish a center for criminal justice at his alma mater, Lamar University (located in his Texas congressional district).

Despite the charges of pork, the bill's progress was impeded primarily by the assault-weapons ban and the inclusion of a provision that barred the use of statistics to help prove racial bias in criminal cases involving the death penalty. This latter measure alienated many members of the congressional Black Caucus, who would have otherwise provided key support for President Clinton. Because of the concern that the death penalty is applied disproportionately against black men, a provision adding more than fifty new federal crimes for which the death penalty could be applied also dismayed blacks in Congress.

Anxious to win final approval, and with an eye toward the fall elections, Clinton and his congressional allies pushed for an early vote in the House. This proved to be a serious tactical blunder because they had not lined up the necessary support. In a dramatic reversal on a procedural vote to adopt a rule for the bill, the House rejected the crime bill on August 11 by a vote of 225 to 210. Especially embarrassing was the vote against the bill by fifty-eight Democrats. As with other gun votes, opposition was strongest in the South. Sixty-four percent of the defecting Democrats (thirty-seven of the fifty-eight) were from the South; most of the rest came from strong gun states in the Midwest and West. Eleven Republicans supported the bill. Although twenty-seven members of the congressional Black Caucus supported Clinton on the vote, eleven did not (including the lone Republican member of the caucus, Gary Franks of Connecticut).

Under normal circumstances a defeat on a rules vote would spell the end of the legislation. Yet President Clinton would not accept defeat, vowing to "fight and fight and fight until we win this battle for the American people." Clinton launched an intensive public campaign, enlisting the assistance of police organizations and several members of his cabinet. Congressional leaders vowed to bring back the bill, and in another departure from normal procedure, they negotiated a new version of the bill, this time cutting the bill's spending by about 10 percent ($3.3 billion), including Representative Brooks's $10 million allocation for Lamar University. In addition, in order to sway some moderate Republicans, a provision was added to allow evidence of previous sex crimes to be introduced in subsequent such trials. Throughout the negotiations process, many supporters of the bill urged Clinton to drop the assault-weapons ban from it in order to ensure passage, but Clinton refused to budge on the matter. Throughout this period the NRA lobbied intensively to kill the assault-weapons provision.

On August 21, after three days and two nights of negotiation, the revised bill was brought before the House in a highly unusual Sunday session. This time, with the help of moderate Republicans and four members of the Black Caucus—Cleo Fields (D-LA), Gary Franks (R-CT), John Lewis (D-GA), and Charles Rangel (D-NY)—who were persuaded to vote with the president, the bill passed by a vote of 235 to 195 (after two other affirmative procedural votes for the bill). This time forty-six Republicans supported the bill in a bipartisan effort that led many to proclaim "a new era of cooperation" between the parties. Key moderate Republicans, including junior House members, played an uncharacteristically major role in the negotiations process with the White

House. Stubborn opposition from anti–gun control Democrats made such bipartisan bargaining necessary.

The bill then went to the Senate, where the bipartisan spirit quickly evaporated as opponents expressed dismay over the House's highly unusual action of altering the original conference committee version. Bill opponents sought to bring back the original conference version, a move that would have effectively ended the bill's chances for 1994. In the Senate as well as the House, the primary focus of contention was the assault-weapons ban.

On August 23, Senate minority leader Robert Dole announced that forty Republicans (plus Dole himself) had agreed to stop the crime bill, which would have killed the measure because a bloc of forty-one could prevent any move to end debate, thereby ending chances for bill passage. Two days later, however, in a crucial procedural vote, bill supporters won the votes of sixty-one senators, with thirty-nine voting in opposition. Six Republicans defected to support the bill; one Democrat voted against it. The six Republicans were John Chafee of Rhode Island; John Danforth of Missouri; James Jeffords of Vermont; Nancy L. Kassebaum of Kansas; William Roth of Delaware; and Arlen Specter of Pennsylvania. The one defecting Democrat was Richard Shelby of Alabama. After an additional procedural vote, the Senate passed the bill, and Clinton signed HR 3355 on September 13, 1994, as Title XI of the Violent Crime Control and Law Enforcement Act (PL 103–322; 108 *Stat.* 1796).

In its final form the assault-weapons ban outlawed for ten years the manufacture, sale, and possession of nineteen specified types of weapons, as well as dozens of "copycat" weapons that possessed two or more characteristics of the nineteen named types. It also specifically exempted 661 sporting rifles and limited magazines to those that could hold no more than ten bullets. Existing assault-style rifles were exempted from the ban, and Congress was given the power to review the inclusion of additional weapons under the terms of the measure.

Thus, in a five-year period the assault-weapons ban was submitted to a vote six times on the floor of the Senate and six times on the House floor. The significance of these votes is underscored by the virulent politics surrounding congressional deliberations (comparable to that described in this chapter for the other gun bills), the bypassing of usual procedures, and the admitted reluctance of many in Congress to deal with any gun control measure. As Representative Hughes noted about the gun issue: "It's one of those issues that members would be just as happy if it would go away. A lot of people have said to me, 'I hope we don't have to take it up next year.'"[36]

That prediction failed to come true. When Republicans won control of both houses of Congress in the 1994 elections, gun control foes found close allies among Republican leaders. Early in 1995 Senate majority leader Dole and House Speaker Newt Gingrich (R-GA) both publicly pledged to make repeal of the assault-weapons ban a top priority. A vote was planned for late spring, but the terrorist bombing of a federal office building in Oklahoma City on April 19 derailed those plans. Although the 170 people killed died from a fuel oil and fertilizer bomb rather than gunfire, public sentiment turned fiercely against the venomous antigovernment rhetoric that had accompanied efforts to repeal the weapons ban. This sensitivity was heightened because of evidence that the explosion was the work of one or more Americans who were motivated by a fierce antipathy to US governmental authority (as represented by the federal office building). As time went on, support for repeal of the ban waned.[37] By 1996 Majority Leader Dole had become the Republican front-runner for the presidential nomination, which prompted him to downplay his earlier promise to seek repeal. Nevertheless, a vote to repeal the ban was brought to the floor of the House on March 22, 1996. The repeal passed by a vote of 239 to 173 (not enough to override an expected veto from President Clinton). As in other gun control votes, the parties split on the issue; 183 Republicans voted for repeal and 42 voted against; 56 Democrats voted for repeal and 130 against. This division of party loyalties was especially significant because party-line voting reached record high levels in 1995 and 1996. Finally, regional differences again emerged, in that a majority of Northern Democrats voted against repeal, whereas a majority of Southern Democrats voted for repeal. Of 69 Southern Republicans, all but 4 voted for repeal. Despite the successful vote, it was clear by early 1996 that the Senate would not take up the measure, because Dole realized that a prominent stand against the ban might hurt his chances in the presidential election. This ensured that the measure would never reach the president's desk during the 104th Congress. The vote was nevertheless held to fulfill the Republican promise to the NRA.[38]

Critics derided the assault-weapons ban as purely symbolic politics. Yet crime statistics revealed that assault weapons had a certain criminal appeal. Federal law-enforcement officials reported that although assault weapons made up only about 1 percent of all weapons owned nationwide, 5.9 percent of weapons traced to crime use in 1990 were assault weapons; in 1993 the figure rose to 8.1 percent. An Urban Institute study found that assault weapons accounted for 8 percent of guns at crime scenes during a seven-year period in the 1990s, and the Violence Policy Center reported that one in ten law-enforcement officers killed in the line of duty died from an assault weapon. A follow-up study found that one in five officers were killed with assault weapons from 1998 to 2001 and that assault-weapons crimes studied in selected cities declined from 17 to 72 percent during the ban. Another indication of the appeal of such weapons to criminals came in May 1996, when federal agents broke up a gun smuggling ring that involved efforts to smuggle Chinese AK–47 assault rifles into the United States. The investigation was prompted when the weapons began turning up among members of violent California gangs. By 2004 seven states (California, Connecticut, Hawaii, Maryland, Massachusetts, New Jersey, New York, and the District of Columbia) along with several cities had enacted their own bans on assault weapons. An additional seven states have considered enacting the ban.[39]

The assault-weapons ban remained popular with the public as its September 2004 deadline for expiration neared: 68 percent of Americans favored the measure. Yet Republican congressional leaders opposed the extension, and President Bush, who claimed to support it, did nothing to aid the law's renewal. Political pundits concluded that he preferred to see the bill die before it reached his desk. Those plans nearly went awry when, in March 2004, ban supporters in the Senate attached ban renewal to a bill to shield gun manufacturers and dealers from lawsuits (which had already passed the House and had more than fifty Senate cosponsors); the bill passed by a 52–47 vote (see discussion later in this chapter). Infuriated that their top legislative priority now had this measure included, along with another to require background checks for gun purchases at gun shows, the NRA ordered the plug pulled on the entire bill. The abrupt turnaround resulted in the defeat of the whole bill by a vote of 90 to 8. The rapidity of the turnaround stunned veteran Senate watchers. Senator Dianne Feinstein (D-CA), a ban supporter, said of the NRA, "They had the power to turn around at least sixty votes in the Senate. That's amazing to me." Senator John McCain (R-AZ) noted, "I've been around here eighteen years, and I've never seen anything quite this bizarre."[40] After the bill expired in 2004, periodic, unsuccessful efforts to renew it were made. For all the attention focused on assault weapons, another gun issue received even more attention in Congress during the early 1990s: the debate over the imposition of a national waiting period for gun purchases.

The Brady Bill

From 1987 to 1993 gun control proponents placed their primary emphasis on the enactment of a national waiting period for handgun purchases. The purpose of such a rule would be twofold: first, to provide authorities with the opportunity to conduct a background check on the prospective purchaser in order to prevent handgun purchases by felons, the mentally incompetent, or others who should not have handguns, and second, to provide a cooling-off period for those who seek to buy and perhaps use a handgun in a fit of temper or rage. On its face such a procedure certainly represents a modest degree of government regulation, for it merely postpones a handgun purchase by a few days and denies handguns only to those who everyone agrees should not have them. Yet the ground being fought over in the bitter power struggle between regulation opponents and proponents was far less important than the struggle itself.[41]

Act One

The Brady bill was introduced in early 1987 in the Senate by Howard Metzenbaum and in the House by Representative Edward F. Feighan (D-OH). It quickly became the top priority of HCI and Sarah Brady, James Brady's wife and the HCI leader. The NRA opposed the measure, saying that it would simply be a prelude to stronger regulation, that it would not stop criminals from getting guns, and that it merely inconvenienced those entitled to guns. As late as the mid-1970s, however, the NRA had supported such a waiting period. This change can be taken as one example of the NRA's increasingly hard line on any and all gun controls.

The Brady bill was put up to a chamber-wide vote for the first time in the House in September 1988, when opponents led by the NRA succeeded in defeating the bill (by substituting an NRA-backed amendment for the waiting period, approved by a vote of 228 to 182), despite a concerted effort by HCI and a coalition of police organizations called the Law Enforcement Steering Committee. By its own account, the NRA spent between $1.5 million and $3 million in the successful effort to kill the bill, mostly on a media campaign and grassroots efforts. Assessing the failed effort, Representative Feighan noted that at least two dozen House members had privately spoken of their support for the bill but had refused to vote for it, not because they feared losing their seats but because of "the aggravation" that accompanied opposing the NRA (what was discussed in chapter 4 as the "hassle factor").[42]

Act Two

Two years later both chambers voted to approve the Brady bill. Initial House approval for a seven-day waiting period came in May 1991 (by a 239–186 vote), with Senate approval (by a 71–26 vote) following a month later. Before passing the Brady bill, the House defeated an NRA-backed substitute, sponsored by Representative Harley O. Staggers (D-WV), that called instead for an instant computerized background check of prospective handgun purchasers. Such a system would, in theory, eliminate the need for waiting yet still bar gun purchases by those not eligible.

The problem with such a proposal at the time was that successful operation of such a system required that pertinent records from all the states be fully automated. Yet in 1991 only ten states had such automation; eight states still handled files manually, and nine states did not even maintain the necessary felony records. Moreover, according to an analysis by Congress's Office of Technology Assessment, the time lapse between the conclusion of a criminal case and its logging in state records runs from weeks to months. Thus, the actual development of a viable system would take years and would cost hundreds of millions of dollars. The political strategy behind the Staggers proposal was based on the principle that a motion is easier to defeat if the opposition has something to offer in its place. By proposing an alternative of little or no feasibility, the NRA and its allies were offering a plan that seemed to offer a meaningful reform yet posed no actual change in gun-purchasing procedures for many years to come.[43] The Staggers proposal became Brady bill opponents' chief rallying point.

The Senate version, approved in June 1991, differed from that of the House in two important respects. First, it called for a five-day, instead of a seven-day, waiting period. Second, the Brady provision was attached to an omnibus crime bill, over which the two chambers wrangled throughout the year.

A conference version was hammered out in November that rolled the Brady provision (with a five-day waiting period) and a compromise crime bill together. The House narrowly approved that bill on November 27. The Senate finally brought the compromise bill to the floor for a vote on March 19, 1992, but Republicans used the unique Senate device of the filibuster (i.e., unlimited debate) to force bill sponsors to withdraw the measure after a vote to end debate (to invoke "cloture") failed. Such a cloture vote to end a filibuster poses a special problem because it requires an extraordinary majority of sixty votes to pass instead of the normal majority of fifty-one required for most Senate actions.

Democratic leaders brought the bill back a second time in the fall, but the failure to end a second filibuster in a vote on October 2 killed the bill. Majority Leader George Mitchell (D-ME) also attempted unsuccessfully to force a separate vote on a seven-day waiting period. By this point, however, concern over the impending elections overshadowed further efforts.

President Bush publicly opposed the Brady bill throughout 1991 and 1992 but linked it with the larger crime bill, saying that he would sign the measure even if Brady was included—but only if the larger crime bill was to his liking. Bush's veto threat hung over the bill, yet it also opened the door to presidential approval because it provided a means whereby he could have signed the measure into law without seeming to abandon his inclination to oppose most gun control measures entirely. In the end Bush's qualified veto threat had little effect on the outcome except to the extent that it buttressed the cause of Senate Republicans, who succeeded in blocking the measure.[44]

Act Three

The Brady bill struggle climaxed in 1993 when supporters promoted a five-business-day waiting period. House Judiciary Committee approval was won on November 4, despite the objections of committee chair and gun control opponent Jack Brooks, who also boosted the bill's chances by consenting with reluctance to separate the measure (HR 1025) from a new crime bill. Six days later the full House approved the Brady bill after fending off several amendments (sponsored by Republicans and Representative Brooks) designed to weaken the bill. One such amendment, to phase out the waiting period after five years, was adopted. The final vote to pass the bill (HR 1025) was 238 to 189.

Following the lead of the House, the Senate separated the Brady bill (S 414) from the larger crime package. The bill faced a Republican filibuster almost immediately, but an agreement between the political party leaders to allow floor consideration of a substitute version that included two NRA-backed provisions forestalled this move. The first called for the federal five-day waiting period to supersede all state waiting periods (twenty-four states had waiting periods of varying lengths in 1993; twenty-three also had background checks). This was objectionable to Brady supporters because many states had waiting periods longer than five days, and the move was seen as a violation of states' rights. This amendment was stricken from the bill by a Senate floor vote. The second measure, added to the bill successfully, called for ending the five-day waiting period after five years. The Senate then faced another filibuster, which looked as though it would be fatal to the bill. Brady supporters and congressional allies all conceded that the bill was dead for the year. The postmortems proved to be premature, however; within a couple of days, on November 20, the Republicans decided to end their opposition, sensing a rising tide of impatience and the inability to win further concessions from Democratic leaders. The bill was passed that day by a 63–36 vote.[45] The bill then went to a contentious House-Senate conference on November 22. The House passed the conference version early the following morning. Senate Republican leader Robert Dole, however, balked at the compromise, calling it unacceptable. Senate Democratic leader George Mitchell threatened to reconvene the Senate after the Thanksgiving break in order to obtain final action. The two finally reached an accommodation, and the bill was approved in the Senate by voice vote on November 24, with a promise to consider several modifications in early 1994. President Clinton signed the Brady Handgun Violence Prevention Act (PL 103–159; 107 *Stat.* 1536) into law on November 30.

As enacted, the Brady law codified a five-business-day waiting period for handgun purchases. It also authorized $200 million per year to help states improve and upgrade their computerization of criminal records, increased federal firearms license fees from $30 to $200 for the first three years and $90 for renewals, made it a federal crime to steal firearms from licensed dealers, barred package labeling for guns being shipped (to deter theft), required that state and local police be told of multiple handgun sales, and stated that police must make a "reasonable effort" to check the backgrounds of gun buyers.

Foes of the Brady law, including the NRA, challenged its constitutionality, not as a violation of the Second Amendment but as a violation of states' rights under the Tenth Amendment. In 1997 a sharply divided Supreme Court struck down the provision of the Brady law requiring local police to conduct background checks. In a 5–4 ruling in the case of *Printz v. US* (521 US 898), the Court held that Congress had overstepped its power, violating state police power. The ruling did not challenge the propriety of barring handgun sales to those with criminal backgrounds or those deemed mentally incompetent. In the aftermath of the case, President Clinton urged the states to continue to conduct the background checks voluntarily.

After the Brady law went into effect, several surveys verified that the law was operating as expected. In its first three years the law blocked about 250,000 gun sales. In addition, the increase in license fees for gun dealers decreased the number of dealers, from 285,000 before the law to 224,000 one year later (about 80 percent of these dealers were individuals with no storefront). By 1996 the number of licensed dealers had dropped to about 103,000; by 2007 there were about 50,000 licensed dealers. In 2013, there were about 65,000 dealers.[46] In 1998 the five-day waiting period lapsed, as per the terms of the law, and was replaced by the FBI's National Instant Criminal Background Check System (NICS). This system is designed to allow an immediate background check to occur. The check must be completed within three days, but over 95 percent of the background checks are completed within seconds, according to the FBI. From 1994 to 2000 almost six hundred thousand handgun purchases were blocked as the result of background checks. In 2000, twenty-six states conducted their own background checks; the rest relied on FBI data. By 2008 about 1.8 million handgun sales had been blocked (about 2 percent of all handgun purchases). In 2009 the government passed its 100 millionth background check. By 2013, 180 million background checks had been conducted and more than 2 million sales blocked. State checks resulted in a slightly higher rejection rate, probably owing to better and more complete state data. Even though the national government no longer requires waiting periods, nineteen states have their own, ranging from a few days to several months. These states are Alabama, California, Connecticut, Florida, Illinois, Indiana, Kansas, Maryland, Massachusetts, Minnesota, Missouri, New Jersey, New York, North Carolina, Ohio, Rhode Island, South Dakota, Washington, and Wisconsin. Control proponents have argued for a restoration of a national three-day waiting period, in part because of the perceived value of a cooling-off period before handgun purchases.

One area of gun sales continued to be omitted from nationally mandated background checks. In most places "secondary market" gun sales by unlicensed individuals can occur without background checks. Generally referred to as the gun show loophole, these sales at gun shows, flea markets, and other unregulated venues account for as much as 40 percent of gun sales. As of 2008, seventeen states required background checks for all handgun purchases, even those from unlicensed sellers. Since 2004 federal law has required the destruction of background check data within twenty-four hours (known as the Tiahrt Amendment, named after Representative Todd Tiahrt [R-KS], who sponsored the measure), making it unavailable for law enforcement examination.

One nagging problem related to the NICS system was resolved in 2007. In the wake of the Virginia Tech State University shooting in April 2007, when a mentally unstable student shot and killed thirty-three people (see introduction), many were outraged because a loophole in reporting practices in Virginia resulted in the shooter's ability to legally purchase two handguns despite having been judged mentally incompetent by a judge. In fact, only twenty-two states submitted mental health records to the federal NICS system at the time, as the Brady law did not penalize noncomplying states. As a result, and in a moment of unprecedented cooperation, the NRA and the Brady Campaign combined forces to support a bill in Congress to improve state record keeping and enforce compliance. The result was the NICS Improvement Amendments Act of 2007 (PL 110-180). Signed by President Bush in January 2008, the law now requires all states to submit appropriate mental health records and also provided a procedure whereby those judged mentally incompetent to own a firearm could petition to have the right restored. In addition, it provided federal funding to help states come into full compliance with record keeping and reporting requirements. Congress considered further action to again improve record gathering and reporting relating to mental incompetence and guns in 2011 in the aftermath of the shooting of Representative Gabrielle Giffords (D-AZ) in Tucson by a deranged man (see the introduction).

Yet another problem drew public attention in 2011. Even though the Brady law barred those judged mentally incompetent from acquiring guns, no systematic procedures existed to take guns from those who purchased them legally but who were later judged incompetent. The problem was illustrated dramatically when a California man with mental problems, Roy Perez, shot and killed his mother, a neighbor, and the neighbor's daughter in 2008. Perez had purchased a Glock handgun legally in 2004 but was later held involuntarily for psychiatric evaluation, a step that disqualified him from gun ownership. Yet overwhelmed police had had few resources to follow up in such cases. According to the state, in 2011 over 18,000 Californians owned guns that they were no longer legally eligible to have, and only a handful of states even possessed the data necessary to track down the estimated 180,000 people nationwide who fall into the same category.[47]

Political Assessment

The political consequences of the Brady law far outstripped its policy consequences. As noted earlier, no gun control measure was put to a vote in either house from 1972 until 1988 (not including McClure-Volkmer, which was a measure to lift gun controls). From 1988 through 1993, eight floor votes were taken on the Brady bill alone (five were votes in favor, three were against; four in the House and four in the Senate). A crucial swing in favor of the Brady bill occurred in the House between 1988 and 1991. About thirty-five House members actually switched their votes to support the bill, citing repugnance at the NRA's continued strong-arm tactics and the modest nature of the regulation being proposed. In addition, the 1991 House vote helped to deflate the NRA's image of invulnerability. According to Representative Charles E. Schumer (D-NY), a Brady supporter, "people realized that there's life after voting against the NRA."[48]

The common partisan pattern observed in other gun bill votes emerged here as well. More Democrats than Republicans supported the Brady bill, but both parties were split. In the House 184 Democrats supported Brady and 69 were opposed (77 percent Democratic support); the Republican split was 54 in favor and 119 opposed (31 percent Republican support). Northern Democrats provided the greatest support for Brady (82 percent); Southern Democrats provided the lowest Democratic support (55 percent).[49] As has been true with other gun bill votes, the strongest opposition came from Southern, Western, and rural representatives (rural districts are concentrated in the South and West), regardless of party. The strongest support came from urban representatives.

As was true of the other gun bills analyzed in this chapter, consideration of the Brady bill was fraught with contention from beginning to end. The version passed in 1993 had ten roll-call votes in the House and five in the

Senate. Consideration was marked by intense lobbying, numerous filibusters in the Senate (despite its reputation, the filibuster is still relatively unusual), many attempts to amend the bill, use of conference committees, and limited presidential influence.

Outside Congress, popular support for the Brady bill continued to swell, especially as concerns over crime once again rose. Moreover, leaders of all ideological stripes voiced Brady bill support, including former presidents Nixon, Ford, Carter, and Reagan, as well as conservatives such as William F. Buckley.

The election of Bill Clinton put a president in the White House who was much more sympathetic to the aims of gun control proponents. Still, even though the bill's near passage in 1992 clearly suggested that time for enactment had come, Clinton's primary focus in his campaign and his first year in office was on a plethora of domestic policy issues other than gun control. Indeed, many of Clinton's people were caught by surprise when Clinton began to aggressively promote gun control in late 1993.[50]

Finally, passage of the Brady law did have one effect predicted by the NRA: it opened the door to further regulations, to the extent that it showed the NRA could be beaten and depicted it as an extremist organization opposed to any regulation, no matter how modest or limited. Similarly, enactment was empowering for the Brady Campaign, police organizations, and others fighting for the control cause. But control opponents renewed their commitment to block further regulation and reaffirmed their resolve to fight on.[51] As the public turned its attention to other matters, the likelihood that further significant controls would be enacted began to diminish. Commenting on the NRA's continued ability to apply political pressure, one member of Congress noted that "it's a lobby that can put 15,000 letters in your district overnight and have people in your town hall meetings interrupting you."[52]

The Post-Columbine Reaction

The April 20, 1999, massacre at Columbine High School in Littleton, Colorado, was the most shocking in a series of high school shootings that occurred in the late 1990s (see chapter 3). In the aftermath of the incident, national shock and outrage put unprecedented pressure on Congress to respond. Senate leadership, headed by gun control foe Trent Lott (R-MO), seemed unsure about the Senate's mood on the issue, but, yielding to pressure, Lott advanced a juvenile justice bill to which were added several gun control measures. On May 12 the Senate rejected a measure to require background checks for gun show sales, but two days later the Senate reversed itself and adopted the measure, although it was not as strong as Democratic leaders had sought. That same day the Senate rejected a measure to bar Internet sales of guns by unlicensed dealers. On May 20 the Senate passed a bill that would have required background checks to occur within three days for firearms purchases at gun shows, flea markets, and pawn shops (closing the so-called gun show loophole); revoked gun ownership for those convicted of gun crimes as juveniles; toughened penalties for juvenile offenders who used guns in crimes and also for those who provided such guns to juveniles; and required locking devices or boxes to be sold with all new handgun purchases. The bill also would have blocked legal immunity to those who sold guns to felons, and it would have banned the import of high-capacity bullet magazines (those that could hold more than ten bullets). The final version included a tougher background check provision than had been added by Republicans on May 14, and the bill was adopted by an unusual 51–50 vote, when Vice President Al Gore, as president of the Senate, cast the tie-breaking vote for the amendment. The final package was approved by a 73–25 vote. As a measure of shifting sentiment, the Senate had defeated attempts to require gun locks and ban the import of high-capacity magazines the previous year.

Columbine Fizzles

The bill passed by the Senate met a chilly reception in the House of Representatives, although the initial reactions of House Speaker Dennis Hastert (R-IL) and House Judiciary Committee chair Henry Hyde (R-IL) were positive, as both expressed support for many of the elements of the package. Yet Republican House leaders had long records of opposition to stronger gun laws, and House majority whip Tom DeLay (R-TX) led the NRA-backed counterattack. By early June House majority leader Dick Armey (R-TX) and DeLay had publicly broken with Hastert, vowing to defeat the measure. After several weeks of bargaining and delay, during which time control foes marshaled their resources, the House took three decisive floor votes on June 18. The first vote narrowly approved (218–211) a weakened gun control package that was sponsored by former NRA board member John Dingell (D-MI) and drafted with the guidance of the NRA. This version would have weakened the gun show background check system and opened the door to the interstate sale of handguns, thereby rolling back a restriction that had been on the books for thirty years. The second vote defeated (193–235) a version similar to the tougher Senate-passed bill sponsored by Representative Carolyn McCarthy (D-NY). The final vote on the overall gun package was defeated (147–280) by a coalition of procontrol representatives who considered the bill too weak and anticontrol representatives who opposed any new controls. The House thus sent to a House-Senate conference committee a juvenile justice bill without any gun control provisions. The bill was never reconciled with the Senate version, and thus the legislation died. After the 2007 Virginia Tech shooting (mentioned earlier), Congress did act to improve record keeping, but this action occurred with the cooperation of both the NRA and the Brady Campaign, a highly unusual action that did not presage any change in Congress's heightened opposition to new gun control legislation.

Political Assessment

House stalling tactics gave foes of the bill, led by the NRA, the time they needed to mobilize opposition and hope for declining public interest as schools let out, families went on vacation, and the country's attention began to turn to other matters. From mid-May to mid-June the NRA spent $750,000 on mass mailings and $300,000 on phone banks. HCI spent about $350,000 on similar activities. Part of the effort to defeat the new measure included diverting attention away from gun control measures and toward issues of media violence. Still, passage of the Senate bill marked the first successful effort to pass any new gun law since 1994, indicating the effect of public pressure. Following on the contentious political patterns of the other bills discussed in this chapter, chamber leaders were able to exercise relatively little control; committee preeminence, a hallmark of congressional activity, was contradicted, in that committee preferences were altered or overturned on the floor. Extended and heated debate, numerous votes, procedural wrangling, and intense political pressures all marked the politics of this effort.[53]

Lawsuit Protection for Gun Manufacturers

From the time of the election of George W. Bush as president in 2000, the National Rifle Association's top legislative priority was to obtain legislation to protect the gun industry and gun dealers from litigation. For several decades sporadic lawsuits had been filed against gun manufacturers seeking damages to compensate gun-crime victims. The legal basis for such actions is the tort law principle that individuals or other entities can be held responsible for selling products that, although legal, needlessly or willfully expose others to great risk of harm. For example, the Ford Motor Company was held civilly liable in the 1970s for its design and production of the Ford Pinto because the Pinto's gas tank was located in such a way that the car was likely to explode when hit from behind. The poor design feature was not illegal, but Ford executives knew of the defect and sold millions of the cars anyway.

In lawsuits regarding guns, litigants argued that handgun manufacturers knew that, because of their sales and distribution practices, a disproportionate number of their guns wound up in criminal hands (leading to claims of "negligent distribution practices"). In addition, the failure of some companies to install simple and inexpensive safety features yielded additional legal charges. For example, the installation of a fifty-cent part on some types of handguns could save lives by preventing the gun from being fired if the bullet magazine or clip were removed even when a bullet remains in the chamber.[54]

Such litigation met with limited success until 1999. In the landmark case of *Hamilton v. Accu-Tek,* a Brooklyn jury awarded money damages to families of gun violence victims based on the claim that several gun manufacturers, whose guns had been used in the shootings, had been negligent in their marketing and distribution practices, such that the companies had reason to believe that their guns would be obtained and used by criminals. Although the verdict was eventually overturned on appeal, it encouraged a spate of new lawsuits against gun manufacturers and dealers around the country. More than thirty cities brought similar suits. Among the best-known cases was a $433 million suit brought by the city of Chicago against gun dealers located just outside of the city limits who were caught on videotape illegally selling numerous guns to undercover officers dressed as gang members. These cases were strengthened when a government report was released in 1999 revealing that in the previous three years, 0.3 percent of gun dealers were responsible for the sale of over 57 percent of guns used in crimes committed during this period. In 2007, 57 percent of guns used in crimes were traced back to 1 percent of all gun dealers. Clearly, some dealers were far more responsible in their sales practices than others.[55]

A case in point was successful litigation against Bushmaster Firearms Inc. of Windham, Maine, and Bull's Eye Shooter Supply store of Tacoma, Washington. In 2002, two men were arrested (and later convicted) for committing ten fatal sniper shootings in the Washington, DC, area. One of the men purchased the gun they used, a .223 Bushmaster rifle (a slightly altered, civilian version of the military M-16), at Bull's Eye. Subsequent investigations revealed that at least 238 guns "disappeared" from the shop—that is, investigators assumed that at least some of the guns had been sold without proper paperwork. Among the 238 missing guns was the one used in the shooting spree. The Tacoma gun store agreed to pay $2 million to eight plaintiffs; Bushmaster agreed to pay $550,000. The gun company's liability was based on the assumption that it could have required the store to implement simple security measures by threatening to withdraw its stock.[56]

Gun control foes decried this litigation, arguing that it was an abuse of the civil justice system that would only bankrupt gun manufacturers and pad lawyers' bank accounts and that it amounted to back-door gun control. Supporters argued that some in the gun industry were, indeed, culpable and that they should be subject to the same civil law standards as rogue companies in other areas. And they argued against granting any special protection to the gun industry by pointing out that no other business sector enjoyed similar protections. Indeed, litigation proponents were emboldened by a similar effort against cigarette manufacturers, who agreed to pay major settlement costs because of a variety of deceptive and improper practices related to the chemical manipulation and marketing practices pertaining to cigarettes. NRA efforts to legislate gun manufacturer immunity were not limited to Congress, however. By 2005 thirty-three states had also passed laws barring such lawsuits by localities (called "preemption" laws).[57]

Yet the public had, at best, mixed feelings about such litigation efforts aimed at perceived industry wrongdoing, and Republican leaders highly sympathetic to the gun lobby controlled both Congress and the presidency. In 2003 momentum to provide federal liability protection finally resulted in passage of a bill by the House of Representatives. The Senate was slower to act, but in March 2004 it was poised to approve the same bill. Gun control proponents, however, after failing to block the bill, managed to attach to it amendments to extend the assault-weapons ban (by a 52–47 vote), slated to expire that September, to require background checks for all gun purchases at gun shows (closing the so-called gun show loophole, added by a 53–46 vote), and to require safety locks to be sold with new handguns (approved 70–27). Infuriated, NRA leaders insisted that the bill be defeated rather than accept the "poison pill" amendments; within hours it failed by a vote of 8–90.

The failure of the 108th Congress to enact the bill was remedied in the 109th. Fortified with an increase in Republicans in both houses, in July 2005 the Senate passed the measure by a 65–31 vote, partly thanks to key support from fourteen gun-sympathetic Democrats, including Minority Leader Harry Reid of Nevada. Senate majority leader Bill Frist of Tennessee avoided the problems from the previous year by employing a procedural tactic to limit amendments. The measure also got a lift when officials in the American military sent a letter to Congress in July saying that companies providing weapons to the military needed to be protected for national security reasons. The House passed the bill in October by a 283–144 vote. The bill passed with bipartisan support from 223 Republicans and 60 Democrats; voting against were 140 Democrats and 4 Republicans.[58] As passed and signed by the president, the Protection of Lawful Commerce in Arms Act of 2005 (PL 109-92; 119

Stat. 2095) bars civil suits against gun manufacturers, distributors, dealers, and importers of firearms and ammunition, although it makes an exception for certain cases involving defective guns or expressly criminal behavior by manufacturers or dealers, as, for example, when a gun is knowingly sold to someone not legally entitled to own a gun. The immediate effect of the law was to halt more than a dozen ongoing cases in states around the country. The law did not affect cases that had already been resolved. The measure also included a requirement that handguns be sold with locks, and it barred the manufacture or importation of armor-piercing bullets. In the aftermath of winning this unique protection for the gun industry, other businesses lobbied Congress to win similar immunity.

Sandy Hook

On the morning of December 14, 2012, twenty-year-old Adam Lanza shot and killed his mother as she lay in bed asleep, using a gun she owned. Lanza had lived with his mother in her Newtown, Connecticut, home but had not spoken with her in two years, insisting that they communicate by email only. Lanza had exhibited significant mental health problems for many years and, among other things, had been obsessed with stories of past mass shootings. All of the guns Lanza had in his possession on that day belonged legally to his mother, who had been an avid shooter. She had tried to interest her son in shooting as a way to bond with him. After killing his mother, Lanza drove to nearby Sandy Hook Elementary School, taking four of his mother's guns with him. He entered the school, shooting out its glass front entrance and proceeded into the building, where he shot and killed twenty elementary school children, as well as six adult teachers and staff, using a Bushmaster XM15-E2S .223-caliber semiautomatic assault rifle along with several thirty-bullet magazines. He fired 154 shots in less than five minutes. All of those killed were shot with the assault rifle and each was shot at least three times. About a minute after the first police arrived, Lanza shot and killed himself with a 10mm Glock handgun. He also had another handgun with him, a 9mm Sig Sauer, which he did not fire. Additionally, a 12-gauge semiautomatic shotgun was found in Lanza's car, which he also did not use in the killings. No motive for the attack was ever established.[59]

The Sandy Hook shooting followed several other senseless mass shootings that had occurred in the previous months, yet the pointless, savage cruelty of such violence directed at children shocked the nation in a way recent past shootings had not. The last mass shooting to have a similarly traumatizing effect on the country was the 1999 Columbine High School shooting. For President Barack Obama, as for many newly mobilized because of this event, this was a watershed moment. During his first term, Obama had largely avoided the gun issue, but after a convincing re-election campaign the previous month, bringing with it a renewed electoral mandate, and his January inauguration and the State of the Union both in sight, Obama decided to move on the issue. Within days of the shooting, Obama appointed Vice President Joe Biden to head a task force to study the gun issue and make recommendations for change. Within a month, the group presented its report, calling for universal background checks for gun purchases, restrictions on assault weapons and high-capacity bullet magazines, mental health and school safety initiatives, increased funding for police protection in schools, and stronger measures to stop straw gun purchases and gun trafficking. In mid-January, Obama also issued nineteen executive orders to enhance and fund research on gun violence, improve federal gun trafficking databases, examine gun safety measures, and other steps involving federal agencies.

The measure was first taken up in the Democratic-controlled Senate, with bill supporters hoping that passage of at least some of the bills would pressure the Republican-controlled House to at least take up the measure. In March 2013, the Senate Judiciary Committee approved measures to criminalize straw gun purchases, a uniform background check measure, and an assault-weapons ban. At about this time, a junior member of the Senate, Joe Manchin (D-WV) took up the cause of championing some version of a gun bill, partly at the behest of more-liberal Senate leaders who felt that a more-conservative sponsor would give the bill greater legitimacy. Manchin was considered one of the most-conservative Democrats in the Senate, was a gun owner, and had been endorsed by the NRA throughout his thirty-year political career. Yet, he broke with the NRA in this effort. He persuaded Pennsylvania Republican Pat Toomey—who had been elected with the help of over a million dollars from the NRA—to cosponsor the measure. The Manchin-Toomey bill that emerged in April called for universal background checks for gun purchases, including gun show and Internet sales, excepting transfers to relatives and friends, and it facilitated the gathering of mental health and other relevant data from the states to be submitted to the national background check (NICS) database. Yet, it also reduced the background check waiting period from seventy-two hours to forty-eight hours (if no report came back within that time, the gun sales would go through); made interstate transport of weapons easier; allowed interstate sale of handguns from licensed dealers; made the use of gun records for creating a registry a felony; and established a national commission on mass violence. Throughout this period, bill advocates, including

Judiciary Committee Chair Pat Leahy (D-VT) and Manchin, worked closely with representatives of the NRA; indeed, the provisions added to expand gun access came at the behest of the NRA. While the gun group did not trumpet its involvement, the Manchin-Toomey bill was constructed with, and won the quiet approval of, the NRA.[60]

Almost immediately, however, word of the compromise bill and the NRA's role leaked out on gun-rights websites, and gun groups hostile to the NRA, such as the Gun Owners of America and the National Association for Gun Rights, began to pummel the NRA for selling out the cause. Within days, NRA leaders ceased communicating with Manchin; shortly thereafter, they announced their opposition to the bill, vowing to do everything they could to defeat it. On April 17, the full Senate voted on seven gun-related measures; each needed to garner sixty votes—not a simple majority of fifty-one—because at the time, a bill could only proceed if it first received sixty votes, which was enough votes to end debate (called invoking cloture). The Manchin-Toomey bill thus garnered majority support, but still failed, by a vote of fifty-four in favor and forty-six against. A separate measure to ban assault weapons, championed by Senator Dianne Feinstein (D-CA), failed 40–60; the magazine limits bill failed 46–54; the straw-purchase gun trafficking bill failed 58–42. The NRA trumpeted the bills' defeat as a great victory for gun rights, but never mentioned to its membership that it had helped craft the bill that it later helped defeat. Bill supporters decried the NRA, noting that public opinion polls consistently showed that 90 percent of Americans supported universal background checks.[61]

As noted, Senate passage was no guarantee that the bill would have made its way to the president's desk. In fact, as the Senate was working on these measures, House Republican leaders advanced four measures to roll back gun regulations, including provisions to bar the Bureau of Alcohol, Tobacco, Firearms, and Explosives (ATF) from requiring gun dealers to conduct annual inventories of their stock to make sure that guns had not been lost, stolen, or improperly sold; to broaden the definition of guns that could be imported into the United States; to prevent the ATF from canceling a gun dealer's license for lack of business; and to add a disclaimer to government gun data saying that it could not be used to draw conclusions about gun crimes.

Three political reactions emerged from this tumultuous political moment. First, gun rights groups extolled their victory. Second, gun control groups redoubled their efforts. Third, legislative activity exploded throughout the United States: in 2013, twenty states enacted tougher gun laws, while twenty-seven states loosened gun regulations; some states enacted both types of measures.[62]

The Bureau of Alcohol, Tobacco, Firearms, and Explosives

The ATF traces its history back to 1791, when Treasury Secretary Alexander Hamilton created a tax on spirits that had to be collected by the department. That tax was ended in 1802 but was reintroduced to help finance the Civil War. Even then, the department had to hire people to track down tax evaders. In 1919 the enactment of Prohibition prompted the creation of the Prohibition Unit, which then became the Bureau of Prohibition, still part of the Treasury Department. (It was under this office that Elliot Ness of *Untouchables* fame operated in the 1920s and 1930s.) The unit became the Alcohol Tax Unit when Prohibition ended in 1933. The unit was renamed the Alcohol and Tobacco Tax Division in 1951, when it was given jurisdiction over newly instituted tobacco taxes. (By this time it was a part of the Internal Revenue Service [IRS] in the Treasury Department.) Although first gaining jurisdiction over guns in 1942, arising from the gun regulations enacted in the 1930s, the agency was given important additional jurisdiction over guns—and its current title—in 1968 as a result of the Gun Control Act of that year, which required the ATF to issue licenses to firearms dealers and oversee proper record keeping. In 1972 the ATF was transferred from the IRS and given bureau status within the Treasury. In 2003, the ATF was moved to the Department of Justice as part of the reorganization of homeland security-related agencies.[63]

Although the bureau's headquarters are located in Washington, DC, its operations are relatively decentralized, as most ATF personnel operate from regional offices around the country. The bureau is organized into two sections: regulatory enforcement and criminal enforcement. Matters dealing with gun regulations, including licensing, gun tracing, illegal firearms transport and possession, and explosives, are handled by criminal enforcement. Although long involved in criminal investigations, the ATF possesses neither the size nor the reputation of other federal law enforcement agencies such as the FBI or the Secret Service. Virtually no other government agency is subject to the same degree of vilification and denigration by gun groups.

The central political question regarding the ATF's enforcement activities revolves around two contradictory charges. The NRA and its allies charge that the ATF ruthlessly and arbitrarily harasses honest gun owners and dealers and that the agency is a loose cannon. Thus, the NRA has publicly and repeatedly attacked the ATF over the years. In the late 1970s and early 1980s this campaign against the ATF became both mean and angry. In a 1981 NRA-produced film called *It Can Happen Here*, ATF agents were depicted as "Nazi gestapos" and "jackbooted fascists."[64] During congressional hearings the following year Representative John Dingell, also an NRA board member, called ATF agents "knaves and rogues," saying, "I would love to put them in jail. I would dearly love it." He continued, "I think they [the agents] are evil."[65] The demonizing of the ATF reached a fever pitch in the mid-1990s, as the NRA and other opponents tarred the agency with claims of murder and persecution of allegedly innocent citizens. In a full-page newspaper ad run in several national papers in March 1995, the NRA said that the ATF "deserves public contempt." Representative Harold Volkmer called the ATF "one of the most Rambo-rogue law enforcement agencies in the United States." In one instance, radio talk show host G. Gordon Liddy counseled his listeners to fire "head shots" at ATF agents who approached them because "they've [the agents] got a vest underneath." In 1995 more than one hundred ATF agents received death threats, which in some instances included threats against agents' children. Many attributed these vituperative attacks to the NRA's bellicose rhetoric, even suggesting that such rhetoric might have contributed to extremist actions, including the bombing of the federal office building in Oklahoma City in 1995. A former NRA board member, David Edmondson, said of the NRA's attacks on the ATF that "I think these ads, which are going in a direction of radicalism and the militias, are embarrassing to the traditional market of the N.R.A.—Joe Gun Owner."[66]

In contrast, gun control proponents and others have argued that the ATF is a weak and relatively ineffective agency that has been buffeted by the prevailing political winds, especially those stirred up by the NRA. The multiple and relatively unpopular goals of the agency carve out a difficult bureaucratic mission. And given the characteristics of social regulatory agencies, we would expect agency behavior to conform more closely to this view than to that of ATF critics.

ATF Performance

Much of the reputed laxity of ATF enforcement can be traced to its stated objective of relying on voluntary compliance with many of the laws it is charged with enforcing. Yet the enforcement problem predates even the ATF's modern incarnation.

During congressional hearings in 1965, for example, Treasury Department officials acknowledged that only five employees were assigned full time to enforce the 1934 and 1938 gun laws. In the previous thirty years the department had obtained only one conviction involving the improper mailing of firearms to individuals in states that required purchase permits. An ATF representative reported that during 1980 the bureau had conducted only 103 investigations of firearms dealers and that only ten dealer licenses had been revoked. In 1985 the ATF fielded only 400 inspectors to monitor what were then more than

200,000 gun dealers. In 1994 about 250 agents were responsible for overseeing 280,000 dealers, and then-ATF director Steve Higgins testified to Congress that, with existing understaffing problems, it would take the agency 750 years to conduct background checks on all new federal firearms license applicants. From 1972 to 2005 the ATF averaged fewer than twenty license revocations per year; throughout the 2000s corrupt gun dealers who violated criminal laws were almost never prosecuted.[67]

To cite a different kind of regulatory lapse, in 1979 the ATF's firearms technology branch examined the Ingram MAC-10 pistol and recommended that it be classified as a machine gun. This classification would have placed strict controls on the weapon under the National Firearms Act of 1934, but the agency's firearms classification panel overturned the recommendation, instead putting it in the semiautomatic category, thereby freeing it from significant regulation. At the time fewer than one thousand of these weapons had been produced. But in the next three years production increased and the weapon was used in a variety of crimes, including the murder of a Missouri state trooper. In 1982 the ATF reassessed the status of the weapon and this time classified it as a machine gun (the weapon is easily converted to either semi- or fully automatic use).[68] But in the reclassification process, ATF exempted the thirty-two thousand MAC-10s produced or sold before 1982. Subsequently, RPB Industries, Inc. in Texas has produced a variation of the MAC-10.

In the mid-1980s ATF and other government officials admitted that gun smuggling and other illegal gun trafficking, as well as the Firearms Owners Protection Act of 1986 (discussed earlier in this chapter), which limited the ATF to conducting one random inspections of a gun dealer per year—even dealers caught violating the law—had not been high enforcement priorities.[69] An investigation in 1994 found that the United States was a major source of illegal gun shipments to other countries, in part because the ATF lacked the personnel to monitor the country's then 280,000 gun dealers. The Associated Press reported that Colombian drug lords, Japanese gangsters, Croatian nationalists, Irish gunrunners, Argentine and Philippine rebels, and Mexican drug gangs were among many international groups that had obtained arms from the mostly unregulated US dealers. Government officials expressed concern that the illicit gun trade was on the verge of a significant expansion to nations of the former Soviet bloc.[70]

The Political Balancing Act

The key bureaucratic trait of the ATF is its dependence on executive branch superiors. Unlike other federal agencies, the ATF has no constituency to stand behind it in politically troubled times, nor does it possess statutory independence, as do independent regulatory agencies (for example, the Food and Drug Administration).

During the Carter administration political attacks on the ATF were largely fended off. In 1978, however, after the ATF announced plans to computerize its records to facilitate gun tracing—a task legally delegated to the agency—the NRA flooded Congress and the Treasury Department with angry mail aimed at what it labeled the "gun police." As a consequence, Congress denied ATF the $4.2 million appropriation to implement the program. When the ATF then said that it could still fund the program from other budget lines, Congress cut the agency's appropriation by that amount.[71] ATF opponents found an ally in Ronald Reagan, who moved early in 1981 to abolish the agency entirely, a fate avoided only because of the intervention of Treasury secretary Donald Regan, who did allow significant budget cuts. In the fall of 1981 Reagan proposed to shift some ATF responsibilities (such as tax collection) back to the IRS, with the ATF's special agents to be transferred to the Secret Service. At the time the ATF employed thirty-nine hundred people and had an operating budget of $160 million.

The proposal initially met with approval from the NRA and dismay from the ATF. One employee commented, "The N.R.A. has finally won." The agency director said that the ATF was being "destroyed by cuts that are in large measure due to the N.R.A. campaign against us."[72] Despite the initial outcry, the ATF's days seemed numbered until the NRA and its congressional allies realized that the cure might be worse than the disease (they were tipped off in part by the curious reticence of some gun control proponents to speak out against the plan). Instead of keeping gun control in the hands of a beleaguered, low-prestige agency, the new proposal would lodge this authority in the hands of the highly respected, efficient, and fully computerized Secret Service. Labels such as "jack-booted fascists" would never stick to the agency that guards the life of the president.

What followed was furious backpedaling. The plan was suddenly found to be "ill advised" and "unworkable." Representative Dingell claimed that the plan would sully whatever new agencies adopted the ATF mission and employees. "Mix dirty water with clean water ... and you get dirty water every time," he said. The plan was thus killed, although the agency underwent further budget cuts.[73] According to the *Congressional Quarterly,* the proposal died because it met with "fierce opposition from gun owners ... led by the National Rifle Association, a frequent harsh critic of the BATF."[74] The NRA's subsequent "shrill attacks" on the Reagan administration for continuing to promote the plan before the final agreement to kill it earned the ire of Reagan adviser Edwin Meese, among others.

By the end of Reagan's administration the ATF had grown to nearly the size it had maintained in the 1970s and had improved its reputation by successful investigations of abortion clinic bombings and crime activities of armed neo-Nazis and other extremist groups.[75] Even so, it still trod carefully where gun activities were concerned. For example, it stopped monitoring the thousands of gun shows held yearly around the country, despite the general acknowledgment that widespread illegal gun trafficking occurred at such shows. "If we wanted to," said ATF head Stephen Higgins, "we could go to a gun show and arrest people coming out and just line 'em up."[76]

Further, the ATF suffered a serious loss of prestige in 1993 over its handling of a raid in February on the heavily fortified and armed compound of the Branch Davidian cult near Waco, Texas. (Some have erroneously tied the ATF to the botched raid on Ruby Ridge, Idaho, in 1992, where the agency was not involved.) Four ATF agents were killed and twenty were wounded in an initial assault on the compound, leading to a two-month standoff. FBI agents eventually stormed the fortress, and the cult leader ordered the structure burned to the ground, killing nearly all of those inside. A subsequent report sharply criticized the ATF for mishandling the raid and then lying to cover up its mistakes. Later in 1993 Vice President Al Gore headed a committee that proposed merging the ATF into the FBI (along with the Drug Enforcement Agency). This time, the plan was motivated not by animus toward gun control but by concern for budget efficiency. The plan was dropped, however, and the new ATF director, former Secret Service director John Magaw, worked to improve agency morale and effectiveness. Magaw's organizational reforms and a backlash of sympathy for the agency after the Oklahoma City bombing (in which ATF agents were killed and which was also investigated by the ATF) helped the agency's reputation.[77]

The Clinton administration's support for gun controls meant an expanded mission for the ATF. In 1994, for example, ATF extended the prohibition on armor-piercing bullets to certain bullets that formerly could not be fired from handguns. Rapid-fire, "street sweeper" shotguns were subjected to strict ATF regulation on the directive of Treasury Secretary Lloyd Bentsen. Owners of the eighteen thousand such weapons in circulation were required to submit to registration, fingerprinting, and photographing (the weapon had been developed for military and riot-control purposes in South Africa). Dealers in such weapons were also subjected to new fees and regulations.[78]

Under the George W. Bush administration the ATF was renamed the Bureau of Alcohol, Tobacco, Firearms, and Explosives (although most references to the agency continued to use the acronym "ATF") to accommodate investigations related to explosives. Yet the agency underwent sharp budget cuts, despite the government's greater commitment to fighting terrorism after 9/11. This trend was consistent with the administration's general hostility to gun regulation and sympathy with the goals of the ATF-hostile NRA. In 2006 ATF director Carl J. Truscott was forced to resign amid allegations that he had expended extravagant sums of agency money on building construction, office furniture, and other building upgrades at a time when agency allocations for new cars, bulletproof vests, and other basic items were being cut. For the next seven years the ATF functioned without a permanent agency head, as the NRA and allies successfully opposed any nominee offered up to the Senate for confirmation until President Obama won approval of then-acting director Todd Jones as part of a deal with Senate Republicans to approve a package of nominees. By one account, the absence of a permanent agency head hampered the ATF's ability to monitor the ten thousand gun shops operating in America along the Mexican border that have become a primary source of assault weapons and other firearms that have fueled the escalating gang-led drug war in Mexico.[79]

The agency was pummeled for its botched handling of a covert operation dubbed Operation Fast and Furious when congressional committees launched what turned out to be over a dozen investigations, beginning in 2011 and spanning over four years. Fast and Furious was the name for the ATF's operation to trace illegal gun trafficking from the United States to Mexican gangs. Agents allowed about two thousand guns to cross into Mexico in order to trace their course and move against the trafficking ring. While law enforcement will sometimes allow illegal activity to occur (drug trafficking, for example) in order to ensnare an entire criminal network, as was the case here, some of the two thousand guns turned up at Mexican crime scenes, including two at the location where an American agent was killed. The operation, begun in 2009, was shut down at the end of 2010; the Bush administration had conducted a similar operation, Operation Wide Receiver, in 2007 and 2008. Again, the ATF suffered a black eye and a tarnished reputation.[80]

Political Assessment

The NRA's depiction of the ATF as an out-of-control agency that has exceeded its mandate is a claim that is virtually without foundation.[81] Although it has no doubt instituted some unjustified prosecutions (an inevitable consequence for any law enforcement agency), its overall record suggests a contrary conclusion. The exaggerated and even wild claims leveled by the NRA are explainable as (1) part of the NRA's political tactic of identifying and attacking an external "enemy" around which it can rally its partisans, (2) a political tactic to put the ATF on the defensive in an effort to hobble its watchdog activities, and (3) the NRA's longtime opposition to any and all government regulation of guns.

The ATF has labored under several bureaucratic and political handicaps. First, it has no native constituency to provide political support from outside the government. Similar agencies, such as the FBI, the Secret Service, and the CIA, are in similar circumstances, yet these agencies have been able to compensate for this political deficiency by building strong national reputations for crime fighting and national security work that have insulated them from budget cuts and political attacks. The smaller ATF (its 2013 budget was $1.15 billion, virtually unchanged from its $900 million from ten years earlier, but still only a fraction of the size of the FBI's) has generally been considered a "second-string" enforcement agency, dealing with less glamorous elements of law enforcement. This becomes clear when the ATF is compared with other federal law enforcement agencies, including the FBI, the Drug Enforcement Agency, the Secret Service, Immigration and Naturalization, and the Bureau of Customs. In 1970 the ATF had the fourth-largest budget; by 1995 it had the smallest budget of the six agencies.[82]

Second, the agency's disparate and seemingly marginal purposes have further undercut its bureaucratic standing. Stated more simply, an agency with a "glamorous" and clearly focused mission is more likely to be effective and respected than one whose mission is less well focused and less glamorous. Indeed, a key reason for the ATF's survival as a separate agency was that J. Edgar Hoover did not want agents whose job was tracking down illegal liquor to be a part of the FBI.[83] This problem is summarized by a derisive spinoff of the ATF's name: the Bureau of "Whiskey, Cigarettes, and Pistols."

Third, the agency lacks statutory independence, making it subject to the political preferences of the president and the secretary of the treasury. Thus, the agency's fortunes improved under sympathetic presidents such as Carter and Clinton and declined under less sympathetic presidents such as Reagan, yet it continued to suffer during the second Bush and Obama presidencies. Such a roller-coaster existence has undercut agency morale and therefore its effectiveness.

Fourth, the ATF does not possess the resources to do its job. For example, the agency is charged with regulating those who apply for and obtain federal firearms licenses (i.e., a license to deal in guns, which allows the dealer to obtain guns at wholesale prices through the mail and also exempts the dealer from background checks and waiting periods). The number of such licenses increased 59 percent from 1980 to 1993, yet the number of ATF inspectors actually dropped 13 percent during the same time. As a consequence, 90 percent of these applicants were never interviewed by an ATF inspector. In 1990 the ATF inspected only 2 percent of all gun dealers. Violations are frequently uncovered in the rare inspections that do occur, suggesting widespread violation of federal laws. Even with the dramatic drop in the number of licensed dealers, the ATF still lacks the necessary resources to conduct routine checks on most dealers. As of 2013, it employed five thousand people, roughly the same number it had in 1972. And the Firearms Owners Protection Act of 1986, discussed earlier, included a provision weakening the ATF's ability to regulate gun dealers, limiting them to one unannounced on-site visit per year, regardless of the dealer's past record. Even now, the ATF is barred by law from computerizing its records. Background checks are still conducted by hand, laboriously and slowly, sifting through microfiche and paper records, mostly at the ATF's National Tracing Center in Martinsburg, West Virginia. A routine trace takes about five days—a process that would take seconds by computer. In fact, when a gun is connected to a crime, the ATF must first call the gun's manufacturer to identify that gun's wholesaler, then contact that company by phone to trace the gun to the retail dealer, and will then search the dealer's files by hand (again, using paper records). The ATF is also barred from creating a database of what guns were sold to whom and when. When Obama asked for a report on lost and stolen firearms in the United States, a first-ever such report was delivered in 2013. It showed that the government had received information on over 190,000 lost and stolen firearms in 2012 alone, with 9 percent of these lost by licensed gun dealers; the actual number was considered much higher since there is considerable non-reporting of lost and stolen guns.[84]

Clearly, the ATF's inability to carry out the law encourages much suspicious gun trafficking. This has become a major problem along the Mexican-American border. From 2007 to early 2010, of 31,946 guns seized by the Mexican government, 80 percent came from the United States. In 2008 the Arizona attorney general charged a Phoenix gun dealer with selling more than seven hundred AK-47s and other guns to Mexican gang straw purchasers, but the case was dismissed because the state's law was so weak that any prosecution was virtually impossible. From 2007 to 2010 more than twenty-eight thousand people have been killed in Mexico in drug- and gang-related violence. Similarly, the ATF has been steadily pressured to de-emphasize gun control activities and concentrate instead on the war on drugs.[85] A close look at ATF appropriations patterns from 1970 to 1995 confirms this analysis, revealing that ATF appropriations have grown more slowly than those of other, comparable federal law enforcement agencies (including the FBI, Drug Enforcement Agency, Secret Service, Immigration, and Customs). As for charges that the ATF has recklessly used deadly force, a comparative analysis reveals that the ATF's record is no different from other federal law enforcement agencies' records. Further, federal law constrains the ATF more strictly than other federal law enforcement agencies. In short, "the ATF is not a powerful bureaucracy" but rather "the weak sister of federal law enforcement agencies."[86]

Like other agencies involved with social regulatory policy, its political opponents, congressional critics, and even others in the executive branch have whipsawed the ATF. Regardless of the course of future national gun control efforts, the ATF will continue to be subject to prevailing political winds.

Conclusion: Furious Politics, Marginal Policy

I noted at the start of this chapter that the proposal advanced by the Roosevelt administration in the 1930s, national gun registration, represented a far more ambitious policy goal than the celebrated (among control advocates) victory of proponents in the early 1990s, a waiting period for handgun purchases. These lowered policy objectives have resulted in the achievement of some legislative successes for control supporters. Yet the fury of gun politics has hardly abated. If anything, that fury has become more intense in recent decades, even though the policy turf has narrowed. As shown in Table 5.1, the scope of gun legislation has, if anything, narrowed over time. How do we explain the changes in policy focus from the 1930s to the 2000s and the divergent trends of sustaining-to-escalating political intensity versus the regressing policy objectives of control supporters?

The first and most important response is to underscore the common political traits of national institutions as they struggle with social regulatory policy. As expected, Congress has been the primary focal point for efforts to revise national gun policy. Presidents have maintained interest in gun issues but have played a relatively marginal role. The ATF has behaved as an agency besieged. Its fate has hung on the preferences and disposition of its sole political benefactors, the president and the secretary of the Treasury—since 2003, the Department of Justice and the attorney general. When dealing with social regulatory policy, the presidency, Congress, and the agency have assumed political roles that differ markedly from the common understanding of how these institutions behave; that is, the president leads, Congress follows, and federal agencies operate, within bounds, by their own discretion and organizational mission. That these three institutions behave in an entirely contrary fashion when it comes to gun control—Congress's role is preeminent, the president's role is marginal, and the federal agency is whipsawed by outside interests—speaks to the intractability of the issue and the power of the social regulatory framework.

Second, as to the political forces brought to bear on these national institutions, the NRA has obviously been the dominant actor. After an influence peak in the 1980s, its influence soared in the 2000s, even with Democrat Obama in the White House, largely as a result of its successes during the gun-friendly presidency of George W. Bush, culminating in the 2005 passage of the gun industry liability immunity bill. Although the NRA's influence has been cyclical, the organization remains one of the most feared and fearsome interest groups in American politics.

The nature of interest-group politics is such that the energized and intense backers of the NRA have repeatedly proved the axioms that a highly motivated, intense minority operating effectively in the interest group milieu will usually prevail in a political contest over a larger, relatively apathetic majority, and that it is easier to prevent policy enactment than cause it, which has more often been the NRA's policy approach. The difficult task for control proponents has been to inspire the apathetic majority sufficiently to overcome the inertia of inaction, a tactic that has become even more difficult with an array of pro-gun policy changes in the 2000s. Yet if control supporters have been hampered by the greater difficulty of offensive rather than defensive policymaking, they did benefit from the political backwash of popular revulsion arising from a series of massacres in the late 1980s and 1990s, from Long Island to California, that served as a catalyst for change in the way that political assassinations did in the 1960s.

Third, the prior success of the NRA in controlling political outcomes, including its notable yet little-noticed ability to keep gun issues off the legislative agenda altogether, explains the sustained-to-escalating intensity of gun politics juxtaposed with regressing policy objectives. In other words: *to control the agenda is also to control the outcome.* Gun control supporters needed to establish political credibility and puncture the NRA's image of invulnerability by logging a win—any win—against it. The more modest a policy proposal is, the more likely is success.

The sea change in the gun policy struggle is best exemplified by the shift in agenda control in Congress. From 1972 to 1988 no bill to expand gun controls came to a vote on the floor of either house of Congress. From 1988 to 1993, thirteen floor votes on gun bills were taken (on assault weapons, banning handgun sales to minors, and the Brady bill). Of those, nine passed and four failed. The NRA's best strategy has always been to keep gun bills bottled up in committee or otherwise off the floor of Congress, where bills receive wider public attention and control proponents are more able to tap into broad popular sentiments supporting stronger gun measures. The political scientist E. E. Schattschneider identified this phenomenon as expanding the scope of

Table 5.1 Major gun legislation enacted into law, 1968–present

Law name and number	Shortened name or nickname	Major provisions
The Gun Control Act of 1968 (PL 90-618; 82 Stat. 1226)	Gun Control Act	The Gun Control Act of 1968 (PL 90-618; 82 Stat. 1226) • Banned interstate shipment of firearms and ammunition to private individuals • Barred gun sales to minors, felons • Strengthened licensing and record keeping for gun dealers and collectors • Regulated other destructive devices (bombs, etc.) • Increased gun-crime penalties • Barred import of foreign-made surplus firearms
The Firearms Owners Protection Act of 1986 (PL 99-360; 100 Stat. 449)	McClure-Volkmer bill	Repealed elements of the Gun Control Act: • Allowed interstate sale of long guns • Eased record keeping for ammunition dealers • Allowed gun dealers to do business at gun shows • Kept ATF from gathering centralized gun dealer records • Limited unannounced ATF inspections of gun dealers to one per year • Barred future possession/transfer of machine guns • Kept handgun restrictions

The Brady Handgun Violence Prevention Act of 1993 (PL 103159; 107 Stat. 1536)	Brady bill	• Started national five-day waiting period for handgun purchases (eliminated in 1998 when instant-check system instituted) • Helped states pay for criminal records computerization; continued increased federal firearms license fees • Made gun thefts from dealers a federal crime • Barred package labeling for guns shipped through mail • Required local police to conduct background checks (struck down in *Printz v. U.S.*, 1997)
The Violent Crime Control and Law Enforcement Act of 1994 (Title XI; PL 103-322; 108 Stat. 1796)	Assault-weapons ban	• Barred for ten years possession and sale of nineteen types of assault weapons, along with similar "copycat" models (law lapsed in 2004) • exempted 661 sporting guns • limited gun magazines to those holding ten bullets (restrictions not applied to assault weapons/magazines already owned)
The Protection of Lawful Commerce in Arms Act of 2005 (PL 109-92; 119 Stat. 2095)	Gun Manufacturers Liability Protection Bill	• Barred civil suits against gun manufacturers, distributors, dealers, and importers • Required handguns to be sold with locks • Barred manufacture, import of armor-piercing ammunition

conflict in order to change the outcome (in this case, to the benefit of control supporters).[87] The final step in this process was the NRA's successful political offense in the 2000s, joining successful policy changes in Congress with favorable administrative decisions by the Bush administration, and success before the Supreme Court capped this final step. In the final chapter we turn to the policy prospects for gun control and a proposal for a new way to think about the gun issue.

Chapter 6

Gun Policy

A New Framework

> The greater the difficulties, the greater is the task of a policy of restraint and the merit of those who ... would know how to forgo the "easy" solution, the "Gordian knot" solution of force, in favor of a peace that would be neither appeasement and abdication nor the Carthaginian result of a war which might spell the destruction of our civilization.
>
> —*John H. Herz, "Idealist Internationalism and the Security Dilemma,"* World Politics

THE GUN CONTROL BATTLE IS, above all, a struggle over public policy. As the many elements and cases of the gun issue analyzed in this book reveal, the gun policy struggle is one in which elephantine political forces battle over policy mice. This conclusion is surely no surprise to anyone with a passing acquaintance with the gun issue. At the same time, only a full understanding of the policy issue's scope and its political consequences can hope to yield any sort of policy synthesis.

The purposes of this chapter are, first, to draw together the primary findings of the previous chapters, and second, to use them as a springboard to propose a new framework for conceptualizing the gun issue, based precisely on its inflammatory nature, grounded as it is in the social regulatory policy dynamic. I draw such a framework from an unlikely but entirely logical source—international relations. Before considering these primary purposes, however, we need first to address one final, crucial matter: the relationship between federalism and gun control.

Federalism: The Great Regulation Dilemma

America's thousands of gun regulations belie the central, often ignored, fact that nearly all these regulations exist at the state and local levels. There is reason to believe that some of these regulations have had an effect on behavior. Nevertheless, despite our country's geographic size and diversity, the ease of long-distance travel means that the flow of arms from low-regulation to high-regulation states continues nearly unabated.[1] Therefore, the question of how state powers and regulations relate to national government powers and regulations (a practical definition of federalism) undergirds any analysis of national gun policy.[2]

The New York Case

The situation in New York State provides a classic example of the federalism dilemma. New York enacted the nation's first modern gun law in 1911. Known as the Sullivan law, the measure imposed strict requirements on the sale, possession, and carrying of concealable weapons.[3] Despite resistance from rural upstate interests, the state has generally maintained among the toughest gun laws in the nation. In order to obtain a handgun license in New York, an individual must be at least twenty-one years old, have no felony convictions or other serious offenses or mental illness, be of "good moral character," submit photos and fingerprints, and pay an application fee of $115. The entire process can take at least several months, and all licenses must be renewed every five years. Even so, guns continue to pose a major problem, especially in New York City. According to data compiled by the Bureau of Alcohol, Tobacco, Firearms, and Explosives, 80 to 90 percent of the guns used in crimes throughout the state come from out of state. Virginia is the source of more than one-quarter of these guns, followed by Florida, Texas, Georgia, Connecticut, West Virginia, and Ohio. This flow of guns into New York is referred to as the "iron pipeline." According to the Brooklyn district attorney's office, half of all the guns recovered in this one New York City borough in 1999 came from Florida, Georgia, and Virginia alone.[4] All these states have more lax gun laws. Frustrated at the federal government's continued sporadic and ineffective enforcement efforts, New York began a cooperative effort with Virginia in 1993 to stem the flow of illegal guns between the two states. It also decided to devote more state resources to stemming the illicit gun trade.

New York's cooperative effort with Virginia showed some results. After Virginia imposed a limit of one handgun purchase per month in 1993, the percentage of Virginia-purchased handguns used in crimes fell by 61 percent in New York, 67 percent in Massachusetts, and 38 percent in New Jersey. The nation's capital, which retains strict gun laws, faces a similar problem. A 2000 ATF study found that half of all guns used in Washington, DC, crimes were purchased from dealers in Maryland and Virginia. A 2010 study found that states with lax gun laws exported guns used in crimes at a far higher rate than states with strict gun laws.[5]

In 2006 New York City Mayor Michael Bloomberg and Boston Mayor Thomas Menino convened a summit of fifteen big-city mayors to coordinate an effort to combat the flow of illegal firearms into their cities. The effort was organized expressly because of frustration with the federal government's inaction. At the same time, Bloomberg announced that the city would be filing lawsuits against fifteen gun dealers located in Georgia, Ohio, Pennsylvania, South Carolina, and Virginia who were targeted because a large number of guns bought from these dealers were eventually used in New York City crimes. Relying not only on gun record data but also on sting operations launched against the dealers, the city pursued both criminal prosecution and monetary damages. Despite federal legislation enacted the previous year protecting gun dealers from lawsuits (see chapter 5), the city's efforts resulted in a voluntary settlement with two of the dealers (both in Georgia), who agreed to strict monitoring of gun sales. The dealers consented to the appointment of "special masters" to monitor their activities, as well as to the provision of records to authorities to verify their compliance with the agreement. This early success encouraged other cities to join in the effort. By the end of 2013, over one thousand mayors in nearly every state had joined in the Mayors against Illegal Guns Coalition, which has expanded its gun-tracing activities.[6]

This inherent federalism problem was recognized early in the twentieth century when progressives and other reformers proposed "model legislation" to be adopted by the states voluntarily to deal with gun regulation and other emerging national concerns. If the states could all be persuaded to adopt their own versions of model regulations, no federal action would be necessary. The problem with this theory, of course, was that its success depended on complete or nearly complete voluntary state compliance—an unattainable goal in almost any policy area. With the coming of the New Deal, the old inhibitions about federal regulation abated.

Recent State Activity

Paralleling an upswing in support for stronger regulations at the national level in the late 1980s and early 1990s, a flurry of state and local gun regulation efforts attracted wide attention. In a move that proved to be a political water-shed, Maryland passed a measure (which also survived a tumultuous statewide referendum) in 1988 barring the sale of cheap handguns. In 1989 California became the first state in the nation to enact an assault-weapons ban, followed by New Jersey in 1990, Connecticut in 1993, and New York State in 2000 along with such cities as Cleveland, Denver, Los Angeles, New York City, and Philadelphia. California banned the sale and possession of .50-caliber sniper rifles in 2004. As discussed in chapter 5, in the year following the Sandy Hook Elementary School shooting, nearly every state enacted measures to strengthen or weaken (and in the case of some states, both) state gun laws. The failure of Congress to act in April only encouraged state-level efforts.

As is true of parallel federal efforts, these state measures are more impor-tant for their political consequences (i.e., the defeat of gun control opponents) than for their effect on policy.[7] Still, the upsurge in state action is notable. According to the National Council of State Legislatures, about one thousand gun control bills were introduced in state legislatures in 1993, a record number. The number of gun control bills introduced in just the first half of 1994 was over two thousand.[8]

A counter-trend in the states has been a low-visibility but relatively suc-cessful effort by the NRA and its allies to enact state preemption legislation, designed to nullify or bar enactment of tougher gun laws by counties, cities, and other local jurisdictions. As of 2000, thirty-nine states had passed such legislation. The political motive for such action is that it allows regulation opponents to concentrate their efforts in state capitals, where conservative forces are traditionally stronger, rather than dealing with scores of localities around the country. In 2009 and 2010 some grassroots gun groups around the country accelerated open gun-carrying activities—carrying handguns openly in public, a practice allowed in thirty-eight states. The matter grabbed national headlines when gun carriers began to hold so-called meet-ups at food establishments like Starbucks coffee bars and pizza parlors, among other places. Although the extremist Gun Owners of America supported these activities, the NRA quietly opposed them, fearing an adverse public reaction to civilians on the streets openly carrying handguns.[9]

Gun Policy Alternatives

In its simplest terms two beliefs buttressed the press for stronger gun laws from policy advocates and the general public: (1) that such laws will contribute to a diminution of the crime problem, even if such a contribution is marginal; and

(2) that guns are inherently dangerous implements of destruction, and regardless of their impact on crime, they should be subject to restrictions similar to any product or hazard that imposes comparable (or less) risk—especially given that guns, unlike products ranging from automobiles to knives, serve no other, counterbalancing purpose. This latter belief garners its chief support from the long-held view that government does and should do whatever is feasible to protect its citizens from harm. Although the gun debate is typically framed in criminological terms, this reasoning makes clear that the gun problem is not just criminological, although fear of crime has provided much of the momentum for gun-law reforms. Any effort to define the gun issue solely in criminological terms ignores the larger, if more diffuse, issue of safety.

Opposing this view is the set of values, beliefs, and practices embodying the American gun culture, discussed in chapter 1. Buttressed today primarily by the hunting-sporting ethos, the gun culture resists further efforts at regulation. As public opinion polls reveal (see chapter 4), resistance is based less on objections to the content of proposed regulation than on (1) the slippery-slope concern that regulation, whether reasonable or not, will inevitably lead to more regulation and, ultimately, the banning of many, if not most, weapons (the NRA's primary clarion call); and (2) the deeply felt belief that such regulations may or do infringe on "rights." Even though no such rights infringement exists from a constitutional perspective as defined by the Supreme Court in 2008 (see chapter 2), the belief itself is an intense motivator.

Thus, the very actions advocated by control proponents, animated by the desire to improve the safety and quality of American life, are viewed by control opponents as inimical to the same quality (although differently defined) of American life. It is a conundrum closely analogous to John L. Gaddis's analysis of why the Cold War evolved at the end of World War II, when he asserted that the very actions pursued by America and its allies in Europe to ensure security and forestall a new war were interpreted by the Soviet Union as provocative and warlike. Similarly, the Soviet Union's actions to develop a loyal ring of buffer nations for its own security were seen by the West as provocative and warlike.[10]

What I have described is the inherent problem of social regulatory policy, where the clash of values plays itself out in the political and, especially, the legislative arenas. An additional insight arising from social regulatory policy analysis is that even if the weight of policy rationality lies with regulation proponents, no meaningful policy resolution can afford to ignore the sensibilities of those whose barricades are the gun culture. It is certainly possible that, with the long-term projected decline of hunting (discussed in chapter 1) and of rural populations (and therefore related cultural norms), the control coalition may eventually succeed in rolling over the NRA and its allies in order to adopt sweeping national gun control reform of the sort found in other Western nations. Yet that outcome seems unlikely in the foreseeable future because control opponents have indicated that they have no intention of giving up the fight, despite having been in the numerical and opinion minority almost from the beginning of the modern gun control fight. Thus, we return to the likelihood of a protracted standoff between the two sides.

The Barriers to Gun Control

As revealed in chapter 2, there is no constitutional barrier to most gun laws. The weight of criminological analysis assessed in chapter 3 leads to the conclusion, based on the preponderance of admittedly incomplete evidence, that gun control is a functional approach to the problems guns pose in society.[11] Chapters 4 and 5 included analyses of the political forces brought to bear on the state of gun policy, noting the political successes of gun control foes and countervailing influence of control supporters, as well as the long-standing public support for tougher gun laws. The often reluctant national institutional players—Congress, the president, the ATF—have found themselves reacting to political tides that seem to wash over the nation's capital like periodic, fierce storms blown in from the Atlantic. The bottom-line conclusion for the state of gun control policy is that barriers to further regulation are fundamentally political.

The primary substantive argument opposing further gun regulations is that such regulations will only make it more difficult for law-abiding citizens to obtain weapons, especially for purposes of self-defense, whereas criminals will continue to gain access to weapons regardless of the law. Remember that this individualistic view of the role of the citizen is deeply rooted in the nation's past, as described in chapter 1.

The Good Guy–Bad Guy Myth

This assertion contains within it one fallacy: that one can readily differentiate between "good guys" and "bad guys"; stated differently, the assumption is that guns in the hands of good guys are good, whereas guns in the hands of bad guys are bad. If the latter are controlled (e.g., through deterrence or imprisonment), the problem is essentially solved.

Yet the statistics on gun-related deaths discussed in chapter 3 make clear that this Hollywood-cultivated dichotomy bears little relation to the reality of most gun-related homicides, in that many homicides are the result of impulsive actions taken by individuals who have little or no criminal background or who are known to the victims. A study of murder trends in 1988 found that 64 percent of murderers were friends or acquaintances of the victims, and 16 percent were members of the victims' families. Strangers committed only 20 percent of murders. According to the Bureau of Justice Statistics, from 1976 to 2005, a relative or acquaintance of the victim committed 51 percent of all murders; strangers committed 14 percent, and the relationship between murderer and victim could not be determined in 35 percent of the murders. Arguments often precipitated murders.[12]

These trends are exemplified in journalistic tallies of gun deaths. An examination of the 11 gun fatalities that occurred during the month of January 1989 in San Jose, California, noted that 4 of the deaths involved justified police shootings; 4 were murders of spouses or roommates, all arising from domestic disputes; 2 were accidental shooting deaths; and 1 was a suicide.[13] A *Time* magazine compilation of all 464 gun deaths that occurred nationwide during the week of May 1–7, 1989, found that the majority of the murders "typically involved people who loved, or hated, each other—spouses, relatives or close acquaintances." Only 13 of the gun deaths were law enforcement related, 14 were self-defense, 22 were accidents, and 216 were suicides. In general, the majority of murders are committed against people known to the perpetrators; the large majority of women murdered are killed by spouses or other intimates.[14]

The good guy–bad guy myth thus evaporates when most murders are examined. Even when we consider that persons with criminal backgrounds are more likely to commit gun crimes such as murder, we are still left with the conclusion that such individuals ought not to have ready access to guns. This becomes even more apparent when suicides and gun accidents (fatal and nonfatal) are added to the cumulative harm guns cause. For gun use (especially nonfatal gun use) in other crimes, such as robbery and theft, the good guy–bad guy principle retains some usefulness because such crimes (especially when guns are involved) are infrequently attributable to impulse and are almost never attributable to accident. Nevertheless, based on existing patterns of gun use, the consequences of a citizenry armed to stave off crime would inevitably be more gun crimes and gun deaths.

The Armed Citizen

To return to the argument against gun control, one can still plausibly argue that widespread citizen possession of guns for self-defense retains logic at both the societal and individual levels. On the societal level one may argue that a cumulative deterrent effect may arise from an armed civil society and that some crimes will be thwarted, even though death is more likely to occur when victims resist or are armed. Indeed, some might be more than willing to accept such a trade-off. On the individual level it seems commonsensical that a crime victim has a better chance of self-protection and crime suppression if the citizen is armed. During the 1992 Los Angeles riots, for example, some storeowners saved their places of business by displaying and even using weapons. During Hurricane Katrina in 2005 some Louisiana gun owners similarly protected property with guns, although widespread looting and gun violence impelled law enforcement to take guns from citizens as well. Yet this bit of apparent common sense is never held up to examination in the gun debate. That is, to have any meaningful effect, such an arming process must take place systematically, on a societal scale. We must then ask, What is the cumulative consequence of an implicit or explicit policy that encourages civilian arming to counteract crime and lawlessness in a modern, developed society? An answer to this question can be found in international relations theory.

The Security Dilemma

Students of international relations concern themselves with how nations behave and interact. Not surprisingly, a central concern of these analysts is armed conflict—in particular, the causes and prevention of war. Throughout history, nations have been forced to rely on themselves, sometimes with the help of allied nations, to ward off the aggressions of other nations. Unlike citizens or communities within a nation, sovereign nations usually operate within an international framework of anarchy, meaning that nations must look out for themselves.[15] (Note that this definition of anarchy is not the one popularly used, in which indiscriminate disorder, confusion, and mayhem are the norm.) The international relations expert Kenneth Waltz notes that "self-help is necessarily the principle of action in an anarchic order."[16]

Anarchy in the international system prevails because of the absence of any authoritative governing body or structure. As the international security expert Bruce Russett writes, "There is no higher authority, such as a world government, to which they [nations] can appeal for protection. Rather, they must try to provide security through policies that heavily emphasize military strength and military deterrence."[17] International politics is, quite simply, "politics in the absence of government."[18]

The great dilemma of this behavior among nations is that, as nations arm and fortify themselves in an effort to stave off conflict, they in turn fan the flames of insecurity in other nations. Emphasizing the universality of this problem, international expert John Herz wrote of the "security dilemma" of men, or groups, or their leaders:

> Groups or individuals ... concerned about their security from being attacked, subjected, dominated, or annihilated ... [s]triving to attain security from such attack ... are driven to acquire more and more power in order to escape the impact of the power of others. This, in turn, renders the others more insecure and compels them to prepare for the worst. Since none can ever feel entirely secure in such a world of competing units, power competition ensues, and the vicious circle of security and power accumulation is on.[19]

As the security analyst Robert Jervis says, "the means by which a state tries to increase its security decrease the security of others."[20] This, in a nutshell, is the "security dilemma."

When a nation takes actions that it considers to be purely defensive (and therefore not threatening to other nations), other nations may perceive some of those actions as an offensive threat to their security. If, for example, a nation builds up its army to deter an attack from a neighboring nation, the neighboring nation is likely to assume that the buildup is designed for attack, not defense, and is therefore likely to respond by increasing its forces, an action that may accelerate the first nation's buildup, and so on, until war breaks out. A classic example of such a cycle is that preceding World War I, as described in Barbara Tuchman's revealing book *The Guns of August*.

One might suppose that such a cycle could be prevented if nations developed solely defensive weapons. But there are two problems with this solution. First, virtually all weapons can be construed as having an offensive purpose (although some defensive *actions* may avoid this problem). Second, even those weapons considered purely defensive, such as antimissile missiles, can be considered threatening to other nations because they suggest that the nation developing them may use them to defend its territory against retaliation in the aftermath of an initial offensive strike. For this reason, defensive weapons are often considered destabilizing in a balance-of-power situation.[21]

Thus, the classic response to the security dilemma is for nations "to expand their *individual* power."[22] Yet the cumulative consequence of this seemingly rational response to international anarchy is the escalation of arms races and an ever-increasing likelihood of war.

Arms races are problematic for three reasons: they are costly and wasteful, they ratchet up the degree of destruction likely to occur if conflict does break out, and they are a primary cause of war. Although arms races are not necessarily the sole causes of war, the historical correlation between the two is high. And arms races are undeniably a bad way to prevent conflict.[23]

These threats to security have driven nations to form alliances, make treaties, and engage in other actions to reduce the likelihood of war. The most prominent such example is the formation of the United Nations at the end of World War II. Central to this effort in recent years has been negotiation of arms control agreements designed to limit the development and spread of nuclear arms, although the security dilemma is not unique to the nuclear age. In fact, arms control "is virtually as old as weapons themselves."[24]

As international security specialists well understand, the constant threat the security dilemma poses would be no threat at all if a powerful international authority existed that could impose order and accompanying standards of behavior on the nations of the world. It is precisely because international systems are "decentralized and anarchic," whereas domestic political systems are "centralized and hierarchic,"[25] that one does not find anarchy to be a prevalent mode of interaction within most nations. Obviously, such an authority exists within the borders of the United States.

The Security Dilemma and the Gun Debate

The startling parallels between the behavior of nations and that of citizens within the United States is less surprising when one considers the fulfillment of the primeval need for order, described at the start of chapter 1, as the first purpose of governments. The desire of citizens to own guns for the purpose of self-defense underscores the government's inability to provide a greater degree of public order. The domestic "anarchy" many fear is the anarchy of elements of the inner city, the darkened lonely street, the random killer, the vicious rapist.

The problem of widespread gun ownership and proliferation in society lies precisely in the seemingly rational desire of the individual to own a gun for self-defense, even though the cumulative consequence of such ownership is likely to be more detrimental than helpful to societal order, and in the reality that guns can be used as easily for offense (e.g., to commit a robbery) as for defense (e.g., to thwart a robbery). Although the purpose of a gun purchase may be defensive, it is impossible for others to feel secure unless they already trust the gun owner. No matter how defense-minded the gun owner, the very act of gun ownership and especially that of gun display are invariably offensive in nature. As a Spanish diplomat noted between the two world wars: "A weapon is either offensive or defensive according to which end of it you are looking at."[26] As one international security expert observed, the only way to ensure that others would interpret gun ownership as purely defensive in nature would be somehow to chain the gun to one's house.[27] Even then, the dangers of suicide and accident would persist.

Bearing in mind the differences between international and domestic political systems, the standoff and conflagration that consumed the Branch Davidian compound near Waco, Texas, in early 1993 dramatically illustrates the applicability of the security dilemma to the American gun situation. The fringe group had amassed an enormous quantity of arms and explosives, insisting that they were for defensive purposes only. One can accept their claim of defense and still understand why the mere acquisition of these materials aroused alarm among government officials and others. This is admittedly an extreme example, but it almost precisely parallels the security dilemma in international politics.

Offense versus Defense

The mere act of gun possession, then, is offensive *regardless of intent* because weapons are inherently offensive and because it is "hard to convince most people that they [through weapons acquisitions] may be inadvertently threatening others."[28] Bearing this in mind, one can still refine the distinction by borrowing from international relations the principle that weapons may be distinguished by their relative degree of offensive or defensive capability, applying the distinction to different types of guns.

Handguns pose an even greater offensive risk than long guns because of their concealability, portability, and ease of use. Supporting this proposition is the fact that handguns are more than three times as likely to be used in violent crime as long guns, even though long guns are easier to obtain and outnumber handguns nationwide by a ratio of roughly two to one. About 15 percent of the 2.1 million handguns made in the United States in 1995 were used in a violent crime within the next five years. In 2006, for example, guns were used to commit about four hundred thousand crimes. Also in 2006, 68 percent of all murders, 42 percent of robberies, and 22 percent of aggravated assaults involved guns. The vast majority of these crime guns were handguns.[29] Moreover, the most frequently cited reason for handgun ownership is self-protection, whereas those who own long guns cite hunting and sporting purposes as the primary reason for ownership. Obviously, long guns may have offensive and defensive purposes as well, but just as international relations specialists distinguish between weapons that have more versus less offensive capabilities, one may do the same when considering types of weapons owned by Americans.

Following this line of logic, assault weapons may be considered to pose a greater offensive threat than other long guns. Even though assault weapons are infrequently used by criminals and constitute a relatively small percentage of total firearms, they have gained in popularity among drug traffickers, urban gangs, extremist groups, and others in recent years and have also gained considerable notoriety when used in highly publicized mass killings. Especially popular among criminals are assault-style semiautomatic pistols, such as the TEC-9.[30] Sales to law-abiding citizens have also increased in recent years. As discussed in chapter 5, assault weapons are distinguishable from other semi-automatic weapons, and they are generally considered to have no legitimate hunting or sporting use. Yet the firepower they deliver (i.e., the ability to fire a bullet per trigger pull from magazines holding thirty rounds or more and to do so by laying down "spray fire") makes them useful for offensive purposes, as reflected in the military reason for their development.[31] Moreover, physicians report more serious injuries from assault weapons than from handguns (because of the greater muzzle velocity of bullets fired from assault weapons, the bullets' tendency to tumble and thus cause more damage, and the assault weapons' ability to fire more bullets before requiring reloading) and an upsurge of such wounds requiring treatment in urban hospital emergency rooms.

Further, for the defense-minded citizen, gun acquisition is not the only available means of defense. The citizen seeking self-protection can instead turn to an array of indisputably defensive *actions* designed to increase personal safety and yet, unlike guns, pose no offensive capability or threat. As discussed in chapter 3, these include installing better outdoor lighting, bars on windows, and home alarm systems; using guard dogs; and forming neighborhood alliances.

Based on the security dilemma principle, a national policy that encourages and implements weapons ownership as a recognized means of self-defense invites a domestic arms race. Of the three problems with arms races mentioned earlier, the first, cost, is probably the least significant for the American gun issue. A government policy encouraging civilian gun possession could easily make weapons available at prices affordable to most. The second and third problems, however—escalation of the degree of destruction and increase in the likelihood of conflict—are severe problems for the domestic arms race advocates.

Escalation

As the security dilemma posits, arms proliferation among citizens would inexorably lead to an escalation of gun-related violence, injuries, and deaths.[32] Those who emphasize the desirability of widespread weapons ownership and carrying among the civilian population never consider, for example, that aside from a likely rise in incidental injuries and deaths, such a policy would invite criminals, as well as law-abiding citizens now more fearful of their safety, to carry increasingly destructive weapons.[33] The security dilemma predicts this pattern of mutual escalation.

Such a phenomenon is observable in the rearming of police forces around the country, where the traditional six-shot service revolver has been replaced by higher-capacity semiautomatic handguns, notably 9mm pistols capable of holding fifteen- to nineteen-round magazines. From the mid-1980s to 1990 nearly half of America's police forces made the switch. By 1995 the 9mm gun was found in nearly all police forces. The reason for the switch is that police have found themselves increasingly outgunned, especially as street violence and semi-automatic weapons have proliferated. Echoing the parallel to international relations, the executive director of the Police Executive Research Forum said, "We've got a full-blown arms race going on in the streets today." Yet police authorities have been concerned about the consequences of this arms escalation. Police in New York City have been "firing too many shots" with the new semiautomatic pistols, according to authorities, which in turn has led to increased training. In an eleven-year study of the thirty-six thousand–member New York City Police Department (the nation's largest city force), officers who fired their weapons in the line of duty hit their targets about 34 percent of the time.[34]

Some might be tempted to cite this phenomenon as a justification for arming citizens to assist the police. Yet it must be noted that the great majority of police officers nationwide never fire their guns in the line of duty, so to exaggerate the actual threat to the police and the public would be a mistake. Beyond this, containment is a key to arms control, and unlike the international sphere, as a means of limiting the arms race, the powers of the state can be brought to bear against those who either own or use weapons improperly. That is, to escalate a domestic arms race beyond law-enforcement officers, whose specific and professional function is the maintenance of societal order, to the general population is to make a quantum leap in the abnegation of government authority. The option of arms escalation among the general population also invites comparable escalation by the criminal population, and it widens the scope of those participating in the escalation process and therefore also the scope of gun-related mayhem. As Jervis notes, "there is no policy and level of arms that is mutually satisfactory [to opposing sides]."[35] Such an approach would feed, not reduce, the security dilemma. This does not mean that citizens have no role in the law enforcement process, but rather that widespread gun carrying is neither the only nor the most desirable option. Indeed, that police organizations have lined up consistently in favor of gun control in recent years provides clear evidence that police are not sanguine about more widespread gun ownership, even among the most law-abiding segments of the population.

To summarize, despite the difficult plight law enforcement agencies face, to bring citizens into a domestic arms race against crime would, as the security dilemma predicts, (1) invite and broaden an arms race that could only result in the escalation of violence (both intentional and unintentional) and cultivate anarchy of the sort found in the international system and in some inner cities, and (2) undercut the legitimate role of the state as arbiter of public order. The Hobbesian world within nations such as Lebanon in the 1980s, Somalia in 1992, and Rwanda in 1994 are extreme, if exemplary, cases in which the state's responsibility to maintain order was passed on de facto to its respective citizens. The resulting chaos and carnage are adequate testimonials to the virtue of leaving the maintenance of public order to the state.

To take a less extreme and more specific example, Texas state law has long included a provision sanctioning citizen use of deadly force against intruders and thieves during nighttime hours. On February 25, 1994, a man who had failed to keep up with his automobile payments shot and killed the worker who was in the process of repossessing the vehicle. The shooter, Jerry Casey, admitted that he was not acting in self-defense when he killed the repossessor with a .30-30 telescopic rifle, and there seemed little doubt that Casey knew why his Ford truck was being towed away. Even though the repossessor was acting legally, no charges were brought against Casey by the district attorney of Harris County, who argued that state law did and should protect such a use of deadly force by citizens because of its general deterrent value to crime. These laws were expanded with the "stand your ground" movement begun in Florida in 2006, discussed in chapter 3.[36]

These examples hint at the broader consequences of a population armed with recognized discretion for the purpose of deterring crime. To return to the good guy–bad guy myth, the Texas instance in particular involved two "good guys"—one, a "repo man" simply doing his job; the other, a citizen without a past criminal record who committed a murder that the state would not prosecute under a law sanctioning wide citizen discretion to use deadly force as a means of deterring and thwarting crime.

Even if one accepts the good guy–bad guy myth, the security dilemma underscores the simple lesson, extracted from countless wars over many centuries, that people (and nations) with the best of intentions still find themselves inevitably drawn into escalating arms races and conflicts when they have no overarching government or authority in which to vest the responsibility for public order. The Texas law just described, enacted at a time when the existing government could provide little help to ward off horse thieves, enmeshes American citizens a little more deeply in the security dilemma.

The self-defense question begs the most important issue distinguishing international politics from domestic politics: Americans have a government that possesses the legitimacy, power, resources, and, above all, obligation to address crime and related defense problems. Admittedly, a government of limited powers that places great store in individual rights and liberties is also limited in the solutions it can pursue; such is the price of living in a free society. Yet living under a government means also that the individual accedes to the authority and legitimacy of the state.

Concealed-Carry Laws

As discussed in chapter 3, forty states have enacted liberalized laws allowing qualified citizens to carry concealed weapons. A primary argument on behalf of such laws is the claim that private citizens should have the right to protect themselves with firearms if necessary. Although the consequences of such laws are yet to be fully understood (and clearly the consequences will be marginal in states where few citizens seek such permits), a key distinction is made between "may carry" and "shall carry" laws. That is, states with a "may carry" law give the government considerable discretion over who may obtain a carry permit, so that only those who can demonstrate both a compelling need and the necessary skill are given such permits. Not surprisingly, relatively few such permits are granted. "Shall carry" laws, in contrast, stipulate that the government must grant carry permits as long as the applicants meet a set of prespecified criteria. Permits are easier to obtain in such circumstances.

A study of three states—Florida, Mississippi, and Oregon—that changed their laws from "may carry" to "shall carry" concluded that homicide rates rose as the result of the relaxation of carry laws. Part of the explanation for the rise in homicides is that criminals are more likely to carry weapons if they believe that average citizens are more likely to be armed.[37] Thus, regardless of whether one supports or opposes gun-carry laws (whether limited or permissive), observed behavior supports the arms race principle.

A similar lesson comes from recent practices of police departments around the country. Police forces in general dislike concealed-carry laws and have been moving more aggressively to deter weapons carrying, especially in urban areas. Police in such cities as Indianapolis, Kansas City, and New York have directed patrol officers to watch for any infractions that might allow stopping and searching individuals and cars. Kansas City reported a 49 percent drop in gun crimes in the areas where this policy was carried out and a 65 percent increase in gun seizures. New York City reported a 41 percent drop in handgun murders in precincts where this was tried, surpassing a 31 percent drop in the overall murder rate. Criminologists such as James Q. Wilson have become strong advocates for this kind of police tactic.[38] Returning to the international relations framework, police forces are applying an effective arms control strategy.

As the French philosopher Jean-Jacques Rousseau observed, "Man loses, through the social contract, his natural liberty, along with an unlimited right to anything that he is tempted by and can get. He gains civil liberty ... which is limited by the general will." A policy that surrenders a significant degree of state police power to individuals pushes society toward, rather than away from, the chaotic state of nature.

Nonproliferation and Arms Control

A rejection of the armed-citizen argument returns us to the original question of this chapter and book: government regulation of guns. Just as some individuals visualize an idyllic world without armies or nuclear weapons, some envision a nation without guns. Although some might argue on behalf of citizen disarmament, it is clear that a host of legal, practical, and other problems all but eliminate the citizen disarmament option, just as world nuclear disarmament can only be considered a fantasy. The most obvious of these problems is the sheer number of weapons in America, along with the difficulty of tracking and retrieving them, as well as clear legal protections established by the Supreme Court. Moreover, the current state of armament among the general population is the product of a long and deeply rooted social tradition that cannot simply be legislated out of existence. Indeed, such a tradition is entitled to respect.

A logical policy framework that balances competing values and preferences between hostile opponents is, to borrow again from international relations theory, *nonproliferation* of new weapons and technologies combined with *arms control* for existing weapons. Nonproliferation is designed to fend off the proliferation of new, more destructive weapons, based on the assumption that it is far easier and more practical to block the distribution of new types of weapons *before* rather than after they flood the market.

Such a strategy is justifiable for limiting the criminological use of guns because of the inherent desirability of applying brakes to the domestic arms race and because the active life of guns used in crime may actually be substantially less than for guns not used in crime.[39] The effort to regulate assault weapons (especially assault-style pistols) falls loosely into this category. Although such weapons have been available, the purpose of regulation would be to stem their distribution before they become more widespread. A similar example is that of the regulation of large-capacity gun clips or magazines (usually defined as those holding more than ten bullets).[40] The assault-weapons ban barred the sale and possession of new magazines (see chapter 5), but when the law lapsed in 2004, they again became legal. Several instances of mass shootings (especially the 2007 Virginia Tech and 2011 Tucson shootings), where the perpetrators used such high-capacity mags, heightened concern about their legality. The best argument opponents of a ban renewal could muster was that many were already in circulation and that the possession of such magazines simply did not matter.

Critics of those seeking such regulations have argued that because assault weapons represent only a small percentage of weapons used in crimes, there is no reason to regulate or restrict their acquisition. Yet their destructive capabilities, offensive nature, and superfluousness to hunting and sporting purposes undercut this argument, even if they are never used in crime. That many such weapons are being adopted for criminal purposes simply emphasizes the desirability of applying the nonproliferation principle to assault weapons before they spread further.

The effort in the 1980s to ban armor-piercing bullets (see chapter 5) represents another, more successful effort along these lines. In the 1990s Senator Daniel Patrick Moynihan (D-NY) spearheaded an effort to ban hollow-point pistol bullets (except for use by the police and the military), which are designed to expand on impact into a sharp-edged, starlike pattern that causes considerable damage to the victim. These bullets were designed for police use because they provide greater stopping power yet are less likely to pass through the body of the intended target and hit a bystander. Like armor-piercing ammunition, these bullets were designed solely to increase the damage to individuals or targets being shot. A similarly destructive bullet was developed in 1994 by Signature Products Corp. of Huntsville, Alabama. Because this bullet was made from a plastic material (a polymer), it escaped existing federal regulations. According to the company's chief executive officer, the bullet was developed because the company had lost business at the end of the Cold War. According to the developer, the bullet "causes a horrific wound."[41]

Arms control has played a vital role in limiting the international nuclear arms race. At the same time, it has offered no panacea and has been most important as a means "to avoid the most provocative actions and limit the most provocative weapons."[42]

Applied to gun regulation, the arms control principle similarly attempts to impose a greater degree of security by controlling guns' deployment, characteristics, uses, safety, and the like. Most recent gun regulation efforts, including those discussed in chapter 5, fall into this category. That is, they are relatively modest measures generally designed to create a greater degree of stability. Even though these measures are marginal as policy, they make sense in an arms control framework, just as international arms agreements may call for only marginal substantive changes yet are still important for their contribution to international security. An example of a new weapons technology that calls for strict regulation is the Barrett .50-caliber sniper rifle. Weighing about twenty-eight pounds, this weapon is highly accurate from more than a mile away, and it must be fired while resting on a bipod. Designed for military applications, US Marines used the weapon to knock out Iraqi armored vehicles during the 1991 Persian Gulf War. A 1995 Rand Corporation report noted that the weapon was highly effective against parked aircraft and has the capability of piercing reinforced armor used to protect airplanes, fuel tanks, toxic chemicals, and ground facilities. The NRA has thwarted efforts by Congress to regulate or restrict civilian purchase of the weapons, arguing that they are used legitimately for sharpshooting. Yet the rifles also have been found in the possession of right-wing American terrorists and even Muslim extremists, fanning law enforcement fears that terrorists both abroad and within America's borders might use the weapons. In fact, in the 1980s American companies sold at least twenty-five such rifles to Osama bin Laden's group al-Qaeda, as America was supporting the Afghani war against the Soviet Union at the time. Yet with the exception of their unavailability in California, which banned the weapon in 2005, these sniper rifles are easier to obtain than handguns, and at least fifteen different companies now produce them.[43] Another example of a recently developed, exotic gun is a two-barrel, credit card–sized firearm, about a half inch thick, capable of firing seven steel BBs per shot. Touted as a self-defense weapon, immediate concerns were raised about its concealability and the absence of regulations regarding sale and use.[44]

More stringent regulations and higher fees imposed on gun dealers and meaningful regulation of gun shows are two obvious and, until relatively recently, overlooked means to impose greater control over the general flow of guns into the national market. Although gun control opponents view these and other such measures simply as a prelude to disarmament—and, indeed, this is surely the intent of at least a few proponents of gun control—disarmament is a separate and distinct purpose. *The only way to reconcile the fears of control opponents with the efforts of control proponents is to recognize the fundamental distinction between arms control and disarmament.*

To deprive citizens of assault weapons and to make handgun acquisition extremely difficult, to cite two control objectives, are justifiable from a security dilemma perspective. Yet the achievement of these objectives could and should occur only with a concomitant guarantee of ownership protection of traditional hunting and sporting weapons for hunters, target shooters, collectors, and sports enthusiasts. It would mean, for example, that a hunter could use a standard semiautomatic hunting rifle but not an AK–47.

An express bargain could be negotiated along these lines: gun control supporters would affirm that their goal excludes gun disarmament and would expressly recognize the legitimate hunting and sporting traditions in America. Gun control foes, in turn, would accept a degree of regulation, but they could be secure in the knowledge that such regulation would not extend to confiscation or disarmament yet would include arms control that focused on handguns and on new, exotic weaponry.

It is obvious that many control opponents, and especially the NRA, would recoil from any such agreement, although the NRA would be shrewd to press for, say, exclusive control over mandatory national gun training programs for all gun owners in exchange for its support of a limited menu of gun regulations. Given the drift of events and changing national demography, the time may come when the NRA and its allies face the prospect of accepting either such an agreement or a more draconian (from their perspective) alternative. One can, indeed, argue that the hunting-sporting tradition legitimately warrants protection, but no such protective agreement can ignore the multiplicity of gun issues and problems that beset the American consciousness.

The theoretical elegance of an arms control approach to this security dilemma problem is that it provides a structure through which bargaining and accommodation can take place between opposing, hostile interests. It offers no magic solution but rather an ongoing process with which both sides can learn to live. That is, it offers a key to the social regulatory paradox.

Notes

Introduction

1. John M. Broder, "32 Shot Dead in Virginia: Worst US Gun Rampage," *New York Times,* April 17, 2007; Michael Luo, "Mental Health and Guns: Do Background Checks Do Enough?" *New York Times,* April 19, 2007; Michael Luo, "Law Overlooked in Handgun Sale to Campus Killer," *New York Times,* April 21, 2007.

2. Michael Dreisser, "Law Didn't Hamper Suspect's Gun Buy," *Baltimore Sun,* April 18, 2007.

3. Alex Koppelman, "Why Democrats Dumped Gun Control," Salon.com, April 18, 2007, www.salon.com/news/feature/2007/04/18/dems_and_guns; Jonathan Weisman and Jeffrey H. Birnbaum, "Democrats Wary of Tightening Laws," *Washington Post,* April 18, 2007.

4. William Saletan, "Friendly Firearms," *Slate,* January 11, 2011, at http://www.slate.com /articles/health_and_science/human_nature/2011/01/friendly_firearms.html; "Senate Judiciary Committee Hearing on Gun Violence," January 30, 2013, at http://articles.washingtonpost .com/2013-01-30/politics/36628109_1_gun-violence-gabby-giffords-senator-grassley.

5. Jo Becker et al., "Police Say They Visited Tucson Suspect's Home Even before Rampage," *New York Times,* January 12, 2011; Marc Lacey and Serge F. Kovaleski, "'Creepy,' 'Very Hostile,' 'Dark': A College Recorded Its Fears," *New York Times,* January 13, 2011.

6. Andrea Kelly and Rhonda Bodfield, "Her Plot Will Unfold at Council Meetings," *Arizona Daily Star,* June 10, 2010.

7. Matthew Lysiak, "Aurora Shooting Suspect James Holmes Jailed in Solitary," *New York Daily News,* July 12, 2012; John Schwartz, "Colorado Gun Laws Remain Lax, Despite Some Changes," *New York Times,* July 20, 2012.

Chapter 1

1. See *Gun Law Failures* (NRA Institute for Legislative Action, 1982). The twenty thousand figure traces back to Richard Hofstadter, "America as a Gun Culture," *American Heritage* 21 (October 1970): 85, but see Philip J. Cook and Kristin A. Goss, *The Gun Debate* (New York: Oxford University Press, 2014), 97–98.

2. American history is, of course, pockmarked by civil strife, from the Whiskey Rebellion of 1794 to the 1992 Los Angeles riots following the Rodney King incident, when police who

were filmed beating motorist King were found not guilty. Our greatest threat to public order, the Civil War, nearly destroyed the United States. Despite these and other instances, however, American society has been among the most ordered, notwithstanding its size, diversity, and democratic values.

3. The philosophical and practical problems of balancing order and freedom are nicely discussed in Theodore J. Lowi and Benjamin Ginsberg, *American Government: Freedom and Power* (New York: Norton, 1994).

4. Samuel Huntington, *Political Order in Changing Societies* (New Haven, CT: Yale University Press, 1968), 7–8.

5. Thomas R. Dye, *Understanding Public Policy* (Englewood Cliffs, NJ: Prentice Hall, 1984), 2. Dye insightfully discusses the many efforts to define public policy properly (efforts he understandably labels "exasperating").

6. See Carl J. Friedrich, *Constitutional Government and Democracy* (Boston: Little, Brown, 1941), 88–89. See also Theodore J. Lowi, *The End of Liberalism* (New York: Norton, 1979), 273. According to the *Oxford English Dictionary,* "policy" and "police" share the Latin root *politia.* Henry C. Black defined police power as securing "generally the comfort, safety, morals, health, and prosperity of its citizens by preserving the public order, preventing a conflict of rights in the common intercourse of the citizens, and insuring to each an uninterrupted enjoyment of all privileges conferred upon him or her by the general laws." *Black's Law Dictionary* (St. Paul, MN: West, 1983), 603.

7. Lowi and Ginsberg, *American Government,* 76.

8. Larry N. Gerston, Cynthia Fraleigh, and Robert Schwab, *The Deregulated Society* (Pacific Grove, CA: Brooks/Cole, 1988), 66. See also Joyce M. Mitchell and William C. Mitchell, *Political Analysis and Public Policy* (Chicago: Rand McNally, 1969), 207–9.

9. Lowi and Ginsberg, *American Government,* 640.

10. Bear in mind that the use of words such as *control* and *coercion* when applied to the government is not meant to be pejorative. Governments may exert too much control or use it perniciously, but government control through the exercise of coercion is indispensable to modern society and is inherently neither positive nor negative.

11. This discussion is a simplified version of Lowi's arenas-of-power scheme. A more detailed examination can be found in Theodore J. Lowi, *The Arenas of Power* (Boulder, CO: Paradigm Publishers, 2009); Robert J. Spitzer, *The Presidency and Public Policy: The Four Arenas of Presidential Power* (Tuscaloosa: University of Alabama Press, 1983); Spitzer, "Promoting Policy Theory: Revising the Arenas of Power," *Policy Studies Journal* 15 (June 1987): 675–89; and Randall B. Ripley and Grace A. Franklin, *Congress, the Bureaucracy, and Public Policy* (Pacific Grove, CA: Brooks/Cole, 1991).

12. This rank ordering is confirmed in Theodore J. Lowi, "Decision Making vs. Policy Making," *Public Administration Review* 30 (May–June 1970): 314–25; Robert J. Spitzer, *Presidency and Public Policy;* and Ripley and Franklin, *Congress, the Bureaucracy, and Public Policy.*

13. For more on this distinction, see William Lilley III and James C. Miller III, "The New 'Social Revolution,'" *Public Interest* 47 (Spring 1977): 52–53; Lester M. Salamon, "Federal Regulation: A New Arena for Presidential Power?" in *The Illusion of Presidential Government,* ed. Hugh Heclo and Lester M. Salamon (Boulder, CO: Westview, 1981), 150–51; Gerston, Fraleigh, and Schwab, *The Deregulated Society,* 27–34; and James Q. Wilson, ed., *The Politics of Regulation* (New York: Basic Books, 1980).

14. Gerston, Fraleigh, and Schwab, *Deregulated Society,* 23.

15. Raymond Tatalovich and Byron Daynes, "Introduction: Moral Conflicts and the Policy

Process," in *Moral Controversies in American Politics,* ed. Tatalovich and Daynes (Armonk, NY: M. E. Sharpe, 2011), xxxii.

16. This corresponds to the distinction between "style" and "position" issues arising from the study of public opinion. Style issues, such as social regulation, are defined as those dealing with matters of taste and manner derived from cultural, religious, or ethnic values (and thus tap stronger and deeper feelings). Position issues, paralleling economic regulation, involve material or economic benefits. The distinction comes from Bernard R. Berelson, Paul F. Lazarsfeld, and William N. McPhee, *Voting* (Chicago: University of Chicago Press, 1954), 184. See also Robert E. Lane and David O. Sears, *Public Opinion* (Englewood Cliffs, NJ: Prentice Hall, 1964), 75–76.

17. Claude Blair, ed., *Pollard's History of Firearms* (New York: Macmillan, 1983), 27–33 and passim.

18. The Consumer Product Safety Commission maintains data on injuries treated in hospital emergency rooms that patients say are related to various products, excluding firearms.

19. "Guns in America: National Survey on Private Ownership and Use of Firearms," *National Institute of Justice,* May 1997; Bureau of Justice Statistics, *Sourcebook of Criminal Justice Statistics* 1999 (Washington, DC: Government Printing Office, 2000), 138; Philip J. Cook, Jens Ludwig, and Adam M. Samaha, "Gun Control after *Heller,*" *UCLA Law Review* 56 (June 2009): 1041–49; "A Shrinking Minority: The Continuing Decline of Gun Ownership in America," *Violence Policy Center,* April 2007. The VPC report is based on data from the General Social Survey of the National Opinion Research Center, University of Chicago.

20. Some see a parallel between efforts to regulate guns and the country's experiment with Prohibition in the 1920s, when public policy was altered to try to end the consumption of alcoholic beverages. A good, brief summary of the policy problems Prohibition raised is found in Cynthia E. Harrison, "Appendix: The Prohibition Experience," in *The Abortion Dispute and the American System,* ed. Gilbert Y. Steiner (Washington, DC: Brookings Institution, 1983).

21. The concept of culture, arising from anthropology, is defined as "knowledge, belief, art, morals, law, custom, and any other capabilities and habits acquired by man as a member of society"; "the essential core of culture consists of traditional ... ideas and especially their attached values." Milton Singer, "Culture," in *International Encyclopedia of the Social Sciences,* ed. David L. Sills (New York: Macmillan, 1968), 3:527, 528. These and other offered definitions conform to what is described in this and other works as the culture of guns. See Scott Melzer, *Gun Crusaders: The NRA's Culture War* (New York: NYU Press, 2009).

22. The gun culture is recognized by such gun control proponents as Robert Sherrill, *The Saturday Night Special* (New York: Charterhouse, 1973), 324; Carl Bakal, *The Right to Bear Arms* (New York: McGraw-Hill, 1966), ch. 5; Hofstadter, "America as a Gun Culture," 4–11, 82–85; and Franklin E. Zimring and Gordon Hawkins, *The Citizen's Guide to Gun Control* (New York: Macmillan, 1987), ch. 7. Among gun control opponents, see, for example, David B. Kopel, *The Samurai, the Mountie, and the Cowboy* (Buffalo, NY: Prometheus Books, 1992), 419–22; and James D. Wright, Peter Rossi, and Kathleen Daly, *Under the Gun: Weapons, Crime, and Violence in America* (New York: Aldine, 1983). One gun control opponent, William R. Tonso, attempts to argue that there is no unique American gun culture, but he winds up using the synonym "gun attachment" to summarize his observation that "firearms come close to being central to the lifestyles of large numbers of Americans." See Tonso, *Gun and Society* (Washington, DC: University Press of America, 1982), 11, 15.

23. Cook, Ludwig, and Samaha, "Gun Control after *Heller.*"

24. See, for example, Hugh Davis Graham and Ted Robert Gurr, *Violence in America: Historical and Comparative Perspectives* (New York: Bantam Books, 1970); William E. Burrows,

Vigilante! (New York: Harcourt Brace Jovanovich, 1976); and Zimring and Hawkins, *Citizen's Guide to Gun Control.*

25. Richard Slotkin notes about cultural myth making that it "exists 'for the culture' that it serves, and we therefore speak of it as if it were somehow the property or production of the culture as a whole. But the actual work of making and transmitting myths is done by particular classes of persons." *Gunfighter Nation: The Myth of the Frontier in Twentieth-Century America* (New York: Atheneum, 1992), 8.

26. Alexander DeConde, *Gun Violence in America* (Boston: Northeastern University Press, 2001), 17–25 and passim.

27. Quoted in Daniel J. Boorstin, *The Americans: The Colonial Experience* (New York: Vintage, 1964), 350.

28. Alden Hatch, *Remington Arms in American History* (New York: Rinehart, 1956), 5; see also Jervis Anderson, *Guns in American Life* (New York: Random House, 1984), 12; and Leonard Kriegel, "A Loaded Question: What Is It about Americans and Guns?" *Harper's*, May 1992, 45–51.

29. Lee Kennett and James LaVerne Anderson, *The Gun in America* (Westport, CT: Greenwood Press, 1975), 48. Even during early instances of urban unrest before and after the Revolution, citizens rarely carried or used guns (48–49).

30. Hatch, *Remington Arms in American History,* 29. See also Kennett and Anderson, *The Gun in America,* 138–41; and Hofstadter, "America as a Gun Culture," 82.

31. Erik Eckholm, "Working to Keep a Heritage Relevant," *New York Times,* September 26, 2010, 16. The US Bureau of the Census reported about fourteen million hunters in 1991 and 1996.

32. Reported in Ted Kerasote, *Bloodties: Nature, Culture, and the Hunt* (New York: Random House, 1993), 211–12. Kerasote, an author and hunter, provides as eloquent a defense of hunting as any. He asks, "Can a cultural being ethically participate in these natural cycles, cycles that may entail taking the lives of individual animals, animals who are as bright, as bold, and tenderly aware of sunshine and storm as we are? Can one be both cultural and natural?" (178). Kerasote's answer is yes. "Hunting, along with procreation," he says, "is the oldest expression of our genetic nature" (xix).

33. See Decker, Enck, and Brown, "The Future of Hunting: Will We Pass on the Heritage?" *Human Dimensions Perspectives,* no. 16 (Colorado Division of Wildlife, 1993); and Pam Belluck, "Girls and Boys, Meet Nature. Bring Your Gun," *New York Times,* September 18, 2005, A1; US Fish and Wildlife Service, National Hunting and Wildlife Report, 2013, at http://wsfrprograms .fws.gov/Subpages/LicenseInfo/HuntingLicCertHistory20042013.pdf.

34. Kennett and Anderson, *The Gun in America,* 43–48, 58, and Boorstin, *The Americans,* 352–57.

35. A thorough analysis of the militias in the postcolonial period is found in John K. Mahon, *The American Militia: Decade of Decision, 1789–1800* (Gainesville: University of Florida Press, 1960). See also Hofstadter, "America as a Gun Culture," 83; and James M. McPherson, *Battle Cry of Freedom* (New York: Oxford University Press, 1988), 317.

36. Kennett and Anderson, *The Gun in America,* 38–42. First developed in Lancaster, Pennsylvania, in the early 1700s, this American rifle was lighter and less ornamental, had a longer barrel, and fired a smaller-caliber bullet loaded with a greased patch, making it easier to use and more accurate at longer distances than the guns brought over from Europe (38–39).

37. Jack Rohan, *Yankee Arms Maker: The Story of Sam Colt and His Six-shot Peacemaker* (New York: Harper and Brothers, 1948), 298.

38. James Wycoff, *Famous Guns That Won the West* (New York: Arco, 1968), 5–6. See also Harold F. Williamson, *Winchester: The Gun That Won the West* (Washington, DC: Combat Forces Press, 1952), 3; Martin Rywell, *The Gun That Shaped American Destiny* (Harriman, TN: Pioneer Press, 1957), 4; and James B. Trefethen and James E. Serven, *Americans and Their Guns: The National Rifle Association Story through Nearly a Century of Service to the Nation* (Harrisburg, PA: Stackpole Books, 1967). Carl Russell asserted that "the gun had a greater influence in changing the primitive ways of the Indian than any other object brought to America by the white man." Of far greater consequence to the life of Native Americans, however, was the spread of European diseases accompanying the massive influx of European settlers, whose sheer numbers exceeded the significance of their weapons. *Guns on the Early Frontier* (Berkeley: University of California Press, 1957), vii.

39. Lewis Atherton, *The Cattle Kings* (Bloomington: Indiana University Press, 1961).

40. Richard Shenkman, *Legends, Lies, and Cherished Myths of American History* (New York: Morrow, 1988), 112. See also Robert R. Dykstra, *The Cattle Towns* (New York: Knopf, 1968).

41. For an excellent analysis of vigilantism, see Craig B. Little and Christopher Sheffield, "Frontiers and Criminal Justice: English Private Prosecution Societies and American Vigilantism in the Eighteenth and Nineteenth Centuries," *American Sociological Review* 48 (December 1983): 796–808.

42. Ray Allen Billington, *Westward Expansion: A History of the American Frontier* (New York: Macmillan, 1974), 587.

43. Joe B. Frantz and Julian Ernest Choate Jr., *The American Cowboy: The Myth and the Reality* (Norman: University of Oklahoma Press, 1955), 78.

44. Billington, *Westward Expansion,* 787. See also Frank Richard Prassal, *The Western Peace Officer* (Norman: University of Oklahoma Press, 1972), 22, and the numerous works cited by Billington.

45. An excellent summary treatment of this subject is found in Billington, *Westward Expansion,* ch. 30. For a more general treatment of Western violence, see W. Eugene Hollon, *Frontier Violence* (New York: Oxford University Press, 1974). Hollon notes that "of all the myths that refuse to die, the hardiest concerns the extent of the unmitigated bloodletting that occurred in the Western frontier during the closing decades of the nineteenth century" (x).

46. Richard Slotkin, *The Fatal Environment: The Myth of the Frontier in the Age of Industrialization, 1800–1890* (New York: Atheneum, 1985), 15–16. See also Slotkin's other two authoritative works on the myth of the frontier, *Regeneration through Violence* (Middletown, CT: Wesleyan University Press, 973), and *Gunfighter Nation.*

47. This is a primary theme of Richard Slotkin's trilogy. As film director Joel Schumacher noted, "Guns are as much a part of the movies as they are of American culture." Quoted in Jeff Silverman, "Romancing the Gun," *New York Times,* June 20, 1993. Silverman argues that guns are increasingly eroticized and prominently featured in American movies, a fixation that persists despite Hollywood's liberal leanings.

48. Tom W. Smith, "The 75% Solution: An Analysis of the Structure of Attitudes on Gun Control, 1959–1977," *Criminology* 71 (Fall 1980): 309, 311.

49. Wright, Rossi, and Daly, *Under the Gun,* 112–20; Gregg Lee Carter, *The Gun Control Movement* (New York: Twayne, 1997).

50. Belluck, "Girls and Boys"; Angela Leddy, "DEC Checks Hunters' Trophies," *Cortland (N.Y.) Standard,* November 17, 1998, 3.

51. Josh Sugarmann, *National Rifle Association: Money, Firepower and Fear* (Washington, DC: National Press Books, 1992), 27.

52. For more on these incidents, see Osha Gray Davidson, *Under Fire: The NRA and the Battle for Gun Control* (New York: Henry Holt, 1993), 3–19, 272–73.

53. Ibid., 194. According to Davidson, one leader of gun control forces called the Brady bill "a nice, innocuous piece of legislation." During the 1970s even the NRA supported a waiting period (194).

54. Dye, *Understanding Public Policy,* 14.

55. Theodore J. Lowi, "The State in Politics: The Relation between Policy and Administration," in *Regulatory Policy and the Social Sciences,* ed. Roger G. Noll (Berkeley: University of California Press, 1985), 68, emphasis in original. See also Lowi, "What Political Scientists Don't Need to Ask about Policy Analysis," *Policy Studies Journal* 2 (1973): 61–67.

56. This list is a summary of the hypothesized political patterns of social regulatory policy described in Raymond Tatalovich and Byron Daynes, "Introduction," in Tatalovich and Daynes, *Moral Controversies in American Politics,* xxxiii–xxxix.

Chapter 2

1. Lucilius A. Emery, "The Constitutional Right to Keep and Bear Arms," *Harvard Law Review* 28 (March 1915): 473.

2. Mary Ann Glendon, *Rights Talk: The Impoverishment of Political Discourse* (New York: Free Press, 1991), 3–4.

3. Ibid., 8, 12, 14, 77, 171.

4. State right-to-bear-arms provisions and a more detailed examination of the Second Amendment are found in Robert J. Spitzer, *The Right to Bear Arms: Rights and Liberties under the Law* (Santa Barbara, CA: ABC-CLIO, 2001), and Spitzer, *Gun Control: A Documentary and Reference Guide* (Westport, CT: Greenwood Press, 2009).

5. Thomas Babington Macaulay, *The History of England from the Accession of James II,* 5 vols. (New York: Crowell, 1879), 1:117, 269.

6. Quoted in Roy G. Weatherup, "Standing Armies and Armed Citizens: An Historical Analysis of the Second Amendment," *Hastings Constitutional Law Quarterly* 2 (Fall 1975): 973.

7. Lois Schworer, "To Hold and Bear Arms: The English Perspective," in *The Second Amendment in Law and History,* ed. Carl T. Bogus (New York: New Press, 2001), 226. See also Emery, "The Constitutional Right to Keep and Bear Arms," 473–77; Peter Buck Feller and Karl L. Gotting, "The Second Amendment: A Second Look," *Northwestern University Law Review* 61 (March–April 1966): 48–49; Joyce Lee Malcolm, *To Keep and Bear Arms* (Cambridge, MA: Harvard University Press, 1994); Wilbur Edel, *Gun Control* (Westport, CT: Praeger, 1995), 1–9; and Ralph J. Rohner, "The Right to Bear Arms: A Phenomenon of Constitutional History," *Catholic University of America Law Review* 16 (September 1966): 53–84.

8. Feller and Gotting, "Second Amendment," 48–49; Rohner, "Right to Bear Arms," 58; David T. Hardy, *Origins and Development of the Second Amendment* (Southport, CT: Blacksmith, 1986), 35; Lawrence D. Cress, "The Right to Bear Arms," in *By and for the People: Constitutional Rights in American History,* ed. Kermit L. Hall (Arlington Heights, IL: Harlan Davidson, 1991), 64–66; *National Commission on the Causes and Prevention of Violence* (Washington, DC: Government Printing Office, 1969), app. J; and Carl T. Bogus, "The Hidden History of the Second Amendment," *U.C. Davis Law Review* (Winter 1998): 375–86.

9. Macaulay, *History of England,* 1:269.

10. Keith Ehrman and Dennis A. Henigan, "The Second Amendment in the Twentieth Century: Have You Seen Your Militia Lately?" *University of Dayton Law Review* 15 (1989): 8–10. Firearms have been closely regulated in Britain from medieval times to the present.

11. Daniel J. Boorstin, *The Americans: The Colonial Experience* (New York: Vintage, 1964), 356; and Stephen Halbrook, *That Every Man Be Armed: The Evolution of a Constitutional Right* (Oakland, CA: Independent Institute, 1984), 58.

12. Lee Kennett and James L. Anderson, *The Gun in America* (Westport, CT: Greenwood Press, 1975), 61. See also Stephen Halbrook, "To Keep and Bear Their Private Arms," *Northern Kentucky Law Review* 10 (1982): 13–39.

13. Richard L. Perry, ed., *Sources of Our Liberties* (New York: American Bar Foundation, 1959), 7th in series, 34; 11th in series, 11.

14. Clinton Rossiter, *Seedtime of the Republic* (New York: Harcourt, Brace and World, 1953), 386–87. John K. Mahon defines militia (composed of "irregulars" or "citizen soldiers") as adult male citizens of fighting age (between eighteen and forty-five) obligated to enroll with the government for military service, serve for a few months every year, meet or train rarely when there was no impending emergency, only partially covered by military law, and usually under state command. Professional soldiers were volunteers who enlisted for several years, served even in peacetime, were under federal control, and were fully subject to military law. *The American Militia: Decade of Decision, 1789–1800* (Gainesville: University of Florida Press, 1960), v.

15. According to the historian James Flexner, "Utopian thinking backed the political preferences of state leaders by postulating that the best fighting force would be made up of militiamen who exerted their God-given natural gifts as they took turns defending their fields." *Washington: The Indispensable Man* (New York: New American Library, 1984), 111.

16. Merrill Jensen, *The New Nation* (New York: Vintage, 1965), 30. Despite common impressions to the contrary, service in colonial militias was not universal. See John Shy, *A People Numerous and Armed* (New York: Oxford University Press, 1976), 21–33; and Don Higginbotham, "The Federalized Militia Debate: A Neglected Aspect of Second Amendment Scholarship," *William and Mary Quarterly* 55 (January 1998): 39–58.

17. Boorstin, *The Americans,* 355–56, and Mahon, *American Militia,* 3.

18. Quoted in Weatherup, "Standing Armies and Armed Citizens," 979–80. At a later point, Washington said of the militias that they "consume your provisions, exhaust your stores, and leave you at last in a critical moment." Quoted in Mahon, *American Militia,* 5. According to Washington, the militia "system" was "sinking the cause" of the Revolution. See Flexner, *Washington,* 85; also 67, 83–84, 111.

19. During the Revolution, Congress was extremely reluctant to accede to General Washington's repeated requests for a larger professional force because of the fear that it "weakened the soldiers' state ties and seemed a possible instrument of tyranny." Flexner, *Washington,* 111.

20. Max Farrand, *The Framing of the Constitution of the United States* (New Haven, CT: Yale University Press, 1913), 49. Charles Pinckney argued that the states would see the wisdom of some degree of federal control over the state militias. For himself, Pinckney had "but a scanty faith in Militia. There must be (also) a real military force—This alone can (effectually) answer the purpose). The United States had been making an experiment without it, and we see the consequence in their rapid approaches toward anarchy [a reference to Shays's rebellion]." Max Farrand, ed., *The Records of the Federal Convention of 1787,* 4 vols. (New Haven, CT: Yale University Press, 1966), 2:332. Theodore J. Lowi and Benjamin Ginsberg assert that "it is quite

possible that the Constitutional Convention of 1787 in Philadelphia would never have taken place at all except for ... Shays's Rebellion." *American Government: Freedom and Power* (New York: Norton, 1994), 34.

21. Farrand, *Records of the Federal Convention,* 2:326.

22. Ibid., 2:388; see also 1:465; 3:616–17.

23. Ibid., 4:59.

24. Ibid., 3:319.

25. Ibid., 3:420.

26. Ibid., 3:209.

27. Bernard Schwartz, *The Bill of Rights: A Documentary History,* 2 vols. (New York: Chelsea House, 1971), 2:773, 831.

28. New Hampshire, New York, North Carolina, and Virginia all recommended a bill of rights that included wording regarding militias and the right to bear arms. See Spitzer, *Gun Control,* 32–34.

29. Schwartz, *Bill of Rights,* 2:842. Other states that tacked on militia-related wording when they approved the Constitution used similar language.

30. Mahon, *American Militia,* 6. See also the remarks of Luther Martin to the Maryland ratifying convention in Farrand, *Records of the Federal Convention,* 3:207–8.

31. Helen E. Veit, Kenneth R. Bowling, and Charlene Bangs Bickford, eds., *Creating the Bill of Rights* (Baltimore, MD: Johns Hopkins University Press, 1991), x, xiv, xv, 12, 30, 38, 48. Unlike the House, the Senate met in secret, so no official debate records exist. Supreme Court Chief Justice Warren Burger wrote that the Second Amendment "must be read as though the word 'because' was the opening word" of the amendment. "The Right to Bear Arms," *Parade,* January 14, 1990, 5.

32. Veit, Bowling, and Bickford, *Creating the Bill of Rights,* 182, 183–84, 198–99.

33. Ibid., 182. Gerry's reference to "the late revolution" was to Britain's Glorious Revolution of 1688.

34. For the common law basis of personal self-protection, see, for example, Joel Samaha, *Criminal Law* (St. Paul, MN: West, 1993), ch. 6. The irrelevance of such activities as hunting, sporting, and personal protection to the Second Amendment are discussed in Andrew D. Herz, "Gun Crazy: Constitutional False Consciousness and Dereliction of Dialogic Responsibility," *Boston University Law Review* 75 (January 1995): 65–67.

35. 1 *US Stat.* 271 (1792). The act went on to direct that "commissioned officers shall severally be armed with a sword or hanger and esponton [a long, pointed weapon with a hook], and that from and after five years from the passing of this act, all muskets for arming the militia as herein required, shall be of bores sufficient for balls of the eighteenth of a pound. And every citizen so armed, and providing himself with the arms, ammunition, and accoutrements required as aforesaid, shall hold the same exempted from all suits, distresses, executions or sales, for debt or for the payment of taxes."

36. Farrand, *Records of the Federal Convention,* 2:385. This wording, of course, allowed the government to provide arms, which it has done since the mid-nineteenth century.

37. Mahon, *American Militia,* 21–22, 25. Nevertheless, militia forces suffered their most devastating defeat in American history at the hands of Native Americans, known as St. Clair's defeat, in 1791. See Arthur M. Schlesinger Jr. and Roger Bruns, eds., *Congress Investigates: A Documented History, 1792–1974,* 5 vols. (New York: Chelsea House, 1983), 1:3–101.

38. Local militias continued to gather for "musters" throughout much of the nineteenth century, but such gatherings were primarily social occasions that were important for their

entertainment, sporting, and social consequences at a time when Americans had few forms of amusement or entertainment. See Mahon, *American Militia*, 67–68, and William Riker, *Soldiers of the States: The Role of the National Guard in American Democracy* (Salem, N.H.: Ayer, 1979; first published 1957).

39. Ehrman and Henigan, "The Second Amendment in the Twentieth Century," 36; Mahon, *American Militia*, 48–49, 66–67.

40. Donald M. Snow and Dennis M. Drew, *From Lexington to Desert Storm* (Armonk, NY: M. E. Sharpe, 1994), 261–62. See also Frederick B. Wiener, "The Militia Clause of the Constitution," *Harvard Law Review* 54 (December 1940): 188–89.

41. Stephen Skowronek, *Building a New American State* (Cambridge: Cambridge University Press, 1982), 315n17.

42. James D. Richardson, *Messages and Papers of the Presidents*, 2 vols. (Washington, DC: Bureau of National Literature, 1913), 9:66–70.

43. 32 *Stat.* 775–80 (1903), also known as the Dick Act.

44. 39 *Stat.* 166 (1916); see 197–203.

45. 32 *US Code* 7014–16 (1959). Today the national government pays and equips the National Guard.

46. See 10 *US Code* 311 (1983). The organized militia today includes the National Guard and the Naval Militia.

47. Saul Cornell, *A Well-Regulated Militia: The Founding Fathers and the Origins of Gun Control in America* (New York: Oxford University Press, 2006). See also H. Richard Uviller and William G. Merkel, *The Militia and the Right to Arms* (Durham, NC: Duke University Press, 2002).

48. There was a militia call-up at the start of the Civil War, but as the Civil War historian James M. McPherson noted, "By the 1850s the old idea of militia service as an obligation of all males had given way to the volunteer concept." Those militia outfits still meeting at all "spent more time drinking than drilling." *Battle Cry of Freedom* (New York: Oxford University Press, 1988), 317.

49. According to the constitutional scholar Frederick B. Wiener, "the Second Amendment, which purportedly guarantees the right to bear arms, is now substantially a dead letter in the face of police power necessities and a recession from the frontier." "Militia Clause of the Constitution," 186. This history and interpretation of militias is confirmed in *Maryland v. US*, 381 US 41 (1965) and in *Perpich v. Department of Defense*, 496 US 334 (1990).

50. 92 US at 553. The only dissenter in the case was Justice Nathan Clifford. The three men in this case were charged under the Force Act of 1870, a civil rights act that made conspiring to intimidate or injure citizens in order to prevent them from exercising their constitutional rights a federal crime.

51. The case was *Chicago, Burlington and Quincy Railroad Co. v. Chicago*, 166 US 226 (1897), in which just compensation in cases of eminent domain from the Fifth Amendment was applied to the states using the Fourteenth Amendment.

52. Justice Hugo Black argued for total incorporation, but the idea never found wide acceptance on the Court or elsewhere. Daniel A. Farber, William N. Eskridge Jr., and Philip Frickey say, for example, that "the Supreme Court never accepted Justice Black's theory as a matter of constitutional interpretation." *Constitutional Law* (St. Paul, MN: West, 1993), 398. See Black's dissenting opinion in *Adamson v. California*, 332 US 46 (1947), at 68–123.

53. In *Twining v. New Jersey*, 211 US 78 (1908), the Supreme Court cited *Presser* to underscore that the Second Amendment was not incorporated: "The right of trial by jury in civil

cases, guaranteed by the 7th Amendment ... and the right to bear arms, guaranteed by the 2nd Amendment (*Presser v. Illinois* ...), have been distinctly held not to be privileges and immunities of citizens of the United States, guaranteed by the 14th Amendment against abridgment by the states" (at 98).

54. "The right of the people to keep and bear arms (art. 2) is not infringed by laws prohibiting the carrying of concealed weapons" (281–82). The Court also ruled in *Patsone v. Commonwealth,* 232 US 138 (1914), that a Pennsylvania law prohibiting unnaturalized, foreign-born persons from possessing firearms was constitutional.

55. Nelson Lund, "The Second Amendment, Political Liberty, and the Right to Self-Preservation," *Alabama Law Review* 39 (1987): 109. Sawed-off shotguns were used in trench warfare during World War I.

56. *US v. Miller,* 307 US 174; 26 *US Code* 1132c. One reason the Court may not have addressed these broad issues more completely is that the defendants did not send a representative to argue their side before the Supreme Court in oral argument.

57. *Adams v. Williams* did not involve the Second Amendment as an issue. In it, Justice William O. Douglas objected to what he considered an illegal search of a suspect, which uncovered a gun. This prompted Douglas to question the ease with which Americans can obtain guns: "A powerful lobby dins into the ears of our citizenry that these gun purchases are constitutional rights protected by the Second Amendment.... There is under our decisions no reason why stiff state laws governing the purchase and possession of pistols may not be enacted. There is no reason why pistols may not be barred from anyone with a police record. There is no reason why a State may not require a purchaser of a pistol to pass a psychiatric test. There is no reason why all pistols should not be barred to everyone except the police." Douglas then cited *US v. Miller* as precedent and discussed the history behind the Second Amendment. Justice Thurgood Marshall joined in the dissent. *Lewis v. US* involved a man convicted for unlawfully possessing a weapon under the Omnibus Crime Control and Safe Streets Act of 1968. In his majority opinion Justice Harry Blackmun recognized the propriety of the gun control provisions in the act, saying that they did not violate the Second Amendment: "These legislative restrictions on the use of firearms are neither based upon constitutionally suspect criteria, nor do they trench upon any constitutionally protected liberties. See *United States v. Miller.*"

58. NRA lawyer Stephen P. Halbrook alone has written four books and dozens of law journal articles on gun control and the Second Amendment. See Bogus, "Hidden History of the Second Amendment," 318. The National Rifle Association and other gun rights groups have provided extensive support for this writing; see, for example, Scott Heller, "The Right to Bear Arms," *Chronicle of Higher Education,* July 21, 1995, A12; Herz, "Gun Crazy," 138n358.

59. In the case of *US v. Emerson* (270 F.3d 203; 5th Cir. 2001), a lower federal court accepted the individualist interpretation of the Second Amendment but did not use it to strike down the gun restriction that gave rise to the challenge.

60. *Parker v. District of Columbia* (478 F.3d 370; D.C. App. 2007). The appeals court accepted the individualist view in a 2–1 ruling against the DC law.

61. *D.C. v. Heller,* at 678.

62. Ibid., at 675.

63. Ibid., at 684.

64. Ibid.

65. Ibid., at 685.

66. *McDonald v. Chicago,* at 926.

67. Ibid.

68. Ibid.

69. *Slaughter-House Cases* (83 US 36, 1873). Only Justice Clarence Thomas supported using the "privileges or immunities" clause as the basis for incorporation. For more on incorporation and the Second Amendment, see Robert J. Spitzer, "Why Gun Ruling Is a Teachable Moment," *CNN Opinion,* June 30, 2010, http://www.cnn.com/2010/OPINION/06/29/spitzer .guns.supreme.court/index.html?iref=storysearch.

70. *McDonald v. Chicago,* at 921.

71. Ibid., at 991.

72. "Post-*Heller* Litigation Summary," *Law Center to Prevent Gun Violence,* April 24, 2014 at http://issuu.com/lcav/docs/post-heller_litigation_summary_-_ap?e=3502204/7639713#search; Philip J. Cook and Kristin A. Goss, *The Gun Debate* (New York: Oxford University Press, 2014), 97.

73. *US v. Nelson,* 859 F.2d 1318 (8th Cir. 1988), at 1320. The other federal court of appeals cases include *Cases v. US,* 131 F.2d 916, 922–923 (1st Cir. 1942), cert. denied sub nom *Velazquez v. US,* 319 US 770 (1943); *US v. Tot,* 131 F.2d 261, 266 (3d Cir. 1942), reversed on other grounds, 319 US 463 (1943); *US v. Johnson,* 441 F.2d 1134, 1136 (5th Cir. 1971); *Stevens v. US,* 440 F.2d 144, 149 (6th Cir. 1971); *US v. McCutcheon,* 446 F.2d 133, 135–36 (7th Cir. 1971); *US v. Decker,* 446 F.2d 164 (8th Cir. 1971); *US v. Synnes,* 438 F.2d 764 (8th Cir. 1971), vacated on other grounds, 404 US 1009 (1972); *Cody v. US,* 460 F.2d 34, 36–37 (8th Cir. 1972), cert. denied, 409 US 1010 (1972); *Eckert v. City of Philadelphia,* 477 F.2d 610 (3d Cir. 1973), cert. denied 414 US 839 (1973); *US v. Day,* 476 F.2d 562, 568 (6th Cir. 1973); *US v. Johnson,* 497 F.2d 548, 550 (4th Cir. 1974); *US v. Swinton,* 521 F.2d 1255 (10th Cir. 1975), cert. denied, 424 US 918 (1976); *US v. Warin,* 530 F.2d 103, 106 (6th Cir. 1976), cert. denied, 426 US 948 (1976); *US v. Graves,* 554 F.2d 65, 66–67 (3d Cir. 1977); *US v. Oakes,* 564 F.2d 384, 387 (10th Cir. 1977), cert. denied, 435 US 926 (1978); *Quilici v. Village of Morton Grove,* 695 F.2d 261, 270 (7th Cir. 1982), cert. denied, 464 US 863 (1983); *Thomas v. Members of City Council of Portland,* 730 F.2d 41 (1st Cir. 1984); *US v. Toner,* 728 F.2d 115 (2d Cir. 1984); *Farmer v. Higgins,* 907 F.2d 1041 (11th Cir. 1990), cert. denied, 498 US 1047 (1991); *US v. Hale,* 978 F.2d 1016 (8th Cir. 1992), cert. denied, 507 US 997 (1993); *Fresno Rifle & Pistol Club v. Van de Camp,* 965 F.2d 723 (9th Cir. 1992); *US v. Friel,* 1 F.3d 1231 (1st Cir. 1993); *Love v. Pepersack,* 47 F.3d 120, 124 (4th Cir. 1995), cert. denied 516 US 813 (1995); *US v. Farrell,* 69 F.3d 891 (8th Cir. 1995); *Hickman v. Block,* 81 F.3d 168 (9th Cir. 1996), cert. denied, 519 US 912 (1996); *US v. Rybar,* 103 F.3d 273 (3d Cir. 1996), cert. denied, 522 US 807 (1997); *US v. Wright,* 117 F.3d 1265, 1273 (11th Cir. 1997), cert. denied, 522 US 1007 (1997); *Peoples Rights Organization, Inc. v. City of Columbus,* 152 F.3d 522, 539 (6th Cir. 1998); *Gillespie v. City of Indianapolis,* 185 F.3d 693 (7th Cir. 1999), cert. denied, 528 US 1116 (2000); *US v. Napier,* 233 F.3d 394 (6th Cir. 2000); *US v. Metcalf,* 221 F.3d 1336 (6th Cir. 2000); *US v. Finitz,* 234 F.3d 1278 (9th Cir. 2000), cert. denied, 531 US 1100 (2001); *US v. Hancock,* 231 F.3d 557 (9th Cir. 2000), cert. denied, 532 US 989 (2001); *US v. Baer,* 235 F.2d 561 (10th Cir. 2000); *US v. Lewis,* 236 F.3d 948 (8th Cir. 2001); *US v. Haney,* 264 F.3d 1161 (10th Cir. 2001); *US v. Henry,* 288 F.3d 657 (5th Cir. 2002); *US v. Bayles,* 310 F.3d 1302, 1307 (10th Cir. 2002); *Silveira v. Lockyer,* 312 F.3d 1052 (9th Cir. 2002), cert. denied 540 US 1046 (2004); *Nordyke v. King,* 319 F.3d 1185 (9th Cir. 2003), cert. denied 543 US 820 (2004); *US v. Parker,* 362 F.3d 1279 (10th Cir. 2004), cert. denied 543 US 874 (2004); *Bach v. Pataki,* 408 F.3d 75 (2nd Cir. 2005), cert. denied 546 US 1174 (2006). In a case appealed to the Supreme Court from New Jersey, *Burton v. Sills,* 394 US 812 (1969), a challenge to a gun law alleging a violation of the Second Amendment was "dismissed for want of a substantial federal question."

74. Burger, "Right to Bear Arms," 4–6. Burger describes the militia-based history of the

Second Amendment, noting that a "huge national defense establishment has taken over the role of the militia of 200 years ago" (5).

75. See John Levin, "The Right to Bear Arms: The Development of the American Experience," *Chicago-Kent Law Review* 48 (Fall–Winter 1971): 159–62, and Dennis A. Henigan, "Arms, Anarchy and the Second Amendment," *Valparaiso University Law Review* 26 (1991): 108–9, 127. Forty-four state constitutions make some mention of a right to bear arms. See Spitzer, *Gun Control*, 296–303.

76. *Quilici v. Village of Morton Grove*, 532 F.Supp. 1169 (1981); 695 F.2d 261; *Quilici v. Village of Morton Grove*, 695 F.2d 261 (1982). The federal district court and court of appeals also found the law to be consistent with the Illinois state constitution (art. 1, sec. 22), which recognizes "the right of the individual citizen to keep and bear arms." The ordinance also exempted licensed gun collectors and owners of antique firearms. Brushing aside arguments of those opposing the law, the court of appeals confirmed that possession of handguns by individuals was not part of the right to keep and bear arms, that this right pertained only to militia service, that the local law was a reasonable exercise of police power, and that the Second Amendment did not apply to the states, "even if opponents to gun control find it illogical." See also Eric S. Freibrun, "Banning Handguns: *Quilici v. Village of Morton Grove* and the Second Amendment," *Washington University Law Quarterly* 60 (Fall 1982): 1087–118. Residents are not denied their handguns but must keep them in licensed gun clubs. The ordinance does not affect long guns.

77. A physician named Timothy Joe Emerson was charged with violating a federal law that barred him from possessing firearms because he was under a domestic violence protection order, prompted when he brandished a gun in the presence of his estranged wife and child. The appeals court majority's individualist interpretation of the Second Amendment did nothing to help Emerson, as his case was sent back to trial in Texas, where in 2002 he was convicted of unlawful firearms possession. Robert J. Spitzer, "The Second Amendment 'Right to Bear Arms' and *United States v. Emerson*," *St. John's Law Review* 77 (Winter 2003): 1–27. The Supreme Court refused to hear an appeal of the *Emerson* case (*Emerson v. US*, 536 US 907 [2002]).

78. Saul Cornell, "St. George Tucker and the Second Amendment," *William and Mary Law Review* 47(February 2006): 1123–55. Tucker viewed the Second Amendment as a civic right and a right belonging to the states. He also addressed personal self-defense but not as coming from the Second Amendment. Joseph Story, *Commentaries on the Constitution* (Durham, NC: Carolina Academic Press, 1987; first published 1833), 708; and Thomas M. Cooley, *General Principles of Constitutional Law* (Boston: Little, Brown, 1898), 298–99. Cooley's book did not include discussion of the important *Presser* case until the subsequent (fourth) edition of this book, published in 1931, which buttressed the standard interpretation found in the writings of other constitutional scholars. Both Story and Cooley describe the broader, more general nature of keeping and bearing arms arising from the old-style unorganized militias and musters of the pre–Civil War era.

79. Irving Brant, *The Bill of Rights* (Indianapolis, IN: Bobbs-Merrill, 1965), 486.

80. Robert A. Rutland, *The Birth of the Bill of Rights* (Chapel Hill: University of North Carolina Press, 1955), 229.

81. See *American Law Reports, Federal* (Rochester, NY: Lawyers Co-Operative, 1983), 700–29. In 1975 the American Bar Association endorsed the understanding that the Second Amendment is connected with militia service. See Lund, "The Second Amendment, Political Liberty, and the Right to Self-Preservation," 105.

82. Paul Finkelman, "District of Columbia v. Heller: It Really Was About a Well Regulated Militia," *Syracuse Law Review* 59 (2008): 267.

83. *D.C. v. Heller,* at 657.

84. Garry Wills, *A Necessary Evil* (New York: Simon and Schuster, 1999), 257, 258, 259.

85. Richard A. Posner, "In Defense of Looseness," *The New Republic,* August 27, 2008, www.tnr.com/article/books/defense-looseness. For more on "law office history" and the Second Amendment, see Robert J. Spitzer, *Saving the Constitution from Lawyers* (New York: Cambridge University Press, 2008), ch. 5.

86. Posner, "In Defense of Looseness"; J. Harvie Wilkinson III, "Of Guns, Abortions, and the Unraveling Rule of Law," *Virginia Law Review* 95 (April 2009): 253–323; Douglas Kmiec, "Guns and the Supreme Court: Dead Wrong," *Tidings Online,* July 11, 2008, http://www.the-tidings.com/2008/071108/kmiec_text.htm; Kmiec, "What the Heller?" *Slate,* July 8, 2008, http://www.slate.com/blogs/blogs/convictions/archive/2008/07/08/what-the-heller-is-only-the-supreme-court-s-liberty-enhanced.aspx.

87. To pick an example, Stephen Halbrook, in *The Founders' Second Amendment* (Chicago: Ivan R. Dee, 2008), quotes Patrick Henry as saying during the Virginia ratifying convention "that every man be armed" (4) as evidence that the country's founders favored "the ideal of an armed populace" (3). This quote would seem to support the view that at least some early leaders advocated general popular armament aside from militia purposes. Yet here is the full quote from the original debates: "May we not discipline and arm them [the states], as well as Congress, if the power be concurrent? so that our militia shall have two sets of arms, double sets of regimentals, &c.; and thus, at a very great cost, we shall be doubly armed. The great object is, *that every man be armed.* But can the people afford to pay for double sets of arms, &c. Every one who is able may have a gun. But we have learned, by experience, that, necessary as it is to have arms, and though our Assembly has, by a succession of laws for many years, endeavored to have the militia completely armed, it is still far from being the case" (emphasis added). Jonathan Elliot, *Elliot's Debates, on the Adoption of the Federal Constitution,* 4 vols. (New York: J. B. Lippincott, 1937), 3:386. It is perfectly obvious that Henry's comments are in the context of a discussion of the militia and of the power balance between the states and Congress.

88. *D.C. v. Heller,* at 646.

89. See 10 *US Code* 311 (1983). Current code lists the lower age as seventeen, but in colonial times, the age range was of necessity wider.

90. *D.C. v. Heller,* at 650.

91. Stuart R. Hays, "The Right to Bear Arms, a Study in Judicial Misinterpretation," *William and Mary Law Review* 2 (1960): 381–406.

92. See Robert J. Spitzer, "Lost and Found: Researching the Second Amendment," *Chicago-Kent Law Review* 76 (2000): 349–401; Spitzer, *The Right to Bear Arms,* 72.

93. *D.C. v. Heller,* at 662, emphasis in original.

94. David Thomas Konig, "The Second Amendment and the Right to Bear Arms after *D.C. v. Heller,*" *UCLA Law Review* 56 (June 2009): 1297.

95. See Samaha, *Criminal Law,* ch. 6.

96. American Law Institute, *Model Penal Code and Commentaries* (Philadelphia, PA: American Law Institute, 1985), vol. 1, pt. 1, 380–81. See also the definition of self-defense in Henry C. Black, *Black's Law Dictionary* (St. Paul, MN: West, 1991), 947.

97. *D.C. v. Heller,* at 661, 662.

98. Robert E. Shalhope says the Second Amendment protects weapons possession for Americans in part "for the purpose of keeping their rulers sensitive to the rights of the people." Would this make, say, Lee Harvey Oswald, John Wilkes Booth, and David Koresh true democrats?

"The Ideological Origins of the Second Amendment," *Journal of American History* 69 (December 1982): 614. See also Halbrook, *That Every Man Be Armed*, 68, 194–95; Lund, "The Second Amendment, Political Liberty, and the Right to Self-Preservation," 111–16; Wayne LaPierre, *Guns, Crime, and Freedom* (Washington, DC: Regnery, 1994), 19–20; and Glenn H. Reynolds, "The Right to Keep and Bear Arms under the Tennessee Constitution," *Tennessee Law Review* 61 (Winter 1994): 668–69.

99. Roscoe Pound, *The Development of Constitutional Guarantees of Liberty* (New Haven, CT: Yale University Press, 1957), 90–91. See also Wendy Brown, "Guns, Cowboys, Philadelphia Mayors, and Civic Republicanism: On Sanford Levinson's 'The Embarrassing Second Amendment,'" *Yale Law Journal* 99 (December 1989): 661–67.

100. Saul Cornell, *Whose Right to Bear Arms Did the Second Amendment Protect?* (Boston: Bedford/St. Martin's, 2000), 19–20. Stuart R. Hays goes so far as to cite with approval the Civil War as an instance of "the right to revolt when the laws of the government began to oppress." Whatever one thinks of that conflict, the effort of Southern states to break away from the Union was not within the bounds of the Constitution but an attack on the document and was a threat to the Union's continued existence. "Right to Bear Arms," 382.

101. The Calling Forth Act states as its purpose "to provide for calling forth the Militia to execute the laws of the Union, suppress insurrections and repel invasions." Section 1 of the act says, "in case of an insurrection in any state, against the government thereof, it shall be lawful for the President of the United States, on application of the legislature of such state, or of the executive (when the legislature cannot be convened) to call forth such number of the militia of any other state or states, as may be applied for, or as he may judge sufficient to suppress such insurrection." Section 2 says, "That whenever the laws of the United States shall be opposed, or the execution thereof obstructed, in any state, by any combinations too powerful to be suppressed by the ordinary course of judicial proceedings ... it shall be lawful for the President of the United States to call forth the militia of such state to suppress such combinations, and to cause the laws to be duly executed. And if the militia of a state ... shall refuse, or be insufficient to suppress the same, it shall be lawful for the President, if the legislature of the United States be not in session, to call forth and employ such numbers of the militia of any other state or states most convenient thereto."

102. Greg Sargent, "Sharron Angle Floated Possibility of Armed Insurrection," June 15, 2010, http://voices.washingtonpost.com/plum-line/2010/06/sharron_angle_floated_possibil.html.

103. See Joshua Horwitz and Casey Anderson, *Guns, Democracy, and the Insurrectionist Idea* (Ann Arbor: University of Michigan Press, 2009).

104. In his *McDonald* concurring opinion, Justice Clarence Thomas raises this very argument. See also Robert J. Cottrol and Raymond T. Diamond, "The Second Amendment: Toward an Afro-Americanist Reconsideration," *Georgetown Law Journal* 80 (1991): 309–61; and Stefan B. Tahmassebi, "Gun Control and Racism," *George Mason University Civil Rights Law Journal* 1 (Winter 1990): 67–99. Blacks were undeniably deprived of the fundamental right of self-protection pertaining but not limited to weapons possession. Yet extending weapons ownership to a subdominant group in society at a time when the group was deprived of most other basic freedoms and protections would in all likelihood be a formula for racial annihilation, as was the case with Native Americans: it would give the dominant group an excuse to attack. A discussion of women and the Second Amendment can be found in Jeffrey R. Stone, Richard A. Epstein, and Cass R. Sunstein, eds., *The Bill of Rights in the Modern State* (Chicago: University of Chicago Press, 1992).

105. Cottrol and Diamond, "The Second Amendment," 335.

106. Bogus, "Hidden History of the Second Amendment." See also Carl T. Bogus, "Race, Riots, and Guns," *Southern California Law Review* 66 (May 1993): 365–88.

107. According to the historian Ralph Ketchum, "the anti-federalists saw in the enlarged powers of the central government only the familiar threats to the rights and liberties of the people." *The Anti-Federalist Papers and the Constitutional Convention Debates* (New York: New American Library, 1986), 16.

108. Garry Wills, "To Keep and Bear Arms," *New York Review of Books,* September 21, 1995, 68. Wills's article is as careful and detailed an account of the meaning of the words behind the Second Amendment as exists in print.

Chapter 3

1. Michael Moriarty, "Get Rid of Guns, Says Father of Boy Killed in Accident," *Syracuse (N.Y.) Post-Standard,* October 16, 1989; and John O'Brien, "Family: Lax Gun Rules Led to Death," *Syracuse Post-Standard,* April 26, 1991.

2. "Women Find Security Behind a Gun," *Syracuse (N.Y.) Herald American,* September 9, 1990. Marion Hammer later became the first female president of the National Rifle Association.

3. Robert Reinhold, "After Shooting, Horror but Few Answers," *New York Times,* January 19, 1989; and Osha Gray Davidson, *Under Fire: NRA and the Battle for Gun Control* (New York: Holt, 1993), 3–19.

4. Gary Taubes, "Violence Epidemiologists Test the Hazards of Gun Ownership," *Science* 258 (October 9, 1992): 213–15; and Jane Gross, "Joining War over Guns, New Voices: Physicians," *New York Times,* November 16, 1993.

5. Murray Edelman, *The Symbolic Uses of Politics* (Urbana: University of Illinois Press, 1964), 121. Edelman also says that "language is not an independent variable but a catalyst in the shaping of perception.... People can potentially see an issue in several alternative lights, and the language form itself evokes some one of the potentialities." *Politics as Symbolic Action* (Chicago: Markham, 1971), 68.

6. Michael Luo, "Sway of N.R.A. Blocks Studies, Scientists Say," *New York Times,* January 26, 2011. By 2001 CDC spending on research related to firearms was $400,000. Kristin A. Goss, *Disarmed: The Missing Movement for Gun Control in America* (Princeton, NJ: Princeton University Press, 2006), 88; Neil A. Lewis, "N.R.A. Takes Aim at Study of Guns as Public Health Risk," *New York Times,* August 26, 1995; Jim McElhatten, "US Quietly Begins to Study Gun Safety," *Washington Times,* October 19, 2009, http://www.washingtontimes.com/news/2009 /oct/19/nih-funds-study-of-teen-firearms/.

7. "US Easily Leads World in Gun-Related Deaths," *New York Times,* April 17, 1998; Wendy Cukier and Victor W. Sidel, *The Global Gun Epidemic* (Westport, CT: Praeger, 2006).

8. Peter Applebome, "Verdict in Louisiana Killing Reverberates across Nation," *New York Times,* May 26, 1993.

9. David E. Sanger, "After Gunman's Acquittal, Japan Struggles to Understand America," *New York Times,* May 25, 1993; and Adam Nossiter, "Judge Awards Damages in Japanese Youth's Death," *New York Times,* September 16, 1994. America's gun habits continued to receive considerable attention in Japan. The country closely followed the enactment of the Brady bill in 1993, and its passage in November was front-page news throughout the country. Japan also began distributing pamphlets to Japanese planning to visit the United States, discussing how to avoid

danger and explaining such phrases as "Freeze" and "Get your hands up." "Japan Hopes Brady Bill Is First Step," *Syracuse Post-Standard,* November 26, 1993.

10. See Philip J. Cook, "The Technology of Personal Violence," in *Crime and Justice: A Review of Research,* ed. Michael Tonry (Chicago: University of Chicago Press, 1991), 4, 6–7, 28; and Philip J. Cook and Jens Ludwig, *Gun Violence: The Real Costs* (New York: Oxford University Press, 2000), viii; "Gun Violence," National Institute of Justice, October 26, 2010, http://www.nij.gov/topics/crime/gun-violence/. I do not propose to answer the chicken-and-egg question of whether guns cause or are merely incidental to violence. In all probability the actual relationship incorporates elements of both. But one need not resolve this dilemma to note that the two are closely and inextricably linked in both image and fact. The homicide rate began to rise dramatically in the 1960s, as did the production and sale of handguns, which play a disproportionately large role in gun injuries and deaths.

11. Francis X. Clines, "As Gunfire Gets Closer, Fear Comes Home," *New York Times,* December 12, 1993; and Richard L. Berke, "Fears of Crime Rival Concern over Economy," *New York Times,* January 23, 1994.

12. See "Firearm Injury in the US," *Firearm and Injury Center at Penn,* 2009, at www.uphs .upenn.edu/ficap/; http://www.fbi.gov/stats-services/crimestats; "Gun Deaths and Injuries," Legal Community Against Violence, http://www.lcav.org/statistics-polling/gun_violence _-statistics.asp#3; Michael Planty and Jennifer L. Truman, "Firearm Violence, 1993–2011," Bureau of Justice Statistics, May 2013; "Crime in the United States, 2011," FBI, at http://www .fbi.gov/about-us/cjis/ucr/crime-in-the-u.s/2011/crime-in-the-u.s.-2011/tables/expanded -homicide-data-table-14. The peak year of gun deaths was 1993, which logged 39,595.

13. Garen J. Wintemute, Stephen Teret, and Jess F. Kraus, "The Epidemiology of Firearm Deaths among Residents of California," *Western Journal of Medicine* 146 (March 1987): 374–77; Sabra Chartrand, "Gunshot Wounds Labeled Epidemic," *New York Times,* June 11, 1992; "After Dark," *Economist,* March 5, 1994, 25–26; and "Guns and Crime," Crime Data Brief, US Department of Justice, April 1994.

14. National Research Council, *Firearms and Violence* (Washington, DC: National Academies Press, 2005), 62–63; David Hemenway, *Private Guns, Public Health* (Ann Arbor: University of Michigan Press, 2004), 113–14; *National Vital Statistics Reports* 57, no. 14 (April 17, 2009): table 19, p. 91; M. Heninger and R. Hanzlick, "Nonnatural Deaths of Adolescents and Teen-agers: Fulton County, Georgia," *American Journal of Forensic Medical Pathology* 29, no. 3 (2008): 208–13.

15. Philip J. Hilts, "Gunshots Killing More Teenagers," *New York Times,* June 10, 1992; "Study: Firearms Killed 4,200 Teens in 1990," *Syracuse Post-Standard,* March 24, 1993; "Guns Are No. 2 Cause of Death among the Young, Data Show," *New York Times,* April 9, 1996; Cook and Ludwig, *Gun Violence,* 18; Gregg Lee Carter, "Dueling Statistics," *Forum for Applied Research and Public Policy* (Winter 2000): 70; Office of Juvenile Justice and Delinquency Prevention, *Report to Congress on Juvenile Violence Research,* US Department of Justice, July 1999, x. These data are available from several sources, including the Children's Defense Fund and the National Center for Health Statistics.

16. Quoted in "As Cities Reach Record Number of Killings, Youths Play Grim Role," *New York Times,* January 1, 1994; US Department of Justice, Office of Juvenile Justice and Delinquency Prevention, "Challenging the Myths," *Juvenile Justice Bulletin,* February 2000, 5.

17. See, for example, James D. Wright, Peter H. Rossi, and Kathleen Daly, *Under the Gun: Weapons, Crime, and Violence in America* (New York: Aldine de Gruyter, 1983), 170. The policy expert Philip Cook has produced an estimate of a little more than five injuries for every gun

death, based on a variety of data sources. See Cook, "The Case of the Missing Victims: Gunshot Woundings in the National Crime Survey," *Journal of Quantitative Criminology* 1 (1985): 91–102, and Cook, "Technology of Personal Violence," 12. According to a 1993 report issued by the New York State Legislative Commission on Science and Technology, the nationwide ratio of gun injuries to deaths is closer to 7.5 to 1. Luther F. Bliven, "Committee Studies Report on Firearms Crime," *Syracuse Post-Standard,* June 1, 1993. A new system for reporting all firearms injuries was to be implemented in 2003. Under the previous system many firearms-related injuries were not reported. In New York City, for example, hospitals were not required to report gunshot injuries treated in emergency rooms or on an outpatient basis.

18. Nancy Gibbs, "Up in Arms," *Time,* December 20, 1993, 21; Albert J. Reiss Jr. and Jeffrey A. Roth, eds., *Understanding and Preventing Violence* (Washington, DC: National Academy Press, 1993), 256; Cook and Ludwig, *Gun Violence,* 11.

19. "Firearm Injury in the US," 6. Data from 2003–2005.

20. Erik Eckholm, "Ailing Gun Industry Confronts Outrage over Glut of Violence," *New York Times,* March 8, 1992. See also National Institute of Justice, "Guns in America: National Survey on Private Ownership and Use of Firearms," *NIJ Journal,* May 1997; Bureau of Justice Statistics, *Sourcebook of Criminal Justice Statistics 1999* (Washington, DC: Government Printing Office, 2000), 138–39; Philip J. Cook and Mark H. Moore, "Guns, Gun Control, and Homicide," in *Homicide: A Sourcebook of Social Research,* ed. M. Dwayne Smith and Margaret A. Zahn (Thousand Oaks, CA: Sage), 278; National Research Council, *Firearms and Violence,* 56–58; Violence Policy Center, "A Shrinking Minority: The Continuing Decline of Gun Ownership in America," April 2007; Philip J. Cook and Kristin A. Goss, *The Gun Debate* (New York: Oxford University Press, 2014), 13.

21. Data from the National Opinion Research Center—General Social Survey Data File 1998, 2008; "Gun Ownership Trends and Demographics," *Pew Research Center,* March 12, 2013, http://www.people-press.org/2013/03/12/section-3-gun-ownership-trends-and-demographics/.

22. Franklin E. Zimring, "Firearms, Violence, and Public Policy," *Scientific American* 265 (November 1991): 50. Cook offers similar numbers; see "Technology of Personal Violence," 23; Zawitz, "Guns Used in Crime," 2; "Handgun Use Rose in 1993, Reports Show," *New York Times,* July 10, 1995; Josh Sugarmann, *Every Handgun Is Aimed at You* (New York: New Press, 2001).

23. Philip J. Cook, "Guns and Crime: The Perils of Long Division," *Journal of Policy Analysis and Management* 1 (1981): 120–25. When divided out, however, the per-year use of handguns in crime as a percentage of all handguns is small, as guns have a long shelf life. Gary Kleck provides an estimate of 0.9 percent of handguns involved in crime in any one year, a figure consistent with Cook's estimate. *Point Blank: Guns and Violence in America* (New York: Aldine de Gruyter, 1991), 44.

24. For more on the relationship between handguns and crime, see Bureau of Alcohol, Tobacco and Firearms, *Project Identification: A Study of Handguns Used in Crime* (Washington, DC: Bureau of Alcohol, Tobacco, and Firearms, 1976); Comptroller General of the United States, *Handgun Control: Effectiveness and Costs* (Washington, DC: General Accounting Office, 1978); and Bureau of Justice Statistics, "Handgun Crime Victims," *Special Report* (Washington, DC: US Department of Justice, 1990). On the importance of bullet caliber and speed, see Jeremy J. Hollerman, "Gunshot Wounds," *American Family Physician* 37 (1988): 231–46; Franklin E. Zimring, "The Medium Is the Message: Firearm Caliber as a Determinant of Death from Assault," *Journal of Legal Studies* 1 (January 1972): 97–124; Sugarmann, *Every Handgun Is Aimed at You.*

25. From a 1978 survey, reported in Wright, Rossi, and Daly, *Under the Gun,* 96.

26. Cook, "Technology of Personal Violence," 28–29.

27. The study by James D. Wright and Peter H. Rossi is based on self-administered questionnaires to 1,874 prisoners in ten states. The sample was not random but was based (for reasons the authors discuss) on convenience. Thus, the group studied cannot be considered representative of prisoners or of those who do or do not use guns in crimes. Nor does it reflect those who use guns illegally but are not caught and imprisoned. Still, it is an important research effort. *Armed and Considered Dangerous: A Survey of Felons and Their Firearms* (New York: Aldine de Gruyter, 1986). As Daniel D. Polsby noted, those in prison "are remarkable neither for honesty nor acute introspection." "Reflections on Violence, Guns, and the Defensive Use of Lethal Force," *Law and Contemporary Problems* 49 (Winter 1986): 97. See also Gary S. Green, "Citizen Gun Ownership and Criminal Deterrence: Theory, Research, and Policy," *Criminology* 25 (February 1987): 70–71.

28. Wright and Rossi, *Armed and Considered Dangerous,* 15–17, 128.

29. Gary Kleck and Karen McElrath, "The Effects of Weaponry on Human Violence," *Social Forces* 69 (March 1991): 669–92, and Philip J. Cook and Mark H. Moore, "Gun Control," in *Crime,* ed. James Q. Wilson and Joan Petersilig (San Francisco: ICS Press, 1995), 272–75.

30. Franklin E. Zimring, "Is Gun Control Likely to Reduce Violent Killings?" *University of Chicago Law Review* 35 (Summer 1968): 721–37. See also Zimring, "Medium Is the Message"; Philip J. Cook, "The Effect of Gun Availability on Robbery and Robbery Murder: A Cross Section Study of Fifty Cities," in *Policy Studies Review Annual,* ed. Robert H. Haveman and B. Bruce Zellner (Beverly Hills, CA: Sage, 1979); Philip J. Cook, "Robbery Violence," *Journal of Criminal Law and Criminology* 78 (Summer 1987): 357–76; and Franklin E. Zimring and Gordon Hawkins, *Crime Is Not the Problem* (New York: Oxford University Press, 1997). Wright, Rossi, and Daly are more cautious in their support of this principle. *Under the Gun,* 203, 209.

31. In 1989, for example, the success rate for noncommercial robberies was 70 percent when guns were used, 55 percent when knives were used, and 49 percent when clubs or other instruments were used. Cook, "Technology of Personal Violence," 21.

32. Leonard Berkowitz and Anthony Le Page, "Weapons as Aggression-Eliciting Stimuli," *Journal of Personality and Social Psychology* 7 (October 1967): 202–7; Leonard Berkowitz, "Impulse, Aggression and the Gun," *Psychology Today* 2 (September 1968): 19–22; and Berkowitz, "How Guns Control Us," *Psychology Today* 15 (June 1981): 11–12.

33. Alfred Blumstein and Richard Rosenfeld, "Assessing the Recent Ups and Downs in US Homicide Rates," *NIJ Journal* 237 (October 1998): 10.

34. Philip J. Cook, "The Effect of Gun Availability on Violent Crime Patterns," *Annals of the American Academy of Political and Social Science* 455 (May 1981): 63–79; Cook, "Technology of Personal Violence," 4, 28; Kleck and McElrath, "Effects of Weaponry on Human Violence"; Franklin E. Zimring, "Reflections on Firearms and the Criminal Law," *Journal of Criminal Law and Criminology* 46 (Fall 1995): 7; Zimring and Hawkins, *Crime Is Not the Problem.*

35. Gerald D. Robin, *Violent Crime and Gun Control* (Highland Heights, KY: Academy of Criminal Justice Sciences, 1991), 3–4; Hemenway, *Private Guns, Public Health,* 47. An important factor in at least some such incidents may be alcohol. For more on the link between alcohol and homicide, see Robert N. Parker and Linda-Ann Rebhun, *Alcohol and Homicide: A Deadly Combination of Two American Traditions* (Albany: State University of New York Press, 1994).

36. On policymakers and guns, see Kleck, *Point Blank,* 223. Percentages are from John Henry Sloan et al., "Firearm Regulations and Rates of Suicide," *New England Journal of Medicine* 322 (February 8, 1990): 369. On increasing use of guns in female suicides, see Wright, Rossi, and Daly, *Under the Gun,* 167–68.

37. J. J. Card, "Lethality of Suicidal Methods and Suicide Risk: Two Distinct Concepts," *Omega* 5 (1974): 37–45, and Kleck, *Point Blank,* 258.

38. Kleck, *Point Blank,* 225, 226, and Cook, "Technology of Personal Violence," 24.

39. See Mark S. Kaplan, Margaret E. Adamek, and Scott Johnson, "Trends in Firearm Suicide among Older American Males: 1979–1988," *Gerontologist* 34 (February 1994): 59–65; Cook and Ludwig, *Gun Violence,* 23; Madeline Drexler, ed., "Guns and Suicide: The Hidden Toll," *Harvard Public Health,* Spring 2013, 26–28.

40. Julie Sullivan, "The Oregonian: A Case in Umatilla County Shows That for Veterans, Suicide Is a Mortal Enemy," Portland State University, September 11, 2010, http://www .beta .www.pdx.edu/news/the-oregonian-a-case-in-umatilla-county-shows-that-for-veterans -suicide-is-a-mortal-enemy.

41. As Cook observes, "Surely someone who purposefully points a gun at a vital area and pulls the trigger expects to die." "Technology of Personal Violence," 25.

42. Ronald V. Clarke and David Lester, *Suicide: Closing the Exits* (New York: Springer Verlag, 1989), vii. The difficulties of studying displacement are discussed on 76–77.

43. Arthur L. Kellerman et al., "Suicide in the Home in Relation to Gun Ownership," *New England Journal of Medicine* 327 (August 13, 1992): 467.

44. Robert E. Markush and Alfred A. Bartolucci, "Firearms and Suicide in the United States," *American Journal of Public Health* 74 (1984): 123–27; David Lester, "An Availability-Acceptability Theory of Suicide," *Activitas Nervosa Superior* 29 (1987): 164–66; and David Lester, "Restricting the Availability of Guns as a Strategy for Preventing Suicide," *Biology and Society* 5 (1988): 127–29; Hemenway, *Private Guns, Public Health,* 38.

45. Card, "Lethality of Suicide Methods and Suicide Risk"; Richard Seiden, "Suicide Prevention: A Public Health/Public Policy Approach," *Omega* 8 (1977): 267–76; Myron Boor, "Methods of Suicide and Implications for Suicide Prevention," *Journal of Clinical Psychology* 37 (1981): 70–75; Clarke and Lester, *Suicide;* Kellerman et al., "Suicide in the Home in Relation to Gun Ownership"; Garen J. Wintemute et al., "Mortality among Recent Purchasers of Handguns," *New England Journal of Medicine* 341 (November 1999): 1583–89. In his tabular synthesis of the existing literature, Kleck summarizes a lengthy list of studies, yet he fails to include any of the studies listed here, all of which militate against his arguments, and he omits others as well. *Point Blank,* 265–67.

46. Clarke and Lester, *Suicide,* 72; see also chs. 4 and 5 of this book.

47. Kellerman et al., "Suicide in the Home in Relation to Gun Ownership." Rather than rely on aggregate statistics, this study was based on an intensive analysis of the counties incorporating Memphis, Tennessee, and Seattle, Washington, from 1987 to 1990.

48. Sloan et al., "Firearm Regulations and Rates of Suicide." This study was based on a comparison of the counties incorporating Seattle, Washington, and Vancouver, British Columbia, Canada.

49. Cook, "Technology of Personal Violence," 26.

50. Hemenway, *Private Guns, Public Health,* 44–45.

51. Matthew Miller et al., "Household Firearm Ownership and Rates of Suicide across the 50 United States," *Journal of Trauma* 62 (April 2007): 1029–34; Matthew Miller and David Hemenway, "Guns and Suicide in the United States," *New England Journal of Medicine* 359 (September 4, 2008): 989–91; Drexler, "Guns and Suicide."

52. David A. Brent, Joshua A. Perper, and Christopher J. Allman, "Alcohol, Firearms, and Suicide among Youth," *Journal of the American Medical Association* 257 (June 26, 1987): 3369; and Jane E. Brody, "Suicide Myths Cloud Efforts to Save Children," *New York Times,* June 16,

1992. For more on suicide and children, see Cynthia R. Pfeffer, *The Suicidal Child* (New York: Guilford Press, 1986).

53. Brody, "Suicide Myths Cloud Efforts to Save Children."

54. Ibid.; study conducted by the University of North Carolina at Chapel Hill Injury Prevention Research Center, December 15, 2004, http://www.unc.edu/news/.

55. Mark L. Rosenberg, James A. Mercy, and Vernon N. Houk, "Guns and Adolescent Suicides," *Journal of the American Medical Association* 266 (December 4, 1991): 3030.

56. David A. Brent et al., "The Presence and Accessibility of Firearms in the Homes of Adolescent Suicides: A Case-Control Study," *Journal of the American Medical Association* 266 (December 4, 1991): 2989–95; Rosenberg, Mercy, and Houk, "Guns and Adolescent Suicides," 3030; Sean Joe and Mark S. Kaplan, "Firearm-Related Suicide among Young African-American Males," *Psychiatric Services* 53 (March 2002): 332–34.

57. Daniel W. Webster et al., "Association Between Youth-Focused Firearm Laws and Youth Suicides," *Journal of the American Medical Association* 292 (August 4, 2004): 594–601; Catherine A. Okoro et al., "Prevalence of Household Firearms and Firearm-Storage Practices in the 50 States and the District of Columbia," *Pediatrics* 116 (September 2005): 370–76.

58. Brent, Perper, and Allman, "Alcohol, Firearms, and Suicide among Youth," 3372. This finding was based on an earlier analysis of the blood and urine of suicide victims in Australia.

59. Wright, Rossi, and Daly, *Under the Gun,* 168–70; Cook, "Technology of Personal Violence," 8, 12–13. According to one study, the ratio of accidental gun injury to accidental gun death in 1992 was thirteen to one. See Joseph L. Annest et al., "National Estimates of Nonfatal Firearm-Related Injuries," *Journal of the American Medical Association* 273 (June 14, 1995): 1751.

60. Zimring, "Firearms, Violence and Public Policy," 52; Wright, Rossi, and Daly, *Under the Gun,* 169; and Garen J. Wintemute et al., "When Children Shoot Children," *Journal of the American Medical Association* 257 (June 12, 1987): 3107–09; Cook and Ludwig, *Gun Violence,* 27. See Kleck, *Point Blank,* 309. Kleck rails against those who use the word "children" to apply to those up to the age of eighteen, viewing the use of the term as serving "no purpose other than the propagandistic one of duping people into believing that accidental gun deaths are common among small children" (277). According to the *Britannica World Language Dictionary,* "child" is defined as "a young person of either sex at any age less than maturity, but most commonly one between infancy and youth." Clearly, the concern is with "minors," those who have not reached the age of majority, generally eighteen.

61. Wintemute et al., "When Children Shoot Children."

62. David McDowall and Colin Loftin, "Collective Security and Fatal Firearm Accidents," *Criminology* 23 (August 1985): 401, 403; Okoro et al., "Prevalence of Household Firearms."

63. See Kleck, *Point Blank,* ch. 7. Kleck places little emphasis on the nonfatal injury rate.

64. Jane E. Brody, "Keeping Guns Out of Children's Hands," *New York Times,* August 17, 2004; Michael Luo and Mike McIntire, "Children and Guns: The Hidden Toll," *New York Times,* September 29, 2013.

65. Douglas A. Smith and Craig D. Uchida, "The Social Organization of Self-Help: A Study of Defensive Weapon Ownership," *American Sociological Review* 53 (February 1988): 94–102. See also McDowall and Loftin, "Collective Security and Fatal Firearm Accidents," 401–16. A useful discussion of self-defense and its relationship to deterrence is found in Green, "Citizen Gun Ownership and Criminal Deterrence."

66. Cook, "Technology of Personal Violence," 57–58. According to the National Crime Survey, from 1979 to 1987 burglaries were successful when the victim was home in 33 percent of the instances, compared with a success rate of 14 percent when the victim used a gun.

67. See Wright and Rossi, *Armed and Considered Dangerous,* 148. But see also Cook, "Effect of Gun Availability on Robbery and Robbery Murder"; and Cook, "Technology of Personal Violence," 60. In two actual instances in which localities promoted gun possession to combat crime, Orlando, Florida, and Kennesaw, Georgia, the available data provide no reliable evidence that crime patterns were altered. Gary Kleck and David J. Bordua note that the rape rate dropped at the time of the Orlando intervention program. "The Factual Foundation for Certain Key Assumptions of Gun Control," *Law and Policy Quarterly* 5 (1983): 271–98. But Gary Green found fault with the city's police data on which the study was based, noting that the rape rate was reported at zero three years before the city program and that it recorded drops even larger than that attributed to the Orlando gun program before the program was implemented. "Citizen Gun Ownership and Criminal Deterrence," 73–75. For the Kennesaw case, see Kleck, "Crime Control through the Private Use of Armed Force," versus Cook, "Technology of Personal Violence," 61.

68. For example, Green, "Citizen Gun Ownership and Criminal Deterrence," 70–77; Zawitz, "Guns Used in Crime," 3; National Research Council, *Firearms and Violence,* 74; Philip J. Cook and Jens Ludwig, "5 Myths about Gun Control," *Washington Post,* June 13, 2010.

69. Kleck, *Point Blank,* 107; Kleck produced a figure of 645,000 defensive handgun uses in 1980, compared with 580,000 criminal handgun uses in the same year, leading him to conclude that the two uses balance each other out. "Crime Control through the Private Use of Armed Force," *Social Problems* 35 (February 1988): 1–21. The NRA reported that Kleck was now estimating "as many as 2.4 million defensive uses of firearms each year in America." "Gary Kleck Honored," *American Rifleman,* January 1994, 7.

70. Kleck's estimate assumes that the National Crime Victimization Survey, which in past years reported an average of about 55,000 defensive uses of guns per year, somehow failed to report another 945,000 defensive uses of guns per year. Kleck relied primarily on a 1981 Hart poll and a 1990 Mauser survey that asked if members of the respondents' households had used a handgun (the Mauser survey included any gun) for protection any time at work, home, or elsewhere in the previous five years. The results, based on extrapolation from the sample, suggested that guns had been used for self-defense about three million times over five years. Yet such recall data are inherently unreliable in survey research, and the vagueness of the question makes the results highly suspect. The additional surveys he cites as corroborating evidence pose even greater problems, for example, by failing to distinguish between uses against animals versus people or by extending the retrospective period to "ever." Moreover, self-protection was defined so broadly that it would include such circumstances as investigating a noise in the basement. In essence, Kleck makes no distinction between actual and imagined instances of self-defense uses of guns. The numerous problems with Kleck's data are ironic in light of his harsh criticism of the methodologies of those with whom he disagrees. *Point Blank,* 105–8, 146, 467–68. Kleck amplifies such criticisms in *Targeting Guns* (New York: Aldine DeGruyter, 1997). See also Cook, "Technology of Personal Violence," 54–55; and Robin, *Violent Crime and Gun Control,* 62. The Kleck and Gertz poll, reported in "Armed Resistance to Crime," improves on the previous suspect polls, yet the survey's reliability is suspect because it was conducted privately (although a professional telephone polling firm did the telephoning) rather than by a professional survey organization, such as Gallup. Further, response validity was not verified by an outside, impartial expert unconnected with the research project. Kleck and Gertz dismiss the idea that their respondents would lie, yet they fail to consider another alternative: that their respondents believed they had encountered a serious self-defense instance when in fact the belief might not jibe with the objective circumstances. That is, the self-defense belief might

not coincide with an actual protection instance that would not have occurred without a gun. Philip Cook suggests, "It is quite possible that most 'self-defense' uses occur in circumstances that are normatively ambiguous: chronic violence within a marriage, gang fights, robberies of drug dealers, encounters with groups of young men who simply appear threatening." Cook and Moore, "Gun Control," 272. The results of a study of gun ownership among urban gang members, in which self-protection was the most commonly cited reason for gun ownership, illustrates an additional problem raised by Kleck's inability to verify the legitimacy of the alleged gun defense incidents. See Beth Bjerregaard and Alan J. Lizotte, "Gun Ownership and Gang Membership," *Journal of Criminal Law and Criminology* 86 (Fall 1995): 37–58. See also Richard D. Alba and Steven E. Messner, "*Point Blank* against Itself: Evidence and Inference about Guns, Crime, and Gun Control," *Journal of Quantitative Criminology* 11 (1995): 391–410; William Wells, "The Nature and Circumstances of Defensive Gun Use," *Justice Quarterly* 19 (March 2002): 127–57. When the Harvard School of Public Health conducted its own similar telephone surveys and had the reported instances of defensive gun uses analyzed by a panel of judges, they concluded that 51 percent of them were "probably illegal." David Hemenway et al., "Gun Use in the United States," *Injury Prevention* 6 (December 2000): 265. The study also reported that far more people reported being threatened or intimidated by a gun than using one for self-defense.

71. Cook, "Technology of Personal Violence," 56, 61–62. According to the data Cook obtained, from 1979 to 1987 an average of 6.8 million residential burglaries occurred per year. Of those, someone was home in about a million instances. Residents took some kind of self-defensive action in half these instances. They used guns in about 3 percent of the instances (a knife or other weapon was used in 2 percent). This yields a figure of thirty-two thousand uses of guns. This figure is added to the fifty thousand other defensive uses of guns to produce the eight thousand total. The thirty-two thousand figure is significant because Kleck argues that most defensive gun uses occur in the home. See also Wright, Rossi, and Daly, *Under the Gun*, 149. Cook's numbers of defensive gun uses as well as those of the National Crime Victimization Survey have remained relatively constant at eighty to eighty-five thousand per year. See Cook and Moore, "Gun Control," 270–72.

72. David Hemenway, "Survey Research and Self-Defense Gun Use: An Explanation of Extreme Overestimates," *Journal of Criminal Law and Criminology* 87 (Summer 1997): 1430–45; Tom W. Smith, "A Call for a Truce in the DGU War," *Journal of Criminal Law and Criminology* 87 (Summer 1997): 1462–69; and National Institute of Justice, "Guns in America"; National Research Council, *Firearms and Violence*, ch. 5.

73. Gary Kleck and Marc Gertz, "Armed Resistance to Crime: The Prevalence and Nature of Self-Defense with a Gun," *Journal of Criminal Law and Criminology* 86 (Fall 1995): 150–87; Kleck and Gertz, "The Illegitimacy of One-Sided Speculation," *Journal of Criminal Law and Criminology* 87 (Summer 1997): 1460.

74. Gordon Witkin, "Should You Own a Gun?" *US News & World Report*, August 15, 1994, 28. Cook went on to observe, "I don't understand why people would be so much more forthcoming with Kleck's survey callers than with the government's. I find that absurd." See also Dennis A. Henigan, *Lethal Logic* (Washington, DC: Potomac Books, 2009), 114–21.

75. Tom W. Smith, "A Call for a Truce in the DGU War," *Journal of Criminal Law and Criminology* 87 (Summer 1997): 1465. See also Kleck and Gertz, "The Illegitimacy of One-Sided Speculation"; Hemenway, "Survey Research and Self-Defense Gun Use," 1430–45; Philip J. Cook, Jens Ludwig, and David Hemenway, "The Gun Debate's New Mythical Number," *Journal of Policy Analysis and Management* 16 (Summer 1997): 463–69; Carter, "Dueling Statistics"; Deborah Homsher, *Women and Guns* (Armonk, NY: M. E. Sharpe, 2002), 88.

76. According to one study, among robbery victims who used guns for self-defense, 17 percent reported injury, compared with an overall injury rate of 33 percent. Reiss and Roth, *Understanding and Preventing Violence*, 266. See also Robin, *Violent Crime and Gun Control*, 70.

77. Reiss and Roth, *Understanding and Preventing Violence*, 267 (based on data from the FBI); and Sue M. Holmes, "Weapons That Will Not Fire for Just Anybody," *Cortland (N.Y.) Standard*, April 19, 1995, http://www.fbi.gov/about-us/cjis/ucr/leoka/2009.

78. Mike McAndrew, "Taking Aim under Fire," *Syracuse Post-Standard*, March 13, 1996; Marc Santora, "Bystanders' Shooting Wounds Caused by the Police," *New York Times*, August 26, 2012.

79. Al Baker, "11 Years of Police Gunfire, in Painstaking Detail," *New York Times*, May 8, 2008.

80. Cheryl W. Thompson, "Guns Used to Kill Police Officers," *Washington Post*, November 21, 2010.

81. Robert E. Drinan, "The Good Outweighs the Evil," in *The Gun Control Debate*, ed. Lee Nisbet (Buffalo, NY: Prometheus Books, 1990), 58.

82. Arthur L. Kellerman and Donald T. Reay, "Protection or Peril? An Analysis of Firearm-Related Deaths in the Home," *New England Journal of Medicine* 314 (June 12, 1986): 1557–60. For similar findings covering 1958 through 1973, see N. B. Rushforth et al., "Accidental Firearm Fatalities in a Metropolitan Area," *American Journal of Epidemiology* 100 (1975): 499–505.

83. Arthur L. Kellerman et al., "Gun Ownership as a Risk Factor for Homicide in the Home," *New England Journal of Medicine* 329 (October 7, 1993): 1084–91. The study covered 1987 through 1992 for Washington State and Tennessee, and 1990 through 1992 for the Ohio county. The analysis was of 444 homicides committed in the home out of a total of 1,860 committed in the three counties during the time periods cited.

84. John Henry Sloan et al., "Handgun Regulations, Crime, Assaults, and Homicide," *New England Journal of Medicine* 319 (November 10, 1988): 1260.

85. Arthur L. Kellerman et al., "Weapon Involvement in Home Invasion Crimes," *Journal of the American Medical Association* 273 (June 14, 1995): 1759–62. Wintemute et al., "Mortality among Recent Purchasers of Handguns"; Mathew Miller, Deborah Azrael, and David Hemenway, "Firearm Availability and Unintentional Firearm Deaths, Suicide, and Homicide among 5–14 Year Olds," *Journal of Trauma* 52 (February 2002): 267–75; Mark Duggan, "More Guns, More Crime," *Journal of Political Economy* 109 (October 2001): 1086–114. David McDowall and Brian Wiersema report that from 1987 to 1990 fewer than two crimes in a thousand met armed resistance from victims. "The Incidence of Defensive Firearm Use by US Crime Victims," *American Journal of Public Health* 84 (1994): 1982–84.

86. Douglas J. Wiebe, "Homicide and Suicide Risks Associated with Firearms in the Home," *Annals of Emergency Medicine* 41 (2003): 771–82; Linda L. Dahlberg et al., "Guns in the Home and Risk of a Violence Death in the Home," *American Journal of Epidemiology* 160 (November 15, 2004): 929–36; Matthew Miller et al., "State-Level Homicide Victimization Rates in the US in Relation to Survey Measures of Household Firearm Ownership, 2001–2003," *Social Science and Medicine* 64 (2007): 656–64; Charles C. Branas et al., "Investigating the Link between Gun Possession and Gun Assault," *American Journal of Public Health* 99 (November 2009): 2034–40; Dana Loomis et al., "Employer Policies Toward Guns and the Risk of Homicide in the Workplace," *American Journal of Public Health* 95 (May 2005): 830–32.

87. Robert A. Sprecher, "The Lost Amendment," *American Bar Association Journal* 51 (June 1965): 668.

88. Larry Pratt, "Gun Laws Cost Lives," *Syracuse Post-Standard*, January 8, 1994. Pratt is vice president of the Gun Owners Foundation.

89. David McDowall, Colin Loftin, and Brian Wiersema, "Easing Concealed Firearms Laws: Effects on Homicide in Three States," *Journal of Criminal Law and Criminology* 86 (Fall 1995): 193–206; Center to Prevent Handgun Violence, "Legal Action Report," February 1998; *License to Kill, and Kidnap, and Rape, and Drive Drunk* (Violence Policy Center, 1999); Ralph Blumenthal, "Bull's-Eyes of Texas: Getting a Gun License," *New York Times*, July 14, 2006; Philip Cook et al., "Gun Control after *Heller*," *UCLA Law Review* 56 (June 2009): 1078–85; "Concealed Weapons Permitting Policy Summary," *Law Center to Prevent Gun Violence*, August 28, 2013, http://smartgunlaws.org/concealed-weapons-permitting-policy-summary/; Michael Wines, "Alabama Ruling Hobbles Ban On Guns in the Open at Polls," *New York Times*, July 13, 2014.

90. Robert J. Spitzer, "More Permits Mean Less Crime … Maybe, but Not in Cities," *Los Angeles Times*, February 19, 1996. See also James Q. Wilson, "Just Take Away the Guns," *New York Times Magazine*, March 20, 1994; Rebecca Voelker, "States Debate 'Carrying Concealed Weapons' Laws," *Journal of the American Medical Association* 273 (June 14, 1995): 1741; L. Sherman, J. W. Shaw, and D. P. Rogan, *The Kansas City Gun Experiment* (Washington, DC: National Institute of Justice, 1995); D. M. Kennedy, A. M. Piehl, and A. A. Braga, "Youth Violence in Boston," *Law and Contemporary Problems* 59 (1996): 147–96; Michael Janofsky, "Decline in Gun Violence Bypasses Philadelphia," *New York Times*, May 10, 1998; Bob Herbert, "A Winning Strategy," *New York Times*, March 7, 2002.

91. John R. Lott Jr., *More Guns, Less Crime* (Chicago: University of Chicago Press, 2010). Lott's argument appeared in an earlier coauthored article, John R. Lott Jr. and David B. Mustard, "Crime, Deterrence, and Right-to-Carry Concealed Handguns," *Journal of Legal Studies* 26 (January 1997): 1–68.

92. Dan A. Black and Daniel S. Nagin, "Do Right-to-Carry Laws Deter Violent Crime?" *Journal of Legal Studies* 27 (January 1998): 209–19; Kleck, *Targeting Guns*, 372. Kleck's discussion refers to Lott and Mustard, "Crime, Deterrence, and Right-to-Carry Concealed Handguns." Kleck does argue that the Lott study undercuts other studies showing that concealed-carry laws produce an *increase* in crime, particularly murder. See also Jens Ludwig, "Guns and Numbers," *Washington Monthly* (June 1998): 50–51; Daniel W. Webster et al., "Flawed Gun Policy Research Could Endanger Public Safety," *American Journal of Public Health* 87 (June 1997): 918–21.

93. Hashem Dezhbakhsh and Paul H. Rubin, "Lives Saved or Lives Lost?" *American Economic Review Papers and Proceedings* 88 (May 1998): 468–74. They based their analysis on Lott and Mustard, "Crime, Deterrence, and Right-to-Carry Concealed Handguns." My thanks to Mark Prus and Kathleen Burke for their insights on this matter.

94. Lott, *More Guns, Less Crime*, ch. 3. Bureau of Justice Statistics, *Sourcebook of Criminal Justice Statistics* 1999, 138–39; Kleck, *Targeting Guns*, 98–99; Harry Henderson, *Gun Control* (New York: Facts on File, 2000), 230.

95. Ted Goertzel, "Myths of Murder and Multiple Regression," *Skeptical Inquirer*, January–February 2002, 19–21; Duggan, "More Guns, More Crime." Goertzel's article argues that econometric modeling has failed to live up to its promise of resolving such controversial national issues as gun control and capital punishment.

96. Ian Ayres and John J. Donohue III, "Shooting Down the 'More Guns, Less Crime' Hypothesis," *Stanford Law Review* 55 (April 2003): 1194–312; John J. Donohue, "Guns, Crime, and the Impact of State Right-to-Carry Laws," *Fordham Law Review* 73 (November 2004): 623–52; Ian Ayres and John J. Donohue, "More Guns, Less Crime Fails Again: The Latest Evidence from 1977–2006," *Economic Journal Watch* 6 (May 2009): 218–38.

97. Lott, *More Guns, Less Crime*, 24–25, 112.

98. Jens Ludwig, "Do Carry-Concealed Weapons Laws Deter Crime?" *Spectrum* 70 (Spring 1997): 29.

99. Lott, *More Guns, Less Crime*, 3.

100. Richard Morin, "Scholar Invents Fan to Answer His Critics," *Washington Post*, February 1, 2003, C1; Timothy Noah, "The Bellesiles of the Right?" *Slate*, February 3, 2003, http:// slate.msn.com/id/2078084/; David Glenn, "Scholar's Most Vigorous Defender Turns Out to Be Himself," *Chronicle of Higher Education*, February 14, 2003; "Who Is Mary Rosh?" http://www .whoismaryrosh.com; Jon Weiner, "Gun-Research 'Freak'-out," *Los Angeles Times*, May 31, 2006.

101. Cook and Goss, *The Gun Debate, 86–88;* Benjamin Hayes," Stolen Guns: Why You Should Worry," *The Crime Report*, September 10, 2013, http://www.thecrimereport.org /viewpoints/2013-09-stolen-guns-why-you-should-worry.

102. Moore, "Keeping Handguns from Criminal Offenders," 92–109. Second study reported in Cook, "Technology of Personal Violence," 60.

103. David McDowall, "Firearm Availability and Homicide Rates in Detroit, 1951–1986," *Social Forces* 69 (June 1991): 1085–101; James Lindgren, "Organizational and Other Constraints on Controlling the Use of Deadly Force by Police," *Annals of the American Academy of Political and Social Science* 455 (May 1981): 110–19; and Wilson, "Just Take Away the Guns," 47.

104. George D. Newton and Franklin E. Zimring, *Firearms and Violence in American Life* (Washington, DC: Government Printing Office, 1970); Llad Phillips, Harold L. Votey Jr., and John Howell, "Handguns and Homicide: Minimizing Losses and the Costs of Control," *Journal of Legal Studies* 5 (April 1975): 463–78; and Joseph Magaddino and Marshall H. Medoff, "An Empirical Analysis of Federal and State Firearm Control Laws," in *Firearms and Violence*, ed. Don B. Kates Jr. (San Francisco: Pacific Institute, 1984), 255. The Newton and Zimring study has been criticized for not analyzing causality or considering other social forces.

105. Cook, "Technology of Personal Violence," 44.

106. Franklin E. Zimring, "Firearms and Federal Law: The Gun Control Act of 1968," *Journal of Legal Studies* 4 (January 1975): 196.

107. Fox Butterfield, "Cities Finding a New Policy Limits Guns," *New York Times*, November 20, 1994; Fox Butterfield, "New Data Point Blame at Gun Makers," *New York Times*, November 28, 1998; George J. Benston and Frank J. Vandall, "Legal Control over the Supply of Handguns," *Pace Law Review* 26 (Spring 2006): 394–95.

108. Police Executive Research Forum, *A Gathering Storm—Violent Crime in America*, October 2006, 7, http://www.policeforum.org/news/detail.dot?id=46057.

109. Wright, Rossi, and Daly, *Under the Gun*, 149. See also Matthew G. Yeager, "How Well Does the Handgun Protect You and Your Family?" in Nisbet, *Gun Control Debate*, 234.

110. David Hemenway, Sara J. Solnick, and Deborah R. Azrael, "Firearms and Community Feelings of Safety," *Journal of Criminal Law and Criminology* 86 (Fall 1995): 121–32; D. Hemenway, D. Azrael, and M. Miller, "National Attitudes Concerning Gun Carrying in the United States," *Injury Prevention* 7 (December 2001): 282–85.

111. David Olinger, "Massacre Energizes Gun Debate but Not Lawmakers," *Denver Post*, April 19, 2000; Robert J. Spitzer, *The Right to Bear Arms* (Santa Barbara, CA: ABC-CLIO, 2001), 1–2; Ralph W. Larkin, *Comprehending Columbine* (Philadelphia, PA: Temple University Press, 2006); Dave Cullen, *Columbine* (New York: Twelve, 2009).

112. Robert J. Spitzer, "The Gun Dispute," *American Educator*, Summer 1999, 10–15; James Alan Fox and Marianne W. Zawitz, "Homicide Trends in the United States," *Bureau of Justice Statistics Crime Data Brief*, January 1999, NCJ 173956.

113. Margaret Weigel, "Violence in Schools," *Journalist's Resource,* April 9, 2014, http://dev.journalistsresource.org/author/margaret-weigel; Kimberly Heflin, "School Shootings Pace Continues Despite Emphasis on Safety," *Syracuse Post-Standard,* February 3, 2014.

114. "Guns in Schools," *Huffington Post,* January 15, 2013, http://www.huffingtonpost.com/2013/01/15/guns-in-schools-firearms-_n_2482168.html; Sarah A. Buck, et al., "Teachers with Guns," *Center for Homicide Research,* August 1, 2013; "Guns in Schools Policy Summary," *Law Center to Prevent Gun Violence,* November 1, 2013, http://smartgunlaws.org/guns-in-schools-policy-summary/.

115. Patricia King and Andrew Murr, "A Son Who Spun Out of Control," *Newsweek,* June 1, 1998, 33; Timothy Egan, "From Adolescent Angst to Shooting Up Schools," *New York Times,* June 14, 1998; Ford Fessenden, "How Youngest Killers Differ," *New York Times,* April 9, 2000; Jack M. Bergstein et al., "Guns in Young Hands," *Journal of Trauma* 41 (November 1996): 794–98.

116. Theodore Day et al., "Guns Make Colleges Safer," *Dallas Morning News,* April 22, 2009. See also Marshall Lewin, "The New Campus Revolt," *America's First Freedom,* January 2008, 27–29.

117. "Guns on Campus," *National Conference on State Legislatures,* March 7, 2014, http://www.ncsl.org/research/education/guns-on-campus-overview.aspx.

118. Scott Jaschik, "Campus Crime Rates Fell from '94 to '04," *Insider Higher Ed,* February 25, 2008, http://www.insidehighered.com/news/2008/02/25/crimestats; Robert Birnbaum, "Ready, Fire, Aim: The College Campus Gun Fight," *Change,* September–October 2013; "Crime on College Campuses in the US," *Students for Concealed Carry,* May 2009, http://concealedcampus.org/campus-crime/. The International Association of Campus Law Enforcement Administrators, Inc., expressed its opposition to civilian concealed carrying on campus in statements in March and August 2008 (www.iaclea .org). Between 2000 and 2005 campuses nationwide averaged four homicides per year; in 2006 it was eight, and in 2007 the number was twelve, plus the thirty-two killed at Virginia Tech. In 2008 the number was thirteen. Even at its highest in 2007, that number was a tiny fraction of national homicide rates. Alex Johnson, "College Security Tighter, but Is It Enough?" MSNBC, November 17, 2008, http://www.msnbc.msn.com/id/2766800/.

119. Will Buchanan, "Three Years after Virginia Tech Shooting, College Gun Bans Prevail," *Christian Science Monitor,* April 16, 2010, http://www.csmonitor.com/layout/set/print/content/view/print/295243. See also "No Gun Left Behind: The Gun Lobby's Campaign to Push Guns into Colleges and Schools," Brady Center to Prevent Gun Violence, May 2007, http://dev.bradycenter.org/legalaction/bcereports/nogunleftbehind; David B. Kopel, "Pretend 'Gun-Free' School Zones: A Deadly Legal Fiction," *Connecticut Law Review* 42 (December 2009): 515–84.

120. Manuel Roig-Franzia, "Fla. Gun Law to Expand Leeway for Self-Defense," *Washington Post,* April 26, 2005; Abby Goodnough, "Florida Expands Right to Use Deadly Force in Self-Defense," *New York Times,* April 27, 2005; Patrik Jonsson, "Is Self-Defense Law Vigilante Justice?" *Christian Science Monitor,* February 24, 2006.

121. Adam Liptak, "15 States Expand Right to Shoot in Self-Defense," *New York Times,* August 7, 2006.

122. The account that follows is drawn from Robert J. Spitzer, *Guns across America* (New York: Oxford University Press, 2015), ch. 4.

123. Kleck says, "Prospective violent offenders unable to easily obtain handguns would presumably seek substitutes, and for many of them the most satisfactory substitute would be a long gun." *Point Blank,* 91. Kleck thus concedes, although not explicitly, that some prospective

criminals would not turn to long guns if handguns were less available. This is an assumption supported by existing patterns of gun use, as discussed in this chapter.

Chapter 4

1. For more material on the rhetoric of gun control, see Andrew Jay McClurg, "The Rhetoric of Gun Control," *American University Law Review* 42 (Fall 1992): 53–113; and Raymond S. Rodgers, "The Rhetoric of the NRA," *Vital Speeches of the Day,* October 1, 1983, 758–61.

2. Larry J. Sabato, "How Direct Mail Works," in *Campaigns and Elections,* ed. Sabato (Glenview, IL: Scott, Foresman, 1989), 96. See also R. Kenneth Godwin, *One Billion Dollars of Influence* (Chatham, NJ: Chatham House, 1988).

3. The literature on social movements supports this analysis. See, for example, Neil J. Smelser, *Theory of Collective Behavior* (New York: Free Press, 1963); Michael Useem, *Protest Movements in America* (Indianapolis, IN: Bobbs-Merrill, 1975); Robert J. Spitzer, *The Right to Life Movement and Third Party Politics* (Westport, CT: Greenwood, 1987); and Kay Lehman Schlozman and John T. Tierney, *Organized Interests and American Democracy* (New York: Harper and Row, 1986), 52.

4. Raymond Tatalovich and Byron Daynes, "Introduction," in *Moral Controversies in American Politics,* ed. Tatalovich and Daynes (Armonk, NY: M. E. Sharpe, 2011), xxxiv.

5. Other groups that have worked or are working against gun control laws include the Citizens Committee for the Right to Keep and Bear Arms (which includes a research arm, the Second Amendment Foundation), formed in 1971 by a group of gun enthusiasts who thought that the NRA was not being tough enough on the gun issue, and the Gun Owners of America (GOA), founded in 1975. The GOA is headed by Larry Pratt and claims a membership of three hundred thousand. The Coalition to Stop Gun Violence (formerly the National Coalition to Ban Handguns) receives brief treatment in this chapter. The Violence Policy Center, headed by Josh Sugarmann, has engaged in high-visibility research to promote gun control arguments. Because of the money required to have a direct impact on the political process, these groups have focused most of their efforts on education and research activities. Robert J. Spitzer, "Gun Control: Constitutional Mandate or Myth?" in Tatalovich and Daynes, *Moral Controversies in American Politics,* 163–67.

6. L. Sandy Maisel, ed., *Political Parties and Elections in the United States,* 2 vols. (New York: Garland, 1991), 2:687.

7. Edward L. Schapsmeier and Frederick H. Schapsmeier, *Political Parties and Civic Action Groups* (Westport, CT: Greenwood, 1981), 310.

8. Carol Skalnik Leff and Mark H. Leff, "The Politics of Ineffectiveness: Firearms Legislation 1919–38," *Annals of the American Academy of Political and Social Science* 455 (May 1981): 60; Lee Kennett and James LaVerne Anderson, *The Gun in America* (Westport, CT: Westview, 1975), 138–41, 205–6; and Richard L. Worsnop, "Gun Control," *CQ Researcher,* June 10, 1994, 512.

9. Osha Gray Davidson, *Under Fire: The NRA and the Battle for Gun Control* (New York: Holt, 1993), 29–30.

10. Edward F. Leddy, *Magnum Force Lobby* (Lanham, MD: University Press of America, 1987), 147, 197. The content analysis of the magazine spans 1926 through 1983.

11. Neil A. Lewis, "N.R.A. Meets Call for Gun Control with a Muzzle," *New York Times,* March 12, 1992; Fox Butterfield, "Aggressive Strategy by N.R.A. Has Left Its Finances Reeling,"

New York Times, June 26, 1995; Richard Keil, "NRA Loses 300,000 Members since January," *Cortland Standard,* August 2, 1995; Jill Smolowe, "Go Ahead, Make Our Day," *Time,* May 29, 1995, 18–24; Michael Powell, "The Revival of the NRA," *Washington Post,* national weekly edition, August 28, 2000; Eric Lichtblau, "Beyond Guns: N.R.A. Expands Political Agenda," *New York Times,* July 13, 2010; Josh Sugarmann, "NRA Misplaces a Million Members," *Huffington Post,* April 24, 2008, http://www.huffingtonpost.com/josh-sugarmann/nra-misplaces-a-million-m_b_98429.html; Philip J. Cook and Kristin A. Goss, *The Gun Debate* (New York: Oxford University Press, 2014), 190–191.

12. Jack L. Walker Jr., *Mobilizing Interest Groups in America* (Ann Arbor: University of Michigan Press, 1991), 31. See also Graham K. Wilson, "American Interest Groups in Comparative Perspective," in *The Politics of Interests,* ed. Mark P. Petracca (Boulder, CO: Westview, 1992), 82.

13. The NRA concedes as much. See James Trefethen and James E. Serven, *Americans and Their Guns* (Harrisburg, PA: Stackpole Books, 1967).

14. Davidson, *Under Fire,* 22, 27–28. As Kennett and Anderson noted about the NRA, "Government sales of surplus arms were a vital element in the organization's growth." *The Gun in America,* 205.

15. Josh Sugarmann, *National Rifle Association: Money, Firepower and Fear* (Washington, DC: National Press Books, 1992), 111.

16. Robert Sherrill, *The Saturday Night Special* (New York: Charterhouse, 1973), 219–23, and Bill Keller, "Powerful Reputation Makes National Rifle Association a Top Gun in Washington," *CQ Weekly Report,* May 9, 1981, 799.

17. Sugarmann, *National Rifle Association,* 111.

18. Brooke A. Masters, "Rifle Program under Fire on Hill," *Washington Post,* July 26, 1989; Pete Stark, "Army Division Serves as NRA Recruiting Tool," *Syracuse (N.Y.) Post-Standard,* March 12, 1990; James W. Davis, "We've Heard of Targeted Subsidies, but ...," *New York Times,* June 20, 1990; "The Democrats' Big Guns," *New York Times,* October 18, 1993; and George Will, "Termination Is Not a Viable Concept within Congress," *Cortland Standard,* November 12, 1993.

19. Paul Rauber, "Home on the Rifle Range," *Sierra,* May–June 1994, 42–43.

20. *The NRA Member Guide,* 20; and Jan Hoffman, "Fund Linked to N.R.A. Gave $20,000 for Goetz's Defense," *New York Times,* April 16, 1996. The NRA established the fund in 1978.

21. Sugarmann, *National Rifle Association,* 87.

22. These activities are carefully chronicled in Carl Bakal, *The Right to Bear Arms* (New York: McGraw-Hill, 1966), ch. 6.

23. Michael J. Harrington, "The Politics of Gun Control," in *American Politics, Policies, and Priorities,* ed. Alan Shank (Boston: Allyn and Bacon, 1984), 146.

24. B. B. Drummond Ayres Jr., "Gun Maker on MayLem: That Is Not Our Doing," *New York Times,* March 19, 1994.

25. Sugarmann, *National Rifle Association,* 88.

26. Erik Eckholm, "Ailing Gun Industry Confronts Outrage over Glut of Violence," *New York Times,* March 8, 1992; Tom Diaz, *Making a Killing* (New York: New Press, 1999).

27. Joseph P. Fried, "9 Gun Makers Called Liable for Shootings," *New York Times,* February 12, 1999; Sharon Walsh, "The NRA Fires Back," *Washington Post,* March 8, 1999; Robert J. Spitzer, "Gun Industry Doesn't Know What's Good for It," *Syracuse Post-Standard,* April 20, 1999; Michael Janofsky, "Pressured by Suits, Gun Makers Turn to Political Effort," *New York Times,* January 19, 2000; Fox Butterfield, "Suit against Gun Makers Gains Ground in Illinois,"

New York Times, January 3, 2002; Carl T. Bogus, "Gun Litigation and Societal Values," *Connecticut Law Review* 32 (Summer 2000): 1353–78; Wayne V. McIntosh and Cynthia L. Cates, "Cigarette, Firearms, and the New Litigation Wars," in *The Interest Group Connection,* ed. by Paul S. Herrnson, Ronald G. Shaiko, and Clyde Wilcox (Washington, DC: CQ Press, 2005), 356.

28. Sugarmann, *National Rifle Association,* 89–99; Drummond Ayres Jr., "US to Seek Rise in Fee for Gun Dealers," *New York Times,* January 4, 1994. The license fee increase was part of the Brady Act, passed by Congress in November 1993; "Blood Money: How the Gun Industry Bankrolls the NRA," *Violence Policy Center,* April 2011; Peter H. Stone and Ben Hallman, "NRA Gun Control Crusade Reflects Firearms Industry Financial Ties," *Huffington Post,* January 11, 2013, http://www.huffingtonpost.com/2013/01/11/nra-gun-control-firearms-industry-ties _n_2434142.html

29. Michael Barone, Grant Ujifusa, and Douglas Matthews, *The Almanac of American Politics* (Boston: Gambit, 1972), 321, 679. As is so often the case in interest-group politics, other factors in their reelection bids hampered Clark and Tydings, probably outweighing the NRA's role.

30. Quoted in Davidson, *Under Fire,* 39.

31. Peter H. Stone, "Under the Gun," *National Journal,* June 5, 1993, 1335; Glenn H. Utter and Robert J. Spitzer, "Institute for Legislative Action," *Encyclopedia of Gun Control and Gun Rights* (Amenia, NY: Grey House Publishers, 2011).

32. Quoted in Davidson, *Under Fire,* 149.

33. Ibid., 151–52.

34. Joan Biskupic, "Handgun-Control Advocates Keep on Shooting Blanks," *CQ Weekly Report,* December 2, 1989, 3313–14. For example, NRA advertising erroneously reported that bills before Congress in 1989, S.747 and S.386, would require gun owners to pay a $200 tax for certain types of guns. The NRA also claimed falsely that owners of semiautomatic weapons would be required to submit to fingerprinting and an FBI investigation.

35. Michael Blood, "Organizations Spend Millions on Partisan 'Communications,'" *Cortland Standard,* January 13, 1994. See also Ted Gest, "Battle over Gun Control Heats Up across US," *US News & World Report,* May 31, 1982, 35; Darren Samuelsohn, "Why Gun Lovers Still Fear President Obama," *Politico,* July 19, 2012.

36. Carol Matlack, "Under Assault," *National Journal,* April 22, 1989, 980; Cook and Goss, *The Gun Debate,* 191.

37. Stone, "Under the Gun," 1336, and data provided by the Federal Election Commission; Kelly D. Patterson and Matthew M. Singer, "The National Rifle Association in the Face of the Clinton Challenge," in *Interest Group Politics,* ed. Allan J. Cigler and Burdett A. Loomis (Washington, DC: CQ Press, 2002), 68–71; James Dao, "N.R.A. Tightens Its Embrace of Republicans with Donations," *New York Times,* April 26, 2000; James Dao, "National Rifle Association Unleashes Attack on Gore," *New York Times,* May 21, 2000. NRA spending to elect or defeat members of Congress is not necessarily devoted to appeals dealing with the gun issue. In two House races in 1992, for example, the NRA sponsored vigorous campaigns to unseat incumbents who supported a waiting period for handgun purchases. Yet these NRA-financed campaigns never mentioned gun control; instead, they focused on other issues, such as the balanced budget amendment and flag burning. See Richard E. Cohen, "NRA Draws a Bead on Incumbents," *National Journal,* September 19, 1992, 2134; Kenneth P. Vogel, "NRA Takes Flak for Ties with Left," *Politico,* July 12, 2010.

38. Peter H. Stone, "Is the NRA Bleeding Internally?" *National Journal,* March 13, 1993,

626–27. This was a spurious argument to some extent, as the ratio of initial cost to dues payment tends to follow this pattern for most organizations. Organizations make back their money through renewals and ancillary contributions or purchases, although the NRA's member renewal rate has been low in recent years. See, for example, Andrew S. McFarland, *Common Cause* (Chatham, NJ: Chatham House, 1984), 81. See also Jack Anderson, *Inside the NRA* (Beverly Hills, CA: Dove Books, 1996), 31–34; Robert Dreyfuss, "Good Morning, Gun Lobby!" *Mother Jones*, July–August 1996, 38–47; Barbara Vobejda, "NRA Is Said to Lay Off Dozens," *Washington Post*, September 23, 1996; and Richard Feldman, *Ricochet* (New York: John Wiley, 2008).

39. Butterfield, "Aggressive Strategy by N.R.A. Has Left Its Finances Reeling"; and David C. Morrison, "From the K Street Corridor," *National Journal*, July 8, 1995, 1774.

40. "NRA Rated 'Risky,'" *Syracuse Post-Standard*, June 5, 1995.

41. Katharine Q. Seelye, "National Rifle Association Is Turning to World Stage to Fight Gun Control," *New York Times*, April 2, 1997; Raymond Bonner, "US, in a Shift, Backs U.N. Move to Curb Illicit Trade in Guns," *New York Times*, April 25, 1998; and Raymond Bonner, "U.N. Panel May Approve Limit on Guns Despite N.R.A. Pleas," *New York Times*, April 30, 1998; Robert J. Spitzer, "Gun Rights for Terrorists?" in *Transformed by Crisis: The Presidency of George W. Bush and American Politics* (New York: Palgrave Macmillan, 2004), 158–59; and Arshad Mohammed, "US Reverses Stance on Treaty to Regulate Arms Trade," Reuters News Service, October 14, 2009; Rachel Stohl, "Tell the Truth About the Arms Treaty," *New York Times*, April 12, 2013; Kathy Wiemers, "Is President Obama Trying to Take Away Americans' Weapons Through a Treaty With Other Countries?" *The Fact Finders*, November 18, 2012, http://www.thefactfinders.org/1/post/2012/11/-reader-question-is-president-obama-trying -to-take-away-americans-weapons-through-a-treaty-with-other-countries.html.

42. Joshua Kurlantzick, "Global Gun Rights?" *New York Times Magazine*, September 17, 2006, 28; and David Morton, "Gunning for the World," *Foreign Policy* 152 (January–February 2006).

43. Schlozman and Tierney, *Organized Interests and American Democracy*, 88–106; and Graham Wootton, *Interest Groups: Policy and Politics in America* (Englewood Cliffs, NJ: Prentice Hall, 1985), 221–22. According to John T. Tierney, the NRA has "a huge budget and a large, excitable membership." "Organized Interests and the Nation's Capitol," in Petracca, *Politics of Interests*, 207.

44. "NRA: More Bang for the Buck," *Washington Post*, March 4, 1986. See also Jonathan D. Salant, "Analysis Ties Vote, NRA Money," *Syracuse Post-Standard*, May 9, 1991, which reports on findings from Public Citizen's Congress Watch. *Common Cause* offers the same kind of analysis. For example, it reported that among House members who supported an NRA-backed amendment to water down a bill criminalizing the use of weapons parts to make assault-style semiautomatic weapons (the amendment exempted domestic-made parts), 93 percent received NRA PAC contributions within the previous five years. Sixty-nine percent of those who did not receive NRA PAC money voted against the amendment. The amendment passed 257–172 on October 4, 1990. *Common Cause News*, October 17, 1990.

45. Laura I. Langbein and Mark A. Lotwis found that money was important in influencing votes on the Firearms Owners Protection Act of 1986 in the House of Representatives. They found not only NRA contributions but those of HCI to be important, along with lobbying and grassroots efforts, especially those of police organizations in conjunction with HCI. Yet these findings do not necessarily contradict the prevailing view that money does not normally buy votes because Langbein and Lotwis found that representatives' votes on this bill had no effect on their home constituents, making it a relatively low-visibility issue—that is, one in which

money is more likely to be important. In addition, the study found lobbying to be an extremely effective counterforce. Finally, these patterns may be quite different for the Senate. "The Political Efficacy of Lobbying and Money: Gun Control in the House, 1986," *Legislative Studies Quarterly* 15 (August 1990): 413–40.

46. Frank Sorauf comes to this conclusion in part by examining specifically the case of the NRA. Sorauf even questions the solidity of the link of money to access. See *Money in American Elections* (Glenview, IL: Scott, Foresman, 1988), 307–14. Laura I. Langbein examined the impact of gun PAC spending on the Firearms Owners Protection Act of 1986 and noted that "NRA donations to pro-gunners clearly prevented many from switching away from a pure pro-gun position." "PACs, Lobbies and Political Conflict: The Case of Gun Control," *Public Choice* 77, no. 3 (1993): 569. See also Elisabeth Gerber, *The Populist Paradox* (Princeton, NJ: Princeton University Press, 1999); Frank R. Baumgartner et al., *Lobbying and Policy Change* (Chicago: University of Chicago Press, 2009).

47. Keller, "Powerful Reputation Makes National Rifle Association a Top Gun in Washington," 799; and Steven V. Roberts, "Rifle Group Viewed as Key to Gun Law," *New York Times*, April 5, 1981.

48. James Q. Wilson, *Political Organizations* (New York: Basic Books, 1973), 33–35. For more on purposive incentives, see Jeffrey M. Berry, *The Interest Group Society* (Glenview, IL: Scott, Foresman, 1989), 53–54.

49. Wilson, *Political Organizations,* 35. This concern is reflected in the NRA's stated purposes, the first of which is "to protect and defend the Constitution of the United States, especially with reference to the inalienable right of the individual American citizen guaranteed by such Constitution to acquire, possess, transport, carry, transfer ownership of, and enjoy the right to use arms, in order that the people may always be in a position to exercise their legitimate individual rights of self-preservation and defense of family, person and property, as well as to serve effectively in the appropriate militia for the common defense of the republic and the individual liberty of its citizens." The NRA's other four stated purposes are promoting "public safety, law and order, and national defense"; training others in the use of weapons; promoting shooting sports; and advancing hunter safety. See "The NRA Member Guide."

50. Ronald J. Hrebenar and Ruth K. Scott, *Interest Group Politics in America* (Englewood Cliffs, NJ: Prentice Hall, 1990), 103.

51. Berry, *Interest Group Society,* 60. NRA grassroots activity is described in Tom Loftus, *The Art of Legislative Politics* (Washington, DC: CQ Press, 1994), ch. 7; and Ronald G. Shaiko and Marc A. Wallace, "Going Hunting Where the Ducks Are," in *The Changing Politics of Gun Control,* ed. John M. Bruce and Clyde Wilcox (Lanham, MD: Rowman and Littlefield, 1998).

52. "Consumer Product Safety Agency Created in 1972," *CQ Almanac, 1972* (Washington, DC: Congressional Quarterly, 1972), 141–50.

53. "Testing, Testing, Testing," *60 Minutes,* March 20, 1994; and Jeff Brazil and Steve Berry, "Federal Safety Law Targets 15,000 Items, but Not Guns," *Los Angeles Times,* February 1, 1998.

54. Quoted in Harrington, "Politics of Gun Control," 148.

55. The armor-piercing capabilities of such bullets are derived from replacing soft-metal lead tips with hard metal, such as bronze, that is coated with Teflon.

56. "Kill the 'Cop-Killer' Bullets," *New York Times,* August 29, 1983.

57. Stephen Kleege, "Brookhaven Eyes Bullet Ban," *New York Times,* August 15, 1992. For more on the Brookhaven case, see Jervis Anderson, *Guns in American Life* (New York: Random House, 1984), 102–4.

58. Davidson, *Under Fire*, 88–95. The revised bill included exemptions for target shooting and sporting ammunition. See Public Law 99–408, *US Statutes at Large*, 1986 (100 *Stat.* 920).

59. Quoted in Carol Matlack, "Under Assault," *National Journal*, April 22, 1989, 978.

60. "Letter-Writing and Campaigns," *CQ Weekly Report*, March 9, 1991, 605. See also Stephanie Saul, "NRA Takes Aim at Brady Bill," *Newsday*, April 16, 1991.

61. Ian Brodie, "High Price to Pay for Defying the Gun Threat," *Times of London*, October 18, 2000.

62. Eric Lichtblau, "Terror Suspects Buying Firearms, US Report Finds," *New York Times*, March 8, 2005; Richard A. Clarke, "Things Left Undone," *Atlantic Monthly*, November 2005, 38.

63. Robert J. Spitzer, "Gun Rights for Terrorists?" in *Transformed by Crisis: The Presidency of George W. Bush and American Politics*, ed. by Jon Kraus et al. (New York: Palgrave Macmillan, 2004), 141–65.

64. "Boarding? Denied. Lock and Loading? Sure," *New York Times*, May 9, 2011; Eric Lichtblau, "On Terrorist Watch List, but Allowed to Buy Guns," *New York Times*, June 20, 2009; Mike Lillis, "Dem Bill Would Close Gun Sales 'Terror Gap,'" *The Hill*, March 6, 2013.

65. Davidson, *Under Fire*, 36, see also 30–36.

66. This fierce intraorganizational struggle between a moderate faction seeking a broader, more pragmatic, and outer-directed approach and a more extreme inner-directed faction seeking greater purity and homogeneity on the gun issue is remarkably similar to the "broad" versus "narrow" bifactional splits that have characterized the internal struggles of single-issue minor parties in American history (including such third parties as the Liberty, Free Soil, Prohibition, Greenback, and Right to Life Parties). Each arose from single-issue social movements that paralleled many of the traits of the NRA. See Spitzer, *Right to Life Movement and Third Party Politics*, 29–31, 51–52, 70.

67. "NRA Reportedly Threatens Bennett's 'Political Future,'" *Syracuse Post-Standard*, March 18, 1989, and Matlack, "Under Assault," 979–80.

68. Stephen Labaton, "House Kills Sweeping Provisions in Counterterrorism Legislation," *New York Times*, March 14, 1996.

69. Sam Howe Verhovek, "An Angry Bush Ends His Ties to Rifle Group," *New York Times*, May 11, 1995.

70. "Wayne LaPierre, on the Ropes," *New York Times*, May 20, 1995; and "The G.O.P. and the N.R.A.," *New York Times*, May 12, 1995.

71. Emilie Raymond, *From My Cold, Dead Hands: Charlton Heston and American Politics* (Lexington: University Press of Kentucky, 2006).

72. Katharine Q. Seelye, "Close Votes in N.R.A. Elections Quash Hope for Internal Unity," *New York Times*, May 6, 1997; Seelye, "Heston Asserts Gun Ownership Is Nation's Highest Right," *New York Times*, September 9, 1997; Robert J. Spitzer, "Door No. 1: Muskets? Or Door No. 2: Free Speech?" *Christian Science Monitor*, September 19, 1997; Michael Janofsky, "N.R.A. Tries to Improve Image, with Charlton Heston in Lead," *New York Times*, June 8, 1998; Powell, "The Revival of the NRA." In his book *Inside the NRA* Jack Anderson argues that the NRA has alienated itself from most hunters and sportspeople.

73. Brian Doherty, *Gun Control on Trial* (Washington, DC: Cato Institute, 2008), xxiii, see also 62.

74. W. James Antle III, "Caught in the Crossfire," *The American Spectator*, September 2010, http://spectator.org/archives/2010/09/17/caught-in-the-crossfire.

75. Antle, "Caught in the Crossfire"; Vogel, "NRA Takes Flak for Ties with Left"; Vanessa O'Connell, "Gun Advocates Open a New Front," *Wall Street Journal*, April 19, 2010.

76. In 1993 and 1994 CSGV worked closely with such broadcast networks as MTV and Nickelodeon and with movie studios including Walt Disney Co., Paramount, Sony Corp., and Warner Brothers to produce and promote an antiviolence campaign (which would presumably include a strong gun-warning component). MTV has provided free air time for public service spots sponsored by CSGV. See W. John Moore, "Lights! Camera! It's Gun Control Time," *National Journal,* December 18, 1993, 3007.

77. Pete Shields wrote about his experiences in *Guns Don't Die—People Do* (New York: Arbor House, 1981). Shields stepped down as chair in 1989 and died in 1993.

78. Robert Curvin, "Is the NRA in Trouble?" *New York Times,* October 11, 1982. Figures from data provided by the Federal Election Commission; Adam Clymer, "House Approves Repealing of Ban on Assault Guns," *New York Times,* March 23, 1996; Patterson and Singer, "The National Rifle Association," 69.

79. Wayne King, "Target: The Gun Lobby," *New York Times Magazine,* December 9, 1990, 82. The 1994 membership figure was obtained from the HCI national office. See also Michael Isikoff, "The Brady Bill: Success and Growing Pains," *Washington Post,* May 31, 1991.

80. Barbara Gamarekian, "Fighting the Fight on Gun Control," *New York Times,* February 11, 1987; Philip Shenon, "Wife of Aide Cut Down with Reagan Scoring Hits against the Gun Lobby," *New York Times,* May 25, 1990; and King, "Target."

81. Lisa Girion, "Gun Violence Moves Moms to Action," *Los Angeles Times,* April 3, 2000; James Dao, "New Gun Control Politics," *New York Times,* March 11, 2001; James Dao, "Gun Control Groups Use N.R.A. Tactics for Fall Elections," *New York Times,* July 24, 2000; Deborah Homsher, *Women and Guns* (Armonk, NY: M. E. Sharpe, 2002); Kristin Goss, *Disarmed: The Missing Movement for Gun Control in America* (Princeton, NJ: Princeton University Press, 2006), 184.

82. Michael M. Grynbaum, "Bloomberg Says His Push Against Guns Will Grow," *New York Times,* December 21, 2012; Francine Kiefer, "Bloomberg-backed Gun Group Turns to Midterms," *Christian Science Monitor,* July 7, 2014; Philip Rucker, "Bloomberg's Gun Group to Start 2014 Midterms Strategy by Surveying Candidates," *Washington Post,* July 6, 2014; Robert Draper, "Inside the Power of the N.R.A.," *New York Times Magazine,* December 15, 2013; http://everytown.org/; http://www.momsdemandaction.org/; Alec MacGillis, "This is How the NRA Ends," *The New Republic,* May 28, 2013, http://www.newrepublic.com/node/113292/

83. "2014 Gun Sense Voter Federal Candidate Questionnaire," *Everytown for Gun Safety,* http://gunsensevoter.org/wp-content/uploads/Gun-Sense-Voter-Questionnaire-FINAL.pdf; http://americansforresponsiblesolutions.org/

84. This account is taken from Goss, *Disarmed.*

85. Standard books on the 1988 elections do not even mention gun control as a salient issue that year. See, for example, Paul R. Abramson, John H. Aldrich, and David W. Rohde, *Change and Continuity in the 1988 Elections* (Washington, DC: CQ Press, 1990); Peter Goldman and Tom Mathews, *The Quest for the Presidency 1988* (New York: Simon and Schuster, 1989); and Gerald M. Pomper et al., *The Election of 1988* (Chatham, NJ: Chatham House, 1989). The gun issue might have been important in swinging Pennsylvania to Bush in 1988, a state Dukakis lost by about 2 percent of the vote. Pennsylvania has the second-highest NRA membership of any state in the country. Even so, this one state would have made little difference in altering Bush's wide margin in the electoral college.

86. Noam Scheiber, "Gun Shy," *New Republic,* January 29, 2001, 15–16; E. J. Dionne Jr., "Guns and Votes," *Washington Post,* February 13, 2001; Robert J. Spitzer, "NRA Loses Its Political Firepower," *Los Angeles Times,* April 12, 2004.

87. Noam N. Levey, "NRA's Political Clout Is Waning," *Los Angeles Times,* June 14, 2008;

Jonathan Martin, "National Rifle Association Will Seek to Portray Obama as Threat to Second Amendment," *Politico,* July 1, 2008; Lindsay Young, "Outside Spenders' Return on Investment," *Sunlight Foundation,* December 12, 2012, http://sunlightfoundation.com/blog/2012/12/17 /return_on_investment/.

88. Quoted in Worsnop, "Gun Control," 520.

89. Hazel Erskine, "The Polls: Gun Control," *Public Opinion Quarterly* 36 (Fall 1982): 455.

90. This discussion relies in part on Gallup poll results. Gallup's results are generally consistent with those of other mainstream national and academic pollsters, such as the National Opinion Research Center and the Institute for Social Research. Gallup poll updates cited in this section are from Gallup's website, http://www.gallup.com. Gary A. Mauser and David B. Kopel complain that polls sponsored by large media outlets are less reliable than those conducted by survey research organizations and tend to be "slanted, loaded, or technically incompetent." "'Sorry, Wrong Number': Why Media Polls on Gun Control Are Often Unreliable," *Political Communication* 9 (April 1992): 86. They mistakenly lump Gallup and Harris polls together with all other media polls, failing to distinguish between polls conducted by these and other respected polling organizations as part of their regular polling and instances when these organizations join with one or more media outlets to pursue particular issues or questions. The explosion of media polling does, indeed, pose accuracy and reliability problems, but the problems identified with media polling extend to subjects other than gun control. Although Mauser and Kopel are correct in urging that media polls be interpreted with care, their selective analysis of such polls exaggerates problems that are endemic to all polling, and they fail to take into account the broad range of such polling, which finds general concurrence with what is known about public sentiment on the major features of the gun issue. For a balanced and detailed discussion of the virtues and problems of media polling, see Thomas E. Mann and Gary R. Orren, eds., *Media Polls in American Politics* (Washington, DC: Brookings Institution, 1992).

91. Erskine, "The Polls: Gun Control," 455, 460. This fact is well established in the public opinion and interest-group literature. See, for example, Robert Weissberg, *Public Opinion and Popular Government* (Englewood Cliffs, NJ: Prentice Hall, 1976), 130; Herbert Asher, *Polling and the Public* (Washington, DC: CQ Press, 1992), 18; Wootton, *Interest Groups,* 317–18; and Schlozman and Tierney, *Organized Interests and American Democracy,* 36. Gary Kleck disputes the notion that opinion on gun control has been relatively consistent and supportive, calling it "very volatile." To support this argument, he cites some Massachusetts state polls taken in 1976 concerning a state gun issue. Aside from the very limited geography and time period he cites to support his conclusion, Kleck fails to recognize or appreciate the relative consistency of national gun opinions when compared with other key national issues across the last seven decades as well as the inherent volatility of state polls concerning state issues. *Point Blank* (New York: Aldine de Grnyter, 1991), 363.

92. Kevin Johnson, "Homicides Fall in Big Cities," *USA Today,* December 29, 2010.

93. As V. O. Key noted, "markedly unimodal distributions of supportive opinion are associated with most public policies and services." *Public Opinion and American Democracy* (New York: Knopf, 1961), 31. Kleck considers these general data to be "meaningless" because there may be little concurrence between what citizens consider adequate gun control and the actual controls that exist. *Point Blank,* 361–62. Although such a disjunction may exist, Kleck fails to note, first, that this principle applies to public opinion on virtually any policy issue, from health care to welfare to international trade. It is a truism of public opinion that "the level of political information of the mass electorate" is "abysmally low." David H. Everson, *Public Opinion and Interest Groups in American Politics* (New York: Franklin Watts, 1982), 59. Second,

despite this, the durability and visibility of the gun issue as a federal, state, and local concern as well as the prevalence of guns in American society increase confidence that American opinion on this subject is as well informed as that regarding any policy issue. And third, the political and policy mandate of a citizenry that prefers stronger controls than currently exist is perfectly clear to officeholders and decision makers. That this preference has not been translated into more policy enactments is a function of the myriad political forces that intervene between the citizen and the state. See Bernard C. Hennessy, *Public Opinion* (Belmont, CA: Duxbury, 1970); and Robert S. Erikson, Norman Luttbeg, and Kent L. Tedin, *American Public Opinion* (New York: Macmillan, 1991). Kleck also argues that "there was little long-term trend in support for gun control over the period 1959–1990" and that "there was little that could be described as a strong long-term trend" (367). Yet even Kleck's own data contradict this false conclusion, as his data compilation shows national support in favor of gun purchase limits to range from 67 to 79 percent and support for federal handgun registration to range from 66 to 80 percent during the 1959–1990 period (378). The short-term fluctuations that prompt Kleck's comments are ubiquitous in American public opinion.

94. Lawrence L. Knutson, "Poll Finds Wide Support for Gun Control," *Cortland Standard,* December 30, 1993; and George Gallup Jr. and Alec Gallup, "Handgun Waiting Period," *Syracuse Post-Standard,* November 11, 1988. Updates from the Gallup website and Tom W. Smith, "Public Attitudes towards the Regulation of Firearms," NORC/University of Chicago, March 2007.

95. Carol D. Foster, Mark A. Siegel, and Nancy R. Jacobs, eds., *Gun Control—Restricting Rights or Protecting People?* (Wylie, TX: Information Plus, 1993), 71–73; Ann L. Pastore and Kathleen Maguire, eds., *Sourcebook of Criminal Justice Statistics,* 2002, http://www.albany.edu/sourcebook; Emily Swanson, "Half of Americans Support Stricter Gun Laws," *Huffington Post,* April 17, 2014, http://www.huffingtonpost.com/2014/04/17/gun-control-poll_n_5161905.html.

96. "Sentiments on Gun Issues," *New York Times,* March 12, 1992; "A Little Gun Control, a Lot of Guns," *New York Times,* August 15, 1993; Knutson, "Poll Finds Wide Support for Gun Control"; Smith, "Public Attitudes towards the Rebulation of Firearms."

97. Jill Smolowe, "Go Ahead, Make Our Day," *Time,* May 29, 1995, 21; "Gun Owners: NRA Gun Owners and Non-NRA Gun Owners," Survey Taken for Mayors Against Illegal Guns, December 2009. Republican pollster Frank Luntz's polling organization, The Word Doctors, took the survey.

98. Leslie McAneny, "Americans Tell Congress: Pass Brady Bill, Other Tough Gun Laws," *Gallup Monthly* 330 (March 1993): 3. Percentages of respondents supporting a handgun ban, from 1980 to 1993, were 31, 38, 39, 41, 42, 41, 43, and 42, yielding a positive correlation coefficient of .69. Gallup did not ask this question from 1994 to 1997.

99. Felicity Barringer, "Majority in Poll Back Ban on Handguns," *New York Times,* June 4, 1993; Benjamin I. Page and Robert Y. Shapiro, *The Rational Public* (Chicago: University of Chicago Press, 1992), 94–96. Updates from Gallup website, www.gallup.com.

100. US Bureau of the Census, *Statistical Abstract of the US: 1992* (Washington, DC: Government Printing Office, 1992), 241. See also "Guns in America: Who Owns Them," *New York Times,* March 9, 1992; and Tom W. Smith, "The 75% Solution," *Journal of Criminal Law and Criminology* 71 (Fall 1980): 307–9.

101. Pauline Gasdow Brennan, Alan J. Lizotte, and David McDowall, "Guns, Southernness, and Gun Control," *Journal of Quantitative Criminology* 9, no. 3 (1993): 289–307. The authors also provide an excellent synthesis of the literature on this variable. Robert M. Jiobu and Timothy

Curry, "Lack of Confidence in the Federal Government and the Ownership of Firearms," *Social Science Quarterly* 82 (March 2001): 77–88.

102. Tom W. Smith, "2001 National Gun Policy Survey of the National Opinion Research Center," NORC, University of Chicago, December 2001.

103. "Gun Owners." For more on historic comparisons between the beliefs of gun owners and the population as a whole, see "Majority Supports Stiffer Handgun Laws," *Gallup Report*, August 1983, 4. According to a 1993 CBS/*New York Times* poll, the difference in support for stronger gun laws between the population as a whole and gun owners was 13 percent (70 percent support by the general population and 57 percent support among gun owners).

104. Shawn Neidorf, "The NRA's Image Improves as Support for Gun Control Slips," Pew Research Center for the People and the Press, April 4, 2007.

105. Wootton, *Interest Groups*, 320, 326.

106. Gerald M. Pomper with Susan S. Lederman, *Elections in America* (New York: Longman, 1980), 168–69. The analysis covers platforms from 1944 to 1976.

107. Dennis S. Ippolito and Thomas G. Walker, *Political Parties, Interest Groups, and Public Policy* (Englewood Cliffs, NJ: Prentice Hall, 1980), 136; Susan Page, "Poll Spots Activism Gap in Gun-Control Debate," *USA Today*, January 15, 2013.

108. All references to the content of party platforms are drawn from copies supplied by the national party committees. The first reference to gun issues appeared in the Republican platform of 1856, which, in discussing the turbulence in the Kansas territory, said that "The right of the people to keep and bear arms has been infringed." The Democratic platform of 1864, which was hostile to the North's vigorous prosecution of the Civil War under Lincoln, bemoaned "the interference with and denial of the right of the people to bear arms in their defense," saying that it was "calculated to prevent a restoration of the Union and the perpetuation of a Government deriving its just powers from the consent of the governed."

Chapter 5

1. For example, Homer Cummings, "New Guns for Old," *The Commentator* 2 (January 1938): 45–49. Cummings was FDR's Attorney General.

2. For example, Peter Woll says that "American bureaucracy is an independent force, and from its independence it draws much of its strength and prestige. It is a powerful and viable branch of government, not properly subject to complete control by Congress, the President, or the judiciary." *American Bureaucracy* (New York: Norton, 1977), 248. Douglas Yates says that "it is widely agreed—even among those who disagree on most other political issues—that something must be done to get the bureaucracy under control." *Bureaucratic Democracy* (Cambridge, MA: Harvard University Press, 1982), 149. Francis E. Rourke chronicles "the extraordinary influence bureaucrats now exert on policy decisions." *Bureaucracy, Politics, and Public Bureaucracy* (Boston: Little, Brown, 1984), 10. See also John J. DiIulio Jr., Gerald Garvey, and Donald F. Kettl, *Improving Government Performance* (Washington, DC: Brookings Institution, 1993), 18–19. The nature of bureaucratic power is nicely detailed in Kenneth J. Meier, *Politics and the Bureaucracy* (Pacific Grove, CA: Brooks/Cole, 1993), 57–79, although Meier points out, apropos of my analysis, that bureaucratic power varies according to the kind of agency.

3. This discussion is drawn from Carol Skalnik Leff and Mark H. Leff, "The Politics of

Ineffectiveness: Federal Firearms Legislation, 1919–38," *Annals of the American Academy of Political and Social Science* 455 (May 1981): 48–62; Franklin E. Zimring, "Firearms and Federal Law: The Gun Control Act of 1968," *Journal of Legal Studies* 4 (January 1975): 133–43; and Lee Kennett and James LaVerne Anderson, *The Gun in America* (Westport, CT: Greenwood, 1975), 201–13.

4. Submachine guns were differentiated from machine guns, as the former were less bulky and more portable. The first and best known of these was the Tommy gun, developed during World War I and then marketed and sold commercially after the war.

5. Roosevelt's attorney general in the 1930s, Homer Cummings, was a staunch advocate of national gun registration. In 1938 he wrote, "Show me the man who doesn't want his gun registered and I will show you a man who shouldn't have a gun." Cummings, "New Guns for Old," 48. Cummings's successor, Robert Jackson, recommended to Congress in 1940 that all firearms be registered, all weapons transfers be recorded, and each transfer be taxed. "A 1940 Proposal: Register Firearms," *New York Times*, April 11, 1989.

6. Leff and Leff, "Politics of Ineffectiveness," 61. The NRA was a prominent part of a broader coalition that included gun manufacturers, the American Legion, the American Wildlife Institute, the American Game Association, the Izaak Walton League, various pistol groups, and other, similar organizations.

7. This observation is supported by Leff and Leff, "Politics of Ineffectiveness," 57–60, and by Kennett and Anderson, *The Gun in America*, 213–15, 252–54.

8. "The Gun under Fire," *Time*, June 21, 1968, 14.

9. All presidents face similar influence cycles, and the final year of a president's term is invariably the low point of presidential influence, a fact especially true for Johnson because he had already announced his intention not to seek another term and was facing ever-increasing hostility over Vietnam. See Robert J. Spitzer, *President and Congress: Executive Hegemony at the Crossroads of American Government* (New York: McGraw-Hill, 1993), 270–71.

10. This analysis is summarized in Robert J. Spitzer, *The Presidency and Public Policy: The Four Arenas of Presidential Power* (Tuscaloosa: University of Alabama Press, 1983), 150. The presidencies studied were those from Eisenhower to Ford.

11. The bill that Johnson signed was studded with features he opposed, including mandatory emphasis on riot control, removal of pressure to integrate local police forces, broad wiretapping provisions, the narrowing of limits on the rights of the accused, a change in the funding formula aimed at upgrading local and state police forces from direct grants to localities to block grants to states, and weakened gun control. See Spitzer, *Presidency and Public Policy*, 68; and "Congress Passes Extensive Anticrime Legislation," *CQ Almanac* 1968 (Washington, DC: Congressional Quarterly, 1969), 225.

12. "Gun Controls Extended to Long Guns, Ammunition," *CQ Almanac* 1968, 552. The following discussion is drawn from this account.

13. See, for example, Woodrow Wilson, *Congressional Government* (New York: Meridian Books, 1956 [1885]); Richard F. Fenno, *Congressmen in Committees* (Boston: Little, Brown, 1973); Charles O. Jones, *The United States Congress* (Homewood, IL: Dorsey Press, 1981), 196–97; and Steven S. Smith and Christopher J. Deering, *Committees in Congress* (Washington, DC: CQ Press, 1990).

14. Spitzer, *Presidency and Public Policy*, 116–18.

15. Ibid., 120–25. When the 165 bills are categorized according to the four policy areas and averages of roll-call votes are calculated, the figures are as follows: in the House, 1.5 roll calls for constituent bills (37), 1.8 roll calls for distributive bills (40), 2.2 roll calls for redistributive

bills (57), and 3.1 roll calls for regulatory bills (31); and in the Senate, 3 constituent, 3.3 distributive, 8 redistributive, and 11 regulatory. Thus, the Gun Control Act's total of 5 roll calls in the House exceeds the regulatory average, and the 11 in the Senate ties the regulatory average. For more on this analysis and its justification, see 115–29. The controversial nature of the gun bill is even more notable when one considers that Congress also considered a prodigious array of controversial and landmark bills during this time, dealing with such areas as civil rights, education, welfare, and Vietnam.

16. "The Gun Control Controversy," *Congressional Digest,* May 1986, 130; and "A Question of Guns," *Newsweek,* June 24, 1968, 81–85.

17. Zimring, "Firearms and Federal Law," 149–70. See also Jervis Anderson, *Guns in American Life* (New York: Random House, 1984), 86. A careful analysis of the legal and implementation-related consequences of this and subsequent legislation is found in William J. Vizzard, *Shots in the Dark* (Lanham, MD: Rowman and Littlefield, 2000).

18. The repeal was enacted in the form of a rider attached to a tax bill. "Equalization Tax, Ammunition," *CQ Almanac,* 1969 (Washington, DC: Congressional Quarterly, 1970), 334–36. Senator Wallace Bennett (R-UT) led the effort.

19. "Federal Gun Law," *CQ Almanac,* 1985 (Washington, DC: Congressional Quarterly, 1986), 228–30; Steven V. Roberts, "Senate Votes Sweeping Bill to Loosen Control of Guns," *New York Times,* July 10, 1985; and Paul Duke, "Bill to Loosen US Gun Law Passes Senate," *Wall Street Journal,* July 10, 1985. All accounts of Senate action emphasize the considerable impact of the NRA's efforts.

20. The last successful discharge petition was in 1983. The two bills so petitioned that were enacted into law were in 1938 and 1960. Randall B. Ripley, *Congress: Process and Policy* (New York: Norton, 1988), 135; and "Congress Relaxes Federal Gun Control Laws," *CQ Almanac* 1986 (Washington, DC: Congressional Quarterly, 1987), 83.

21. Steven R. Weisman, "Reagan Tells of Initial Pain and Panic after Being Shot," *New York Times,* April 23, 1981. Reagan reversed himself after his presidency, coming out in support of the Brady Bill in 1991. Steven A. Holmes, "Gun Control Bill Backed by Reagan in Appeal to Bush," *New York Times,* March 29, 1991; and Ronald Reagan, "Why I'm for the Brady Bill," *New York Times,* March 29, 1991. Reagan also came out in favor of banning assault weapons after his presidency. Osha Gray Davidson, *Under Fire* (New York: Holt, 1993), 201.

22. Linda Greenhouse, "House Adjourns Gun Control Debate to Cut Costs," *New York Times,* April 10, 1986. Greenhouse also noted, referring to the bill, that "the episode was testimony to the power of the National Rifle Association, one of the best organized and most feared lobbies in Washington." "The N.R.A.'s Lobbying Is as Effective as Ever," *New York Times,* April 13, 1986.

23. Linda Greenhouse, "House Passes Bill Easing Controls on Sale of Guns," *New York Times,* April 11, 1986.

24. Ibid. That the NRA viewed these two provisions as serious reverses is evidenced by the fact that one day after McClure-Volkmer was signed into law, NRA executive vice president G. Ray Arnett fired all fifteen members of the NRA's public education division, who were then given two hours to clean out their desks and leave the building. Several explanations have been offered for the firings, but anger over McClure-Volkmer was at least one—if not the primary—reason. Arnett himself was later forced out. Davidson, *Under Fire,* 187–88.

25. See, for example, John Herbers, "Police Groups Reverse Stand and Back Controls on Pistols," *New York Times,* October 27, 1985; and Philip Shenon, "An Alliance Is Slain over Gun Control," *New York Times,* April 9, 1986. See also "House Votes to Weaken US Gun Control

Law," *CQ Weekly Report,* April 12, 1986, 783. As Linda Greenhouse noted, "If the police lobbying was unusual, even more startling was the extent to which it failed." "N.R.A.'s Lobbying Is as Effective as Ever."

26. Quoted in Davidson, *Under Fire,* 65.

27. Laura I. Langbein and Mark A. Lotwis, "Political Efficacy of Lobbying and Money: Gun Control in the US House, 1986," *Legislative Studies Quarterly* 15 (August 1990): 413–40; Laura I. Langbein, "PACs, Lobbies and Political Conflict: The Case of Gun Control," *Public Choice* 77, no. 3 (1993): 551–72; and Richard Corrigan, "Hunters Help NRA Win Showdown," *National Journal,* April 19, 1986, 954.

28. Robert Reinhold, "Effort to Ban Assault Rifles Gains Momentum," *New York Times,* January 28, 1989; and "Bush, a Lifetime NRA Member, Opposes Semiautomatic-Gun Ban," *Syracuse (N.Y.) Post-Standard,* February 17, 1989. One clear indication of this is the author's clipping files: for assault weapons for the year 1989 was by far the thickest.

29. Clifford Krauss, "House Resoundingly Defeats Ban on Semiautomatic Arms," *New York Times,* October 18, 1991. The massacre occurred on October 17. Hennard used a Glock 9mm semiautomatic pistol and a Ruger P89.

30. Nancy Herndon, "Moves to Make Assault Guns Illegal Matched by New Wave of Buying," *Christian Science Monitor,* February 27, 1989; and "Deadly Decision on Assault Rifles," *New York Times,* July 26, 1990. The most common of these assault weapons include (in order of popularity) the TEC-9, the AR-15, the Uzi, the MAC-11, the MINI-14, the AK-47, the MAC-10, the SPAS-12, the HK-91, and the HK-93. About fifty weapons fall under the assault weapon category, but these ten account for nine-tenths of all assault-weapon crime. Jim Stewart and Andrew Alexander, "Assault Weapons Muscling in on the Front Lines of Crime," *Atlanta Journal and Constitution,* May 21, 1989; and Robert J. Spitzer, "Assault Weapons Ban," *Christian Science Monitor,* April 16, 1998. Title XI of the Violent Crime Control Act (108 *Stat.* 199; PL 103–322) defines assault weapons, including both rifles and pistols.

31. Gerald M. Boyd, "Bush Opposes a Ban on Assault Firearms but Backs State Role," *New York Times,* February 17, 1989; Charles Mohr, "US Bans Imports of Assault Rifles in Shift by Bush," *New York Times,* March 15, 1989; and Bernard Weinraub, "Bush Considers Calling in Guard to Fight Drug Violence in Capital," *New York Times,* March 21, 1989. Sensing the mood of the public and the government, Colt Industries voluntarily suspended the sale of its copy of the military M-16 rifle. Charles Mohr, "Impact of Curbs on Guns Debated," *New York Times,* March 16, 1989. The ban immediately affected the import of about 113,000 assault-type weapons. Charles Mohr, "Federal Agency to Begin a Survey on Use of Semiautomatic Weapons," *New York Times,* March 23, 1989. Imported assault weapons accounted for about a quarter of those owned in the United States.

32. Douglas Jehl, "Clinton Undertakes His Drive on Guns and Crime," *New York Times,* August 12, 1993; and John M. Broder, "Clinton to Impose a Ban on 58 Types of Imported Guns," *New York Times,* April 6, 1998.

33. Clifford Krauss, "Senate Approves Ban on Manufacture of Military-Style Weapons," *New York Times,* November 18, 1993; and Clifford Krauss, "Senators Back Ban on Selling Guns to Minors," *New York Times,* November 10, 1993. The measure prompted surprisingly little opposition, passing 99–1.

34. Katharine Q. Seelye, "In Gun Vote, an Odd Hero for Liberals," *New York Times,* May 7, 1994.

35. Seth Mydans, "Freshman Withstands an N.R.A. Fusillade," *New York Times,* May 9, 1994. The representative was Steve Horn (R-CA).

36. "Gun Curbs Stall on Hill; Some Imports Banned," *CQ Almanac* 1989 (Washington, DC: Congressional Quarterly, 1990), 262.

37. Katharine Q. Seelye, "G.O.P. Gains Allies in Move to Repeal Assault-Rifle Ban," *New York Times*, January 26, 1995; Katharine Q. Seelye, "Gingrich and N.R.A. to Delay Bill on Gun Ban," *New York Times*, January 28, 1995; and Jerry Gray, "Dole, in a 2d Nod to Right, Pledges to Fight Gun Ban," *New York Times*, March 18, 1995.

38. Adam Clymer, "House Approves Repeal of the Ban on Assault Weapons," *New York Times*, March 23, 1996; and Alan Greenblatt, "Repeal of Assault Weapons Ban Unlikely to Go beyond House," *CQ Weekly Report*, March 23, 1996, 803.

39. "Legislative History, Violent Crime Control Act, PL 103–322," *US Code Congressional and Administrative News* (St. Paul, MN: West, 1994), 4:1821; David E. Sanger, "Chinese Arms Seized in Undercover Inquiry," *New York Times*, May 24, 1996; Spitzer, "Assault Weapons Ban"; Karen MacPherson, "Ban Ends, Congress Ducks," *Pittsburgh Post-Gazette*, September 13, 2004; and Robert J. Spitzer, "Why the Gun Ban Died Quietly," *San Jose Mercury News*, September 19, 2004.

40. Sheryl Gay Stolberg, "Senate Leaders Scuttle Gun Bill Over Changes," *New York Times*, March 3, 2004; and Spitzer, "Why the Gun Ban Died Quietly."

41. Gwen Ifill, "Hot Debate Magnifies a Modest Gun Law," *New York Times*, May 12, 1991.

42. "NRA Showed It Still Had What It Takes to Overcome Gun-Control Advocates," *CQ Almanac* 1988 (Washington, DC: Congressional Quarterly, 1989), 100–1. For an example of the NRA's "hassle factor" at the state level, see Tom Loftus, *The Art of Legislative Politics* (Washington, DC: CQ Press, 1994), ch. 7.

43. Gwen Ifill, "House Passes Bill to Set Seven-Day Wait to Buy Handguns," *New York Times*, May 9, 1991; "Gun Control's Red Herring," *New York Times*, May 6, 1991; and Gwen Ifill, "Cost Is Put in the Millions for Computer Gun Check," *New York Times*, May 7, 1991. The cost estimate was from the Congressional Budget Office.

44. "Anti-Crime Bill Falls Victim to Partisanship" and "Brady Bill Part of Stalled Crime Package," both in *CQ Almanac* 1991 (Washington, DC: Congressional Quarterly, 1992), 262–70, 271–73; and "No Compromise Forged on Crime Bill," *CQ Almanac* 1992 (Washington, DC: Congressional Quarterly, 1993), 311–13.

45. Clifford Krauss, "Gun Bill Freed from a Logjam; Passage More Likely," *New York Times*, October 28, 1993. The *Times* dubbed the bill's revival "political CPR." Sarah Brady compared it to the Dewey-Truman story, when predictions of Truman's political demise in the 1948 elections proved to be premature. Adam Clymer, "How Jockeying Brought Brady Bill Back to Life," *New York Times*, November 22, 1993; and Karen DeWitt, "Five Years of Struggle by Bradys Pays Off," *New York Times*, November 22, 1993.

46. Fox Butterfield, "Brady Law Halts Permits for 45,000," *New York Times*, March 12, 1995; "Law on Gun Buyers," *New York Times*, September 5, 1997; "An Analysis of the Decline in Gun Dealers: 1994 to 2007," Violence Policy Center, August 2007. For more on the federalism consequences of the Brady Act, see Carol J. DeFrances and Steven K. Smith, "Federal-State Relations in Gun Control: The 1993 Brady Handgun Violence Prevention Act," *Publius* 24 (-Summer 1994): 69–82; Fred Schulte, "ATF's Struggle to Close Down Firearms Dealers," *Huffington Post*, February 1, 2013, http://www.publicintegrity.org/2013/02/01/12117/atfs-struggle-close-down-firearms-dealers.

47. Ed Connolly and Michael Luo, "States Struggle to Disarm People Who've Lost Right to Own Guns," *New York Times*, February 6, 2011.

48. Ifill, "House Passes Bill to Set Seven-Day Wait to Buy Handguns." Prominent defectors

from the NRA included Representatives Les AuCoin (D-OR) and Susan Molinari (R-NY). See Steven A. Holmes, "Rifle Lobby Torn by Dissidents and Capitol Defectors," *New York Times,* March 27, 1991.

49. Voting patterns were similar in the Senate, but regional analysis is more statistically variable for Senate votes because of the smaller number of senators. The eleven southern states send only twenty-two representatives to the Senate.

50. "President's Jump in Favor of Gun Control Startles Aides," *Syracuse Post-Standard,* December 10, 1993.

51. For example, the NRA publication *American Rifleman* featured a cover story in its January 1994 issue (the first to come out after passage of the Brady Bill) under the banner "Anti-gun Frenzy." The cover article's reference to the passage of the Brady Bill was this: "When Bill Clinton signed the Brady bill into law November 30, a drop of blood dripped from the finger of the sovereign American citizen." Oddly, the only photo on the cover of the issue was that of Hillary Clinton, whose role on the gun issue was less prominent than were the roles of other members of the Clinton administration. The lead article was entitled "Line Up and Shut Up. Face Forward. Stay in Line. State Your Name. Last Name First," 32–33.

52. "Brady Bill Part of Stalled Crime Package," 271.

53. Frank Bruni, "Senate Votes Gun Curbs, Hours after Georgia School Shooting," *New York Times,* May 21, 1999; Frank Bruni and James Dao, "Gun-Control Bill Rejected in House in Bipartisan Vote," *New York Times,* June 19, 1999; "Gun Control Agreement Eludes Conferees, Derails Juvenile Crime Legislation," *CQ Almanac* 1999 (Washington, DC: Congressional Quarterly, 2000), 18:3–26.

54. John Tierney, "A New Push to Grant Gun Industry Immunity from Suits," *New York Times,* April 4, 2003; Dennis A. Henigan, "Sue the Gun Makers," *Washington Post,* October 29, 1999. See also Carl T. Bogus, "Gun Litigation and Societal Values," *Connecticut Law Review* 32 (Summer 2000): 1353–78; George J. Benston and Frank J. Vandall, "Legal Control Over the Supply of Handguns," *Pace Law Review* 26 (Spring 2006): 305–96; Timothy D. Lytton, ed., *Suing the Gun Industry: A Battle at the Crossroads of Gun Control and Mass Torts* (Ann Arbor: University of Michigan Press, 2005).

55. Barry Meier, "Cities Turn to US Gun-Tracing Data for Legal Assault on Industry," *New York Times,* July 23, 1999; Daniel Feldman, "Legislating or Litigating Public Policy Change: Gunmaker Tort Liability," *Virginia Journal of Social Policy* 12 (Fall 2004): 153; "Why Criminals Are Still Getting Guns," *Parade Magazine,* November 4, 2007, 10. The Illinois Supreme Court dismissed the Chicago case in 2004.

56. Rebecca Cook, "Bushmaster, Bull's Eye Settle for $2.5 million in D.C. Sniper Shootings Lawsuit," Associated Press, September 9, 2004.

57. Wayne V. McIntosh and Cynthia Cates, "Cigarettes, Firearms, and the New Litigation Wars," in *The Interest Group Connection,* ed. Paul S. Herrnson, Ronald G. Shaiko, and Clyde Wilcox (Washington, DC: CQ Press, 2005), 341–64; Robert J. Spitzer, "Gun Industry Doesn't Know What's Good for It: Regulation," *Syracuse Post-Standard,* April 20, 1999; and Sheryl Gay Stolberg, "Congress Passes New Legal Shield for Gun Industry," *New York Times,* October 21, 2005.

58. Amy Goldstein, "House Passes Ban on Gun Industry Lawsuits," *Washington Post,* October 21, 2005; Richard Simon, "Bill to Shield Gun Makers Is Approved," *Los Angeles Times,* October 21, 2005.

59. "Report of the State's Attorney for the Judicial District of Danbury on the Shootings at Sandy Hook Elementary School and 36 Yogananda Street, Newtown, Connecticut on December

14, 2012," *Office of the State's Attorney Judicial District of Danbury,* November 25, 2013, http://www.nytimes.com/interactive/2013/11/26/nyregion/26newtown-report.html?ref=nyregion. One of the school officials killed was the school's guidance counselor, Mary Sherlach, who was a 1978 graduate of SUNY Cortland.

60. Michael McAuliff, "Bipartisan Gun Control Agreement Announced On Background Checks," *Huffington Post,* April 10, 2013, http://www.huffingtonpost.com/2013/04/10/gun-control-background-checks_n_3052871.html; Robert Draper, "Inside the Power of the N.R.A.," *New York Times Magazine,* December 13, 2013.

61. Jennifer Steinhauer, "Gun Control Drive Blocked in Senate," *New York Times,* April 18, 2013; Draper, "Inside the Power of the N.R.A."

62. Jennifer Steinhauer, "Congressional Committees Make Some Gun-Rights Provisions Permanent," *New York Times,* March 14, 2013.

63. Leslie Maitland Werner, "An Agency Steps Out of Obscurity," *New York Times,* January 27, 1985; and Wayne King, "A Bureau That Battled Bootleggers Is Tough Target for Budget-Cutters," *New York Times,* February 1, 1988. The Treasury Department first exercised jurisdiction over firearms when it was charged with collecting the excise tax on firearms sales in 1919. Josh Sugarmann, *National Rifle Association: Money, Firepower and Fear* (Washington, DC: National Press Books, 1992), 91.

64. " … Any Gun You Want," *New York Times,* October 7, 1981.

65. Quoted in Sugarmann, *National Rifle Association,* 124–25.

66. Peter Maas, "Can John Magaw Save the ATF?" *Parade Magazine,* May 19, 1996, 4, 6; "A Role for B.A.T.F.," *New York Times,* May 4, 1995; and Fox Butterfield, "Long before Bombing, Gun Lobby Was Lashing Out at Federal Agents," *New York Times,* May 8, 1995.

67. "Gun Controls Extended to Long Guns, Ammunition," *CQ Almanac* 1968 (Washington, DC: Congressional Quarterly, 1969), 552; Bill Keller, "Powerful Reputation Makes National Rifle Association a Top Gun in Washington," *CQ Weekly Report,* May 9, 1981, 801; and B. Drummond Ayres Jr., "US to Seek Rise in Fee for Gun Dealers," *New York Times,* January 4, 1994; "Shady Dealings," Brady Center to Prevent Gun Violence, Washington, DC, January 2007, 23–26.

68. According to one account, "even inexperienced gun owners could make the change in a matter of minutes, using only a file." The weapon was first popularized in a 1974 John Wayne movie, *McQ.* Erik Larson, "The Story of a Gun," *Atlantic Monthly,* January 1993, 52. See also Larson, *Lethal Passage: How the Travels of a Single Handgun Expose the Roots of America's Gun Crisis* (New York: Crown, 1994).

69. "US Aides Find Gun Smuggling Is a Low Priority," *New York Times,* September 6, 1985.

70. Charles J. Hanley, "America Is a Mother Lode of Firepower for World of Conflict and Crime," *Cortland Standard,* April 6, 1994.

71. Sugarmann, *National Rifle Association,* 122.

72. "Two Regulatory Units Facing Budget Cuts," *New York Times,* February 14, 1981; and Phil Gailey, "White House Planning to Kill Firearms Enforcement Unit," *New York Times,* September 9, 1981.

73. Davidson, *Under Fire,* 52–53.

74. "Treasury, Postal Funds in Continuing Measure," *CQ Almanac,* 1983 (Washington, DC: Congressional Quarterly, 1984), 273.

75. The agency was given jurisdiction over arson and explosives in the Anti-Arson Act of 1982.

76. King, "A Bureau That Battled Bootleggers Is Tough Target for Budget-Cutters." Higgins

likened such arrests to ticketing jaywalkers, although the volume of improper gun exchanges suggests a more serious problem. See also Robert D. Hershey Jr., "Vigor Wins New Life for Firearms Agency," *New York Times,* December 23, 1985.

77. Stephen Labaton, "Firearms Agency Struggles to Rise from the Ashes of the Waco Disaster," *New York Times,* November 5, 1993, and Maas, "Can John Magaw Save the ATF?" Repeated charges of sexual harassment and racial discrimination within the agency also rocked the ATF. Branch Davidian group leader David Koresh (his real name was Vernon Howell) had amassed an enormous quantity of arms and munitions, including machine guns and explosives. For more on this incident, see Ronald Kessler, *The FBI* (New York: Pocket Books, 1993), 418–29.

78. "Firearms Agency Bans Armor-Piercing Bullets," *New York Times,* February 6, 1994; Steven A. Holmes, "Treasury Imposes New Regulations on Some Shotguns," *New York Times,* March 1, 1994; and "Another Blow to the N.R.A.," *New York Times,* March 2, 1994.

79. Dan Eggen, "ATF Director Resigns amid Spending Probe," *Washington Post,* August 5, 2006; Michael Isikoff, "The ATF's Big Hole," *Newsweek,* April 26, 2010.

80. Adam Berlow, "Current Gun Debate May Not Help Beleaguered ATF," *The Center for Public Integrity,* February 11, 2013, http://www.publicintegrity.org/2013/02/11/12155 /current-gun-debate-may-not-help-beleaguered-atf.

81. In 1993 and 1994 the NRA focused much attention on the fate of the Branch Davidians in Waco and the case of Randy Weaver and his family, armed white supremacist extremists who lived in Idaho. Several family members were killed in an FBI-federal marshal assault on the Weaver home in 1992. The NRA has sought to depict both incidents as cases of innocent, law-abiding citizens set upon by the government because they owned weapons. Indeed, the government mishandled both cases, but in both instances it had ample cause to take action. The NRA's effort to elevate these individuals to martyr status and depict federal law-enforcement officials as fascist tyrants can be seen in the *American Rifleman* issues of September 1993 (in particular Robert K. Corbin's "The President's Column") and November 1993 ("The Randy Weaver Case," 41–43) as well as in the *American Hunter,* October 1993, 43–44. The ATF played no direct role in the Randy Weaver case and did not participate in the final assault on the Waco compound.

82. Wendy L. Martinek, Kenneth J. Meier, and Lael R. Keiser, "Jackboots or Lace Panties?" in *The Changing Politics of Gun Control* (Lanham, MD: Rowman and Littlefield, 1998), 24.

83. Richard Gid Powers, *Secrecy and Power* (New York: Free Press, 1987), 184–85.

84. Michael Winship, "Hundreds of Thousands of Guns Unaccounted for in the US," *Salon.com,* June 29, 2013, http://www.salon.com/2013/06/29/hundreds_of_thousands_of _guns_unaccounted_for_in_the_us_partner/.

85. Philip J. Cook, Stephanie Molliconi, and Thomas B. Cole, "Regulating Gun Markets," *Journal of Criminal Law and Criminology* 86 (Fall 1995): 59–91; William J. Vizzard, "The Impact of Agenda Conflict on Policy Formulation and Implementation: The Case of Gun Control," *Public Administration Review* 55 (July–August 1995): 343; and David Ignatius, "The US Gun Lobby Holds Mexico Hostage," *Washington Post,* August 1, 2010.

86. Martinek, Meier, and Keiser, "Jackboots or Lace Panties?" 41–42. See also William J. Vizzard, *In the Cross Fire: A Political History of the Bureau of Alcohol, Tobacco, and Firearms* (Boulder, CO: Lynne Rienner, 1997); William J. Vizzard, *Shots in the Dark* (Lanham, MD: Rowman and Littlefield, 2000); and James Moore, *Very Special Agents* (Urbana: University of Illinois Press, 2001).

87. E. E. Schattschneider, *The Semisovereign People* (Hinsdale, IL: Dryden Press, 1975).

Chapter 6

1. See, for example, Martin S. Geisel, Richard Roll, and R. Stanton Wettick, "The Effectiveness of State and Local Regulation of Handguns: A Statistical Analysis," *Duke Law Journal* 4 (1969): 647–76; Glenn L. Pierce and William J. Bowers, "The Bartley-Fox Gun Law's Short-Term Impact on Crime in Boston," *Annals of the American Academy of Political and Social Science* 455 (May 1981): 120–37; John Henry Sloan et al., "Handgun Regulations, Crime, Assaults, and Homicide," *New England Journal of Medicine* 319 (November 10, 1988): 1256–62; and Colin Loftin et al., "Effects of Restrictive Licensing of Handguns on Homicide and Suicide in the District of Columbia," *New England Journal of Medicine* 325 (December 5, 1991): 1615–20. See also Erik Larson, "The Story of a Gun," *Atlantic Monthly,* January 1993, 48–78; and Erik Larson, *Lethal Passage* (New York: Crown, 1994).

2. Basic issues and consequences of American federalism are summarized in William H. Riker, *Federalism: Origin, Operation, Significance* (Boston: Little, Brown, 1964); Michael D. Reagan and John G. Sanzone, *The New Federalism* (New York: Oxford University Press, 1981); and David C. Nice, *Federalism: The Politics of Intergovernmental Relations* (New York: St. Martin's, 1987).

3. Lee Kennett and James LaVerne Anderson, *The Gun in America* (Westport, CT: Greenwood Press, 1975), 174–86.

4. Craig Wolff, "In New York, the Brazenness of Illegal Gun Dealers Grows," *New York Times,* November 11, 1990; James Dao, "States Joining in Combating Illegal Guns," *New York Times,* April 26, 1993; Patrice O'Shaughnessy, "Guns on New York's Mind," *New York Daily News,* May 16, 2000; Hannah Glover and Erica Pearson, "Young Gun," *Village Voice,* March 21–27, 2001; Toni Whitt, "Bloomberg Invites Other Mayors to Town to Discuss Gun Crime," *New York Times,* April 19, 2006; Michael A. Bloomberg, "Gun Show Undercover," October 7, 2009, www.nyc.gov/gunshow. The ease of gun purchases in Florida has made it "the hub of a booming illegal trade in arms" for criminals, terrorists, and others in Caribbean and Latin American nations. Guns purchased over the counter in Miami were used to assassinate three Colombian presidential candidates in 1989. According to ATF director Stephen Higgins, "We have the reputation as being the No. 1 supplier of weapons in this hemisphere, and that reputation is probably well deserved." Larry Rohter, "From Brazil to Peru to Jamaica, Gun Smugglers Flock to Florida," *New York Times,* August 11, 1991. See also B. Drummond Ayres, "Virginia Aims to Shed Image as 'Handgun Supermarket,'" *New York Times,* December 23, 1992.

5. "One Gun a Month Is Plenty," *New York Times,* February 10, 1996; Fox Butterfield, "Report Links Crimes to States with Weak Gun Controls," *New York Times,* April 9, 1997; Eric Lichtblau, "Study Ties Lax State Gun Laws to Crimes in Other States," *New York Times,* September 27, 2010; "States with Higher Gun Ownership and Weak Gun Laws Lead Nation in Gun Death," Violence Policy Center, June 2, 2010. A 1997 congressional study found that four states—Florida, Georgia, South Carolina, and Texas—were the source of 25 percent of all guns seized in crimes nationwide and that the ten states with the most lax gun laws accounted for more than half of out-of-state guns used in crimes in 1996.

6. Sewell Chan, "Seeking a National Voice, 15 Mayors Meet on Gun Violence," *New York Times,* April 26, 2006; Diane Cardwell, "2 Gun Dealers Settle Lawsuit with the City," *New York Times,* August 1, 2006; Sewell Chan, "Bloomberg Assails N.R.A. and Supports Lieberman," *New York Times,* October 26, 2006; Lichtblau, "Study Ties Lax State Gun Laws to Crimes in Other States."

7. Kevin Sack, "Gun-Control Battles Reveal Gradual Shifts," *New York Times,* June 13,

1993; and Dirk Johnson, "In Heart of Gun Country, Utah Is Changing Its Mind?" *New York Times,* October 14, 1993. The gun issue figured in the 1993 gubernatorial elections in New Jersey and Virginia.

8. Larry Rohter, "In Wave of Anticrime Fervor, States Rush to Adopt Laws," *New York Times,* May 10, 1994. For more on state gun control efforts, see John M. Bruce and Clyde Wilcox, eds., *The Changing Politics of Gun Control* (Lanham, MD: Rowman and Littlefield, 1998), chs. 5–8.

9. Andrew Kirby, "A Smoking Gun," *Policy Studies Journal* 18 (Spring 1990): 746–48; Richard L. Worsnop, "Gun Control," *CQ Researcher,* June 10, 1994, 517; John Hickman, "Gun Control in the Georgia General Assembly," *Comparative State Politics* 16 (October 1995): 22–34; OpenCarry, www.opencarry.org; Ian Urbina, "Locked, Loaded, and Ready to Caffeinate," *New York Times,* March 8, 2010.

10. John L. Gaddis, *The United States and the Origins of the Cold War, 1941–1947* (New York: Columbia University Press, 1972).

11. Many analysts have noted the need for more and better data on guns and the consequences of gun use. See, for example, James D. Wright, Peter H. Rossi, and Kathleen Daly, *Under the Gun* (New York: Aldine de Gruyter, 1983), 22; and Osha Gray Davidson, "Get the Facts on Gun Deaths," *New York Times,* July 31, 1993.

12. "Most Homicides with Known Victim/Offender Relationships Involved People Who Knew Each Other," Bureau of Justice Statistics, US Department of Justice, http://bjs.ojp.usdoj.gov/content/homicide/relationship.cfm#.

13. Andrew H. Malcolm, "From the Police Blotter: Eight Stories That End in Death," *New York Times,* April 17, 1989. The eleven deaths arose from eight events.

14. "Seven Deadly Days," *Time,* July 17, 1989, 31; David Hemenway, "Risks and Benefits of a Gun in the Home," *American Journal of Lifestyle Medicine* 5 (November/December 2011): 502–511.

15. Arnold Wolfers writes that "the insecurity of an anarchical system of multiple sovereignty places the actors under compulsion to seek maximum power even though this may run counter to real desires." *Discord and Collaboration* (Baltimore, MD: Johns Hopkins University Press, 1962), 84. Herbert Butterfield describes this as a "Hobbesian fear—that you yourself may vividly feel the terrible fear that you have of the other party, but you cannot enter into the other man's counter-fear, or even understand why he should be particularly nervous. For you know that you yourself mean him no harm, and that you want nothing from him save guarantees for your own safety." *History and Human Relations* (New York: Macmillan, 1952), 21. Butterfield's description applies equally well to two strangers passing on a darkened street as to the behavior of nations.

16. Waltz emphasizes that anarchy is an "ordering principle" in international relations. Kenneth N. Waltz, *Theory of International Politics* (Reading, MA: Addison-Wesley, 1979), 88–89, 93. People often mistakenly assume that the "anarchy" of the inner cities, for example, reflects the absence of any codes of conduct and behavior. Such is not the case; instead, it reflects the substitution of conventional civil norms with an intricate and different (and certainly more dangerous) "street culture" or "code of the streets." See, for example, Elijah Anderson, "The Code of the Streets," *Atlantic Monthly,* May 1994, 80–94.

17. Bruce Russett, *The Prisoners of Insecurity* (San Francisco: W. H. Freeman, 1983), 3.

18. William T. R. Fox, "The Uses of International Relations Theory," in *Theoretical Aspects of International Relations,* ed. William T. R. Fox (Notre Dame, IN: University of Notre Dame Press, 1959), 35.

19. John H. Herz, "Idealist Internationalism and the Security Dilemma," *World Politics* 2 (January 1950): 157. See also Herz, *Political Realism and Political Idealism* (Chicago: University of Chicago Press, 1951).

20. Robert Jervis, "Cooperation under the Security Dilemma," *World Politics* 30 (January 1978): 169.

21. Recognizing this problem, the United States and the Soviet Union signed the ABM Treaty in 1972 to prevent both sides from developing and deploying antimissile missiles. See Russett, *Prisoners of Insecurity,* 78–79, 116, 155.

22. Herz, "Idealist Internationalism and the Security Dilemma," 173.

23. Russett, *Prisoners of Insecurity,* 47–66; and Walter S. Jones, *The Logic of International Relations* (Boston: Little, Brown, 1985), 377. John T. Rourke says that "there can be little doubt that arms both create a possibility of war and help create a climate of hostility and anxiety that is fertile ground for war." *International Politics on the World Stage* (Guilford, CT: Dushkin, 1991), 501. A study of the relations between powerful nations from 1815 to the present found that disputes between nations resulted in war 82 percent of the time when accompanied by an arms race. Conversely, only 4 percent of international disputes resulted in war when there was no arms race. The analysis was based on a total of ninety-nine "serious disputes" between nations. See Michael D. Wallace, "Armaments and Escalation: Two Competing Hypotheses," *International Studies Quarterly* 26 (March 1982): 37–56.

24. Rourke, *International Politics on the World Stage,* 503.

25. Waltz, *Theory of International Politics,* 88.

26. Quoted in Jervis, "Cooperation under the Security Dilemma," 201.

27. Conversation with John J. Mearsheimer, April 25, 1994. See his book, *The Tragedy of Great Power Politics* (New York: Norton, 2001).

28. Robert Jervis, *Perception and Misperception in International Politics* (Princeton, NJ: Princeton University Press, 1976), 89.

29. "Shady Dealings," Brady Center to Prevent Gun Violence, January 2007, 6; Bureau of Justice Statistics, US Department of Justice. Data from "Gun Violence," National Institute of Justice, http://www.ojp.usdoj.gov/nij/topics/crime/gun-violence/; "Key Facts at a Glance," Bureau of Justice Statistics, http://bjs.ojp.usdoj.gov/content/glance/guncrime.cfm.

30. Larry Rohter, "Pistol Packs Glamour, Power and Reputation as a Menace," *New York Times,* March 10, 1992. According to the Cox newspaper chain's study of the use of assault weapons in crime, such weapons were twenty times more likely to be used in crimes than other weapons.

31. Hunting enthusiasts point out that many standard hunting rifles are semiautomatic as well. But one can make strong arguments for differentiating such weapons from assault weapons (as recent legislation has done) in order to protect legitimate hunting purposes and for barring large magazine clips. Although the distinction between semiautomatic hunting guns and many assault weapons is mostly cosmetic, an arms control approach, discussed later in this chapter, supports the principle of making such distinctions for the purpose of putting brakes on the domestic arms race.

32. This is the argument Alfred Blumstein makes about the proliferation of gun violence among juveniles. See "Youth Violence, Guns, and the Illicit-Drug Industry," *Journal of Criminal Law and Criminology* 86 (Fall 1995): 10–36. An apparent contradiction to this assertion is the case of Kennesaw, Georgia, which passed a local ordinance in 1982 requiring every household to maintain firearms and ammunition. The town's mayor claimed this action resulted in a decline in local crime without any rise in gun deaths. It turns out, however, that the law was

not enforced and exempted those who did not believe in having or using firearms. In addition, claims that crime declined after the ordinance was passed turned out to be a statistical artifact (based on the small absolute number of crimes in a small town of about nine thousand people). In fact, the average crime rate in the four years following passage of the law was higher than in the four years preceding the law. David McDowall, Brian Wiersema, and Colin Loftin, "Did Mandatory Ownership in Kennesaw Really Prevent Burglaries?" *Sociology and Social Research* 74 (October 1989): 48–51.

33. Gary Kleck paints an idyllic picture of armed citizens serving as helpers or "complements" to police, providing "an additional option for dealing with danger." Kleck fails to consider the multiplication of danger in society from criminal, accidental, and suicidal gun use stemming from introducing into society "millions of people [who] are armed and dangerous to each other." *Point Blank* (New York: Aldine de Gruyter, 1991), 142–43.

34. Andrew H. Malcolm, "Many Police Forces Rearm to Counter Criminals' Guns," *New York Times*, September 4, 1990; Gary Pierre-Pierre, "Police Officials Are Said to Be Rethinking Rapid-Fire Guns," *New York Times*, February 18, 1995; and Clifford Krauss, "Police Plan More Training in 9-mm. Gun," *New York Times*, June 5, 1995; Al Baker, "11 Years of Police Gunfire, in Painstaking Detail," *New York Times*, May 8, 2008.

35. Jervis, *Perception and Misperception in International Politics*, 83.

36. Sam Howe VerHovek, "In Killing of Repo Man, Law Shields the Killer," *New York Times*, March 8, 1994.

37. David McDowall, Colin Loftin, and Brian Wiersema, "Easing Concealed Firearms Laws: Effects on Homicide in Three States," *Journal of Criminal Law and Criminology* 86 (Fall 1995): 193–206. See also the response from Daniel D. Polsby, "Firearms Costs, Firearms Benefits, and the Limits of Knowledge," 193–220; and the response from McDowall and associates in "Additional Discussion about Easing Concealed Firearms Laws," 221–25, in the same journal issue.

38. Blumstein, "Youth Violence, Guns, and the Illicit-Drug Industry," 33; Fox Butterfield, "Cities Finding a New Policy Limits Guns," *New York Times*, November 20, 1994; Clifford Krauss, "Shootings Fall As More Guns Stay at Home," *New York Times*, July 30, 1995; James Q. Wilson, "Just Take Away the Guns," *New York Times Magazine*, March 20, 1994, 47; and Robert J. Spitzer, " … Maybe, but Not in Cities," *Los Angeles Times*, February 19, 1996.

39. According to the New York State Police, the average lifespan for guns on the streets is "less than 30 months." This high turnover rate is attributed to the tendency to lose or throw away guns used in crimes and to their seizure by the authorities. Barnaby J. Feder, "Moynihan Wages Battle on Second Front of Gun War," *New York Times*, March 20, 1992.

40. There continues to be a considerable debate about whether the terms "clips" and "magazines" are or are not synonyms. See, for example, "Firearms Glossary," NRA-ILA, http://www.nraila.org/Issues/FirearmsGlossary/.

41. Smothers, "A Debate in Congress Focuses on the Science of Destruction," *New York Times*, November 7, 1993; Adam Clymer, "Moynihan Asks Big Tax Increase on Ammunition," *New York Times*, November 4, 1993; "Company's Destructive New Ammunition Has Critics," *New York Times*, December 27, 1994; and Daniel Patrick Moynihan, "Just Bit the Bullets!" *Washington Post National Weekly*, January 9–15, 1995. The Winchester Ammunition Company voluntarily withdrew its Black Talon bullets from the market in the face of public criticism, although more than twenty other manufacturers continue to produce such bullets.

42. Russett, *Prisoners of Insecurity*, 189.

43. David Johnston, "Congress Never Even Got to Vote to Ban This Weapon," *New York*

Times, June 20, 1999; James Dao, "In 80s, Afghan Militias Fought with US Rifles," *New York Times,* October 7, 2001; "US Gun Industry Armed Osama bin Laden's Terror Network," Violence Policy Center Press Release, October 7, 2001; Carolyn Marshall, "California Bans a Large-Caliber Gun, and the Battle Is On," *New York Times,* January 4, 2005; "Civilian Sales of Military Rifle Raise Concerns about Terrorism," *New York Times,* November 28, 2005.

44. Steve Karnowski, "Minneapolis Gun Shop Debuts a Credit-Card-Sized Firearm," *Cortland (N.Y.) Standard,* October 8, 2004.

Index

About the Author

Robert J. Spitzer (PhD, Cornell University, 1980) is distinguished service professor and chair of the Political Science Department at the State University of New York, College at Cortland.

Spitzer's books include *The Presidency and Public Policy* (1983), *The Right to Life Movement and Third Party Politics* (1987), *The Presidential Veto* (1988), *The Bicentennial of the U.S. Constitution* (1990), *Media and Public Policy* (1993), *President and Congress* (1993), *Politics and Constitutionalism* (2000), *The Right to Bear Arms* (2001), *The Presidency and the Constitution* (coauthored, 2005), *Saving the Constitution from Lawyers* (2008), *Gun Control: A Documentary and Reference Guide* (2009), *We the People: Essentials Edition* (coauthored; 10th ed. 2015), *Encyclopedia of Gun Control and Gun Rights* (coauthored, 2012), and *Guns across America* (2015). He has contributed more than six hundred articles to a variety of journals, books, and other publications and is often interviewed and quoted in national and international media on gun control and other subjects. He is also series editor for the Book Series on American Constitutionalism for SUNY Press.

In the 1980s, Spitzer served as a member of the New York State Commission on the Bicentennial of the U.S. Constitution. He served as president of the Presidency Research Group of the American Political Science Association from 2001 to 2003 and is a recipient of the SUNY Chancellor's Award for Excellence in Scholarship. He has testified before Congress on several occasions and been cited in federal court cases.